Praise for

Survival Math

"Jackson writes with a keen attentiveness to the social contexts shaping the lives of his family, offering nuanced depictions that upend the stereotypes that often cage us in."

—*The New York Times Book Review*

"A shattering memoir of [Jackson's] mother's love affair with drugs and his own struggle to reconcile the forces of racism, toxic masculinity, the lure of the hustle, and the 'composite Pops' who helped raise him."

—*O, The Oprah Magazine*

"An expansive chronicle as much as his own personal story . . . *Survival Math* is remarkably direct and poignant."

—*USA Today*

"[A] vibrant memoir of race, violence, family, and manhood . . . Jackson recognizes there is too much for one conventional form, and his various storytelling methods imbue the book with an unpredictable dexterity."

—*The Boston Globe*

"In his nonfiction debut, award-winning novelist Mitchell S. Jackson explains what it's like to grow up black in one of the whitest cities in the country: Portland, Oregon."

—*Time*

"The sum of *Survival Math*'s parts is a highly original whole, one that reflects on the exigencies—over generations—that have shaped the lives of so many disenfranchised Americans."

—*Paste*

"Jackson tells the story of his family . . . with radical love and honesty."

—*The New York Times*

"A vulnerable, sobering look at Jackson's life and beyond, in all its tragedies, burdens, and faults . . . Jackson dissects the darker realities of his hometown, [and] his explorations feel strikingly unguarded."

—*San Francisco Chronicle*

"Gripping and harsh and full of passion and heart."

—*Tampa Bay Times*

"Jackson revisits his early years in a black Portland neighborhood, telling the stories of his struggling family members and analyzing the marginalizing cultural forces around them."

—*Entertainment Weekly*

"An extensive and illuminating look at the city of [Jackson's] childhood, exploring issues like sex, violence, addiction, community, and the toll this takes on a person's life."

—BuzzFeed

"Staggeringly smart . . . This book is a vivid and artful exploration of race and legacy in the United States, told in a poetic and piercing voice unlike anything else in the literary world right now."

—*Portland Monthly*

"In recalling his own struggle, what Jackson has created is a monument to the marginalized—and it's every bit as harrowing and beautiful as its architect's life."

—*Willamette Week*

"In prose that is both poetic and brutally honest, Jackson [explores] his family's story as a lens into the history of his community."

—Salon

"Thanks to Jackson's fresh voice, this powerful autobiography shines an important light on the generational problems of America's oft-forgotten urban communities."

—*Publishers Weekly*, starred review

"A potent book that revels in the author's truthful experiences while maintaining the jagged-grain, keeping-it-a-100, natural storytelling that made *The Residue Years* a modern must-read."

—*Kirkus Reviews*, starred review

"Award-winning novelist Jackson reclaims his history through an elegant memoir. . . . The result is an intimate portrayal of what makes us human."

—*Library Journal*, starred review

"[An] inquisitive and unflinching investigation of the conditions that shaped [Jackson's life]."

—*Booklist*, starred review

"This is a mesmerizing book, full of story, truth, pain, lyricism, humor, and astonishment: the stuff of a difficult life, fully lived, and masterfully transformed into art."

—Salman Rushdie, author of *Quichotte*

"Relentlessly clear-eyed and virtuosic, *Survival Math* offers revelation after revelation; in the end, it remakes our understanding of the world and those in it."

—Jesmyn Ward, author of *Sing, Unburied, Sing*

"Mitchell Jackson shows us his youth in Portland with an unforgettable mix of sharp humor, wide interrogation, and indelible tragedy. . . . mesmerizing."

—Piper Kerman, author of *Orange Is the New Black*

"Penetrating social critique, rigorous self-examination, epochs and eras attired with a craftsmanship that seems effortless: by every measure, *Survival Math* is ahead of the curve."

—Greg Pardlo, author of *Air Traffic*

"In *Survival Math*, Mitchell Jackson turns a familial story into an American one, writing with brutal honesty about himself and the men and women who shaped him. . . . Put another way: this book is dope."

—Reginald Dwayne Betts, author of *Felon*

"Jackson's musings skillfully illuminate the bloodlines, both inherited and earned, that pulse through the body of America's gang-graffitied carceral state."

—Tyehimba Jess, author of *Olio*

"This story—this complex history of an American family that could be representative of many—Jackson, undoubtedly, proves is his. It beats like a part of him."

—Jason Reynolds, author of *Long Way Down*

"Mitchell Jackson's *Survival Math* is telling the truth as you've never heard it."

—Leslie Jamison, author of *Make It Scream, Make It Burn*

"With the code-switching agility of Toni Cade Bambara and with the lyric intellect of Albert Murray, *Survival Math* exhibits Mitchell Jackson at his full power, shining a light on the path ahead—indeed, helping us to survive—in one of the most challenging times in recent American history."

—A. Van Jordan, author of *The Cineaste*

"*Survival Math* is a compassionate meditation on the human costs of this country's ongoing war on black lives and—more importantly—the methods we employ to endure despite it all."

—Angela Flournoy, author of *The Turner House*

"After reading dozens of books on race, completing thousands of hours of research, and attending countless conferences, I can confidently say Mitch Jackson is one of the most important voices of our generation."

—D. Watkins, author of *We Speak for Ourselves*

"This story is grit and gilded; a space where individual pasts collide with our collective hopes for America's future."

—DaMaris B. Hill, *A Bound Woman Is a Dangerous Thing*

"Jackson tells an indisputable universal truth that will compel you to question everything you thought you knew about life and living in America."

—Sanderia Faye, award-winning author of *Mourner's Bench*

"In *Survival Math*, Mitchell Jackson pens an honest, firsthand account of a family caught up in the game."

—Jeffery Renard Allen, author of *Song of the Shank*

"Jackson doesn't flinch from the red hot center of the truth."

—Crystal Wilkinson, author of *The Birds of Opulence*

"*Survival Math* is the best memoir I've read in ages."

—Cheryl Strayed, author of *Wild*

"This book is beautiful and vital."

—Terrance Hayes, author of *American Sonnets for My Past and Future Assassin*

ALSO BY MITCHELL S. JACKSON

The Residue Years: A Novel

Oversoul: Stories and Essays

SURVIVAL MATH

NOTES ON AN ALL-AMERICAN FAMILY

MITCHELL S. JACKSON

SCRIBNER

New York   London   Toronto   Sydney   New Delhi

Scribner
An Imprint of Simon & Schuster, Inc.
1230 Avenue of the Americas
New York, NY 10020

First Scribner trade paperback edition February 2020

SCRIBNER and design are registered trademarks of The Gale Group, Inc.,
used under license by Simon & Schuster, Inc., the publisher of this work.

For information about special discounts for bulk purchases,
please contact Simon & Schuster Special Sales at 1-866-506-1949
or business@simonandschuster.com.

The Simon & Schuster Speakers Bureau can bring authors to your live event.
For more information or to book an event, contact the Simon & Schuster Speakers Bureau
at 1-866-248-3049 or visit our website at www.simonspeakers.com.

Interior design by Erich Hobbing

1   3   5   7   9   10   8   6   4   2

Library of Congress Control Number: 2018276116

ISBN 978-1-5011-3170-7
ISBN 978-1-5011-3173-8 (pbk)
ISBN 978-1-5011-3174-5 (ebook)

Selections from this book were previously published in different form, including:
"Revision" by the Center for Fiction and "Composite Pops" in *The Fire This Time*,
published by Scribner. Several of the Survival Files previously appeared in *Tin House*.

For Justice. For Jaden.

In memory of Erin "Jo Jo" Cowan.

"That man who is forced each day to snatch his manhood, his identity, out of the fire of human cruelty that rages to destroy it knows, if he survives his effort, and even if he does not survive it, something about himself and human life that no school on earth—and indeed, no church—can teach."

—James Baldwin

"And there are no new pains."

—Audre Lorde

CONTENTS

Author's Note   xv

Prologue: Dear Markus   1

PART 1

Who are we?

Exodus   15

Composite Pops   25

Matrimony   33

SURVIVOR FILES   53

PART 2

What have we learned?

Apples   67

The Scale   89

SURVIVOR FILES   149

PART 3

What have we endured?

American Blood   161

The Pose   177

Fast Ten, Slow Twenty   205
SURVIVOR FILES   229

PART 4

How do we proceed?

Survival Math   241
Revision   255
SURVIVOR FILES   271

Epilogue: Dear Justice   283
Acknowledgments   291
Notes   293

AUTHOR'S NOTE

We are survivors: descendants of the Africans who endured the wretched march to the west coast of their continent, brutal confinement, a cruel transatlantic passage, and reached—alive, somehow alive—the shores of a new world. Among the future generations of those captured humans are the men on this book cover, all of whom are my family members, each of whom I photographed and asked the same question: What's the toughest thing you've survived? I wrote their responses as second-person narratives and feature them along with their portraits. To grant a measure of anonymity, I forsook noting which story belongs to which man. The portraits and stories together form Survivor Files, which are presented in the interstices of the parts in this book. The narratives of the men in my family are separate from the narratives in the essays, but they are one with the story of black Americans. We are *all*-American, which is to say, our stories of survival are inseparable from the ever-fraught history of America.

SURVIVAL MATH

PROLOGUE

Dear Markus,

Ain't no way you could know this, but you were the first of us to set foot on the land that became the state where I was born—Oregon. And now here we are, strangers but not estranged, more like kindred, more like forevermore tethered to terra firma by a death date and birth date. Yours: August 16, 1788. Mine: August 16, 1975. Here I am centuries after your death, wanting to share with you what has become of the place where you gasped your last breath and I gloried my first.

There's much I don't know about your living-and-breathing in Cape Verde, so I've envisioned what it was like, have pictured you hanging near the ports—burnished, famished, bleary-eyed—proclaiming to anybody with ears that you'd board a ship bound for the New World and change forevermore your fortune. Then Captain Robert Gray and his crew docked their sloop for a little R & R and refitting. The way I picture it, Gray trekked inland and highsighted about how historic his voyage would be, about how he'd captain his *Lady Washington* around Cape Horn and through the Drake Passage to America's west coast to trade trinkets for furs and sail on to China, about how he was looking to add a new member to his small crew. As I imagine it, his notice sounded to you like the ocean looked in your dreams. So, you fat-mouthed to Gray and crew how much you knew about seafaring, how quick you could learn what you didn't know, big-upped how good you were with your hands, how able a swimmer you were, the super thew in your thin arms and legs, declared if there was a challenge to be met, you'd meet it, so help you God!

Whatever your pitch, sure enough you were soon aboard the ship and sailing around the horn for this New World. What were those days like? Did you expect to watch the sunset over the horizon, to witness a full moon in a sky sprent with stars, to hear the music of the sails catching the wind, but instead sorrowed over gales bashing the yards, a tempest tossing the ship on her broadside, Gray yelling, "All hands on deck"? Your

1

shipmate Haswell (Did y'all call him Robbie?) logged in his journal details of your first day in this place we share, your last day on earth. He wrote that the ship landed at Tillamook Bay and he and some of the crew had a meal with the natives while the rest of you were out cutting grass for the livestock, that you took a break, stabbed your cutlass in the sand, and when you turned your back, one of the natives snatched it and broke out. I imagine you dreaded (were it me, I would've been spooked something serious) the prospect of Gray learning you'd lost your tool, of him losing faith in you, and that you wanted to avoid at grave costs the prospect of the crew teasing you something terrible about being green, and-or the haters among them dubbing you a dim-witted black boy for the rest of the voyage. Or maybe it was fear that the cost of the tool would be subtracted from whatever pay Gray had offered, if he pledged any recompense at all. As Haswell told it, there wasn't much time between you peeping your missing cutlass and catching the culprit. Per his pen, while he and some of the other crew raced to your aid, the natives "instantly drenched their knives and spears with savage fury" in you until you released the thief, staggered, and fell dead. Haswell admitted he and the others (punk shit, perhaps) broke for the ship to avoid the same happening to them.

Markus, the second one of us (when I say "us," whom do you take it to mean?) on record to set foot in what became this place we share was a dude named York who traveled with the Lewis and Clark Expedition. York is damn near mythic for his time as Clark's indispensable manservant-slave. We—you and me—should feel proud of the tales of him whipsawing thick-ass logs at Camp Dubois, hefting supplies no one else could, flexing his superior skills at hunting buffalo, geese, brants, being chosen to share his "big medicine" with native women who believed him a dark-skinned and nappy-haired wonder.

York helped the corps map out part of the Oregon Trail in those pre–Civil War days when they called this place the Oregon Country—Oregon being a name anointed in 1822 by the Florida congressmen who proposed a bill to incorporate the area as territory. In the Oregon Country, owning slaves long-term was outlawed, however the autonomous provisional government passing a Lash Law, ephemeral though it was, confirms those Oregon pioneers were still anti-us: "Blacks in Oregon be they free or slave will be whipped twice a year until he or she shall quit the territory." Congress at last voted into existence the Oregon Territory in 1848 and elected a new provisional government or, rather, more men willing themselves white who believed with just the right statutes, one of which was our exclusion, this land could become their paradise. Markus, had you lived long enough to instead emigrate to this paradisiacal place post the repeal of its initial exclusion law, you would've been subject to laws that forbade you voting or acquiring free land or an ordained coupling with any white soul.

Who could and couldn't come, who could or couldn't stay, was tough, tough talk, though—praise, praise—it amounted to but one expulsion. That hapless victim was a fair-skinned man named Jacob Vanderpool. Picture Vanderpool dressed impeccable in a checkered vest and tailored trousers and bucked white shirt with his silk tie bowed just so, him buzzing around his boardinghouse-saloon-restaurant when the sheriff showed up to arrest him because a local white business owner contended him in violation of the exclusion law. Picture Vanderpool's lawyer soon thereafter arguing the charge against his client was out-and-out unconstitutional. Picture the prosecutor calling witnesses—none of whom can say for fact when this not-light-skinned-enough man arrived in their midst—and the judge delivering his verdict: "I being satisfied that the same Jacob Vanderpool is a mulatto and that he is remaining in the territory of Oregon contrary to the statutes and laws of the territory, do therefore order that the said Jacob Vanderpool remove from said territory within thirty days from and upon the service of this order—the said order to be served by showing to the said Jacob Vanderpool this original and at the same time delivering to him a true copy of the same."

Imagine that sheriff serving Vanderpool the verdict at his boardinghouse-saloon-restaurant the same day it was adjudged, and that judgment quavering in Vanderpool's hands as he read it again and again and worried over delivering the news to his workers and finding a state, a city, a people that would accept him. Imagine Vanderpool, a symbol for Oregon's colored folk for decades to come, packing all that he could over the next few days and striking off quiet and stealthy from a white man's land.

Seventy or so miles lie between the beach village where you drew your last breath and the curious city where I drew my first. A city birthed when men surnamed Lovejoy and Overton—fast friends canoeing the Willamette for Oregon City—docked near a well-known grove of trees called The Clearing. In my mind, the men hopped out, swanked inland, turned their hands to visors against a majestic sun, prospected as far as their cerulean (or were they green?) eyes could see, and proclaimed to their munificent God, *This should be ours*. In the next months, they cleared more land, built structures, laid out plans. Within a year, though, a flood hit and spooked Overton into selling his stake in the claim to a man surnamed Pettygrove. Per the lore, both Lovejoy and Pettygrove wanted to christen the settlement after the New England city they hailed from and thrice flipped a coppery penny that decided, Portland it would be.

Portland cityhood preceded Oregon statehood, which congress granted on Valentine's Day in 1859. Should you have lived into your nineties and tried to settle in this nascent state, you would've discovered how unloved, unwelcomed, and unsecured you were, would've found every bit of you opposed by its exclusion law—the lone legislation of its kind for states admitted into the Union: "No free negro, or mulatto, not residing in this State at the time of the adoption of this Constitution, shall come, reside, or be within this State, or hold any real estate, or make any contracts, or maintain any suit therein; and the Legislative Assembly shall provide by penal laws, for the removal, by public officers, of all such negroes, and mulattoes, and for their effectual exclusion from the State, and for the punishment of persons who shall bring them into the State, or employ, or harbor them."

In the history of Oregon, our folks have numbered, most years, less than 5 percent of its residents, so it shouldn't be no big old surprise that in the 1920s, the second coming of the KKK flourished in this blanched state and its cities. Here's proof: one summer night the Portland klavern goaded reporters and civic leaders to a meeting in a hotel with the cryptic message, "learn something to your advantage." Once the invited guests arrived, Klan members ushered them out of the hotel and into cars that chauffeured them to a secret "throne room," where reporters with box cameras and pens and notepads and a pair of Klansmen in full regalia awaited them. That evening, the Klan argued they weren't a hate group, that they'd be a powerful ally to the friends of "law and order." To close the meeting, the King Kleagle—a southern transplant who believed the state a monolithic promised land for his ilk—offered an ominous warning: "Respect for the law and the working of a small army of unofficial detectives who will work with the constituted law are the marks of the Klan character . . . There are some cases, of course, in which we will have to take everything into our hands. Some crimes are not punishable under existing laws, but criminals should be punished." The next day the

papers ran a photo that featured the Exalted Cyclops and King Kleagle
in their gleaming white glory suits beside dark-suited attendees, which
included the chief and captain of police, a sheriff, the US district attorney
and (state) district attorney, reps for the Justice Department and National
Safety Council—even the mayor. That winter of 1922 the Klan held its
first public meeting and lured thousands of curious Portlanders into the
Municipal Auditorium for a keynote speech titled "The Truth about the
Invisible Empire, Knights of the Ku Klux Klan."

Markus, while the Klan flourished in the 1920s, so did we—much
credit due to the Golden West Hotel, the nexus of our social life in the
city, which ain't me in the least dismissing the Freeman Second Hand
store; Rutherford Haberdashery, Barbershop, Cigar and Confectionery
Store, or the Egyptian Theatre, despite folks who looked like us being
forced to sit in the balcony no matter how many seats sat empty below
us. A couple of decades later, the city's infinitesimal black community
boasted activists like Otto and Verdell Rutherford, who from the forties
to the sixties turned their living room into a virtual mimeograph factory
for the NAACP. It also included members of the NACW (National
Association for Colored Women), who once protested for the hiring of
black postal workers. It came to include indefatigable members of the
National Urban League and The Black United Front. And best believe
we needed every single one of them. Back then Portland was a place
where one of us might be searching for a Sunday brunch or dinner spot
and be confronted by a "whites only" or "we cater to white only trade,"
sentiments we hoped we'd escaped.

In this state, in this city, there ain't no escaping the gray, and days
of rain, rain, rain. There was a time when we couldn't escape redlining
neither—or in other words, the Portland Realty Board's corrupt "Code
of Ethics," edicts which forbade Realtors and bankers from selling us
homes in prime neighborhoods for fear we'd plunge their worth. And
should we forget our sanctioned limits, bold-ass bigots would spike hand-
drawn posters on their lawns—"WE WANT WHITE TENANTS IN
OUR WHITE COMMUNITY; WE WANT WHITE TENANTS IN OUR
NEIGHBORHOOD"—to remind us.

Scores of us can trace our roots in this city, the Rose City, to the 1940s,
when one of our kinfolk from down South peeped a Help Wanted ad in
their hometown paper, packed their life into bags and-or suitcases, and
caught boxcars called the Magic Carpet Special or the Kaiser Caravan into

Portland for a chance to build a new life working in one of Henry Kaiser's shipyards. Those relatives locomoted into the City of Roses and found a hovel or shacked up with friends or relatives or in some cases slept on the pool table of a tavern and washed their private parts in a squalid bathroom. Or else moved to a slapdash development dubbed Kaiserville and renamed Vanport City. No matter the shelter they found, they could feel gratified building Liberty ships that would help the Allies beat the Nazis while clocking more dough for work than they ever did where they came from.

Vanport was an incontrovertible boon for our folks, but that changed on Memorial Day—May 30—1948. Picture this: men, women, families living in slipshod housing built on wetlands the year snowmelt and more deluges than even a raintastic city could stand swelled the Columbia River to record heights. Picture residents waking one morning to find a flyer slipped under their door that read, "Remember: Dikes are safe at present. You will be warned if necessary. You will have time to leave. Don't get excited." That late afternoon, air-raid sirens blared and city and college workers and police and men and women and boys on bikes raced through the streets warning, "THE DAM IS BROKEN! THE DAM IS BROKEN! GET TO HIGHER GROUND!" Picture men in sport coats and fedoras humping trunks on their backs and mothers in long print dresses toting shirtless diapered babies or armloads of hangered clothes, all fleeing for higher ground. Taxis and buses, with passengers pushing the limits of physics, tore up a hill to drop their loads until a crush of stalled cars blocked the route. Imagine the Columbia River surging into the city in leviathan waves and men late in minding the mandate to evacuate wading through waist-high muddy water with their toddlers on their shoulders. The water sank cars, snatched buildings off their foundations, rose beyond the tops of stop signs. Dozens gathered along an avenue and gawked at the scene below: at couples stranded on their roofs, men in powerboats breaking through windows for rescues, inconsolable housewives crying, "We lost everything!" What had been moments ago a delta was now a filthy lake teeming with letters, heirlooms, photos. That night the Red Cross opened emergency headquarters in downtown Portland and dozens of hospitals, churches, schools, and strangers' homes became relief centers.

The flood scuttled the lion's share of us for shelter in Northeast Portland's Albina district, which sent the Germans and Scandinavians hightailing for the suburbs. Before long somebody dubbed Northeast

"Tombstone Territory" or "The Tombs," and like other exercises in municipal neglect, it became a threat to our well-being. My mama grew up in the Tombs and testifies not to its menace but to memories of grown folks shambling to Mr. Collins's store to buy greens in a box or waiting for the fruit guy to hit Mississippi Ave with crates of apples harvested in Hood River. To the times that when a child was sick, parents would call the Watkins products man or shuffle down to Rexall drugstore for back-home remedies. Mom recalls my great-grandmama shuttling her and her uncle-brothers and aunt-sisters to the Lloyd Center mall to pick out a winter coat; she reminisces about the days or weekends she and a dusky crew would skip down to the community center for a class on crocheting or knitting or cooking or quilting, for lessons on how to swim or weave a gimp.

Circa the time Mom was rocking pigtails and traipsing to craft classes, the Cotton Club was the hot spot for grown folks. Markus, you would've had to live lifetimes for the chance to pick your Afro planetary, don loud polyester pants and a ruffle or puffed-sleeve shirt, and escort your main squeeze down to the club. Once inside, you might spend the night puffing menthols and ordering libations while you watched the live show of an act you'd seen on *American Bandstand* or *Soul Train*. Other nights you'd swear the room chimerical as you sat tables away from Cab Calloway or Joe Louis or Sammy Davis Jr. Every night, the carousing would end with the club's sailor-capped proprietor touting, "We're the only nightclub on the West Coast with wall-to-wall soul."

Those were good times, good, good times. But since there ain't never been such a thing as celebration enough to null our plight, we rioted in '67, set firebombs in '69. The riots nor the bombs posed a problem of much significance to those in power, since in the scheme and scope of this city, this state, we—deemed *negroes* at the time—have never amounted to much beyond a noisome political nuisance. As proof, I submit to you the time strangers once appeared at the front door of dozens of Northeast residents and warned them to move because the city had approved plans to raze their houses for a hospital expansion and new coliseum. Some of the imminently displaced joined the Emanuel Displaced Persons Association, and one meeting witnessed a neighbor beseeching bureaucrats to treat her with "dignity and care." As further proof, I submit the time Portland's *un*finest dumped three dead possums on the doorstep of the Burger Barn because they believed it a neighborhood treasure.

The city's first black police commissioner fired those officers, and an arbitrator, with the quickness, reinstated their jobs.

Markus, there's the history of ours that's hit the books, what evermore should live in its ledgers, but we must, I must, keep alive the record of where we lived and how we lived and what we lived and died for—lest it slip into the ether. If it's cool with you, I'd like to skip ahead to when I was a wee bit, to the umpteen days I spent decked in a purple robe belting "Goin' Up Yonder" as part of the youth choir of the First AME Zion—the oldest African Methodist church in the state. In those days, my great-grandmother or great-aunt or some other born-again relative would drag my brothers and cousins and brother-cousins and sister-cousins and me to what felt like a yearlong Sunday service or a nightlong Sunday service or holiday service or revival. When service would end, we'd gather in a church hall and gobble, our paper plates soaked through with collard green juice or chicken grease, mountainous church dinners. What I want to tell you about is the one year I played Little League baseball at Peninsula Park (I couldn't hit a fastball for shit), where Saturdays they held games on several diamonds; where four-on-four battles turned the hoop courts across the park into a chain net symphony. Kids my age swam in the park's pool until the whites of our eyes turned devil red or else our aquatic fun was cut short 'cause somebody's baby brother or sister or cousin pissed or shat in the shallow end. Those days included skipping an afternoon to Union Ave—later named MLK Jr. Boulevard—with the coins or loose bills I haggled out of an adult or mined from the bottom of my mama's purse or collected from a couch or change jar to cop hot food or candy from Johnny & Lennie's convenience store. On birthdays or a special day, I had action at a trip to the caramel popcorn shop in the mall or an ice cream parlor or the pizza parlor with the fire engine truck displayed inside. Back then our Biddy Ball seasons birthed hoop dreams (we played for a certain team or else we wasn't as cold as we thought we was), reveries that, if they didn't flame out all too soon, meant balling in spring tournaments held hours elsewhere and spending whole summers practicing in Irving Park. Most of the hoopers I know spent part of their summers working for a nonprofit that serviced at-risk youth. Or all of it being one.

Coming of age in this place meant feeling as though I'd toured damn near every elementary school in Northeast—not because I wanted to, but because there was often something or other that made the rent impossible for my mama or whoever else to pay; it meant attending a few middle schools and a couple of high schools, catching a public bus to school and standing at an uncovered bus stop on an ultra-drenched day with the frail hope somebody I knew would ride by and swoop.

The day after my thirteenth birthday, a carload of Bloods murdered Ray Ray Winston, the city's inaugural gang homicide. Reporters interviewed Ray Ray's mama the next day, broadcasted her standing outside the projects in a shower cap and black jacket with a microphone punched at her shoulder. "He [Ray Ray] was well loved by everybody," she explained. "He didn't mess with nobody." They showed Ray Ray's high school hoop coach with a mess of hair under a baseball cap and sunglasses hanging from the neck of his T-shirt. "He'd [Ray Ray'd] be the kind of kid you'd want for a son," he told reporters. Then there was the spectacle of young Ray Ray's funeral: Police blocking all access roads to the church, police questioning drivers, police conducting targeted searches of people making their way for the entrance. A procession of mourners filing into the church, among them a dude wearing suspendered slacks and a white shirt, somebody's grandpa in muttonchop sideburns and a sharkskin suit, a woman wearing a Leisure Curl and ankle-length leaf-print dress, youngsters in their Sunday best. And hella Crips there to support their fallen comrade: Crips sporting rags tied over their heads and locs, Crips donning blue plaid shirts single buttoned at the throat, Crips wearing sweatshirts with the words "RIP Ray Ray LOC / CVC" ironed on the back, and still another Crip set marching to the church in a uniform of black hats and white tees and blue jeans.

Ray Ray's death heralded our—the *our* being my cohorts and the hardheads who succeeded us—enduring love affair with colors, served as proof we'd become mortal threats to each other. But that same year, the second coming of the KKK known as the skinheads also proved baleful. One night, skins fresh off passing out white power pamphlets and burning hours guzzling beers, accosted an Ethiopian grad student named Mulugeta Seraw who was outside his car chatting with friends. The racists yelled at Seraw and his homies to move, and when they didn't, they hopped out their compact and started wailing on them. That night, a skin named Ken "Death" Mieske grabbed a bat from his trunk and bashed Seraw three times in the skull, the final blow crushing "his head between the bat and the hard pavement."

Seraw was murdered in Southeast Portland, but the nexus of our life (and death) for a few decades more was Northeast Portland, what we rechristened the NEP or The Town. And Markus, had you been born again and lived among us tenderfoot NEP dwellers, we might've called you OG or Big homie or Big Bro or fam or fanley or cuddie or patna.

The Town featured no poverty of dudes disposed to fray: dudes named Peek-a-Boo or Pep or Cowboy or Face or Rabbit or Cluck or Big Red or Champ or Chip or Stitches or T.N. or Nook Nook or M&M or Monie or J.D. or DBo or Devious or South Central or Eastwood or Hollywood or Fastlivin or Lazy or Teaspoon or Chu-Chu or Maniac or Kenny Mack or Blazer or A-Bone or Big Red or No Toes or O-Dog or Quick. Those who put in abundant work received the honor of a deuce: like Little Smurf was to Big Smurf, like Lil Foxy was to Foxy, like Hog Deuce was to T-Hog.

All that work has begot eras of Big homies and lil homies and gang heroes and gang villains and funerals of Big and lil homies and heroes and villains and innocents that include crowds so large they spill out of an Avenue Baptist church and into the street (RIPs). The NEP, The Town, demands ample faith and dozens upon dozens of places to worship. We also homage the rose: the Rose Garden, Rose Quarter, rosebushes in the yards of homes in the West Hills, in neighborhoods where developers build and open to the public, a new Street of Dreams every year—a street that is for someone else's dreams, because the truth is, some of us dream, but far too many dream small, realistic. And when those young dreams desert us some start demanding by force things that ain't ours. Others move to Vegas to pimp, purchase a new ride, and voyage home with the intent of triumphing up and down MLK. Those who stay local, those with aspirations average as shit and abandoned faith, covet restored muscle cars with custom systems, exotic paint, and wire rims with too many spokes to count. Others (oh boy, this was me) cop a sack from a Big homie, a precooked and acetone-cut underweighed dope sack, and stand on a street grown folk warned us off: Failing or Going or Gantenbein or Skidmore or Mallory or Rodney or Church or Roselawn, corners where young boys whose quivering flames were doused previous to ours, carry stolen straps and grudges against the world. We posted on hot blocks all night for damn near nothing, only half of which, if we were lucky, was ours to keep. That was our cosmos, the reason there's been a helluva chance of finding who we've been looking for in the Justice Center, if for months we ain't seen them on the streets.

One summer, recalcitrant dudes known as The Richmonds stealthed among us on a mission to murder my cousin-friend for an alleged heist. Word was they promised to kill members of his family if they couldn't find him. They spied his stepfather at a gas station and shot several bullets into his back. They later found my cousin-friend's car outside the house of a girl who'd just celebrated her twenty-first birthday. They surrounded and fired more than fifty bullets into the house, killing her. Not too long after, they broke into the apartment of my cousin-friend's biological father and beat him for his son's whereabouts. When he wouldn't or couldn't reveal it, they shot him in the leg and groin, put a picture of my cousin-friend in his hand, and shot him one last time in the head.

And I've told you this because I need you to know that the NEP and what's happened in it is as much a part of Oregon, of Portland, Oregon, as pioneers and a copper penny and the Street of Dreams.

But I've been away some years, and denizens of the old NEP have been pushed to the city's periphery, out to a place we call The Numbers. Now the Rose City, home, may damn well be a new city—one whose inheritors post placards that read "KEEP PORTLAND WEIRD" or "KEEP OREGON WEIRD" and tacit, so tacit, charge all those that ain't them with translation.

Markus, I'll close soon, but before I do, I must tell you about a not-so-long-ago day I cruised the arteries of this new city: Alberta, Mississippi, Williams Ave. Saw on Alberta a staffing company and a yoga studio and restaurant-bars. Saw cheery citizens lunching on a patio under the shade of tall trees and a vacant lot transformed into a scaled metropolis of food trucks. There was a clothing store and a bike shop and a sticker shop and a doughnut shop and a place that fixes guitars. That day I rode up and down Mississippi and saw a tattoo shop and tea shop and an art gallery and a bookstore. Witnessed a shabby dude—the lone brown face for blocks in any direction—flitting to destination somewhere. Saw a café that sells crepes and a boutique that hawks high-end eyeglasses. While wheeling the wide berth of an interminable-ass bike lane, I peeped a dude on a mountain bike in khakis and an oxford shirt and a woman tattooed in plural on a cruiser. Every few feet, or so it seemed, construction crews were erecting odes to privilege. On Williams Ave, I beheld more miles of bike lanes and bike shops and bikers and the BikeBar. There was an art deco hospital building under construction and a bakery and a hair studio and a Pilates studio and yet another damn yoga studio. There was a mother pushing a hooded stroller and a couple traipsing the sidewalk hand in hand as if this world would never fail them. But what I didn't see on Williams Ave was a single black face any which way my head turned.

Our absence made me question whether this new city is the yield of what they've sown or what we've reaped? It made me wonder if it's our just due from surrendering our hope too soon or dreaming pragmatic or mashing on somebody's baby girl all winter to glory new wheels down MLK in majestic summer brilliance or being enchanted with colors or transforming from one gang to the other or copping a dope sack on consignment from a head-start-on-prison Big homie and posting all night on a dim side street for a few bucks, if even a buck, of profit or seizing with a strap what don't belong to us or flouting a second or third strike and revolving to prison to serve a mandatory minimum stretch; I asked myself, could this new place—home—which seems so much the locus of our undoing, be the harvest of our collective deeds? The answer is, yes. But the answer is also that you and me and the generations between and beyond us must refuse assuming the greatest weight for what this place has become. Because if these centuries attest to anything, it's to the incontrovertible truth that this ain't our Eden, and won't be, for that was never their intent.

Until,
Mitch, AKA the lil homie

PART 1

Who are we?

Hallowed African blood.
Our fathers brought forth
upon this continent, living and dead,
sold as slaves, so far below
the scale of created beings, altogether unfit
to associate with the white race,
subject to the jurisdiction thereof.
Unfortunate. Uncivilized.
Due certain unalienable rights,
privileges, immunities, guaranteed to the citizen.
Vote denied, abridged by one nation,
indivisible, marked by every act.
Men, women, children [dis]united.

EXODUS

My exodus occurs after years wandering the wilderness of my hometown, the crucible that included working a part-time, and only-time, gig at the *Oregonian*'s downtown insert facility stacking pallet after pallet of inky-ass newspapers. For bread to live. For bread to leave. The day in question, I got a phone call from someone who, for the love (and just maybe his liberty), I'll call Brother A. Brother A called me to plead a ride to his apartment in the burbs to sweep for dope after his dope-dealing roommate, a dude who'd already done a nickel in the pen on a drug charge (which, by the way, is not judgment, but context), had just got knocked by the Feds. Brother A explained he needed the ride because his main squeeze had wrecked his Jeep, and he couldn't think of anyone more fitting than me, of all people on God's verdant earth, me, to be the one to shuttle him.

Heeeeeelllll no! That should have been my answer. But that was not my answer. My answer tugged me out of my job at the end of my shift and into the forest-evergreen Lexus I'd bought in the bygone unblessed days when I sold more than weed. It sent me bolting out of my job and into my ride to swoop Brother A from someplace close and hit Highway 26 with most dubious sense.

Guessing now is as good a time as ever to mention that this was the age during which I might've been selling weed—twenty sacks, eighths, half and whole zips, and in the most blessed of times, half and whole pounds. Selling chronic, stacking newspapers, and throwing parties because evermore this brother, a brother, every brother should diversify his hustle. No mights or maybes to that.

Memories from that age, hypothetical and otherwise, seldom feature date stamps, but I can assure you this incident occurred May 2002 AD, which I know for truth because one of my homeboys and me had just thrown a well-attended Memorial Day shindig, and between my cut of the door and profits from the weed I may have been selling, I had a knot of bills in my inky work jeans—which accounts for why at the time I was feeling at least extra medium about myself. Brother A and I traded lightweight banter en route, and before I knew it, we'd reached his apartment complex, grounds of such expanse, there was plenty of time for my pulse to cease between the moment I pulled into the lot and when I found a place to park my tree-colored ride. Can't speak for Brother A, but in that interstice of arriving and stepping a wary foot out of my ride, I had visions of police swarming us from bushes and vans, seizing discomfited me, slamming my cheek against unforgiving asphalt, and *KABLOWING!* on cuffs.

We did not—word to Yahweh—get ambushed that moment. We hustled past a passel of blithe youngsters and mounted a flight and a flight and a flight of stairs and stood at the threshold of his apartment door (my heart athunder) and asked each other again and for the last time if we should enter, which, inhale, of course we did.

Breathe. Breathe. Breathe.

———

No one was inside. Good sense says I should've left Brother A to brave his fate alone but instead I sat on the living room couch while he proceeded to sweep his roommate's room and the hall closets and every place else he could think to look. He didn't find any meth, but he did find cooking supplies and utensils, which he took straight to the kitchen to scrub and scour. Meanwhile, I sat on the living room couch doing my best impression of ecclesiastical calm.

"Man, I can't believe we was so spooked," I said.

"Yeah, we silly," he said. "Like the police worried about us."

He paused and motioned at me. "Shit, I almost forgot. Come check this out." This is when Brother A led me to his bedroom, pulled a pound of weed from a stash spot, and flaunted a sample. "This some killer," he said. "Smell it." What may or may not have happened next now seems like an act of intercession bestowed by my great-grandmama or some other church-going kin. That act, amen, was using my shirt to grab the plastic bag and inspect a few fluffy, sticky, fragrant stems. I put the weed back and mentioned how fast it would sell and may or may not have asked him if he could cop for me.

He and I strolled back into the living room—me to the couch and Brother A back to washing possible evidence down the drain. Seconds later I heard footsteps on the stairs. *PATTER, PATTER, PATTER!* Heard them and said to myself, *Here come those kids. PATTER, PATTER, PATTER, PAT-TER!* Thought to myself, *Wow, them some heavy-footed-ass kids. PATTER,*

PATTER, PATTER, PATTER, PATTER! Mused, *Boy, there must be more kids than I thought.* That's when Brother A hustled over to the peephole, said, "Oh, shit! POLICE!" and broke for his bedroom.

Before I could move, a mob of police, sheriff, and DEA bum-rushed into Brother A's crib. "Get on the ground! Get on the ground now! Keep your hands where we can see them! Get down! Get down!"

Oh. My. God! I thought, and dropped to my knees then prostrate.

Brother A darted into the living room and ranted, "Let me see your warrant. Let me see your warrant," and in an instant, they spun him face to wall and cuffed him. One officer jerked me off the carpet and asked if I was carrying drugs, if I had anything in my pockets that might cut or poke him. No, I said. And he emptied my pockets, beheld my cell phone and pager and the knot of cash—most of which, let me remind you, I'd made from my Memorial Day shindig and some of which I may or may not have made from serving fat sacks of chronic. More officers appeared, one of them tugging a stout German shepherd. That same officer informed me that if the dog hit on anything from my pockets, he'd confiscate it.

He let his canine loose. It sniffed my wrinkled wad of bills and barked.

Ain't that a bitch! I thought.

The next moment, an officer bopped into the apartment carrying a bag of weed that could've been a motherfucking facsimile of the one Brother A may or may not have flaunted to me thrumming pulses ago. The officer announced he'd found it in a sprinkler outside, asked which one of us it belonged to, and Brother A and me bucked our eyes at each other and damn near shook our heads off our necks. "Huh, what's that? We ain't never seen that in life!" we said.

He crooked his lip and warned if he found either of our fingerprints on the bag he'd charge us.

The officer who searched me marched me into a bedroom and ordered me ass to floor and back to wall while he stood.

He asked me if I knew Brother A's roommate.

"Yes," I said. "Don't know him well, more like 'Hi' and 'Bye,' but yes," I said. "I met him."

He asked if I knew Brother A's roommate sold dope.

"Wow, he did?!" I said. "I had no idea."

He asked if I'd ever been to jail or prison.

"Um, uh—Yes," I said. "One time. Just the one time, though."

He asked me what I'd gone to jail for.

"Um, uh, um, uh, um—for selling drugs," I said, and the rest fell out my mouth: "But it's not what you think. I don't do it anymore, Officer. I'm going to be a writer. Officer, you got to believe me. I'm moving to New York in a few months for grad school. This looks bad, Officer, but it's not how it looks. My word, Officer. Just a few months till I leave," I said. "Please, Officer, please. You've got to let me go!"

———

"Let my people go," Moses and Aaron told the pharaoh of Egypt at the advent of history's most famous exodus. The Hebrew name for Egypt, where Moses's people began their journey, is *Mitzrayim*. For Jews, *Mitzrayim* denotes a place, but it also describes a liberation from psychological limits, the emotional journeys that one experiences all life long. My *Mitzrayim* demanded envisioning a world beyond one that in many ways had been circumscribed; it required believing I could thrive outside where I was born.

The west exodus of my tribe—the Jacksons—began in the 1950s, in the *Mitzrayim* that was Montgomery, Alabama. It could begin with my great-grandparents—Edith "Mama Edie" Larkin Jackson and Samuel "Bubba" Andrew Jackson Sr.—at a mass meeting of the Montgomery Improvement Association, the couple among dozens of spirited negroes filling the hard wooden pews of Dexter Avenue Baptist Church. My great-grandmama styling in a floral-print knee-length dress and cat-eye specs, and my great-grandaddy decked out in a dark worsted-wool suit and wing-tips polished reflective. Picture the whole room hand in hand and swaying as they sing, "Gooooo down, Moses / Waaaay down in Egypt's land / Tell old Pharaoh / Let my people gooooo." The room raises its voice till it shakes the stained-glass windows, then falls hush as MLK, the disciple, prophet, future martyr (go ahead, choose) of an age takes the pulpit in one of his tailored blue suits and a skinny tie and sermonizes on the plans of a Montgomery Transit Authority boycott that, in the days of the Old Testament, might've summoned thunder and lightning. In that meeting or one not too long after, MLK asks for volunteers to carpool members of the boycott and Mama Edie nudges Bubba to raise his hand.

Per familial lore, Mama Edie's mama, Carrie Larkin AKA my great-great-grandmother, was a Montgomery bootlegger par excellence, a savvy woman who invested her ample profits in square miles of terra firma and a restaurant. My great-great-grandmother bore her husband eight children—four girls and four boys—and of that brood, my great-grandmother Edith "Edie" Larkin was the third girl, born in 1916. Edie was beautiful and smart and the daughter most liable to test the house rules. Mama Edie's enterprising mother paid her way through what was then Alabama State College—she did the same for all her daughters. Mama Edie, like every one of her sisters, became a schoolteacher and lived a comfortable life for the time and place thanks to what seemed like inexhaustible deals. They sold tract after tract of family land and divvied up the dividends among their tribe.

Unlike the Larkins, the Jacksons were not a tribe of wealth. My great-grandfather Samuel "Bubba" Andrew Jackson Sr. was born in 1908 in Ada, Alabama, a place so small they call it an unincorporated community of Montgomery County. Bubba was the second to the youngest of his parents' brood of four, and despite being ambitious and hardworking and smart with a miraculous recall for dates, times, and facts, he was forced, like many of his time, to cease his formal schooling before he reached high school. Young Bubba married his first wife, Lillian Dora Arrington, sired his lone biological son, Samuel Andrew Jackson Jr.—my grandfather—and supported his wife and baby boy by running a shoe shop and selling Watkins products door-to-door. Bubba's first wife died of a food-related illness a few years into their marriage, and he met Mama Edie soon after, married for the second time in 1942, and moved to a trailer on Larkin land in a part of town known as the Prairie.

———

The English word *exodus* is derived from the Greek *ex*, which means "out," and *hodos*, meaning "way"—the way out. A year or so before MLK moved from Montgomery to Atlanta and became assistant pastor to his father at Ebenezer Baptist Church, Mama Edie and Bubba made their way out of Alabama to a land that, if not one of milk and honey, promised to be a place less bitter in their mouths. Their migration to Portland began, so one story goes, in the summer of '58 or '59. Mama Edie flew to Portland to visit her sister-in-law and felt so passionate about the city that she phoned Bubba and persuaded him to pack their things and move. Per another story, Mama Edie moved out to Portland with the express intent of helping to integrate the Portland Public Schools, a district that announced soon after the *Brown v. Board of Education* ruling that it would "take no action regarding segregation," despite blacks being relegated almost exclusively to the underfunded and subpar schools in the Albina district. In my mind, the true catalyst for my great-grandparents' migration was somewhere between the stories of love for a new city and wanting to transform it.

In addition to those stories, these facts: Mama Edie and Bubba moved into a house on North Missouri Ave in the Albina district. My activist and missionary-minded great-grandmother got a job teaching at Boise-Eliot Elementary School, a position that began her long career as a beloved Portland teacher. In the City of Roses, Bubba earned his living first as a shoe repairman and, until retirement, as a hospital custodian. In 1960, not too long after they moved to their promised land, they persuaded Sam Jackson Jr., the biological son Bubba fathered by his first wife, to move from Alabama with his wife and four young children—Sam III, George, Anthony, and my mother, Lillie. Meanwhile my great-grands lived sans significant marital quarrels and as loving and supportive friends in plural. They also became active members of St. Andrew Catholic Church and continued their political activism. If there was an asterisk to their marriage, it was the fact that they couldn't conceive a child, an issue they addressed by adopting three children between the late 1950s and the 1960s: Ezekiel and Essie as toddlers and later a grade-school-aged boy named John. Mama Edie and Bubba's adopted children were raised with my mother and her brothers as siblings, as they were close in age and all lived at times under the same roof.

In the summer of 1975, my mother bore Mama Edie and Bubba their first great-grandchild: me. The pair were out of town that August I was born, attending to Mama Edie's niece who had a baby due a month before me. My great-grands traveled back to Portland in September and my mother resumed, with me this time, living with them in a white house the size of a small palace that stands on the corner of Sixth and Mason.

———

The House on Sixth Avenue.

Home.

Let me tell you about the old cherry tree in the front yard of that home, whose stingy yield we'd pluck before it ripened, about the plum and pear trees and blackberry bushes in the backyard, about the garden that Mama Edie tended with love. A hex-web fence surrounded the whole yard, and I'd get scolded for playing on it. If Mama Edie, the family's most austere disciplinarian, chided me more than a few times (which most times meant any more than once), I was commanded to fetch a switch, and if I returned with one too flimsy, I'd be sent for another ad infinitum.

Most folks entered our home through the thick wooden door inset with a large oval glass draped by thin red curtains, an entrance that opened onto a living room with embroidered green couches wrapped in hard plastic and a glass-top coffee table encasing ruby-handled swords. My great-grands had bedazzled the dining room with a chandelier made of a billion oblong crystals and a veneered table that could seat the Last Supper, not to mention a paradise of potted plants lining the window ledges. The kitchen was pasted with a pattern of pots and pans—wallpaper that bubbled in spots and peeled away from the moldings—and some mornings I'd open the kitchen cabinet to search for cornflakes and see a mouse skittering out of sight or else a trail of tiny rodent turds. Mama Edie hobbied on the piano and kept a scratched black upright in a nook that was also decked with earth-toned tweed couches. My great-grands kept their bedroom door locked, but some nights they'd let me inside to sprawl across the bed while Bubba sat in a cracked leather recliner watching the news on an itty-bitty black-and-white TV. Mama Edie kept kiwis, pomegranates, mangoes, and other "special" fruits on her bedroom windowsill, and on the rarest occasions would award one of us kids with a half or whole for minding her commandments. In the mid-eighties—after Mama Edie beat breast cancer but suffered a stroke that paralyzed half her body—she slept in the downstairs room just off the curtained front door of the house. Beaucoup times, I'd tramp past her room, which often smelled of Vicks VapoRub, and she'd beckon me to find her wig or prosthetic breast or to help her into her wheelchair. One night a bullet sang through the window in that room but didn't shatter it, which was the kind of grace I imagined in abundance among the flock who worshipped in the church behind the house.

Weekday evenings or weekend mornings or afternoons, members of the Full Gospel Temple of Prayer Church Inc. would clang cymbals and tambourines, pound drums, smash organ keys; would sing and shout praise that bullied its way through our walls, that might've floated all the way to Bethlehem. Us Jacksons never attended that church. On the other hand, Mama Edie obliged us all to attend Sunday mass. Every. Sunday. And on top of that, whenever the spirit moved her, our matriarch would roam into all the rooms and demand we—Bubba, my mama, an aunt, uncle, cousin, visiting friend—grab our Bibles and haste into the living room, her very own tent of meeting. Once everyone showed, we'd sing from a selected catalog of spirituals: "We Are Soldiers," "Amazing Grace," "Goin' Up Yonder," "Jesus Is on the Main Line," "Soon and Very Soon," "His Eye Is on the Sparrow," "This Little Light of Mine," "Because He Lives." We'd read a Bible verse, and when we finished, Mama Edie would ask us to explain it. She'd request us to choose another verse and read and interpret that too. Near the end of devotion, we'd circle, take up hands, and recite the Lord's Prayer. She'd end by asking us one by one what we were thankful for. And we best be able to give thanks.

My great-grandmother, God rest her soul, would sound a trumpet from heaven for me to fetch the thickest switch on earth if she got wind I'd read word one of Nietzsche's *The Antichrist*, the philippic in which he claims, among other faults of the Christians, that they had weakened the concept of God when they recast the Hebrews' God of Israel into the "god of every man" and "god of a people," into a deity he described as the "good god," as "goodness-in-itself." Nietzsche argues that there is only one way to conceive of a powerful God and that is as the God of a nation, a national God. My great-grands had been taught to believe in that everyman's God, a God who, in due time, would bless the oppressed, the weak, the unfortunate—their people. That teaching was a product of being born in and near the first capital of the Confederacy during what historian Rayford Logan has termed "the nadir of American race relations," the infamous era of American history between the end of Reconstruction and the early twentieth century when racism was worse than any time in post–Civil War America.

How could my great-grands disbelieve in a personal God when they were descendants of Africans who'd been enslaved by Europeans who, as part of willing themselves into a white race, indoctrinated masses of blacks to love and obey a private God, to abide unjust suffering, to weather what seemed an interminable wait for Thy Kingdom Come, and to bequeath that doctrine to their seeds. But as Nietzsche argues, "when a nation is on the downward path, when it feels its belief in its own future, its hope of freedom slipping from it, when it begins to see submission as a first necessity and the virtues of submission as measures of self-preservation, then it *must* overhaul its god." Sometime between Lincoln's symbolic proclamation and the epic battle for civil rights, the people I call my people began to remake their God into a national God that would anoint their quest for liberation. Sometime in those years between winning legal freedom and claiming actual freedoms, black folks transformed themselves—in no small part by forging lives for themselves outside of the South—into as much of a nation as they have ever been (it seems sometimes into as much of one as they may ever be) in the Other America, what has been an Egypt, our *Mitzrayim*.

———————

In the Torah, and in the great good book Mama Edie and Bubba commanded we cherish, heed, and love, God sent word through Moses for the pharaoh to release his chosen people from Egypt. But here's a confession: I've always had trouble conceding that any one group is God's chosen. The forever blathering critic in me, against ample data otherwise, must believe my God, your God, a God bestows egalitarian love, wouldn't give preference to one righteous person over another, one righteous people over another. And while I'm convinced of the sublime power in a person believing their future destined, in a people believing its fortune ordained, in some ways, seeing the impetus for change as outside oneself works to thwart the force needed to mobilize, to sustain the long pursuit of becoming a nation worthy of a revised God's blessings. Because of this, a people—which of course means each person—must translate, "Thus saith the LORD God of the Hebrews, Let my people go," into "Let us go!" They must at some point look no further than themselves for license to prosper, must believe that the true chosen ones are the righteous that choose themselves.

It might sound highfalutin, but "Let us go!" goaded my great-grands to Portland, grandparents too. It's the mantra of a people who subscribe to the belief that to escape the rule of a pharaoh, they must demand of the known world the wealth heretofore usurped from them. It's a chorus for those who profess their destiny as manifest. "Let us go!" fuels all great exoduses, by which I mean journeys that beget for a people chances to thrive, guarantees of justice, a home.

And what people would seek nationhood that fell short of those terms?

———————

Five troubling months after the ordeal with Brother A that ended in my near arrest and me pleading with an officer to "let me go," I boarded a one-way flight for New York and spent hours up, up and wondering what would become of me in this new land. The wheels of our plane burned the runway at JFK, and a pilot announced, "Welcome to New York," along with the local time. I struggled up the jet bridge, a bulging duffel tilting me one-sided, and into the brightness of the terminal. *This is it! You're here*, I thought, and dodged through teeming walkways to baggage claim, where I grabbed one of those carts for people who overpack and tarried for luggage overstuffed with my life to swing into view. Steps from me, a gaggle of suited dudes displayed signs for passenger pickups. On the periphery, cliques of camouflaged guards stood with their rifles pointed hellward. Another officer sported a bulletproof vest over his uniform while clutching the leash of a Belgian shepherd. Outside, a new world. Outside, I felt sticky-damp heat of a kind I hadn't felt in life and followed the signs for taxis past desperate-looking drivers accosting me for a fare. Purgatorial—the time it took for me to reach the front of the winding line waiting for yellow cabs, for an attendant to ask where I was headed, and for me to answer "Manhattan," because I didn't yet know it's called the City. The attendant pointed to a cabbie who also might've hailed from elsewhere.

The cabbie wound out of the airport and onto the expressway and soon he was weaving through traffic at a speed that could wreck us into our afterlives. Still, I lowered my window anyhow, to feel the wind on my face, to read the signs blurring by, to witness as much of this genesis as I could. We drove Atlantic Ave and Flatbush Ave and over a bridge I'd soon learn is the Manhattan. We wheeled onto Canal Street, where hordes milled the sidewalks and traffic stuttered like I'd seldom seen, where at a light, a dude waded between bumpers and demoed an electric bubble gun. My driver motored up Avenue of the Americas in a derby of drivers and turned on West Third and again on MacDougal Street, and in a twinkling, we reached what would be my new home. The cabbie pulled curbside, and I hefted my luggage out of his trunk—heavy as a deconstructed tent of meeting—and carried it piece by piece up steep concrete steps. Then I buzzed the number I'd been given by my future roommate, turned my back to the threshold, and waited—looking off one way, looking off the other. If it were a parable, the perch would be a mountaintop, a summit from which thine eyes witnessed the glory of the second coming, and though it sure enough wasn't one, I was thankful that from this stoop in a land *un*promised, I sensed the advent of another *Mitzrayim*, the boon of a chance to become.

COMPOSITE POPS

The night before my mother push-push-pushed me bawling into the universe, my uncle George, fresh off an army discharge, blew into town and surprised her. Mom was staying with a close elder named Aunt Helen at the time because Mama Edie and Bubba had traveled to New York to comfort a pregnant niece whose August due date was a month earlier than what a doctor predicted for my debut. Uncle George bopped into the house, per what would become his habit, full of that potion. He convinced Mom to turn on the radio and he and she boogied. Mom cut loose without heed to Aunt Helen's warning that if she kept it up, her baby—me—would come early. The next morning, Aunt Helen sent her daughter upstairs to fetch Mom for breakfast, and Mom said she wasn't coming down to eat because she was cramping. Aunt Helen sent her daughter, my cousin, upstairs to ask how far apart were the cramps and when Mom told her, Aunt Helen, who was a nurse, rushed her daughters and Mom into her car and drag raced over to Kaiser Hospital. The hospital workers asked Mom and Aunt Helen for all sorts of check-in paperwork, that is until Aunt Helen flashed: "This girl about to have this baby. She ain't got time for all that." Per Mom's prodigious recall, they rushed her into a hospital room, and there with Aunt Helen, the lone relative present, I was born weighing 6 pounds and 13.5 ounces with pale skin that for a hot second was mistook for jaundice. Just a month or so prior, Mom had informed my biological father she was pregnant. She phoned him from the hospital with news that his second son was born. Instead of visiting the hospital himself, my dad pressed his mother and sister into the role of paternity sleuths. Mom says that Grandma Clara was cordial during the visit but that my aunt inspected newborn me, with a headful of black hair and fair skin, and said, "Why this baby so light? This ain't none of my brother's baby. This a trick baby."

Mom, who's quick-witted and sharp-tongued on most days, was absent the fire for proper condemnation. "Get out. Get," she screamed, and called hospital workers to help eject her unwanted guests.

Mom has spent the lion's share of the years since that day as a single mother—a fact that deserves ovations. Still, no matter how much high-note praise she merits and how much the men who fathered her sons deserve lambasting, my single mama ain't now, nor has she ever been, a father.

Folks have argued differences between a father and a dad, but herein and furthermore I'm considering them the same.

Ours is a revolutionary era of gender fluidness and sexual equality and same-sex parents and girls doubtless need fathers too. Let me repeat: girls need their dads. No way no how no day would I ever diminish or, worse, dismiss the role of a father in his daughter's life. No one, and that includes humans, saints, and extraterrestrials, could convince me that my daughter's life would be better without me in it. However, just as there are some aspects of being a female that my daughter's mother is more comfortable with and equipped to guide her through, there are aspects of being a male that I hope I will have helped my son navigate in a way that only I could.

This is my beating heart: boys need fathers.

Boys need fathers—period, exclamation point.

And if a boy isn't blessed with a dad or gifted with a dynamic stand-in, he must find ways to forge one. He must discern the fatherish men in his life and open himself to their guidance and examples.

It's an act of necessity, and I should know. Not only was my biological father a no-show at the hospital on my born day, despite also living in Northeast Portland, he was absent (the completeness of his absence being a point of dispute) for my first decade of life. To say I had no father, though, is a half-truth. To say my mother was my father would be a sentimental lie. I had a father, and I had one because I made one. Or rather, I composed a father from the men at hand, brothers who kept me long before Obama made it a project.

There was my mother's long-term boyfriend, Big Chris; my maternal grandfather, Sam; my maternal uncle, Anthony; my hoop coach, Dixon; and my biological father, Wesley.

Or I could just call them Pops.

Pops is a group of men who provided a loving example of what it would soon enough mean to be a man. Pops nurtured me. Bestowed me with his wisdom. Pushed me to expand and revise the way I saw the world. He inspired me to dream. He tended my harms. He made sure I knew it was in me to achieve.

BIG CHRIS

My biological father, as I remember it, was absentee from day one through my tenth birthday. Not too long after my first birthday, however, a man named Big Chris heart-throbbed my mama. Big Chris was a recent parolee—bank robbery, what a dreamer!—and a neophyte soon-to-be-prosperous pimp but also a smart, witty, compassionate man whose jokes would have almost anybody guffawing themselves to a bellyache. Mom bore Big Chris two sons and stayed with him off and on for a little more than a decade. For years after they parted, he'd slide through trying to rekindle and-or to spend time with his boys. For absolute fact, whether Mom and Big Chris were official, I was one of those boys. The man never treated me one bit diffcrent from the sons born of his seed. While a critic could knock how he hustled his bread and meat, that critique wouldn't alter the truth. Big Chris was the one who showed me the value and impact of a father's love, that family, real family, often had nothing to do with DNA. And this was a lesson he taught me in life and in death.

In September of 2009, I got a call from Big Chris's daughter, my oldest sister. She said that Dad was sick and I should fly out to Phoenix to see him. In the span of a few days, she went from prodding me to visit soon to imploring me to travel ASAP if I wanted to see him alive. Within a few days, I boarded a flight, bracing for the worst, and muttering prayer upon prayer against it happening. Soon as the flight landed, I powered on my cell phone and received a stream of texts: from my mother, from my brothers, from my sister—all of whom informed me Big Chris was dead. My big sister picked me up from the airport and, between tears, tried to comfort me with Dad's near-to-last words: "I've got to hold on. I've got to hold on so I can see Mitch." What she shared didn't console me in the moment, but later, much later, when my grief begrudged me at least a fingerbreadth, Dad's near-to-last words reaffirmed that I would forever be his eldest boy, that our bond was deeper than even blood.

SAM

Check it: my maternal grandfather, Sam Jackson Jr., honored the duties of his last job for over three decades. He's attended (arriving on time all the time!) Catholic mass each Sunday. He's paid his bills and his tithes. For eras, he's been a pillar at neighborhood rallies and community meetings. He bought and has lived in the same house since the seventies, lived there with his second wife until her death, lives there with his new wife now. Granddad—or as I call him, Dad—rescued my mother countless times with funds because the light company put an apartment of ours on eclipse or the rent had somehow vamoosed out of Mom's purse. Granddad moved me into his home for my last two years of high school, this after I bounced for good from my biological father's house, and soon made it clear to all concerned adults that I was not to be trusted under the charge of my stroke-stricken great-grandmother. Those years I lived with my granddad, he, my cousin-brother, and me ate breakfast together almost every weekday. Those seasons I lived with my granddad, he sat in the bleachers at my home and away high school hoop games, and kept full stats. To boot, as long as my grades were Bs or above, he'd spot me the bucks I requested for hanging with the homies on Fridays and Saturdays. Granddad never once bemoaned being my caretaker—which would've been within reason—not even after he had to slap spit from me for the class-A house crimes of sneaking girls into my basement bedroom. Granddad—Dad—has modeled what it means to be a stand-up man, to honor one's commitments, to shoulder one's obligations and burdens, without seeking praise or recompense.

ANTHONY (ANT)

My maternal uncle Anthony—Ant—is a teeny bit of an eccentric for rocking some style of a Jheri curl well past the great epoch of Jheri curls. Uncle Ant (to my relief, he's a few years into Jheri retirement) is furthermore notable for retelling his I-was-almost-a-high-school-all-American legend to what is now two generations of Jackson family dinner guests. My uncle has recounted his tale so often around me that sometimes I hijack the telling. Let Ant or me preach it, the judges clocked him at 9.7, 9.6, and 9.5 in the 100-yard sprint at a district track meet, but if they had awarded him an official time of 9.5 instead of 9.6, he "would've been an all-American that year."

Ant's story is a tendon to what happened to me in sixth grade, the one year I competed in track. That season, I'd placed second in the district meet to a team rival who'd been besting me in playground race-offs for a couple school years. Ant attended the districts and was disappointed by my finish right along with me. My uncle could've let me play a defeatist, but instead he vowed to train me for the city championship, would swoop me afternoons after school and coach me to run on my toes, lean forward, lengthen my stride; he drilled into my hard head and soft heart the notion that I could beat anybody so long as I ran with good form and believed. The championships took place a couple of weeks later and, sure enough, I lined up against my rival in the 100-meter final. *POW!* We shot off the line, and I pumped as hard and as fast as I could—harder—and still midway through the race, I saw my rival inch ahead of me. That moment, I heard my heart cry, *Nooooooooooo!* The next moment, in what now seems an instance of Prefontaine conjuring, I heard my uncle scream "REACH, Nephew! REACH!" above the din, and reach I did, and won the race with a gap. You should have seen Ant afterward, rejoicing as if, at once, I'd won the city title and Olympic gold and salved the wound of falling short of all-American gloryhood. Thanks to Ant, I felt, short-lived as it was, the pride, joy, confidence of a champion. My uncle was a father that spring day, one who helped instill in me the belief that I could achieve beyond what were once perceived as limits.

DIXON

Dixon was my high school guidance counselor. He'd been working his job—his office walls were a mural of student pictures past and present—for what was almost twenty years by the time I transferred to Jefferson High my junior year. I'd see Dixon at school or at the games decked in Demo blue and gold: be it windbreaker, sweat suit, T-shirt, fitted cap. In those days, Dixon was also the coach of the men's basketball team at Portland Community College, though that job meant little to me my last year of high school hoop, a time when I believed a Division I basketball scholarship was much less of a long shot than it was. Even after that dream was knocked out of bounds, I had little interest in suiting up for my old guidance counselor, playing home games at a campus right across the street from my high school—I'm talking steps! So, what'd I do? What I did was sign on to ball at Clark College, which—haha—was all of a whole six miles from Jeff. And here's more of the rub: I didn't make it a full season at Clark. Blame it on me feeling entitled, above coach reprimand, and too talented for juco comp. Not sure how Dixon discovered that I'd been kicked off that team (or quit, was the story I ran with), but I was thankful he did, and grateful when he offered me a spot on his team, which was a break I wouldn't have recognized as such just months prior, and one I might've mistook as a slight. How ironic, the season I played for Dixon was the best individual ball I played in life, even made honorable mention all-star for the NWAC (Northwest Athletic Conference) South Region despite our squad losing eighteen of our twenty-three games.

While I didn't have a chance in hoop heaven of Kentucky or UCLA or Duke recruiting me, I held fast to the sweat-slick hope that a D-I scholarship offer was still a reasonable ambition. Then, after one of our last practices, Dixon called me into his office. Since Dixon called me into the office close to never, I was thinking he had recruitment news. "Sit down," he said, looking austere. He asked me what were my plans after PCC, and I told him I wanted to play, which, in hindsight, was a partial truth I believed expected of me. Dixon mentioned an academic scholarship at Portland State University called the UMAS (Underrepresented Minority Achievement Scholarship) and suggested I apply—an urging that, in the moment, offended more than inspirited me.

That evening, I dragged out of Dixon's office thinking he disbelieved in my talent rather than being thankful he hadn't gassed me on a hoop dream, because had he done so, I might've ended up like the handful of guys I knew who spent their twenties and thirties chasing insufficient checks in a league overseas. Instead, Dixon kept urging me to apply, and in time, I heeded his advice and, to my surprise, won the scholarship. For a hot second I flirted with walking onto the PSU team but, in the end, conceded I'd never play another college game. The UMAS scholarship was funding my tuition when I got caught the next year selling dope. Days after I found out I was headed to prison, I called up the scholarship's administrators and told them I had a family emergency, which necessitated a year off, and without much probing, they granted me the time. Once one of PCC's assistant coaches borrowed several hundred dollars from me (and paid me back—late), which confirmed for me that he knew what I was up to. It would've been naive of me to believe Dixon was oblivious to my hustling. Shoot, Dixon had to have seen a kazillion dudes like me over the years—bumbleheads hurtling headlong toward a catastrophe unless somebody with sense intervened. He must've gleaned that a blatant reprimand of my enterprise or even an explicit warning would do little to discourage me. So instead, he presented a watershed, an option that proved not just a Godsend but an essential part of what I needed for Godspeed through troubles. And where would I be without Dixon glimpsing into my future and judging what I'd need?

WESLEY

As I said, as I remember it, my biological father became a presence in my life when I was ten years old. One of my most significant memories of him occurred not too long after that time. His wife, my siblings (an older brother and two younger sisters), and me road-tripped to visit Disneyland, SeaWorld, and a few relatives in California. One of those family members lived in an apartment complex with a pool. At that relative's place, we all changed into swimming gear and headed out to the deck, where my dad and siblings began having a grand old time swimming and cavorting and goading me to join them while I gallivanted *around* the pool and at most teased my foot into the shallow end a time or two. My dread was well founded, as this was circa '85, arguably the height of a certain high-water-pants-and-rhinestone-glove-wearing pop star, and I had whips-and-waves befitting a kid who claimed to certain credulous peers that I was a not-so-distant cousin. Or let me put it like this: young Mitch Jackson was not about to get his MJ*esque* do wet, nor (the extent of my swimming skills at the time was a weak dog paddle) was I about to risk my life. But my biological father flexed contrary designs, crept up behind me, scooped me in the air, and tossed me in the pool. He didn't flinch while I flailed and screamed and gulped mouthfuls of overchlorinated water. He said something to me that I can't recall but that my subconscious must've heard because soon I calmed and got my curly head above the surface, and stayed in the pool, and had a damn good day frolicking with my father, brother, and sisters—AKA the Johnsons. My father's lesson took years to reveal itself to me: in troubled water or not, you best learn to swim, cause when your young ass get to drowning, I might not be moved to rescue—a message, by the way, I now count as an act of beneficence.

———

Though their foibles weren't the crux of what I used to compose, best believe not a single man I mentioned has existed in my life beyond critique. And that's all sorts of apropos, since I too am a flawed human striving, striving.

Over the years, I've discovered a thing or more about myself: That who and how I love is not restricted by law or blood. That being a constant presence in the life of those I care for is as much a part of being a man as almost any other act. That wins must be earned and win I will. That I should be cautious of holding fast to old selves. That either I swim or drown and no one impacts that outcome more than me.

Here I am the father of a son and daughter trying my all-out damnedest to mind the lessons of my beloved composite and feeling heartened, so heartened they're rooting for me to best them.

Goooooood lookin, Pops.

MATRIMONY

People might mean well, but benign or not, when somebody asks, How's your mama doing, my impulse is noneya. As in none of your (damn) business, which often construes to "she's fine" or "doing well" or "good," depending on who asked. But to keep it 100, I ain't sure. Let Mom tell it, she's a single woman. Let me tell it, she's a married woman who's been devoted to the most abusive polygamist of all time. Mom, adamant, has filed for dozens of separations and umpteen divorces, but over and over she's found herself reconciled into a union that has lasted beyond its silver anniversary.

CIRCA 1985

Mom's ceremony has been a movie stuck on repeat for more than half my life. Since it's oh so tough, after umpteen years, to tell what's fact and what's fiction, my memory of this story is more or less how it happened. But trust, at its nexus it's all true. All of it. The nuptials occurred the year I was nine, ten—no older than that. That particular night, I blew into Mom's room, found her at the foot of her bed with her head pressed in her hands, and asked her what was wrong. She said nothing. She said she'd be fine. I told her I was hungry and she said she'd fix me something to eat in a few. This answer would have given most any other knucklehead all the excuse they needed to raid the cabinets or the fridge, but for me, a kid who'd been spoiled and couldn't cook, it meant waiting till she shook off enough of what was troubling her to rise.

That didn't happen till late that night, so late it might've been early morning. Mom came into my room, at God knows what hour, and promised me a trip to Burger Barn. Burger Barn burgers, the tastiest burgers in Northeast Portland, the state, maybe on earth, were my favorite thing to eat—period—which is why it took not a word more to coax me out of our crib. We climbed into our yellow Datsun B210 and made a left here and a right there (maybe we listened to the radio, maybe we didn't), and before I knew it, we turned off Interstate Ave into the parking lot of a decrepit-looking motel. The motel's name, I can't call it, but its sign was cracked or buzzing or burned-out. Such were all the motel signs on Interstate back then.

Mom climbed out of the Datsun and, still fiending for my burger, I hopped out and followed her up flights of steps to a room. She knocked and stood back. She seemed composed, but also discomfited. She knocked again and the man who answered, in hindsight, had to be the paragon for his kind, but that night, with zero priors, all I could think was dude's lips looked dusted. "Hey, lil' man," he said, and did something to distract me or Mom or us both from a long, bald gaze.

The room smelled like what they were doing, but again, with no priors, I had little clue. Mom's sister-friend Dawn was in the bathroom, and when she sashayed out, her hair, which most days was relaxed salon straight and combed backward, was a spiky mess and she was dressed in somebody else's oversized shabby gear. The vision of dude and Dawn were all I needed to see the urgency in persuading Mom to leave, to break out, to motor fourth gear to Burger Barn, where my empty stomach would get its fill, and she and I would be safe.

She said soon. She said for me to take a seat and proceeded to elope in a bathroom, where her sister-friend and a dude with frosted lips witnessed her hasty foolish nuptials. I watched a snatch of *Benny Hill* or *Kung Fu Theatre* or whatever former prime-time hit was on the tube that time of night, watched it with my eye twitching like the kids in my class who couldn't sit still and what I didn't recognize as a premonition wrenching my empty gut. The ceremony must've been brief; a commercial break at most, and although I was sheltered from the altar, I have come to believe the following as facts: there was no ring proffered, no kiss between lovers, and no vows vocalized, but in that foggy bathroom, the woman who matters most to me, a woman who up to then I'd never seen drunk or high off nothing, inhaled her "I do."

I DO's

The oldest recorded evidence of marriage between a single man and single woman is from ancient Mesopotamia circa 5000 BCE. Those unions, which by law featured a marriage contract, had the primary intent of ensuring social order. For most of recorded history, starry-eyed romantic love had little to do with whom one married. The ancient Greeks thought lovesickness was a kind of insanity. The Protestant theologians preached that husbands and wives who loved each other too much were sinful idolaters. In the Middle Ages, the Catholic Church's Great Council met and, to combat secret marriages and people marrying in forbidden degrees of consanguinity, ordered that they be announced so that people could make knowing objections to their legitimacy.

The result: whosoever objects to the union of these two people, speak now or forever hold your peace.

Yes, oh yes, I wish I could've objected to Mom's union with science, wish I could've warned Mom what the substance that was her groom would do to the part of her brain called the ventral tegmental area (VTA), explained that when we do something pleasurable, our brain cells release dopamine, a little chemical messenger, which once released travels across a gap between nerve cells called a synapse, binds to a receptor on a neighboring cell called a neuron, and sends a signal to that cell, which produces aaaaaaaaaaaaaah—so much pleasure. Under normal circumstances (meaning, minus the substance), once the dopamine sends the signal, it's reabsorbed into the sender cell by what's called a dopamine transporter. Maybe Mom would've left it at the altar if she'd known that her groom would thwart that cycle, that it would attach itself to the transporter and prevent the normal reabsorption process by the receiver cell. That that disruption would cause the dopamine to build up in the synapse and super-hella overstimulate the receptors, which, in seconds, would feel to her like aaaaaaaaaaaaaaaaaaaaaaaaaaaaaaaaaaah—the bliss of all bliss. The ecstasy would last no longer than a few of her favorite radio songs and then—POW!—her dopamine levels would drop and she'd feel a low like she'd never felt, a crash that would send her chasing that most inimitable high once, twice, for far too long.

If I could return to the night of her nuptials, I would caution her about that fugitive joy, the plunge, and the ultimate damage the substance that was her groom would do to her orbital frontal cortex—the part of her brain that decides the salience of a stimulus—harm that she couldn't undo. Bet she'd've turned runaway bride if she'd known how restless it would make her feel, how paranoid. Or that her groom might give her a stroke or stop her heart. How a weekend getaway with it could waste her from her normal slim to gaunt.

And if the science wouldn't convince her, maybe she would've heeded me presaging all the nights she'd forsake us—three boys she once claimed to love more than herself—the times, after a long absence, she'd sorrow through the door and sleep for days more alone in the dark. Maybe my mother would've refused to give her hand if I prophesized the night she'd break barefoot out of a dope house with a police dog barking at her heels, or the night a stone-fisted neo-barbarian would beat her to gashes and aches everlasting. It's possible I could've persuaded her with a forecast of the stints she'd spend in rehab—in- and out-patient—the months she'd spend serving a prison sentence, the arrests and convictions that, an age later, would prevent her from jobs that would pay what she needs to subsist. There's a chance I could've lobbied her to an adamant "I don't" with the news that her eldest—the baby boy she named for her favorite great-uncle—would end up in prison for selling triple-digit grams of the same substance to which she was about to commit.

CIRCA 1990

It would be foul of me to mention what happened with Mom and not say a word about what happened with me. It happened when I was fourteen, maybe fifteen—when I was an old boy who felt older, who'd resolved I'd exceeded my threshold of mother-where-art-thous. The details: One day after school, I approached a homeboy who I knew sold dope and asked him if he would give me some to sell. He asked me if I was serious, and when I confirmed, he fronted me a few shards, quoted me what I owed him, and sent me on my diffident way. Since I was patient not none, that night or a night in the near future, I crept out of the house with the cream-colored shards stashed on my person and a porous dream of double-up tucked in my chest. It was a Langston Hughes–esque dream if there ever was one, because not only did I *not* double up that first night, I did *not* single up that first night either, a failure that felt as though it might never end. But for a time I kept faith, stood out in the shadows among others determined to clock a dollar. It was frightening and exhilarating all at once. It was near ineffable seeing that world demystified, witnessing firsthand the landscape, which by that time my mother had been roaming for years. There was also a part of me that half hoped I'd see her and that the encounter would coerce her into acknowledging the secret that was secret to fewer of the folks we knew than she or I could've imagined. There was also the feeble promise that if Mom had to confront where her "I do" had delivered us, she'd sue

ASAP for differences irreconcilable, and that would be that. Gavel strike. There was also fleeting comfort in the theory that every night I survived the ruck of rock-toting aspirants was a night my mother too could shamble home from a like scene alive. As I said, though, those first few nights, it was clear my peon sack would not be multiplied. So I hyped myself to return it to my homeboy (lucky for me he really was a homeboy) and explained that I'd made a mistake.

To limit the number of marital mistakes, all major religions have embraced some version of a matchmaker. In Christianity, a cleric or another trusted person is often tapped to connect potential partners. In Buddhism, matchmaking parents—sponsors—of a prospective couple are encouraged to consult an astrologist and, if unsuccessful, are urged to query an innerworld deva. In Judaism, a *shadchan*—whether official or not—has connected partners over the ages. In Islam, a young person makes a *dua* to Allah to find the right person and the family, most often the parents, catalyze the matchmaking by enquiring among their network for prospects. If the couple and the family agree, the couple meets, chaperoned, until such time as they determine their compatibility. If they believe themselves a good fit, the families further investigate the character of the potential mate. Then the couple prays Salat-l-Istikhara—a prayer for guidance—and agrees to pursue marriage or dissolve their dealings. Dawn and her chalk-lipped coconspirator were the ostensible matchmakers of Mom and the substance that, posthaste, became her spouse, but I've come to believe that someone who is of equal if not more culpableness for her union is a man she's never met.

Ricky Donnell Ross, AKA Rick Ross, was born in Tyler, Texas, in 1960 to Annie Mae Ross (maiden name Mauldin), the daughter of an East Texas sharecropper. Rick's father, Sonny Ross—a former army cook and later pig farmer and cleaner of oil tankers—bounced on the family when Rick was a boy, and in 1963, Annie migrated with Rick and his older brother to California, where they lived with his mother's brother. One night that uncle attacked his wife and Rick's mother, and as Rick watched, his mom pulled a pistol from her purse and killed her brother. She spent a brief time in jail before her release and reunion with her boys. Annie Mae and her dead brother's wife bought a house in South Central near where it dead-ended at the 110 Freeway—a home that would shape untold destinies. Rick attended

South Central's Manchester Elementary and Bret Harte Junior High (neither of which taught him how to read), and during that time evinced a penchant for hustling: pumping gas for tips, peddling lemonade, mowing lawns. Though quick, agile, and coordinated, Rick conceded by junior high that he wouldn't grow big enough to star in football or basketball. But then one day, Rick and one of his homeboys moseyed down to a local park where a man was holding tennis clinics. It didn't take many clinics for Rick to realize he'd found his sport, so much so that by ninth grade he was recruited by Dorsey High, a magnet school in Baldwin Hills, known then and now as the Black Beverly Hills, to play for the team. Rick earned all-league tennis honors his first year at Dorsey High and all-city honors every other but quit before he earned his diploma. Rick prevailed upon a man he'd met through tennis to help him enroll in a job training program at the Venice Skills Center, where he wound up studying auto repair—while he stole cars and worked at a chop shop on the side.

Circa late 1979, early 1980, Rick and his homeboy Big Ollie were sitting on his porch. One of his homeboys who was back from college called up. "Man, I got the new thing," he said. "Come thru." Rick jumped in his '66 Impala, pumped a dollar's worth of gas in the tank, and rode out to where his homeboy was staying. Once inside, that homeboy pulled out a baggie with little tubes of white powder. "I'm tellin you, this is the new thing. This here cost fifty bucks." He handed it to Rick to inspect. "Stop lying," Rick said, eyes widening. "This little thing worth fifty bucks?" He gushed how it was so small the police would never catch him with it. "Here, go ahead and take this and see what's what with it," his homeboy said. Rick accepted and he and Big Ollie motored back to the house he lived in with his mom and aunt. They rushed inside and inspected their product, hadn't a clue if they'd gotten their hands on some authentic coca-ine and, if they had, what they'd do with it. So they hopped back in the Chevy, braved their gas peril, and hunted the hood for wisdom.

This was around the time that in South Central on some blocks it was common to see a dozen or more dudes out selling PCP sticks. But coca-ine on the other hand might as well have been some shit from another planet. The homeboys had just about given up on apt consultants when Rick ran into an old pimp he knew from the neighborhood. The pimp was hip to what they had and offered to rock the powder if they let him test it. Post what first appeared a mystical cooking process, the OG produced a small white nugget. He cut a shard off the nugget, smoked it, and smacked his lips. "This taste all right, but I'ma need another piece to make sure it's good," he said. "You don't wanna be out there sellin somethin that ain't right." The old pimp chipped another piece, smoked it, smacked again. "Yeah, this here is proper," he said. "I'm gone go ahead and smoke the rest of it, and I'll get you back on Friday." And just like that, Rick and Ollie had been beat. Rick's career dealing coca-ine, in a few deep inhales, seemed finished. How was he supposed to call up his homeboy to cop more dope when he didn't have the fifty bucks? His boy Big Ollie wanted to kill the OG. "Man, we can't do that," Ross said, and sat around his house brooding.

Hours later, the OG pimp who'd beat him out of the fifty dollars of dope pulled up to the house with someone who wanted to spend a hundred bucks. Rick phoned the homeboy who'd given him the first product. "I ain't got that fifty I owe you, but I got somebody over here that wanna spend a C-note," he said, and his homeboy zipped over to serve the OG pimp. The OG pimp came and went, left and returned, to Ross's mama's house with more people who wanted to cop. Quick, so quick, Rick began clocking a couplefew hundred a day and, all the while, hounding people to teach him how to chef the product he'd soon call "ready rock."

On one of those early days, Rick drove out to visit his old mentor at the Skills Center, someone he hadn't seen since his dope bounty began. "How you doin?" his old mentor asked. "What you been doin?" Rick, after some reluctance, revealed he'd been selling dope, expecting at least a lecture. "Oh yeah? Come with me," his mentor said, and drove him out to his house. "How you think I got this house, this new car, these clothes, all these jewels, all of this on a teacher's salary?" he asked, and told Rick that he used to sell dope, and that he was still connected. That revelation kicked off Rick and his ace Big Ollie buying dope from the mentor, reinvesting their profits, procuring larger and larger quantities till the point they were buying much more than the mentor was willing to sell. The mentor, as amends, introduced them to his connect, a man who, unbeknown to Rick, was a Nicaraguan exile. The Nicaraguan quoted his prices. *Oh shit, I'm finna get rich*, Rick thought, and smiled wide as an LA boulevard. However, months into their transacting, the Nicaraguan got shot in the spine and hospitalized. The convalescence of Rick's Central American connect led to a man named Danilo Blandon, another Nicaraguan exile, who adopted Rick and his homie as customers. It ain't fat-mouthing in the least to claim that Blandon forever changed the course of Rick's life. Blandon was a direct associate of one of the biggest drug traffickers in the world: a Nicaraguan named Nor-win Meneses. Blandon, by way of Meneses, whose coca-ine was as plentiful as California sunshine, helped Rick corner what was then a fledgling crack market in South Central LA. Ricky Donnell Ross from Tyler, Texas, bootstrapped his way to "Freeway" Rick Ro$$, a "ready rock" marketing genius, a South Central drug tycoon who'd claim "[God] put him down [on earth] to be a cocaine man."

Rick's self-sanctified ascension seemed to happen in a flash, but the truth is, it was millennia in the making. Pre-Incan tribes of the Andes chewed the leaves of the coca plant. That cultural practice existed in the region for five thousand years and was exclusive to its inhabitants until the sixteenth-century Spanish conquest of the Incans, whereupon it was introduced into what the Eurocentrists call the Old World. In the nineteenth century, 1859, a talented PhD student isolated the primary alkaloid of the coca plant, and in the custom of other alkaloid nomenclature—morphine, codeine, nicotine, strychnine, quinine—christened the substance coca-ine. Granted he wasn't the one who named it, no one was more instrumental than Sigmund Freud in ushering coca-ine into the public conscious. With the man who wrote "Uber Coca" (dude, go figure, experimented himself into an addict) and other professionals trumpeting the drug as a glorious panacea, it showed up in operating rooms as an anesthetic, was used as a key ingredient in innumerable nostrums and beverages—one of which evolved into Coca-Cola—and became a go-to stimulant for recreational users.

In no time, global companies in countries including Germany and the United States began distributing it. Nevertheless, the plenitude of coca-ine for mass consumption came into question at the top of the twentieth century, a time when America's newspaper of record ran headlines like "Cocaine Evil Among Negroes" and "Negro Cocaine Evil" and the infamous "Negro Cocaine 'Fiends' Are a New Southern Menace." Believe-you-me, pre-civil-rights America couldn't abide the prospect of a superblack anybody on its streets; thus Congress set in motion the eventual criminalization of coca-ine and (opium) with the Harrison Narcotics Tax Act of 1914, a law that imposed a special tax on "all persons who produce, import, manufacture, compound, deal in, dispense, sell, distribute, or give away opium or coca leaves, their salts, derivatives, or preparations, and for other purposes." The legislation, intended to ban all non-medical use of coca-ine, succeeded in making the narcotic scarce for Negroes and almost all else save the mobsters who cornered distributing it on the black market and the Hollywooders who were agreeable to paying a high premium to keep partaking of it.

Notwithstanding the enduring indulgence of the rich and famous, coca-ine usage declined through the 1960s. Mom's eventual matchmaker was born at the top of that decade, and by the time Rick was in junior high, coca-ine use was experiencing a renaissance in places including the Bahamas, Miami, and LA, due in large part to the media dismissing it as harm-less and glamorizing it on the regular in music and film, as well as a new way of consuming the drug dubbed freebasing. That resurgence set the stage for the 1980s proliferation of crack users and, of course, Rick willing himself into a mythic matchmaking magnate. In the Rose City, Rick or his direct emissary, or else somebody who dealt his product second-, third-, or fourth-hand, or else somebody who'd heard of him and wanted to emulate him, or who knew not of him but nurtured kin ambitions, facilitated untold unions (one was too many), my mother's intimate espousal among them.

THE YEAR 1987

Mom proved less committed, thank the good Lord, to the man of flesh and blood she married. In what I intend as benevolence, I'll call him Bo. Mom met Bo while they were both residents of the Hooper Detox Stabilization Center, during the weeks when Mom was awaiting an open bed at the De Paul Treatment Center. Bo, two years Mom's junior, was trying to shake the habit of sipping himself into reeking-drunk belligerence. In a world of good sense, the circumstances of their initial acquaintance would be con-sidered an omen, but this was my mother incipient in the throes of her chemical union, an era during which she made bad judgments about as easy as she breathed.

Bo used to brag to Mom that he was from Gary, Indiana: Michael Jack-son's hometown. Said this, I suppose, because he believed being from else-where conferred him cachet. Bo also used to highsight that he'd one day own a business, which might account for why, every day, he wore a shirt and tie with his slacks and wing-tips and one of the two double-breasted sport coats he owned. (To be fair, when funds allowed, Bo dry-cleaned his digs.)

Once Mom was admitted into De Paul, Bo would swagger into the public recovery meetings—until he got kicked out for coming to one drunk—in his laundered uniform and park beside her. He'd often leave her with notes written during the meetings and would send her love letters between those meetings: missives that promised he'd be Mom's able caretaker, that before he opened a business, he'd land a steady job and buy them a nice home, that she and he would evermore live in comfort. Bo at the time earned his living selling oils and incense on the streets and his wooing included gifting Mom a personal scent. Guessing Bo's courtship felt like the romance novels Mom consumed in her twenties and that, as absurd as it sounds, it made her feel like a belle being charmed by a beau of lesser means. How much in those days could she have felt she deserved? How tough was it to reject her intuition, to dismiss the counselors who warned of Bo's likelihood of relapse, to defy the recovery guidance of waiting till she hit a year sober before entering a romantic relationship? Mom finished her in-treatment program to the "hallelujah" of all who loved her, and Bo persisted, through a short breakup no less, to the great consensual concern of those same people.

Mom moved to The House on Sixth Ave, after her months in rehab. Bo, meantime, had found a room in a downtown hotel for recovering addicts and began working a production gig. He never had much bread but talked often of saving the little bit he earned—the key word: *talked*. The couple would attend parties at a clean-and-sober dance club and afterward stroll across the Burnside Bridge to catch the bus home. On the bridge one of those late nights, Bo professed his love for Mom, got down on a knee, and—ringless (yeah, ringless)—asked for her hand in marriage.

A caesura here for Mom's deliberations:

For certain she didn't love Bo nor want to spend her life with him. She was often repulsed by the pus-filled cystic acne that pocked his face. She'd refused more than one proposal from her life's love, Big Chris, because she disbelieved him husband material. On the other hand, she'd resolved to say yes to the next man who asked.

It also didn't hurt that Bo was raised a Jehovah's Witness and claimed to love the Lord, that in the testing times ahead, he could remind her of NA's step two: "We came to believe that a Power greater than ourselves could restore us to sanity."

Too, too soon, Mom and Bo marched down to H&B pawnshop and picked out rings: a band for him and a half-carat diamond for her. Mom was unemployed at the time and paid for the rings with part of the ten-thousand-dollar settlement she'd won from a department store that accused her of theft. She and Bo married on July 5, 1987, in the Multnomah County Courthouse. A justice of the peace officiated. Mama Edie and Bubba, my grandfather and his second wife, and my brothers and me stood as witnesses, silent, brooding. The ceremony was unremarkable but for the moment the officiant asked Mom to confirm her intent and she stalled.

"Lillie, you gots to say 'yes' or 'I will' or 'I do' or somethin,'" said Bo.

Mom murmured an "I do," and the officiant pronounced them husband and wife. They must've kissed, but somehow, I've been blessed with misremembering it. Neither do I recall a single other endearment. Us Jacksons and Mom's flesh-and-blood husband clambered into an elevator to leave, and no lie, no sooner had we reached the ground floor of the courthouse than I was for certain of one thing: my mother had committed a grave mistake. That weekend, she and Bo borrowed Mama Edie's car and drove to Seattle. There they drank and boogied at the Royal Esquire Night Club— not the most sagacious plan for a pair of recovering addicts—grubbed on fish from a well-known market, and attended a free concert in a park. Their honeymoon suite was a room in Bo's sister's crib.

Upon their return, Bo came to live with us in The House on Sixth Ave, resided with Mom in the dank low-ceiling basement. Bo at the time seemed passionate about God—or else was stricken by the oft-desperate religiosity of the addicted—would pad into Mama Edie's room and spend hours with her reading and discussing scripture. Bo landed a better job at a steel plant, and since it was several miles from Northeast, Mom began waking at dawn, borrowing Mama Edie's ghost-colored station wagon, and chauffeuring him to work. Evenings, she'd borrow the station wagon again to shuttle him home from the end of his shift. As well, about a year prior to Mom and Bo's plagued union, one of his sisters gave birth to a daughter addicted to heroin. The baby had spent the months since she was born in a hospital and was set to be released, but Bo's family couldn't agree on who'd care for her. It seems exceedingly, exponentially, glaringly obvious that a pair of recovering addicts serving as surrogate parents to a baby suffering neonatal abstinence wasn't the brainiest decision in the world, but of course, of course, Mom and Bo weren't the most discerning folks on earth. Furthermore, Mom had told Bo and almost anyone else with ears that she'd always wanted a girl.

Bo's sister brought her baby to Seattle from Indiana, and Mom and Bo once again borrowed the ghost wagon and drove to Seattle to pick her up. For a time, Mom spent her days guarding against the lure of her first spouse, caring for us boys, attending Bo's colicky niece, and ferrying her flesh-and-blood husband to and from work. It didn't take long for Bo to begin disappearing on Friday paydays and drifting through the door at the end of the weekend destitute of even a damn dollar. "Where you been,

Bo?" Mom asked one night in their basement bedroom after Bo's nth vanishing. "You can't keep takin your money and doin whatever you want with it and thinkin you gonna come up in here and eat all the food and live for free," she continued, and Bo responded by knocking her upside her head. She forgave him the first time, persuaded by her inclination to honor her vows, an unwillingness to concede so soon she'd chosen wrong yet again, and the dread of admitting to Mama Edie and Bubba that the obsequious man who'd been reciting scripture with them for hours at a time was, in fact, an abuser.

Bo moved from one job to another. He, on occasion, but occasional at most, brought his paychecks home. One day, Mom found a hoard of empty rotgut wine bottles in the closet of their bedroom. Mom, no punk, confronted him, and Bo's punkass hit her in the face and chest. He stomped outside and tossed their wedding rings into nowhere. He tore their marriage certificate to tiny scraps. "That's the last time you gone put your hands on me, motherfucka," said Mom later that night. "You go ahead and lay down. No, as a matter of fact, you go ahead and go to sleep."

Bo, a punk but not a certain brand of fool, sat awake in a chair while Mom slept. Mom woke with two black eyes. Since they were proof impossible to hide, she crept out of the house wearing sunglasses that morning and caught a bus to check into a motel. Sometime that day, she called Bo's mother and told her it was over. Bo spent not another night in our house. Not more than a week later, Mom borrowed the ghost wagon, drove Bo and his infant niece to Union Station, and slapped tickets in his hand for a bus bound for his and Michael Jackson's hometown. Feeling what I imagine was the greatest relief, she watched him slog toward the depot with his niece in one arm and a tattered duffel packed with every bit of his belongings in the other.

CIRCA 1995

What's the first without the last? Well, this isn't the final, as in end of it all, but it's what signaled for me that I wouldn't have the heart-strength to keep on.

Context: this particular night had to be about a cool seven years (lucky me) before the ordeal with Brother A that almost earned me a return trip to prison, was at least a year prior to my arrest and the Friday the thirteenth in

1997 that his honor Henry Kantor sentenced me to prison in the first place, was a half decade or so after my first barren nights of curb serving.

There was this dude I used to serve: a man who a couple months later would get caught with coca-ine I sold him and, instead of snitching, serve an eight-year prison bid. One night, dude paged me to his crib without hint of what for save that it was urgent. Since I trusted him, I rushed over. Soon as I got there he, who most nights was vociferous as shit, nodded me toward the back room without a word, his face all sorts of somber. When I got in that back room, I discovered my mother, smelling like she smelled, with her eyes gleaming white in the dark. "Mitchell, give me somethin and I'll go home," she said. "Just give me somethin, please."

Maybe I shook her. Maybe I didn't. "Hell no!" I said. "Fuck no!" I said, and felt struck that instant with a brand-new dread. At the time, I'd known dudes who'd served their blood, knew one who'd even sold to his mama, but never mind the next man's deeds, that thought never, and I mean never in life, entered my realm of possibilities. If selling dope to my mama was what it had come to, I knew for absolute certain it would have to come to an end for me.

THE YEAR 2007

Ain't much dubiety on the details here. This was a time I flew home from New York to surprise my family. When I got to Mom's crib, I knocked and waited, expectant for the smile she'd beam the moment she saw me. No one answered, so I knocked and knocked. When it was clear no one was home, I searched under the front mat for the key and let myself in. On a normal day, house empty or not, the TV would've been running with the sound muted and screen flickering. But on that day, the screen was dead gray.

When I came home a few months prior, Mom's living room was plush with a full set of rent-to-own digs: leather couches, coffee and end tables, a sparkle-bordered dining room mirror. But this time, all that fancy new decor was gone, and left in its place was a salvaged leather love seat and not much else. With a bad feeling tumbling around my insides, I set down my bags and rambled into Mom's room—a dim cove fragrant with Mom's cancer stick of choice. The room looked ransacked, and I rooted the chaos for clues. When I didn't find any, I wandered into my brother's room, where I saw wind sucking the curtain through a hole the size of a head in the window. For a better look at the state of things, I hit lights. Up down. Up down—nothing. Hmmm, I wondered, and tried the switches in the kitchen and bathroom, neither of which worked. The light company shutoff was proof enough that Mom was gone once again renewing her vows. I slunk back into the living room, wilted onto the couch, and let my eyes leak.

I don't do *that* often.

The rare times I do, it's *never* for pity.

We—the *we* being Mom and her three boys—don't want nor need no one's pity.

No. One.

None.

Mom, the substance that has been her spouse, my brothers, and me maketh a non-nuclear family whether we acknowledge our ties or not. But things could be far, far worse. We've survived, although not unscathed, Mom's union. Mom has survived, although not unharmed, decades of anniversaries with an abusive spouse. And before anybody gets to criticizing me and mines, know this: My mama ain't no failure. Mom's achieved the triumph of raising three grown boys—all of whom have escaped murder, drug habits, long-term prison terms (ask around, anything less than a nickel is almost unmentionable), illiteracy, gang membership, and much else on the long list of perils that rank us right up there with northern spotted owls.

There's an old recovery maxim, "once an addict, always an addict," the logic being that an addict must choose moment by moment not to abuse. Well, Mom has spent decades of her adult life living moment to moment. Some of those moments have been more successful than others. This is a truth I have come to accept. It's a truth I've had to accept and am stronger for it.

For millennia marriage was considered a civic duty and part of the institution of social responsibility. Recall the Greeks who believed love a psychiatric ailment. The French in medieval times believed love a "derangement of the mind" curable by sex. In fact, the idea of marrying for love didn't take hold in Western culture until the industrial revolution. Mama Edie and Bubba raised Mom to believe in marrying for love: The I-take-you-to-be-my-husband love. To-have-and-to-hold-from-this-day-forward love. For-better-or-for-worse love. Through-health-and-sickness love. Through-good-and-bad-times love. Till-death-do-us-part love. It is a love for all the days of one's life. The love that binds all blessed unions.

History suggests that the pledge Mom exchanged in a shabby motel in the small hours of the morning—the same night that she promised me a Burger Barn burger that I ain't seen to this day—will last on some level till death cleaves her from this earth. Some would call that a fated existence, but what if all these years my mother has been honoring her vow?

THE YEAR 2012

Vow.

That was supposed to be the last word. For drafts and drafts and drafts that was the last word, but now my conscience won't let that be it. Because the night in the motel, the one on Interstate, it seems I either made it up or conflated it with another occasion. On everything I love, for all those years, that's what I *thought* happened. And can you fault me for not having the courage to ask my mother to set me straight? We all know how it goes, right, or we should know or we'll learn: whether we seek or seek not the toughest truths, they'll find us.

As proof, I offer the time Mom and me spent an evening visiting spots in Northeast that were memorable to us and telling each other stories about why each place mattered. That night she directed me to a house on Alberta Street that used to be an after-hours spot. "There," Mom said. "That's where I took my first hit."

CIRCA 1985

Credit due for me at least being spot-on about the year. My great-granddad Bubba—with whom Mom had been charged with caretaking—left on a trip to the supermarket up the street and hours later was presumed lost in a bout of Alzheimer delirium. Mom ventured out with her friend Dawn that night, during what she remembers as family-wide angst. In the wee hours, Dawn dragged Mom to the house that was the after-hours spot in Northeast, and real quick, Mom's sister-friend gave her the shake. Sometime that night, Mom wandered upstairs and into a foggy room where Dawn and a small crew of others were sharing what turned out to be the most ecstatic ephemeral high this side of paradise. On the second floor of that house on Eighteenth and Alberta, in the presence of her best friend and a gathering of future fated spouses, my mother said her doomed "I do" to it-never-was-nor-could-be-right.

Mom stumbled into The House on Sixth the next day. By grace, Bubba had been found, but also by then, the family was on tenterhooks over her. The list of those concerned included her father, who'd made his way to the house. My grandfather pulled Mom aside.

"Where were you?" he said.

"Oh, I was out," Mom said. "Out smokin crack."

"Crack," he said. "And what's that?"

"Well, it's this cocaine," Mom said. "It's like a little rock. And you put it on a pipe and you smoke it."

"I see," he said. "Well, do you think that will be a problem for you?"

"No, I don't think so," Mom said. "I don't think it will," she said. "I'm sure it won't be a problem."

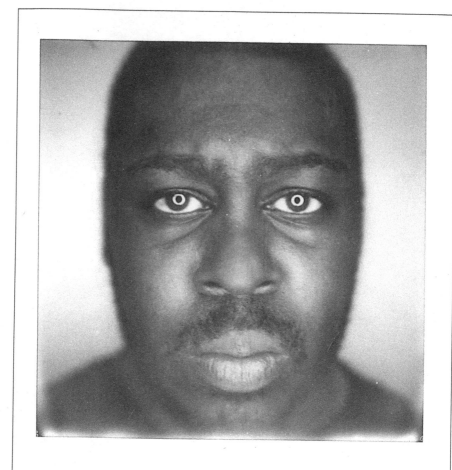

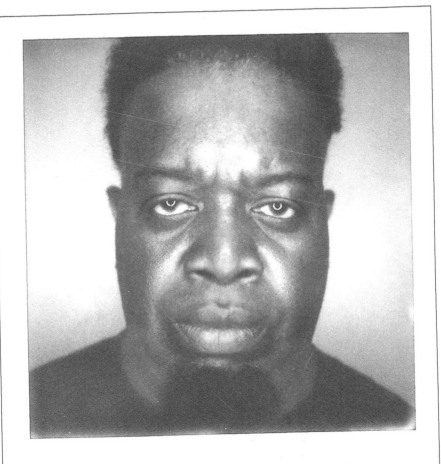

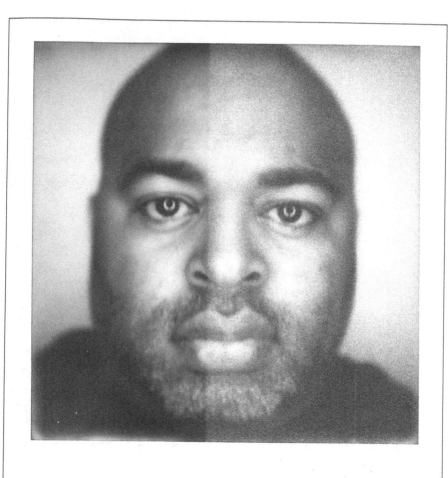

SURVIVOR FILE

You're out one night at the weekend hot spot off too many straight shots to count and therefore the kind of faded you swear manifolds your funny when you hear a dude you don't know say "Blood" to cap a sentence. "Damn, I didn't know niggas was still gangbangin," you say, and search the nearest faces for mirth. But don't nobody smile nor laugh, and in fact dude smacks you upside your dome as if your joke was his cue. In an instant, the two of you take to scrapping inside the club—while neighborhood dudes whose account could damage your rep bear witness—and you best him before being wrenched apart and bounced outside. He paces one way. You pace the other. And in the distance between you lies the tacit truth that the animosity is in no way squashed. The next day, your friend is hosting your brother's moving–to–New York barbecue-fish-fry and you show up hours prior, dump a shoe box carrying your Uzi and a 9mm on the living room table, and shout to the group of gathered men and God, "I heard niggas was looking for me. Well, let niggas know, I ain't hard to find. Somebody gone die!" In your mid-thirties, you'll bust one shot near, but just near, your father inside your crib, not to kill him, but to discourage him from discouraging you against prosecuting what might be your last ballistic beef, but on this day, you're in your late twenties, which in this case is plenty old enough to die. You stomp out of the house and slam yourself into a car driven by your ride-to-beyond-good-sense girlfriend. Your brother calls and cautions you against doing something you'll regret and furthermore against returning to the barbecue-fish-fry. Hours after his call, you flout your disinvitation, which is to say you show up and stalk the yard with a waist-tucked 9mm bulging under your T-shirt and a scowl that ain't got no place near nothing festive. You see a dude who witnessed your scuffle the night before, a dude who's a friend of your new foe, and you flash your 9mm and threaten him into the basement. You lay your pistol in plain view and seethe. "Nigga, we can scrap right here, right now," you say. "Nah, bro, I don't want no problems," he says, and warns your newest archest foe heard word of your whereabouts and is on his way to the barbecue-fish-fry for action. By now almost everyone wants you to leave, including the father of the friend who's hosting, and it's the father's wish you decide to heed. Oh, the timing: you stomp out of the yard, peer down the street, and in the distance, see your new arch foe among a circle of dudes. You pull the pistol from your waist and—men, women, and God's only begotten son be damned—march into the middle of the street. Once, you told a grade-school teacher of your plan to become a hit man, and though you haven't considered that career choice in ages, today could be the day that delivers you to the threshold of that young hope. Before you shoot yourself into that fate, a girl you know from high school darts between you and your new foe. She calls your name, pleads, "Please, don't. Please!" She announces your fast foe is her brother, appeals once more against gunplay, and you pause, seeing an escape out of what a breath before felt destined. "Oh, that's your brother?" you say, and lower your pistol. The next week, you pull into the parking lot of the grocery store with your daughter in the passenger seat, and out of someplace unseen your foe pulls up beside you. Neither hand touches the wheel, and you'd bet blood on why they aren't in view and what one holds. Decisions—of which the most fool would be to reach for what's under your seat. Your daughter is a fifth grader, which is to say, in this instance, plenty old enough to die. You curl over her and brace, and when you don't hear a pistol bark, you raise your head, shake it, no, no, no, look your foe eye-to-assassin-black-eye, and mouth, "Man, I don't want no problems. It's squashed. It's squashed.". . . He idles for what could be the rest of your or your firstborn's life.

SURVIVOR FILE

You: a December baby, so you hit legal grown-ass-manhood midway through your senior year. You: an orphaned son, which is why that birthday you receive an insurance check for a few grand that feels like a bazillion. You get duped into buying a bucket and cop a gold chain, a couple pairs of overpriced jeans, and Jordans—totems of the good life or so you believe. Spring break that year you announce to the uncle who's been your caretaker since you were a tyke, "I'm goin to Seattle. And there ain't nothin you can do about it." You mob to the Emerald City with one homeboy riding shotgun, another in the backseat, the three of you blowing chronic while your speakers *BOOMBLAP!* the whole way up the interstate. You kick it in Seattle for a couple of days, selling dub sacks here and there, hitting the clubs, chasing chicks. Sunday, you and your homeboys puff-puff-pass the last of your chronic the entire return trip, so you're good and loaded when you hit your front door, yell, "I'm back," and swagger upstairs to your room. Your uncle summons you downstairs, his face a whole new stern. "You want to be a man. Go be a man on your own," he says. "You can't live here anymore. You got a week. A week and I want you out." Compunction don't occur to you (not for many years, that is), neither does asking him to reconsider. "Fine, I'll be out before the week's up," you say, and feel an insta-fool for setting yourself on a shorter clock than even your uncle commanded. The next day you apartment hunt as an unemployed, zero-credit eighteen-year-old high school senior. You soon find out how tough it is for somebody jobless and credit-less to be able to see an apartment, much less rent one, whether that somebody's grown-ass-manness is affirmed by law or not. You skip school to widen your search but end up again and again the crestfallen actor in a predictable script: "So where do you work?" they ask. "Right now, nowhere," you say. "Then how are you going to pay rent?" You end up convincing an aunt to let you live with her in an apartment a few blocks from your high school, though that proximity don't keep you from missing, missing, missing days and, in short order, dropping out. All the while, you hang tough with the same homeboys, all of whom are hooligans-in-training. Not to mention, the older cousin you call your brother—the one person you believe addresses you like a person and not a peon—catches a dope case and goes to prison. The aunt in whose apartment you live is either jobless or on the verge of it in perpetuum and collects food stamps, but what the fuck is a federal safety net that catches little to no food for the fridge? What else can you do but supplement the house with minor profits from the weed and bitty grams of crack you sell. Meantime, your crew of goonish homeboys stay kicking up dust, static that sometimes ends with one or more of you dodging bullets. Not to mention, one homeboy robs another one, a breach that births in you a gnawing worry over which of them you can trust, if you can trust any one of them, and about how much you're built for this base new world. Furthermore, you turn your aunt's apartment into a spot, start stashing your triple beam under the sink, inviting customers inside. On the regular, those customers show up late night and the small hours, their cars making a racket, their voices no parts discreet. Often officers appear at the front door of your aunt's apartment and report a neighbor's complaint of drug and gang activity. This occurs for months, until your aunt convinces you to move with her and her kids to Arizona with another uncle. You've considered moving to AZ all of never before this, but that don't stop you from agreeing. You live in AZ's arid heat for a few months burning through your meager bucks on cell phone bills and bullshit. Near broke and homesick, you borrow forever dollars for a flight back and move in with a woman you call your grandmother. The grandmother has no rules about your coming and going, demands only that you "don't disrespect her house," and, wild before you left, your wild spikes to level ten. Soon after, you receive a second insurance payout of several thousand that feels like a million-billion from your mother's long-ago life insurance and restart your fledgling weed-and-dope business. You move out of your grandmother's house into an apartment, let a salesman con you into buying an old Jaguar, drop serious bread on a thick herringbone necklace and bracelet set, and start frequenting car auctions and placing winning bids on hoopties you don't need just to call your homeboys and brag. You feel like a man, like that dude, which is to say, it's all to the good, or so you think, until once, twice, someone tries to kick in your door. That second time, you hear them and dash to grab your .380 from a drawer, flip over a table in front of the door, and convince yourself you're busting at the first motherfucka that steps so much as a toe inside. It becomes clear that you could end up dead, clearer still when your homeboy (the same homie who'll be shot and killed a year later) falls asleep in a dope house and has a crackhead bash his head with a hammer. Quick, you sell the last of your dope and your triple beam and resolve against hustling narcotics for life. But since you're not not job phobic, you begin cashing bad checks and selling heisted video games—petty scam until a fellow scammer gets knocked for the same hustle and faces a seven-year sentence. You perceive his possible verdict as a harbinger. Its message: your grown ass must work, must work or else, because the "or else" you can't bear.

SURVIVOR FILE

You and your patna, after kickin it with some tenders, hike through Northeast for his crib, a route that leads you past a house with a pile of mountain bikes outside it, and inside, a passel of dudes sounding good and saucy. You and your patna slow long enough to glance into the house, glimpse bodies through a naked kitchen window, one of whom spies you and yells, "Hey. Look. Them niggas tryna steal our bikes!" You had no intention of stealing their bikes, but that don't stop you and your patna from breaking. You hear the dudes bust out of the house, slam themselves into a car, and gun the engine. You huff up a hill and around a corner and around another corner and into an alley, keep trucking until you can't hear them. "Damn, bro, that shit was hella close," you say. "What you think they was gonna do?" Your patna shrugs. You slap your hands on your knees, bend, suck wind. You wait a few belabored breaths and motion your patna to follow you out of the alley onto a main street—a street dark and narrow, canopied by trees, flanked by cars. "You think we cool?" your patna asks. "Yeah, we cool," you say. You take a few more mock-confident strides and turn to head your separate ways, but a lanky light-skinned dude with long hair corporeals out of the dark and grabs you by your jacket. Your patna bails. The dude clutching a handful of your jacket hollers for his homies to pull up the car and "bring the dogs." You hear a car growl closer, imagine dogs mauling you, imagine worse, believe yourself doomed until you realize you're less than a block from the house where some of your OGs hang. You manage to magician out of your jacket, dart to the OGs' crib, and *BAM! BAM! BAM!* on the door. One of the OGs answers, double-barreled shotgun in hand. You explain your jam in a burst, and he stomps off the porch with the shotgun. "Where they at?" he says. The OG and you look this- and that-a-way, see no sign of dude or his accomplices. You wait in the OGs' yard for your runagate pulse to slow and dash for home, glancing over your shoulder every few paces. On your way home, you see your patna. You don't bother asking him why he left you, but instead follow him to his house, where you recount the story to each other, call another homeboy, and retell it to him too. Days pass with what happened and might've happened chief in your and your patna's dialogue. Days later your patna's amped, has got his hands on some heat. "We gotta do somethin," he barks. "We can't just let them niggas get away with this shit." Decades from now, you'll feel a deep indebtedness to the angels that have kept you alive, but today your patna's plan looks like the key to life. You draft one of your homeboys as a driver, load heated into his car one late night, and creep down to the house where you first saw the dudes who spooked you. You and your patna hop out your homeboy's ride and dump rounds in the house and the car outside it (a baptism into gunplay) and dash back to the car, and your homeboy smashes away from the scene. Not a single newscast reports the shooting, and neither do you hear word of anybody being shot or killed in the hood that night, and those silences are the extent of your investigation into possible harm.

SURVIVOR FILE

You meet your main squeeze at the park, a park that on this halcyon day is teeming with picnickers and games on all the diamonds and courts. The two of you are strolling outside the park when a carload of Crabs pull up in a Blazer. These are the same Crabs who caught you slipping days before, accused you of putting hands on one of their cousins, and pulled heat on you. That day you denied laying the mitts on their fam, and to your surprised relief, they gave you a pass, but today those same Crabs scream, "Wassup, Cuz," from the window. Since being a punk ain't on no page of your teenage how-to-gangbang handbook, you scream, "What's happenin, Blood. What's goin on?!" The driver idles, and you think you see a passenger reaching for what could put you and your main girl in dirt. You snatch the pistol from your waist and bust—per the police report you'll read later—eight shots. Your girl statues beside you. The Blazer tears off. You duck into the park—what a witness will describe as a saunter—with the gait of a dude who ain't just dumped in daylight, while a dog-walking white man pursues you saying, "HEY! HEY!" Says it till you turn, point the pistol at his life, and squeeze without intent to kill, but should he die, well . . . The gun don't fire but spooks the Samaritan into fleeing. You keep on, your girl at your back. "You can't toss that in the garbage can. You weren't wearing a glove, and your fingerprints are on it," she says, and demands your gun. With no plan whatsoever for disposal, you give it to her. You watch her flit off, see police swarm her near the edge of the park. You bolt out of the park and down the block, see the Crabs you dumped on pull around the corner. Gunless now, you fake reach for heat and they peel off. You sprint between houses, bound a fence into the yard of a woman tending her garden. She stops. You stop. She screams. You break out of the yard, and hustle between houses until you reach the sidewalk, where you snatch off your T-shirt and throw it in a trash can. Sirens scream (for who else in the world but you?) in the distance. You spot a squad car at a red light and jog in place as if, in your tank top and jean shorts, you're out for an afternoon jaunt. Once police creep past, you hotfoot the miles from the park to your house hearing a trumpet in your chest and the wind in your ear, feeling the whir of your life in your neck and wrists. You reach your house and march straight to your room with your mother worrying after you: "What's wrong? What's wrong?" You slam clothes into a bag, grab the couple of bucks left in your stash, and rush past your mother for the door. Your sister catches you before you leave, reports that minutes before you got there, some dudes came to the house looking for you and tried to bully past her, but she broke to the second door and locked them out. Sound advice nor consolation occurs to you, so you offer neither. You instead vault off the porch, dash to the park where the set hangs. You wish you could ring your father, who'd offer counsel, but since he's in AZ, you instead buzz your Big homie. Your Big homie swoops you from the park and shuttles you over to the duplex of a chick who's got a baby by another dude in the set. You sleep in her squalid apartment for days. You see the shooting air on the news and claim the fact they don't list your name as a suspect as a sign of fortune. You end up at your grandparents' house, where you stow a few days, secret till one day your aunt screams, "You gots to get outta here. I don't want you on my couch. Don't want you in my house." You call an uncle and he offers to let you hide out at his place across the river in Vancouver. Over the next few days, your not-quite-flight from the law includes convincing your uncle to ferry you back to the hood to buy bud. On one of those trips, right about the time you're about to blow one with the homies, police pull up. You think: *If I run, where to?* You think: *Who can I call to get me?* You stroll to your uncle's car, climb in, and run down the situation. Your uncle eases away, manages a block or so before an unmarked car hits you with flashers. Your uncle, turrets blaring in his rearview, drives another half block or so and turns into the driveway of your grandfather's house. Police cars (marked, unmarked) screech onto the scene. Officers jump out, draw guns, and bark, "HANDS OUT THE WINDOW! HANDS OUT OF THE WINDOW, NOW! GET OUT OF THE CAR! BACK UP SLOW TO THE SOUND OF MY VOICE!" You wary out of your uncle's car to orders. Officers grab you, slam you facedown, smash knees in your back, flip you over, elbow you in the face, jerk you to your feet. They shove you into the backseat of a squad car. Your mom rushes out of the house. "Hey, that's my son," she says. "That's my son." She barges through the officers to the side of the car. She leans inside. "First thing you tell them when you get there is you want a lawyer," she says. The first thing you do when you get to the county is slumber, hands cuffed, on a bench. A nosebleed frights you awake, and soon officers enter and lead you to an airless room. Right off, they mention your girlfriend's name. "Who that?" you say. They say, "What happened at the park?" You say, "What park?" They say, "How do you think we knew where to come? She told us everything. And we have witnesses saying you shot the gun and she was just there." The officers threaten to charge her if you don't admit to the shooting, and you wonder for moments what's the handbook rule on a girlfriend who snitched. "All right, all right," you say. "This what happened . . ." The moment after you confess, you second-guess it and request a lawyer—ambivalence that you will learn makes your admission inadmissible in court. They book you on three counts of attempted murder and eight counts of unlawful use of a weapon, one count for each shell casing they found at the scene. The DA's office charges you within the week. You own little doubt now that you're headed to prison. The question is, *for how long?* You stew in the Justice Center for three months in a unit that houses violent criminals—kidnappers, rapists, murderers. You're thankful you didn't murder anyone. You're thankful as well for the public defender who discloses you're eligible for a new program called Closed Street, which will allow you to be released if you can find someone to post 10k for bail and offer you a safe home. A friend of the family agrees to put up the ten grand, but the day you're supposed to get out, she reneges. You'll find out later that the family friend believed you'd jump bail, and maybe she's psychic because your plan was to flee and live with your father in AZ, a state you've been told won't extradite. Months after your rescinded chance to blow bail, you meet with your PD to discuss deals and find out that the dudes you dumped on have been caught for another crime and assigned to him. Your PD cites a conflict of interest and decides to drop you instead of them. The court assigns your future to a private lawyer, one whose firm requires pro bono work. This new counsel don't bother pretending overmuch concern with the outcome of your case. He reports that the DA's first plea offer is fifteen years. Or in sentencing parlance 180 months. Your mom pressures you to take the deal, but you do the math on how old you'll be when you parole, and think, *Fuck that!* Meantime, the dudes you dumped on bail out on their new charges and ghost. Lucky you, the year before, the Supreme Court clarified the Sixth Amendment in *Crawford v. Washington*, so when your accusers don't show up to testify at trial, your steeling teenage heart floats to the roof of the courthouse. The prosecutor offers a second deal of eighty-four months. "You better take this one," your mom says. "You need to take this." You weigh her advice, but then the DA's office assigns your case to a new prosecutor, and you resurrect hope for an even lighter sentence. The new DA forbears you the gun minimum of five years. Or in sentencing parlance sixty months. He sweetens the tender with credit for time served. You agree and, anxious, bide time till your sentencing date. That ominous day bailiffs march you into the courtroom, you spot your mother, your sister, your uncle, but not a single homie from the set. Grade-school kids fidget in the benches, a scene resembling your not-that-long-ago class visit to this same courthouse. "You're so young," the judge says. "You do this five years, and when you get out you'll have an opportunity to change your life. However, I'm concerned that you're still in denial." He peers at you, asks if you have anything you'd like to say. "Yes, Your Honor, I do," you say. "I did it. I'm sorry I did it, and I want to accept responsibility for my actions." Your sister leaps to her feet, screams, "Stop it. Stop it. Don't say that. Don't let him say that." The judge orders her seated and his courtroom hushed. "You know, you're either an honorable young man or an idiot," he says. "Because I don't have to accept the DA's recommendation. Not when you just admitted guilt." He calls the DA into his chambers, and you wilt, cursing yourself, refiguring how old you'll be if he gives you the max, wondering if not the max, how long you'll do. A century later, the judge, DA trailing him, strolls out of his chambers and assumes his throne. He lifts a gavel that turns you into the center of the world, and you hostage a deep breath while your heart plummets past the last floor of the courthouse. "Son, consider yourself fortunate," he says. "I've decided to honor your plea."

PART 2

What have we learned?

In the course of human events,
the world will little note,
nor long remember, [our] numberless
afflictions. No refuge could save us
from the terror of flight or gloom of the grave.
The men who framed The Declaration
were principled, free. "People of the United States"
and "citizens" are synonymous,
but [we] were not included,
under the word "citizens."
And no nation so conceived
can long endure. Known facts: [we] had no rights
the white man was bound to respect.

APPLES

One morning Big Chris—Dad—popped up at Mom's job and sold her a grandiose get-rich-in-a-flash scheme and borrowed five hundred dollars. No small sum. Then it was no-hear-from-no-see for long enough to be disrespectful. Two consecutive nights before the morning of this tale, Mom rode by an uncle's apartment (out of love I'll call him Uncle X) and swept for Dad's car. The morning of, she and her sister-friend Dawn (this a few years before Dawn stood witness to Mom's union) and her sister-aunt Essie crowded in her red Triumph Spitfire again to see what they could see, which is to say, who they could find. In matters regarding her one true love, Mom in those days was not of want for grit. She parked on the street, admonished Dawn to wait in the car, and drafted her sister-aunt Essie to accompany her as she waddled up to Uncle X's apartment and knuckled the door. The white woman who would become Uncle X's bottom broad answered.

"Chrissy here?" Mom asked.

"Oh, Chrissy's back there in the room," said Uncle X's broad. Said it, I suppose, because she either didn't know Mom or didn't know better or both—an ignorance that lasted a couple of beats. Or was it a beat? "Oh God," Uncle X's broad said, and tried to close the door, but Mom jammed her foot in the door and forced her way in.

"Essie, watch her," Mom said as she appraised the scene. She stomped toward the kitchen and hunted the drawers for a butcher knife—an act that, as we shall see, might've been coded in her DNA—and kept huffing toward the bedroom. She swung the door open and beheld the soon-to-be father of her second son asleep beside a white woman. A white woman! That white woman popped up and made the kind of face we might expect from a woman awakened to the sight of a crazed person wielding a butcher knife at the foot of her bed.

The white woman nudged Dad. "Chrissy, get up." But Dad and his purgetastic conscious didn't budge. She nudged him again.

"What? What?" he said.

"Chrissy, get up. Somebody's here," she said.

That's when Dad picked his head off the pillow and cracked an eye open.

"Dora!?" He called Mom's middle name as was his custom. Said it as if he'd seen an apparition, an omen.

"You motherfuckin right it's Dora, nigga!" Mom said. "What the fuck is you doin in bed with this white girl?!"

Dad snapped vivid. "Dora, Dora, Dora, Dora," he said. "It's not what you think, Dora."

"How the fuck you think it's not what I think?" Mom said. "I'm six months pregnant with *your* baby, the baby that you been beggin me to have since forever. You come to my job and take my five hundred dollars. Five hundred dollars from your pregnant girlfriend. You take my money and run off for days without a word and now here you is in bed with this white broad!"

"Dora, Dora, Dora, Dora," Dad said. "Wait, wait, let me explain. I can explain."

"You can't explain shit," Mom said.

"But, Dora, listen, we wasn't fuckin," he said. "We wasn't."

"Ooooh, now you want to insult my intelligence," Mom said. She jumped on the bed and snatched the sheets off Dad and the young white woman. She straddled him. "So you layin in bed butt naked with this bitch and you wasn't fuckin?" she said. She kneed Dad's chest and leaned in, her cheek brushing his. "I could kill you. You hear me? I could fuckin kill you right now!" she said. She sat up and raised the butcher knife to near the place where she sent up prayers for the good health of her unborn baby and left it there for what felt like how long it might take for the second coming.

She stabbed it (sharp, dull, no matter) in slow motion right beside Dad's neck. The white woman screamed. Dad screamed. "Shit goddamn, Dora," he said.

"Don't move," Mom warned, her almost-deed shocking her sensate. She hopped off the bed and bolted into the kitchen and called her sister-aunt Essie and together they smashed cups, glasses, plates, saucers. Together they hunted the drawers, tossed utensils, tossed forks, spoons, knives. The sisters in consort swung open the fridge and dumped everything inside it, busted up glass containers when they could. Mom, as a solo act, scratched the kitchen table and chairs with her knife. Meanwhile, Uncle X's bottom broad ran to the bathroom and locked herself in it. Mom raged into the living room, where she stabbed and cut the couches and broke pictures and vases, where she cursed incessant and called, "Oh God! Oh God!" She blustered back into the bedroom where Dad and his white woman hadn't moved. "Oh my God! How could you!" Mom howled. She snatched open the closet and cut and stabbed and ripped all the cloth in sight. "You dirty dog nigga! You take my money. *My* money. And lay up with this white bitch!" she said, and paced in front of the closet. She cut, tore, ripped some more.

"Don't move. Don't say nothin," Dad warned his white woman.

In the midst of the dustup, somebody had called the police. A pair of officers arrived, one of whom, to Mom's benefit, was an old high school classmate. That officer canvassed the havoc. "Wow," he said. "What happened here?"

Dad threw on some of his shredded clothes and stumbled into the front room. "It's just a misunderstanding, Officer. A big, big misunderstanding," he said, and began to explain.

Meanwhile Uncle X's woman peeked her head out of the bathroom. "Misunderstanding my ass. It was her. She did all this," she said, and pointed a finger. "Yeah, bitch, the police here now. You going to jail."

"Bitch. Who you callin bitch?!" Mom said. She leaped for the bathroom door wielding the butcher knife. Unce X's white woman slammed shut the door, but Mom stabbed at it anyhow.

"Miss, miss, put the knife down," one officer ordered. "Miss, put the knife down now!" Mom dropped the knife and sank. The officer that was her old high school classmate sauntered over to her. "Damn, Lillie, you did all this?"

Mom gazed up at him, feeling her tear ducts flood. "Yes, I did," she said. "Here I am pregnant and he came and got my money and ran off and now I find him in bed with a white girl."

"That's no good. No good at all, Lillie," the officer said. "But we're going to have to take you downtown." He helped Mom to her feet and cuffed her. Mom instructed her sister-aunt Essie to drive the Spitfire home and mind the money in her purse in case she needed it for bail. Dad asked what would happen to Mom, and the officers explained that if no one pressed charges there was a good chance the case would be dismissed.

"Don't worry, Dora," Dad said. "Ain't nobody pressin nothin."

The officers scrawled a few more notes and led Mom to their squad car. On the way to the Justice Center, Mom's old classmate glimpsed her sniffling, teary pitifulness in the rearview. "I do believe, Lillie Jackson, that you need to get yourself a new boyfriend," he said.

MYTHS, FAIRY TALES, LEGENDS

Sometimes, in better times, we—the *we* being Mom, Dad, me, and later my bro Chris Jr., whom Mom was carrying—would load into Dad's Cadillac and cruise; we'd wheel for somewhere or nowhere at all, which most times mattered not to me since all the way to wherever, Dad would keep me rapt with knock-knock jokes or a remixed signifying monkey folktale or the story of a good high school hoop game spun into Hellenistic glories. Though I couldn't call a myth from a legend from a fairy or folktale in those days, it's possible those wandering drives and Dad's enchanting-ass storytelling primed my eventual perception of the woman the white man deems his and his alone—the apple.

The apple is part myth, grounded in Hera's garden of the Hesperides and its tree (or trees) bearing immortality-granting golden fruit; we could trace the myth back to Hippomenes tossing those golden apples at Atalanta's feet to win a race of mortal consequence (and her most beautiful hand in marriage). The myth of apple also features elements of Eris crashing Zeus's bridal shower and causing a commotion among the goddesses—and of course the epic beef between the Greeks and Trojans—with that golden apple of discord; and though the jury is forever out on whether it was indeed an apple, I'm counting as part of the apple's genesis the Old Testament myth of Eve coaxing Adam into eating the fruit that evermore ruined our sure shot at an Edenic life.

The apple is part fairy tale. She is never allowed to be a mere woman, or should I say human. She is deemed elegant, pious, sacred, pure, virtuous, virginal, beautiful, moral, sublime, cultured, graceful. She's ethereal, the equal of magical queens and princesses, beings who alone have been blessed with the biological gift of bearing the best of mankind: the white race. And what's a fairy tale without a monster, otherwise known as the swarthy barbarians from which apples must be secured by the men who pledged their safekeep? And what's a fairy tale without an antagonist? The apple's antagonists being uncomely and lascivious colored beings, mere women or less than that, maligned as femme fatales and jezebels and mammies, et cetera—as succubi apt to seduce a guardian into tainting his pure white blood.

The apple is part legend. For proof, I point to colonial times and the unfortunate adulterous apples branded with a scarlet *A* and-or whipped and-or murdered, or the ones who worked tobacco fields or submitted to women's work while their men built the colonies. The Revolutionary War turned scores of women blossoming into applehood into legends, some of whom plodded alongside their independence-minded husbands. Like Martha Washington who shivered beside the future first president through that frigid winter at Valley Forge. Like less-known others who, for the whole of the war, scavenged food or cooked or sewed or nursed the wounded back to health. There were those who disguised themselves as men to join the combat, and those who managed homes and children while their men were off, all the while living as little more than a husband's chattel property that couldn't draft a will or own real estate or vote; shit, who couldn't even sign a contract. Decades later, pale-faced and leisured planter-class apples took high tea in their parlors wearing high-necked, full-sleeved dresses of black-market cotton; they also bolstered their legend by keeping plantations running while their men were off losing a Civil War. The legend of apples reached its zenith following that Civil War, in the post-Reconstruction era some claim is named for Charles Lynch (who married an apple named Anne), i.e., during those terrortastic decades that advanced, among other alibis, the purported protection of an apple's purity—from a whistle or wayward glance or less—as reason enough to turn a black man into a melanoid corpse.

Eras and eras later, that coveted purity catalyzed Dad and his Northern-born let's-defenestrate-the-rules pimp patnas into idolaters of apples and, in many cases, my mama and her ilk into oft-forgiving flagellants. Much, but never enough, has been said about the extreme violence white men have been willing to perpetrate in the name of chivalric and paternal protection of the women they've invested (burdened?) with the expectation of piousness, whom they've weighted with lifetime roles as the incubators and progenitors of the white race. But let me call it, white men were never protecting the purity of white women, for couldn't no mortal woman satisfy his needs nohow. The way I see it, the apple has been essential because, should enough of them betray the white man, the master race as it's known would cease. Indeed, the white man has committed malevolence after malevolence to secure his hegemony over the apple: perforce, his most prized possession. She being vital to his dominion over whomever and whatever he envisaged.

JUST THE TWO OF US

My mother was twenty years old when she met Big Chris: my dad. She was walking home from a day at Western Business College with her best friend (who happened to be Dad's longtime neighbor and childhood friend) when he pulled over and asked them if they needed a ride. They said yes and hopped in. Dad eyed my mother in the rearview mirror, and when he dropped her off, asked her for her digits. He didn't waste no time putting his telephone mack down, though truth be told, Mom needed little convincing: "Your dad had just got out the penitentiary and he had muscles and was fine," Mom told me. "Since I never thought of myself as pretty, it made me feel good that he wanted me. I was like, what this fine nigga want with me?"

Soon Mom was visiting his job (he was on parole and had to keep one) at an adult services center. Dad, being Dad, neglected to mention that he had a girlfriend and a toddler daughter and that his girlfriend would be adamant against his and Mom's quickened hearts. Said girlfriend confronted Mom, but that fracas must've ranked low on Dad's trouble gauge, given later that year, he bought her and Mom the same damn rings for Christmas!

Mom recalls she and Dad hit it off because they were both acute sufferers of middle-child syndrome. She says he spoke often about believing that Uncle X was his parents' favorite and that his younger brother, Uncle Z, was destined for eternal coddling. Plus, Dad was named after an uncle who died at a young age. He confided in Mom that ever since he was a kid, he'd had a recurring dream that he'd die in his thirties. Baring his veins inside out to Mom was a significant wager for Dad, and since Mom would've known or at least sensed that risk, it strengthened their bond. Dad's willingness to reveal his insecurities to my mother might also be why her sense of his intentions was at odds with almost everyone else's: "Your dad used to work. He worked for at least a couple of years at an adult services center; he worked at Montgomery Ward [department store], at Levitz [furniture store]. He never talked about pimping. Most times it wouldn't be any pimping going on until your uncle [X] came to town. That's when he'd up and leave for days. He always looked up to your uncle. After a while, I kind of accepted the pimpin thing. He'd say, 'Well, I bring the money home to you,' and he did."

Those days also call to mind Mom and Dad's atomic love, or should I say their nuclear fights, loud blowups (she screaming more than he) where she would throw lamps and vases and dishes and whatever else she could find that would break or shatter in hi-fi. Mom's rage seemed hella zealous to me back then. Dad was calm for his part (he never once hit her or raised his hand in threat) and sometimes attempted to reason with Mom, but more often than not, would bounce. Mom says around that time his and her favorite songs were Bill Withers's "Just the Two of Us" and Larry Graham's "One in a Million." In retrospect, I can imagine her desperate need for the balm of those songs to sustain her through her fraught amour, through those months she'd hand Dad cash for the bills and he'd blow it, those days when his most brash *hos* would call the house and leave taunting messages with her (sometimes with me). What I couldn't know at the time was how much she needed to believe that he and she were bound to each other in the instances when she'd find another woman's panties in the house, a blatant sign that Dad had committed a transgression high on her list. No trespass was higher, though, than her beloved fucking an apple.

IN THE BEGINNING,
THERE WERE APPLES

The apple tree is an angiosperm, AKA a flowering plant, the appearance of which has been traced to the Cretaceous Period (think Pangaea drifting apart, dinosaurs, the first birds). The apple blossom has both male and female parts but requires cross-pollination—accomplished for the most part by honeybees. Each pollen grain carries two sperm. One fertilizes the egg in the ovule and becomes a zygote and later an embryo. The second unites with other cells in that same ovule and becomes an endosperm, which acts as a nutrient for the embryo. The seed of the apple is formed when the endosperm and the embryo become encased in the part of the ovule that hardens into the seed coat. The ovary and other parts of the flower develop into the fleshy fruit that we eat.

Like the fruit, the seed of the apple as myth/fairy tale/legend is binary. One part, the oldest part, of the apple's seed is the primordial history of man oppressing woman. Witness man's patriarchal yearnings in the Babylonian creation myth where the hero-god strikes down the Great Mother, founds Babylonia, and creates humans. See it in the Epic of Gilgamesh and the king decreeing he must copulate with every young woman (talk about power) *before* she consummated her marriage. There it is again in the Code of Hammurabi, laws that forced a woman to submit to her husband as a slave if she hazarded divorce without his consent, laws where a wife caught cheating would be tied to her lover and drowned unless her husband saved them (what were the chances of that?). The oldest part of the seed is also owed to the Greeks and men like Aristotle, who in *Politics* contends, "as regards the sexes, the male is by nature superior and the female inferior, the male ruler and the female subject." See man's compulsion to subjugate women in the Jewish myth of Lilith—Adam's headstrong first wife, the one made from the same dust as him—who was cast out of Eden for refusing subservience, and later with Eve, who, unlike Lilith, was created from Adam's rib (code for a part of but never a whole or an equal) rather than from the same dust as him. See the notion of man over woman promulgated in umpteen Bible scriptures: "Neither was man created for woman, but woman for man," and "For Adam was created first," et cetera.

The second, younger, part of the apple's seed is the invention of the white race, which, as I see it, is a philosophical phenomenon that emerged centuries ago in Europe—though its roots reach back millennia—and began efflorescing in earnest in colonial America. The white race, which is to say, a collective of conspirators who, by sundry means—political, legal, extralegal, social, artistic, scientific, religious, et cetera—amassed unjust providence over too much of God's bounty. One could argue there'd be no need for apples, the American sort at least, without the white race's epochs-long enterprise of othering, a project inseparable from the deep, deep, deep need to protect and propagate the world's most chimeric self-image.

CHRISTOPHER LEE JONES

My mother, years beyond her time with Dad, years, even, beyond his death, believes (and not a soul could convince her otherwise) that she and he were destined. Christopher Lee Jones Sr. was born May 10, 1954, in Portland, Oregon, to Arthur "Pudding" Jones Jr. and Nancy May Jones. Pudding was a longtime foundry worker, and for a time Nancy was a stay-at-home mother. They were not especially religious, though they did send the kids to church and Sunday school. Pudding had been married prior to Nancy and fathered other children (the exact count is speculative), but my dad was raised among his parents' brood of five, two of whom were girls. Dad was the middle boy of three, which is without doubt a fact of import. He was something of a prodigy, as attest his being bused for a time to a white school with other promising neighborhood kids. It's damn near a consensus of friends and family that Dad was handsome, charming, garrulous, a first-rate "enhanced" storyteller, stand-up-comedian funny, owner of a smile bright as a supermoon, and no small part of a perfectionist. "When we was young, I'd get hungry and slop me a sandwich together," recalls Uncle X. "But your dad would sit and spread his mayonnaise and mustard just so and cut it into the neatest halves. I'd be like, 'Goddamn, Chrissy, you did all that just to eat the muthafucka?!' " Uncle X says. "But that's how he was. Everything he did was meticulous."

My fastidious-ass de facto dad was furthermore a talented dancer and sketch artist, a Pop Warner football phenom, a knockout boxer, and a gifted basketball and baseball player. He was by most measures the kind of universally well-liked and dynamic youngster to whom adults would say, "You can do anything you want," and mean it. But. But. But. To be true, he was also a high-striving hellion. He had a best friend (out of respect, I'm calling him Uncle Y) who lived next door, and together they brawled with kids from elsewhere, stole and stripped bikes for parts, cheated less savvy gamblers in dice and card games, and indulged in sundry other forms of juvenile mischief.

By the time Dad was in his teens, under the tutelage of a friend's older brother—a nefarious gangster, dope dealer, and thief who was known for supplying natural-ass whoopings—Dad and Uncle Y, or just Dad, depending on whose story you favor, had evolved from mischievous youngsters to full-on delinquents.

Recalls Dad's younger brother (for the love, he's Uncle Z), "When I was about a freshman in high school your dad pulled me aside and said, 'Say, it ain't never no reason for you to be broke. Cause you can get some money anytime you need with just three words.'"

"And what words is them, Chrissy?" Uncle Z asked.

"Simple," Dad said. "Stick. Them. Up."

Dad's salad days (go ahead, snicker) featured burglaries and armed robberies and dope dealing and nascent pimping and also it appears a progression from blowing weed to snorting cocaine to sniffing and later shooting heroin, practices that became habits orbiting many years of his life. By this time, my dad's dad had lost an eye in the foundry and suffered a stroke that left him homebound. From then on Pudding, who was all but incapacitated, would sit in his favorite living room chair watching TV with a pistol close at hand. Nancy, for her part, got a job at a tech company and began working the kind of hours you'd expect of a woman who had a house to keep out of foreclosure and five greedy mouths to feed. By necessity, the family dynamics were such that the kids were left ungoverned often and for a long time. The brothers, let me reiterate, had proven what they could do under loose supervision. So imagine what they were into with almost none?

Sometime in high school, Dad was sent to live with his oldest brother, Arthur III (Pudding's son by his previous wife), in LA. Uncle X claims that Dad was shipped off because he punched a principal during a school riot and got expelled. Uncle Z contends it had to do with Dad burglarizing a white boy's apartment for pounds of weed. "They came home while he was in there, and your dad had to jump out a two-story window but broken ankle and all, he got away," Uncle Z says. "But them white boys had seen who it was, and they was after him." Whether it's Uncle X's or Z's reason or both, what's fact is that before Dad graduated (damn skippy, he finished) from Jefferson High School, he spent time in LA.

Those months must've been another harbinger for him. It was the early seventies, which meant he arrived not long after the Watts Riots, which meant it was also circa Tookie Williams and Raymond Washington forming the Crips. And I can just see Dad diving headlong into the mix, soaking up as much G as he could. His older brother worked a job but also pimped on the side, and I imagine modeling chaste living and moral judgment wasn't high on his list of objectives.

Can you envision my dad amid all that past and future tense? Envision his return to Portland after that year spent away. Imagine him, talismans of his California life in hand, returning to a house that was blocks from the city's most infamous *ho* stroll and steps from Ms. Christine's brothel; imagine him once again living among the burglars and boosters and dealers and gangsters and card sharks and gamblers and number runners who must've seemed everywhere at once. The physics of his neighborhood was such that he would've had to have been a superhero to best the inertia, and though Dad had many talents, of this we can all be good and goddamn sure: he didn't sport no cape and dunta-dunts.

So, what did a teenager do who believed himself smarter and more special and more charming and more slick, daring, driven than any local rogue?

He robbed a bank of course!

Per Uncle Z's version, my dad came to the house arguing with his friend about robbing a cigar store.

"Say, why you wanna rob somethin?" said Uncle X.

"Cause I need some real serious thousands," Dad said.

"Well, that ain't no cool play, Chrissy. If you gonna rob something, rob a bank," Uncle X said.

"What bank?" Dad said.

Between the brothers occurs a stark fugitive silence.

"Man, rob the nigger bank," Uncle X said. "Don't nobody give a fuck about that one."

And so was birthed a half-ass impetuous plan for Dad, Uncle X, and a patna to dress up like women and rob Albina Community Bank, AKA the bank run by black folk that was a hop-skip-jump from where they lived. Hasty plan notwithstanding, they made off with nearly thirty grand to split. They invested their score in cocaine, copped a few this-and-thats, and as they said in those days, got the fuck out of Dodge. Word of the heist zipped around the neighborhood in their absence, and before long the police caught the driver and but of course of course (criminal honor, what's that?) the driver snitched. Dad and Uncle X, a pair of smoking-hot sibling suspects, resigned themselves to sure capture, stole back into town, and holed up in one place after another. A couple weeks into their flight, the police busted their (not so) safe house and manifested the brothers' fortune. Because Oregon at the time didn't have a federal prison, the brothers were sent to Lompoc, the World War II disciplinary barracks that had been repurposed into a California federal prison after Alcatraz closed.

Dad and Uncle X were inmates at Lompoc when it was known as the country's most famous "country club prison," the years it was home to H. R. Haldeman and Herbert Kalmbach of Watergate ignominy. The Lompoc of their time had no walls, no fences, no bars, and no armed guards; it was a "camp" where inmates could spend free time jogging and playing tennis or lawn bowling. The Lompoc of their time featured inmate dorms bordered by eucalyptus and pine trees and flower gardens of daisies and roses. It looked and felt, or so I imagine, to its residents like a college dorm, which could explain why Dad (clap for the man) used part of his time to earn his associate's degree.

The questionable punitiveness of their boarding + the comfort of being imprisoned together + the timing of being fresh out their teens (in Dad's case a teen at the outset) and subject to sway = (by my math) circumstances pretty much antithetical to meaningful rehabilitation, if such a thing exists for those *non*habilitated to begin with. It's no wonder why, though Dad achieved a marker of personal progress, by most signs, he and Uncle X also spent beaucoup time working to perfect their pimping. Reminisces Uncle X, "Before I went down, I knocked me a lil old broad who worked at my lawyer's office. Baby girl said she wanted to do my time with me, so I stayed in her ear and eventually put her to work." That "work" lasted all of his and Dad's three and a half years in Lompoc. As if it were written, they were paroled the same day. "When I got out. Baby girl handed me eight grand cash," Uncle X recalls. "So, I gave Chrissy two grand cause that's how we looked out for each other."

They returned to Portland with their egos supercharged off having earned a high grade on the mettle test of prison, returned with the brashness of the bank job in one hand, and in the other, the honorific yield of Uncle X's incarcerated pimp skills. Christopher Lee Jones met Lillie Dora Jackson a few months after his release. It couldn't have been too long after their acquaintance when he met me: the not-yet-one-year-old boy that, for the rest of his days on earth, he'd regard, in word and deed, as his eldest son.

LILLIE DORA JACKSON

Lillie Dora Jackson was born May 28, 1956, in Montgomery, Alabama, to Samuel Jackson Jr. and Mary Alice Jackson (maiden name Reese). Sam was the college-educated son of upper-middle-class blacks. Mary, three years his junior, was a high-school-educated daughter of working-class parents. The couple was married in a shotgun wedding in September of 1955 and welcomed their first child, Sam III, that November. The newlyweds had my mother the following year and named her after her paternal grandmother. Mary Alice delivered another son the next year and their last son the year after that. Though all the children were born near the dawn of the civil rights movement in a state dogged in its defense of Jim Crow, they lived reasonably sheltered lives. Being the lone girl proved advantageous for Mom, at least in the early on. She was the happy recipient of all the dolls she wanted and the proud owner of a closetful of pretty dresses. Her mother would spend mornings styling her hair in meticulous pigtails and would often let her stay up listening to Mahalia Jackson records with her well past the time that her brothers had been sent to bed. Though it might've seemed a blithe existence, it was in fact the South, environs that encouraged Mom's father to follow his parents—Mama Edie and Bubba—to the Northwest.

Mom's good fortune persisted in Portland. Her father found work as a postal clerk and part-time substitute teacher in the Portland Public Schools system, and her mother remained a homemaker. In their house in Southeast, her brothers shared an attic bedroom, but Mom landed her own first-floor bedroom, bathroom included. Mom's habitational comfort, however, belied her parents' discord. Their bedroom was also on the first floor, and many a night Mom heard them bickering. Mom describes her mother as stout, with a quick tongue and quicker temper, and prone to threatening her father with butcher knives (sound familiar?). Their last fight was the night of March 9, 1962. That night, while Mom was in her room, she heard her parents arguing again, and one of them stomp into the kitchen and slam drawers. One parent whisked past her bedroom. The other scrambled by. Then while she lay in bed, she heard their voices booming, followed by someone THUMP THUMP THUMPING down the stairs, and her mother's screams. Maybe her mother called her between those shouts. Maybe my mom burst out of her room at the sound of the tumbling. Whatever the case, my mother found her mother laid out at the base of the steps in her bra and slip, blood coloring her chest. She darted to her mother's side and held her. "Take care of your brothers" were the last words Mary Alice said to her five-year-old daughter.

An ambulance arrived. A neighbor tended Mom and her brothers while the family's pastor drove her father to Providence Hospital. There, doctors pronounced Mom's mom dead from a single stab wound to the chest.

That night, social workers shuttled Mom and her brothers to the Albertina Kerr Nursery, an adoption exchange where they would live for months. Those months in Albertina Kerr offer up few memories save Mom's vigilance in checking on her brothers, who lived in a separate dorm, and the month or so, as protest, she refused to eat. Over the next couple of months, the Reeses (Mom's maternal kin) fought a custody battle with the Jacksons, which is to say Mama Edie and Bubba. In the end, though, the Reeses relented on the condition that, under no circumstance, would the children be split apart. Mom and her brothers were released into the guardianship of Mama Edie and Bubba, their grandparents, and lived there for the four-plus years her father spent in the Oregon State prison. It seems almost if not impossible for me to fathom the extent, over those years, to which Mom and her siblings suffered. How confused and conflicted they must've felt visiting their father in a prison. And what could an adult have told them to ameliorate such hurt? What words, in such a case, can one person say to another?

Mom has trouble recollecting what she was told about the circumstances around her mother's death and father's absence, and a part of me, the part I'm inclined to trust, intuits her misremembering as grace, knows that pushing for details will open wounds that won't heal, wounds that might not have ever healed. Sometimes I try to imagine the course her life would have taken had she been raised by her mother, wonder how the lives of my maternal uncles would've changed if Mary Alice had lived. It's tough to mourn a grandmother I never knew, though realizing how profound that loss has been on my mother and her brothers, I can't help but feel bereft. On the other hand, I haven't asked my grandfather—Dad—about the death of his first wife. Will I ever ask? Um—no, I won't. What should I call my refusal? Answer—a product of the high percentage of high-grade punk in me. As well, though, there were no witnesses that tragic night, so I, nor anyone else save my grandfather, if time, trauma, and penitence hasn't forever effaced his recollection of it, could know what happened. But what I know without doubt is this: for all of my days, my grandfather has been a vital part of Pops, has been a man of integrity, a loving man who hugs me when I walk through his door, and who, for all of my adult years, has wished me Godspeed each time I leave his house. I'll admit that it's easier for me to avoid digging because I've never had to forgive him for my grandmother's death, but I also believe, in that place where my beliefs are strongest, that he's paid penance, and furthermore, that rare is a life deserved of being defined by a single act. And for his sake, the sake of my mom and uncles, and for the sake of all of the rest of us, I prefer to leave it at that.

He was paroled when Mom was a fifth grader at Sacred Heart Catholic School. It didn't take long for him to find love again, this time with the beautiful Mexican woman who worked as a live-in housekeeper for his parents. In short order, the pair eloped and later held a formal ceremony at a Catholic church. The newlyweds found a house in Northeast, and soon after that, my grandfather came to reclaim his children. On the day of that reclamation, he sent his sons to pack, and they hustled off, shouting, "Yay! Yay! We're going to live with Dad!"

"Oh, we are?" Mom said, and began skipping toward her bedroom to gather her things.

Mama Edie caught Mom before she reached her bedroom. She led her into the basement, sat her on a couch, and took up her hands. "Your dad and his new wife found a house and the boys are going to live with them," she said.

"Yes, okay," Mom said.

"But you," she said, "are staying here with us."

"Me," Mom said. "Why me? Why do I have to stay?"

"Because his new wife can't comb your hair," Mama Edie said.

"Can't comb my hair?! But I don't need anybody to comb my hair. I've been combing my hair since my mama died," Mom said. "Look. Look at me. She doesn't have to comb it."

"You're just not going," said Mama Edie. "He's taking your brothers and that's that."

In the following years, Mom's brothers would visit her in The House on Sixth or escort her to their house for a visit. In the years that followed, when Mom had a piano or ballet recital or school program her father would take her shopping and let her pick whatever dress she wanted. Every other summer or so Mom and her brothers would travel to Alabama to visit her mother's kinfolk. The summer before her senior year in high school, however, she arrived in Alabama before her brothers and convinced an uncle to drive her to visit her mother's mother. Her grandmother, Ruth Reese, asked where her brothers were and Mom said she didn't know. She also revealed that she lived with Mama Edie and Bubba. Ruth confronted the man her daughter married the moment he stepped in the door.

"My daughter's dead and I asked you not to split up the kids. And here I find out they're split up," Ruth said. "You all gave me your word. And you need to honor it."

Once the family returned to Portland, Mom moved into her father's home, where she lived until she graduated. But it was a gesture too belated to mend their contemporaneous rift. To trouble matters, it occurred a couple of years after her father and stepmother had adopted a baby girl. "Can you imagine?" Mom says. "You're his biological child and your mom is dead and you think your dad and his new wife don't want you and they go out and adopt a child and raise that child. It was horrible for me." My mother, by then broken in ways no one grasped, finished her senior year of high school in 1974. She bore me by a man she never loved the next summer. The next year, she met Christopher Lee Jones, a man she'd love eternal.

THE FRUIT

The origin of all of the apples on earth can be traced to the genus *Malus* trees that grew over ten million years ago in Central Asia, in what's now Kazakhstan. The hunters and gatherers who passed through mountainous Central Asia helped sow the tasty (sometimes tart) red fruit in areas throughout Asia and Europe. Then a few thousand years ago, an ancient green thumb invented grafting—the botanical practice of joining the tissues of two plants together to produce different varieties—a practice that helped apples become so popular during the Persian empire that when Alexander the Great conquered it, he too propagated them in his kingdom. Love for the apple persisted with much thanks due to the multitudes who traveled the Silk Road trade routes between China and Rome. Apple love became ubiquitous in the Roman Empire, which accounts for why the Romans transported domestic apples to Spain, France, and Britain. Scores of those Europeans sailed across the Atlantic to the new world with a bag of apple seeds in tow, and in the midst of willing themselves into a race, became hardworking expatriates who ate apples and drank alcoholic apple cider as if it was ambrosia. Those soon-to-be-white colonists cut the cider with water and fed it to their kids. They used cider to cook, purchase supplies, pay salaries and debts. Generations ago, striving westward pioneers—none more famous than John "Johnny Appleseed" Chapman, who, often barefooted, traversed miles and miles of midwestern America planting apple orchards to sell to frontiersmen—begot the golden age of American pomology, an era in which Ralph Waldo Emerson mythologized the apple as the "American fruit."

REVELATIONS

One golden afternoon (this, a few years before Mom bore Dad a junior), Uncle Y invited Mom and Dad to a barbecue. Mom and Dad arrived late, and fashionable, by which I mean, there's a high probability they were dressed in matching duds. Once inside, the twinning couple noticed Uncle Y's apartment was quiet, too quiet for there to be a festive barbecue under way. They roamed until they found Uncle Y and his girl in a room with a few others—all of whom were nodding, as dope fiends do, with a heroin kit close at hand. "Oh no, Chrissy. This ain't fixin to be no barbecue. We got to go," Mom said. But Dad, more accustomed to the scene than he could let on, nudged Uncle Y. "Say, Maine, get up," he said. "Thought we was puttin somethin on the grill."

Mom knew everyone in the room save a young white girl. "Say, Dora, this Karen. Say, Karen, this my woman, Dora," Dad said. Uncle Y and crew couldn't rally for the barbecue, so Mom pressed Dad to leave and he conceded. She inquired innocent enough about the white girl on the drive home. "Oh, her," Dad said. "That was Y's girl." Dad explained that the girl had just received her inheritance, what he called "big, big money." He made no further comment on the potential bounty of Uncle Y knocking a tender white girl with big, big bread and a burgeoning dope habit.

Karen was all but inconsequential to Mom until five years or so after the barbecue—that odious morning she found her and Dad asshole naked in the bed and attacked him with the butcher knife. That happened just days before Dad left town on a pimp mission with his older brother, Uncle X. Dad was on that mission when Mom gave birth to her second son in August of 1981. He blew back into town around the time the hospital released Mom and his namesake. Dad swooped Mom and newborn Christopher Lee Jones Jr. from The House on Sixth and drove her the couple of blocks to his parents' place on Seventh Avenue. He parked his Caddy and dawdled, so Mom carried the baby in ahead of him, past Pudding, who spent whole days torpid in his living room recliner, and into Grandma Jones's room. Grandma Jones scooped her grandbaby from the car seat and admired how, at just days old, Chris Jr. resembled his daddy. Grandma Jones got to counting all of her biological grandchildren. "Let's see. X has two. And this makes three for Chrissy and . . ."

"Excuse me, Mrs. Jones," Mom said. "You mean this makes two for Chrissy. Or are you counting Mitchell?"

"Oh no, Lillie. I'm talking about Jeremy. The boy by, um, oh, I forget her name. Oh yes. It's Karen. Yes, the son Chris has by Karen."

"Karen! Chrissy got a baby by Karen?!" Mom said. Said it as an accusation and question at once. Said it to hear herself say it. Said it and felt her insides blaze.

Dad, beaming, danced into his mother's bedroom. "Mama, you see my boy. This my boy. Don't he look just like me?" he said.

"Uh, Chris," Grandma Jones said. "You didn't tell Lillie you had another son?"

"What?!" Dad said. "Um, uh, no, Mama. I didn't tell her."

Mom stood up. She offered him her flaming heart in hopes he'd douse it, that he'd contend Grandma Jones had somehow made a mistake. She remembered Dad describing Karen as Uncle Y's ho. Remembered his non-chalance in introducing them: "Dora, this Karen. Karen, this my woman, Dora." Karen was no threat, just a white girl with the big, big inheritance who'd been nodding off with the rest of them at the barbecue where didn't nobody barbecue. Mom had worked to scrub the memory of discovering Dad and Karen naked in bed that morning, deceiving herself into believing his preposterous-ass plea: "But, Dora, listen, we wasn't fuckin."

Dad glanced from his mom to Mom, from Mom to his mom. "Well," he said. "At least I didn't let her name him after me."

APPLE OF THE WORLD

Despite the numerous traumas, Mom and Dad's love was never unrequited, the two of them never lovelorn; in fact, the couple was steeped in abundant love, boundless love, immutable love, a love that might've loved love too much and too hard and too foolish. But no matter how much he loved my mother and she loved him, no matter how much I love my mama and the infinite value I accord her, no matter how intense I believed the passion between my parents, I know what I know and that's this: she was never his prize, couldn't have been one by no fault of her own. Because worth is always a story, the white race, and in particular white men, became fabulists who spun tales that vaulted white people above all at the expense of most, and that included apotheosizing their women.

But there would also be no apples as they exist without whites maligning black women, without portraying them as depraved, uncomely, as wanton, without them impugning my mother and the line of women before and after her as inept at discouraging their men from worshipping white women. Mom couldn't have been Dad's ultimate reward because in some sense she represented his low rank in the world, because in some respects she served as an emblem of the white race and its skill at subjugating, of the assorted financial, social, mental, physical, spiritual injuries it has inflicted upon the folks we call our folks.

No matter how much he loved her, and I believe in my puny credulous heart that he loved her, Mom had little to no action at being coveted because Dad, his pimp patnas, and untold others had been convinced that the men who'd concocted the white race are the rulers of the universe, and since a white woman (a woman who accepts whiteness as the crux of her identity) is the apple of that man's eye, she could also be viewed as the apple of the world.

For short: apple.

There are athletes and entertainers and well-to-do entrepreneurs (no need to name names) who cherish, court, and marry women they perceive as apples as an emblem of their success so often that the weddings may as well be *SNL* spoofs. There are legions of black men who cherish, court, and marry women they perceive as apples as a diaphanous-ass mode of social climbing. There are untold others who pursue women they judge as apples as a means of mitigating their self-loathing. And before y'all get to excoriating me extra tough, let me say this: I believe there's an abundance of loving, healthy, sincere relationships between black men and white women.

The bond between Dad and his pimp patnas (all pimps?) and a woman they've perceived an apple might be grounded in all of the above, plus envisioning that woman as part of the golden road to their dreams. But politics are the main motive of the most philosophical of the lot. For a political pimp, flaunting the allegiance of a woman believed to be an apple is recompense for the failure of Field Order No. 15—BKA the forty acres and the mule that came later—to make good on righteous redress for their peoples, is the ultimate raised black fist, is proof they were never nohow just three-fifths of a white man's equal.

Trust—you won't catch me circulating conspiracy theories. But ask me if I believe that, save the thousands of Secret Order members and admitted white supremacists, there's a hegemonic group of white men holding clandestine meetings in which they conspire for the downfall of black folks. Ask me if I believe that, and my answer is a resolute no. But ask me if there are men who conceive of themselves as white (to say nothing of The Keepers of The Church), in sundry positions of power, men who subscribe to paradigms about blacks and others and, given those beliefs, make decisions, both conscious and unconscious, which prove detrimental to my folks and me, ask me if I think that happens day in, day out all over our grand old US of A, and my answer is an unequivocal yes.

Since Dad and his pimp patnas believed the same, they must've felt in their half-sentient pimptastic hearts the deep need to employ whatever skullduggery they could to beat stacked odds, to do to the white man's prize what that white man had proven proficient at doing to them: wizening their self-worth down to damn near zilch. Dad and his pimp buddies had managed to transmute their exploitation of the physical and emotional vulnerabilities of women, sometimes young, young women, that they perceived as apples into the fuel that propelled them, to reach the dream. Even if their attainment was evanescent. Even if the dream was that of those circumscribed as other. Plus, a pimp reaps the added satisfaction of having achieved that vision via brains, charm, cunning, coercion, brute force—schemes that, as history attests, have been favored by countless white men. What's more, the pimp who minds the rule of abstaining from sex with a *ho* he perceives an apple—a feat neither Dad nor his patnas seemed to have managed—weakens the theory of an apple being the irresistible and indubitable paragon of beauty. Can you see now how an apple might seem to Dad and his pimp patnas like a gift from on high?

But oh the irony: Dad, the pimps, and other apple idolators were wrong, were misled in believing they could persuade (it ain't a force thing; it's a choice thing, they claim) the apple of the world to do their bidding. Duped because, for all time in all the world, apples exist for the white man and him alone, never for an other. Dad and men kindred in their beliefs were mistaken because the instant an apple consorts with their ilk, with anyone other than a white man, she's no longer a mythic "fairest one"; she's instead a fallen angel; she's rather Adam's unwholesome and unsubmissive first wife, Lilith, uttering Yahweh's name and winging away; or else his seductive second wife provoking her and his banishment from Eden. The moment an apple allies with an other, or God forbid sleeps with him and bears his child, she's corrupted into no more than a mortal white woman.

EVERAFTER

One morning (circa a few years after she had Chris Jr.) Mom got a call from the best friend who was with her when she and Dad first met. "Lillie, Chris is really, really sick," she said. "You need to come see about him." This was one of those months when Dad was staying with one of his *hos* on the second floor of Grandma Jones's house. This was in those days when we—the *we* including Mom, us boys, and whichever one of her brothers had fallen on the toughest times that month—lived in Vancouver, Washington. Distance be damned, Mom hopped in her car, hightailed across the Interstate

Bridge and into Northeast, drove main streets and side streets until she reached the pink house on Seventh and Shaver, a short sprint from where she and Dad first met. She parked and climbed the concrete porch steps and knocked on the front door. No one answered. She knocked again, and again no answer. The second time, though, the door cracked, and she let herself in. She called for Grandma Jones, called for Pudding, called for Dad—and still silence. She huffed past a kitchen sink loaded with dirty dishes to the stairs that led to Dad's room. She climbed them calling, calling, calling his name. Mom discovered Dad lying naked but for his underwear on the filthy carpet with plates of old food littered about him like fallen fruit. She gasped and faltered to him. She kneeled and touched his chest. "Chrissy, you're sick," she said. "You need to come with me." Dad, close to catatonic, mumbled. Mom lifted him onto the couch and cautioned him to stay put. She bustled into the bathroom to find his toothbrush, saw a tub ringed with grime and a toilet stopped with tissue, and backed out. She waded between mounds of dirty clothes into his bedroom, where she found a bag to pack. She rooted through the closet and drawers for something clean. She helped him dress. "Don't worry," she said. "I'm gone get you well." She tugged Dad to his feet, slung his arm over her shoulder, and scooped the bag of clothes with her free hand. Then he and she, Chrissy and Dora, together once more, stumbled for the stairs.

They were mid-descent when a white woman Dad had misbelieved an apple appeared at the foot of the steps.

"Hey, hey, what're you doing?" she said.

"What am *I* doin? What are *you* doin?" Mom said. "You ought to be ashamed of yourself." Mom shouldered Dad down the rest of the steps, steadied him until they reached the last landing, till there they stood, face-to-face, woman-to-woman—mortals, humans, *Homo sapiens*. "This is my sons' father. And I ain't about to let him die," Mom said. "So, move!"

THE SCALE

GENESIS

Figuring the genesis might be an impossible project. That said, the earliest flak I recall occurred while I was a third or fourth grader at King Elementary School. This particular day, we'd taken a field trip. To where escapes me, but I can recall a bus ride and cooling for a part of it with Faith and another part of it with Hope (out of respect, I changed their names). Weeks prior, though it might've been days, Faith, who was one of, if not the, prettiest girl in class, checked the YES box on a love note asking if she'd go with me—an affirmation that had me skippety skipping around the halls with my chest on puff. Hope, however, was also no slacker on the pulchritude— and that truth birthed in me the belief that the committed interest of the both of them would swell me with twice the pride. Thus, I lay down an amateur mack on Hope for a good part of the outing, and guess who had two girlfriends by the end of it?

Yep.

We bused back to the school and I swaggered home to The House on Sixth with my cool quotient on *extra*. That next day at school is hard to recall, but there's a good chance I spent it asserting my amore and working to keep each of them unawares of my two-timing—a tough job made tougher since we shared a homeroom. Then one day soon after, when the final bell sounded, Faith and Hope cornered me near the gym.

"So, what's up. You go with her?!" one said.

"Oh, so now you go with her?!" the other said.

"Um, uh," I stammered, and before I could turn fabulist, they screamed and punched and kicked and stomped, and left me fetal on the dirt-tracked tile. That afternoon, I slumped home aching, preadolescent hubris blooming abundant in my bony chest, thinking of what had been done to me, thinking less, if at all, of what I'd done to them.

OVERVIEW

Player, lover boy, playboy, mack, heartbreaker, pickup artist, skirt-chaser, poonhound, cockhound, tomcat, rake, philanderer, seducer, libertine, ladies' man, cad, Casanova, Romeo, Lothario, Don Giovanni or Juan . . . these last include the names of paradigmatic womanizers, a sort that, from here on, I shall reference as The Men on the Scale (or The Men). The canon of The Men on the Scale reaches back like manifold other aspects of Western culture to classical Athens. Athenian Alcibiades (a member of the Circle of Socrates) was lusted for his remarkable blue eyes, renowned for his war heroics and political savvy, and notorious for his transcontinental playboying. BCE biblical King David (the Goliath-slaying second king of the United Kingdom of Israel and Judah) abandoned, reclaimed, and abandoned again his first wife, married his second wife without ever divorcing his first, and earned disgrace for impregnating a "nubile" mistress named Bathsheba, ordering her husband's murder, and thereafter marrying her. Archetypes of The Men include Lothario from Cervantes's *Don Quixote*. In the seventeenth-century tome, Lothario's homeboy enlists him to seduce his wife as a test of her fidelity, an act that seems to have forever connected him to the mistreatment of women. Literature's ultimate womanizer, however, is Don Giovanni, a character who was first set in writing near the end of the Spanish Golden Age in the dramatist Tirso de Molina's *El burlador de Sevilla y convidado de piedra* (*The Trickster of Seville and the Stone Guest*). No shade to Molina, but Mozart and the librettist Lorenzo Da Ponte's eighteenth-century drama with jokes *Il dissoluto punito, ossia il Don Giovanni* (*The Rake Punished, Namely Don Giovanni*) might be the most indelible interpretation of the legend. Mozart and Da Ponte portray Giovanni as an unscrupulous rake who, in the end, chooses hellfire over repenting for his trespasses against women. The Venetian Giacomo Casanova is one of the Scale's most notable flesh-and-blood archetypes. He evinced his libertine nature as a fourteen-year-old boy by having an affair with a sixteen-year-old girl *and* her fourteen-year-old sister. For years he lived peripatetic, worked assorted jobs, scammed, gambled, and conquered women (and girls); near the end of his life he memorialized his exploits in an autobiography titled *Histoire de ma vie* (*Story of My Life*). The nineteenth-century English poet Lord Byron, another corporeal model of The Men, once wrote to a lover,

"A woman who gives any advantage to a man may expect a lover but will sooner or later find a tyrant." Byron, who claimed to have slept with two hundred women in one year alone, liaised with several aristocrats and, per numerous biographical accounts, a half sister. The index of The Men on the Scale must include Pablo Picasso, a brazen serial adulterer who dealt wicked abuses to all his partners, and once fumed to one of them, "I'd rather see a woman die any day than see her happy with someone else." The modern index of occidental archetypes also includes JFK. In addition to an audacious high-profile affair with Marilyn Monroe, the philandering of America's thirty-fifth president—he once told a friend, "I get a headache if I don't get a strange piece of ass every day"—included other Hollywood starlets, socialites, housewives, his father's ex-mistress, high-class call girls, interns . . . and the list goes on.

For all the prominent names I've mentioned, there are scores of others who could be cited as Western archetypes: the great Dr. MLK, Wilt the Stilt, Gene Simmons, Richard Pryor, a consent-or-not, bigoted, racist, misogynistic cockhound surnamed _____ who bragged to an affirming journalist that his status allowed him "to do anything" to a woman.

The Men on the Scale compass countries and cultures, span (so-called) race, age, class. They too range a gamut: groping megalomaniacs; charismatic misogynists; sexaholics with level 10 libidos; men who chase sex for sport; men who claim themselves insatiable for the presence of women; men who travel itinerate between women on account of commitment dread; single men, boyfriends, betrothed men, married men, men stunted into boys everlasting. They are moguls, executives, athletes, actors, congressmen, mailmen, teachers, students, salesmen, barbers, the jobless, gamblers, scammers, the local dope-dealer.

But no matter their contrasts, every damn one of The Men commit repeated emotional offenses against women, deeds that could be considered criminal.

Since the time of classical Greece, philosophers of law have divided crimes into two categories: *mala prohibita*, crimes "wrong merely because they are punished by statute," and *mala in se*, "acts that are wrong in themselves." *Mala in se* offenses are also known as crimes against moral law or the common law or common right, AKA the law of nature, eternal law, God's law. While the relational wrongdoings of The Men on the Scale are not by and large prohibited by statutes, they are, beyond a reasonable doubt, affronts to morals, the common good, God's law—the gilded rule prophesized in Matthew 7:12: "So whatever you wish that others would do to you, do also to them, for this is the Law."

America's judicial system classifies crimes into three categories: infractions, misdemeanors, and felonies. Each, as a general rule, is judged by its perceived seriousness and, as well, how much potential jail time an offender could face for committing it. Infractions are the least serious. These crimes—jaywalking, traffic tickets, petty theft—are often considered *mala prohibita*. A grade schooler passing love notes to cutie pies on the playground might count as an infraction. Among other mitigating factors, said boy could lay legitimate claim to naïveté, to the likelihood that his harms aren't ruinous. Misdemeanor offenses—in my home state they include harassment, driving while suspended, and false swearing—are considered more serious *mala prohibita* offenses, ones that are punishable by up to a year in jail. Think a teen heartthrob deluged with attention who two- or three-times girls in his high school. A college freshman skirt-chasing their whole first semester. Misdemeanor crimes—which is not to dismiss the hurt of girls (young women)—could, with reason, be defended as the general carousing of youth, a certain level of ignorance or inexperience, a lack of gleaning consequence. The most serious crimes, of course, are felonies, or what were called "true crimes" in the traditional common law on which US jurisprudence is based. Felonies—murder, rape, kidnapping, robbery—are *mala in se* crimes punishable by at least a year and a day in prison, up to death. Just as in criminal courts there are circumstances where prosecutors charge minors with a felony, there could be boys who've begun perpetrating the most serious level of harm. However, the crimes of The Men on the Scale are, in the main, the dominion of grown men.

While the crimes of most of those grown men are not often prosecutable criminal offenses, please believe me when I tell you, their deeds are *mala in se*. Because their acts cause grave injury. Because their acts are perpetrated in perpetuity. Because their learned awareness of probable fallout annuls all justifiable claim to innocence or ignorance. Because. Because. Because.

The worst of The Men on the Scale are heart-and-soul-cidal predators. Their telos is the immaculate, implacable, incontestable, emotional and psychological commitment of a woman—a devotion they exploit to rend her of something vital.

And the *mala in se* means used to achieve that end should also be considered violence.

The *OED* defines *violence* as "the deliberate exercise of physical force against a person, property, etc.; physically violent behavior or treatment; (Law) the unlawful exercise of physical force, intimidation by exhibition of such force." Here, let me draw a distinction between The Men and womanizers who, as part of their relationships with women, commit the *OED* version of physical violence. As I see it, once a man inflicts physical harm—which is not to minimize the impact of psychological abuse—he's another kind of abuser. On the other hand, a narrow definition of *violence* as somatic is a wrongheaded way to judge the wrongdoings of The Men. In his seminal essay on violence "Violence, Peace, and Peace Research," philosopher Johan Galtung stresses the importance of having a broad concept of violence. He distinguishes between physical and psychological violence, defining the latter as including lies, threats, brainwashing, indoctrination—which are, in varying degrees, tools of The Men on the Scale—and locates both the somatic and the mental in the realm of personal violence. Galtung contrasts personal violence with structural or institutional violence and proposes a definition that allows for the interpersonal and the systemic: "Violence is present when human beings are being influenced so that their actual somatic and mental realizations are below their potential realizations." Coercing women to accept living in a world far below their potentials; to abide disappointments, deceptions, affronts; to mute the voice that chides against them expecting better—all violences.

PROFILE

Violent crime birthed the field of criminal profiling: the process of analyzing patterns in the physical and behavioral evidence of crimes and using them to infer characteristics about an offender. Numerous historians argue the field was born in 1888 when Dr. Thomas Bond performed autopsies on two victims of the heretofore unidentified serial killer dubbed Jack the Ripper and submitted a report to investigators that reasoned the perpetrator's behavioral and psychological traits. Criminal profiling didn't get pedagogical until the 1970s, when FBI agent Howard Teten began using unsolved cases to teach courses—grounded in the belief "you'd be able to determine the kind of person you were looking for by what you could see at the crime scene"—at the FBI National Academy. These days, professionals teach several models of criminal profiling. One popular approach is forensic scientist Brent Turvey's Behavioral Evidence Analysis. Turvey's deductive process of profiling includes four steps: (1) Finding meaning in the evidence; (2) Creating a profile of the victim; (3) Analyzing the crime scene characteristics; (4) Creating an offender profile.

Which brings me to myself.

Portland. On an alien-cool August day in 1975, my mother push, push, pushed newborn me into the known world, naming me Mitchell Shunta Jackson—the Mitchell in honor of her favorite great-uncle. In addition to being my mother's son, at present, I'm a father, a brother, a grandson, a nephew, an uncle, a friend, a writer, a professor, a speaker, a dreaming and dreaming dreamer, and for a great many of my forty-three years on earth, a terrible-awful-despicable caretaker of women's hearts. Most, if not all, of those women would testify to my status as a Man on the Scale, and that assessment I confess is an absolute fact. Because I believed there'd be high costs for a flinchless reckoning—not the least of which is what it would prove about my character—and suspicioned myself ill-equipped to bear its judgment, I shirked till now more than superficial reflections of my place on the Scale, on when, how, and why I achieved that rank. But at some point, even a man as prone to cowardice and semi-feeling as me must confront what he's wrought. The profile that follows is an earnest effort at assessing my relational crimes.

Often over the course of reading, reflecting, drafting, and revising (this profile?), I started asking myself what's the difference between a scrupulous wholehearted inquiry and a long-ass exercise in making excuses. And though I'm not sure of an answer, much less *the* answer, the swearable truth, so help me, is this: I mean not a single word of what follows as an attempt to rationalize my violence or paint myself a victim. On the contrary, I hope the women I've harmed will receive these words as at least a measure of atonement, and if not amends, then an inkling of perspective on my misdeeds. But why else? Because I'm mistrustful of volition, know how crucial it is to keep vigilant against the lure of old selves, and believe I can never-nohow lose track of my trespasses. But I'm also motivated by the prospect of casting light on dark parts of myself, of managing one step (forward?) and another with them a little more illumed. Beyond that, I hope whoever sees themselves or their loves in what I write feels encouraged to ask what-when-how-why? And for whosoever else engages with what I set down, I wish at least a trace of something worthwhile.

EVIDENCE

Evidence refers to information or objects that might be admitted into court for judges and juries to deliberate during a case. Before a profile begins, a full forensic—obtained by science—analysis of all available physical evidence must occur. According to pioneering criminologist Edmond Locard's exchange principle, "Any action of an individual . . . cannot occur without leaving a trace." In addition to *Physical Evidence* (dental records, trace chemicals, fingerprints, etc.), reliable sources include witness statements and-or the corroboration of both the physical evidence and testimony. Wound patterns are also an important part of evidence. Wound type may vary from bullet, stabbing, blunt force, etc., but regardless of type, each wound discloses to experts information about how it was inflicted and what inflicted it. For a little over three decades, evidence admissible in court has also included genetic material.

———————

The indisputable proof of a man's presence on the Scale is the class of his crimes—including his number of victims, how often he trespasses them, and his level of callousness. The second most convincing type of evidence are the measures his past or intended victims (or other women) will take to chasten him. One of his sort might draw the comeuppance of a woman shaming him in public. Lord Byron was outed by a scorned lover as a "sodomite" and the ignominious gossip vamoosed him from England. A Man on the Scale might catch a prison bid as penance for his crimes. Casanova was arrested by a Venice Tribunal "primarily" for "public outrages against the holy religion." A Man on the Scale might mosey out his crib one late night and find his tires slashed flat and a window smashed. Or swank home one wee morning—"Don't let daylight catch you!" my crew would warn each other—to find his favorite suits and sweaters and jeans and shirts shredded to scraps and piled on the front porch or else a rent-priced leather jacket and dozens of his favorite kicks dumped into a tub of hot bleach. A Man on the Scale often squanders his marriage or prime romantic bond. Alcibiades spent so much time cavorting with courtesans and hetaerae that, though he in the end thwarted her, his wife braved the public derision of a classical Athens divorce filing and stomped to the courthouse. Almost a decade into their union, the mother of two of Picasso's kids abandoned him for another dude. Several journalists report Joe Kennedy paid Jackie a million bucks to dissuade her from filing divorce papers on JFK—a fee she threatened would compound if her philandering presidential spouse gave her (another?) VD. A man high on the Scale might be cuckolded or earn a slashed face or broomstick beating or a scalding by cooking grease or grits or boiling water and-or, in rarer cases, be forced to abide the constant threat of a worse fate. The jilted lovers of Don Giovanni plotted lethal vengeance against him. A dude from my hometown was shot dead, along with his father, while they sat in a parked car, a murder some rumored was over the son's dealings with a woman.

Men on the Scale often father babies out of wedlock, one, two, three, or more—I know a man who sired more than twenty—kids with different women that result in garnishments for unpaid support and-or the damn near impossibility of maintaining an equitable presence in the lives of his children. I've known women who scorned a Man on the Scale by annulling contact with his child or divulging damning facts or flat-out lies about him to his child. Per the good book, divine reparations might be visited upon the seed of a Man on the Scale. King David's first son by Bathsheba was afflicted as a punishment from God and died as an infant despite the king fasting and praying for his health. Or the lot of one of The Men might be an even more divinable chastening: begetting children who suffer countless troubles, who falter in and out of school, who in time follow his model or fall prey to his kind—generational proof.

———

Though the exact provocations—what at times I experienced as an inexorable compulsion but also must've felt like relentless harm to some women in my life—I've willed into disremembrance, without doubt, some duplicity on my part incited different women on different occasions to vandalize a car I owned. One of them etched "Fuck You" in cursive across my driver's-side door. One woman busted a passenger-side window. One woman slashed my tires while my car sat outside my job. One woman used to pilfer bills from my hustle funds, thieving I learned of years later from a friend. As I imagine it, she saw her thefts as redress for one or more of what might be judged misdemeanor offenses. Once I met a woman at her house after the club. We were in her bedroom when her cell started ringing and ringing. The woman answered a trillion calls into the salvo. "What?" she said. "I can do whatever I want." She hung up. The person called back. "What do you mean, you're outside?" she said. "No, I won't let you in," she said. "You need to leave," she said. "No, you won't do that," she said. "Do I need to call the police?" The woman ended the call and informed me her ex was outside, claiming he'd kill whomever was in the house. And that wasn't the only time a jealous dude threatened serious harm up to murdering me for real or imagined relations with a woman he claimed. Evidence against me includes catching crabs, chlamydia, gonorrhea, chlamydia again, not to mention the scares in between. It seems quite possible that one or more of those women knew she was positive and determined subjecting me to that risk was just due for my crimes. Too many times to count, I've been shoved, slapped, punched, bit for cheating. Over and over, I perpetrated hurt against a woman and sat too close to silent while she wept. Once a woman who'd told me she had her tubes tied (right, I shouldn't have went raw regardless) informed me she was pregnant and she might keep the baby. She asked me what I wanted, and my solipsistic ass told her NO in a tone that couldn't at all be confused for ambivalence. We argued longer, but I was adamant, and soon got up, stomped out of the house, climbed into my car, and stabbed off. At a red light blocks down from her house, I felt a car smack my bumper, and when I looked in the rearview, I saw it was her. Soon as the light hit green, I straight *giddyupped!* She gave chase, and we weaved through traffic, her inching closer block to block, me *ZOOM-ZOOMING!* while I worried over crashing my ride or an arrest for reckless driving. Then I caught another light, hopped out, threw my arms high, and screamed, "What the fuck!" She reversed, shifted gears, waited a piston spark, and launched her car right at me. After discovering text messages and a cache of naked photos, a partner who loved me the best she could keened hours on a bathroom floor and later bared cuts she'd slashed in her leg. That same woman demanded I move out. And I did. Once I visited an on-again-off-again partner at the restaurant-lounge where she worked. She announced she had plans to leave with a famous actor, and it so smote my ego that I argued with her until behemoths in black polos gruffed me downstairs and onto the street. As reproach for cheating, one partner tore my laptop screen off its hinges. Angered over other instances of deceit and-or my unwillingness to honor commitment, that same partner cut my first graduate thesis into scraps a short time before it was due. That same partner found my car parked outside of another woman's apartment—on account of long-shared intimacies and my tacit or expressed pledges of monogamy, the women treated each other as foes—during a night of heavy rain, scattered my clothes in the parking lot, and stabbed my toothbrush in the mud. That same partner, feeling what must've been a legitimate hurt, doused me from sleep one morning with a pot of cold water and warned, "The next time it'll be hot." Once, I mixed up addresses and sent Valentine's gifts *and* handwritten cards to the foes. One on-again-off-again partner—the younger of the foes—showed up to my apartment unannounced and pounded on my door while I lay in bed naked with another woman. That same partner discovered a sex tape I'd made with another woman on my laptop. Once after spending the night with that same partner, a diamond ring I paid thousands for went "missing" from my bedroom. She swears she didn't steal it, but given the countless times I'd wronged her, I can understand if she believed it some small restitution. More than half a decade into our tumultuous union, the same partner caught me on a dinner date with a woman I'd just begun seeing. "Who's she?" she spat. "What the fuck's this?" She tramped out of the restaurant. The new woman decamped soon afterward. And instead of chasing my on-again-off-again partner (the same woman who'd moved from Portland to New York to secure our relationship), I bustled after the new woman and plied her with half-truths. So much deception. So much dastard-ass treachery. And I haven't mentioned what might be the most condemning. The victim was the partner who, about five years prior, was critically injured in a car accident that killed her mother and cousin-sister and paralyzed evermore her five-year-old son. A woman who'd visited me *every* single weekend I was locked down, who never gave me a moment's worry over her fidelity. This was the same partner who, instead of screaming on me or, best yet, bouncing over what she must've sensed were constant infidelities, would cut tiny holes in my shirts and pants, silent protests I wouldn't notice till I was fumbling about the world. The morning it happened, she'd just come home from a graveyard shift and I was conked, lying more on her side of the bed than mine. Most days, she'd float in, quiet, quiet, and I wouldn't know she was home until she rustled the blankets beside me. But that morning, she woke me by twisting the blinds and tossing a letter at me. Maybe it smacked me in the face. If it didn't, it damn sure should've. "What's this? What's this, huh, Mitchell?" she said. Barred light bullied into the room. She hovered in her uniform and hairnet, huffing jagged breaths, her eyes wet but no sign of a loosened tear. "What's what?" I said, grabbed the letter, saw the sender's address, and knew in a thump of my suspect ticker the life I knew was ceased. The sender informed my partner she was pregnant, said other things, true things, I'm relieved (respite I don't deserve) to misremember. There was little to explain and near nothing to deny. "I want you to leave," my partner said. "You need to leave today," she said, and I was out by that evening. Between that morning and the failing light in which I stuffed the last of my belongings into my car, she and I traded few if any words. In the days, months, years since—through the marvel of her benevolence we've become friends—I've thought of asking her to translate that silence. At present, I disbelieve she ever could.

In *The Body in Pain*, Harvard professor Elaine Scarry describes the intelligibility of pain:

> For the person in pain, so incontestably and unnegotiably present is it that "having pain" may come to be thought of as the most vibrant example of what it is to "have certainty," while for the other person it is so elusive that "hearing about pain" may exist as the primary model of what it is to "have doubt." Thus pain comes unsharably into our midst as at once that which cannot be denied and that which cannot be confirmed.
>
> Whatever pain achieves, it achieves in part through its unsharability, and it ensures this unsharability through its resistance to language.

It makes sense now: the women I harmed were certain about their pain yet suffered an inviolable chasm between what they felt and what they could express. And I was some parts incredulous no matter what I'd done, what fallout I witnessed, what feelings they claimed. Them shouting "listen, please," and me again and again muting their pleadings, trepid to the utmost of risking an honest attempt to interpret—even if doomed—their hurt into something intelligible to me. Deciding it safer to dismiss their grieving as maudlin, dramatic, ephemeral. Scarry continues, "Prolonged pain does not simply resist language but actively destroys it, bringing about an immediate reversion to a state anterior to language, to the sounds and cries a human being makes before language is learned." My willful mishearing, determined dislistening to the "anterior language" of the women I harmed—itself a resistance to the effort of empathizing—should be viewed as nothing less than proof of high rank on the Scale. It's a terrible, terrible thing to have to admit about myself, but denying it tempers it none, and the truth is my denials, my refusals might not be the worst of it.

In "Violence and the Word," Yale law professor Robert M. Cover writes, "The deliberate infliction of pain in order to destroy the victim's normative world and capacity to create shared realities we call torture." Torture. For me it'd always existed in a distant universe, a world of war criminals, drug cartels, mob beefs, 9-11 coconspirators in Guantanamo Bay—torment I'd only ever read about or seen in film. Torture on-screen was evil men surrounding a bare-chested, barefoot unfortunate strapped or chained to a chair, was vise grips and hammers and scalpels and forceps and hoods and electric shock and tell-us-what-we-want-to-know-or-else! It was valiant men suffering blows, spitting crimson, and screaming NO! NEVER! in the name of love, honor, nation. But Cover pronounces another kind of torture, one that allows for anguish beyond the corporeal, one that, at bottom, inculpates more of what I'd done. What to make of the partner who, over the years, endured the greatest amount of obvious violence? Yeah, I could claim I never set out to torture her. But what should I call the fact that at no point in our long union was I faithful, that my crimes were damn near ceaseless, that deep down I hoped I could cheat her into accepting my unfaithfulness as our norm? Without question, I was victimizing her, and when she retaliated with her own infidelities—if neither partner is faithful, what's that called?—each time I trusted her less, became less concerned with shielding her from my harms, less penitent, and in some cases spurred to outright maliciousness. All the while, I refused to live with her in a world that was most of my making.

And these facts must also be considered evidence: I'm the father of two children (seventeen and twelve years old) by two different women. The discord I've fostered between those women on account of my ambivalence at making a family with one or the other is proof beyond reasonable doubt of my place on the Scale. It also ain't lost on me one whit that my children have confronted the inheritance of my crimes against their mothers.

Following my breakup with his mother, my son started scuffling on the bus, scrapping on the playground, instigating class chatter—all anew in his school life. Each time, his mother or me or both of us would ask him why he did it and he'd either invent a new-age Greek myth or deep shrug and claim he didn't know. We'd brood, restrict this or that privilege, and hope the last time was the last time till it wasn't. Then a month or so into what was assuming the look of interminable trouble, the principal, a nun, called his mother and asked for an emergency meeting. One dawn soon-come, I caught a train from my apartment in Brooklyn to her house in New Jersey—the slanted rain and dingy cover of the day felt fitting—and she drove the three of us to the school. We buzzed inside and waited on a bench. The principal, a stout woman with a head of short white curls, shuffled out and waved us into her office. She offered us seats around a table sized for kids. "You know we all just love him," she said, once we settled. "He's such a good kid, but as of late, he's just not himself." She touched his hand. He drooped his shoulders, cast his eyes, the eyes we share, low—a boy breakable. The principal asked if there was something going on at home. His mother and I had never made him a "home"—the great divide of our union—and though we didn't mention that fact, we conceded our recent breakup. The next breath he keened, "Why'd you break up? I want my family! Why can't we be a family?" with his wet eyes stabbing between us. In the moment, he seemed inconsolable. His mother's eyes flushed red, then pooled; so did mine. "I'm so sorry," she said. "It'll get better, Son. It'll get better soon, I promise," I said, and felt convicted in an instant of at least a partial lie. That morning remains testament that my transgressions against his mother could harm my son into another kind of boy or, worse, wound him into another me.

And what's more proof than this:

One visit to ATL, my daughter, her mother, and me went to our favorite brunch restaurant. The place was teeming with the usual Sunday crowd—hoary-haired grandparents decked in colorful church threads, yoked couples toting a baby in a detached car seat, youngins Saturday-night live in logo'd denim and dark sunglasses. We signed the list and lady lucked on couches until a waitress called our name and led us to a booth. We ordered our usual: chicken strips, waffles, and fried eggs for her, and for her mother and me, chicken wings roasted a perfect russet, golden waffles, and scrambled eggs. My daughter and her mother sat opposite me watching as I slid the wrappers from straws and dropped them in our ice waters. We chatted about her classes, her sprint times, her new favorite tunes, while I meanwhile bided for the opportune moment to say what'd been balled up in my chest. . . . "You know I'm human. And it hurts when you don't respond to my calls or texts." She fiddled with the salt and pepper shakers, made a shape of the straw wrapper, looked up from her project with puzzled eyes. "What do you mean? When does that happen?" she said. "It happens all the time, sometimes for days or weeks at a time," I said. "That's just not true, Dad. It's just not true," she said. "Oh, it ain't," I said, fished my phone, turned the screen to her, and scrolled through messages. "Look, look, it's all right here. What you call this?" I said, louder than I should. "You're always blaming someone else. What about what *you* do," she said. "You don't listen. Why don't you ever listen?" she said, voice verging on a dirge. Waterworks drizzled down her cheeks. Her mother handed her a napkin, rubbed circles on her back. And I knew in the moment I could do no better than exacerbate what troubled her. We didn't say much of anything else while we ate or on the drive home.

It's occurred to me in the years since that her hurt was at the heart of our exchange. And that as the main source of that grief, as her father—a grown-ass man whose duty it is to protect her from harms—I had no right to question it, had every cause to believe it. But instead, I challenged it, as I'd done the wounds I'd inflicted on her mother. And what must've felt even more criminal was my attempt to shift blame from me—the guilty one who'd failed and failed at listening—to her, an innocent I'd pained into muteness.

VICTIMOLOGY

Victimology is the study and analysis of victims. It's a general term that includes victims—a person who has suffered harm, injury, loss—of any circumstance, and just might be the toughest requisite of authoring a criminal profile. In *Criminal Profiling: An Introduction to Behavioral Evidence Analysis* (second edition) Turvey names as a possible pitfall *Deifying* or *Vilifying* a victim. He describes *Deification* as idealizing victims, a bias he argues prevents seeing a victim in the fullest context. He describes *Vilification* as biasing certain victim populations—sex workers, addicts, runaways, strippers, etc.—as worthless or disposable and therefore less worthy of protection from harm. *Victimology* also includes assessing the amount of risk involved—that is, a person's level of exposure to the possibility of suffering harm or loss. In *Risk Assessment*, profilers classify victims as *Low-risk*, *Medium-risk*, and *High-risk*, categories that describe someone whose personal, professional, and social life seldom subject them to suffering harm or loss through someone whose life exposes them again and again. Three well-known risk assessment theories are *Routine Activity*, *Crime Pattern*, and *Rational Choice*. The *Routine Activity Theory* challenges the belief that crime rates are most affected by macro-level social causes, hypothesizing that for predatory crimes, there must be a convergence in time and space of at least three key elements: an apt offender, a suitable target, and the absence of a capable guardian. The *Crime Pattern Theory*—a central part of environmental criminology and one that yields crime maps for different hours of the day and days of the week—focuses on where crime takes place and the level of daily activity in any given area. The *Rational Choice Theory* focuses on the behavior of an offender, supposing that crime is utilitarian in that an offender weighs means and ends, costs and benefits, and makes a rational choice to pursue a goal in light of those judgments, even if that aim is short-sighted in its forecast of benefits. *Victim Incident Risk* refers to the risk present at the moment an offender acquires a victim. Aspects that increase *Victim Incident Risk* include a victim's lifestyle, state of mind, whether they were under the influence of drugs or alcohol, the time of the occurrence, and the place of occurrence. *Lifestyle Risk* refers to the overall risk present by the virtue of a victim's personality, as well as their personal, professional, and social environment. Turvey cites several personality traits as liable to increase the risk of victimization, but also stresses—as should anyone else with head and heart logic—*Victimology* is *not* the process of finding fault with a victim; rather, it's a practice meant to lend insight into the safeguards an offender will hazard circumventing in hopes of achieving a goal. No matter the risks, the onus of a crime should never be shifted onto a victim. Let me say it this way too: no one, nowhere, nohow, should blame a victim for being prevailed upon by an offender.

———————

The Men on the Scale, ever motivated, choose victims based on how available, vulnerable, and desirable they deem them. The ones with whom I'm most familiar are men of color who've pursued, as if they need more occasions to prove resilient, women from the same (so-called) race. Others with whom I'm acquainted have targeted (is it fair to call it a complex?) women outside their race. Umpteen others are desirous of some physical trait: wide hips, height or its absence, gapped smile, certain-shaped eyes. As might be explained by *Routine Activity Theory*, their victims are often ones with whom they enjoy repeated access: a woman who works at their job, one they peep during an average workday, one who hangs among their circle of homeboys. On the converse, I've known men who've sought victims in the park or the mall or, as we say, in traffic, places where a woman might heed a catcall or a trite-ass script. Other men favor locales that foster higher *Incident Risks*: nightclubs or strip clubs or after-hours, domains where a woman might go wonderstruck over a nefarious dude flashing a grip. The *Rational Choice Theory*, with its focus on an offender's goal(s), might help explain the mental and emotional traits of the victims that Men on the Scale exploit.

Often, The Men will target a passive woman, one they can coerce into believing themselves deserved of less than offered and-or that being treated humane is an act of benevolence. Once Alcibiades declined the dinner invite of a male lover (yes, male-on-male abuse also occurs, though that ain't my focus) in favor of staying home and getting faded with friends. Hours into his drinking, he changed his mind, reveled over to the house of said lover, glimpsed gold and silver through a window, and ordered his slaves to heist half of it and carry it home. The lover's dinner guests were indignant, scolded him that Alcibiades had treated him poorly. "Not so," the lover said. "But with moderation and kindness, he might have taken all there were; he has left us half."

It don't take much more than a cursory look at Alcibiades's life to gather homeboy was hella selfish, that he believed himself Zeus's gift to the world and therefore the feelings of any lover were subordinate to his. That being the case, he would've felt satisfaction in learning of his lover's response and its sure proof of servile worship. But here's what it wasn't: dramatic. And odd as it sounds, that lack of blatant physical drama probably bothered Alcibiades. Competitive as he was, he might've judged what happened to Lord Byron centuries and centuries later as a case of one-upmanship.

One afternoon Lord Byron's lover Lady Caroline popped up at his crib in disguise and confronted him about the slight mind he'd been paying her. He asked her to leave and, not only did she refuse, she found a knife and tried to stab herself. Byron held her until she calmed, at which point he asked his homeboy to escort her to the home of one of her friends. Caroline, who once called Byron "mad, bad, and dangerous to know," said she wasn't going nowhere unless he promised to visit her again before he left town. He agreed. Weeks later, she sent him a love letter with her pubic hair inside it. It's quite possible that Byron chose Lady Caroline *because* he could goad her into what he perceived as theatrics, that he gauged, like others high on the Scale, the valence of his conquest on how strong she reacted to his neglect, slander, breaches.

Men on the Scale use the upshot of their abuse to judge whether or not they've conquered a woman. The most malevolent Men on the Scale subdue victims they can pit against each other and reap pleasure from the fallout over their abuse. While Picasso worked on *Guernica*, his favored mistress-of-the-moment-muse at his side, another mistress showed up to the studio. "I have a child by this man," she announced. "It's my place to be here with him. You can leave now." Said the mistress-of-the-moment-muse, "I have as much reason as you have to be here. I haven't borne him a child, but I don't see what difference that makes." Picasso, meanwhile, kept right on painting. One woman demanded he make up his mind which one had to leave. Picasso later recounted the squabble to another mistress. "I decided I had no interest in making a decision. I was satisfied with things as they were," he said. "I told them they'd have to fight it out themselves. So they began to wrestle. It's one of my fondest memories."

If the cruel-ass Spaniard had recapped this fracas to The Men on the Scale from my era, one of the more obdurate ones would've dismissed it as the women being "in their feelings" and meant by his comment that the women were having more trouble than they should bearing an emotional blow. But what few, if any of us, would've known back then was just how Greek it is to regard a woman's hurt as histrionics. In the essay "Plato and Aristotle on the Nature of Women," philosopher Nicholas D. Smith argues that Aristotle's sexism was based in his philosophy concerning the soul. He points out that Aristotle believed that women possess a deliberative part of the soul (*to bouletikon*) but that in contrast to a masculine soul, it lacks sovereignty. Aristotle called that feminine non-sovereign soul *akuron*. Smith cites philosopher W. W. Fortenbaugh's argument that the lack of dominion of a woman's deliberative part is the result of being susceptible to control by its emotional part (*to orektikon*).

Calling women emotional is common pretext, is at bottom a ski mask and gloves for the criminal, is a man groping for an alibi, is a transparent attempt to acquit himself of the fallout of his trespasses. Defining a woman as emotional locates the locus of her pain outside of her in the non-material world, in a realm beyond perception, and therefore beyond logic and critique. But the truth is, what those men deem maudlin or hysterical—which let me repeat is the language of inexpressible pain—ain't got nothing to do with a woman's soul and in almost all cases has everything to do with what's happened to her in the material world. And as I've seen it, the women most vulnerable to the machinations of Men on the Scale are those whose fathers or father figures doled them flagrant hurt in their formative years. As far as I can see, the most frequent and calamitous accomplice of a Man on the Scale is a victim's father.

Jackie Kennedy was said to believe JFK's conspicuous cheating as a genetic disease bequeathed him by his father and also conduct that could be contextualized by her life before marriage. "Because of my father, I was used to infidelities," she confided in a friend. The woman who's suffered an injurious father (or his substitute) is more prone to pine, knowing or unknowing, for a man who can either ameliorate those wrongs or animate them in the most vivid sense, more apt to abide the resistance, abhorrence, and downright refusal to pledge faithfulness of a Man on the Scale, to see his other failings in failing light, to assume to her peril again and again that a deeper investment will harvest recompense; a woman in search of paternal amends is more liable to risk the ultimate hope that she can be his savior, which is to say, that if she loves the wrong man harder and longer, she can transform him into whom she most yearns for, which, as consequence, compels her to judge her certain repeated failures as her crucible.

Let me address the obvious: no matter what I do, I've privileged my perspective over women, over, in particular, the women I've wronged. That's analogous to allowing the accused or adjudged to testify in court with no word from the victim nor witnesses, with no one to clarify, corroborate, refute. For what took too long of a time for me to claim myself compassionate, I wavered on doing what I gathered, given the circumstance, was the most righteous thing I could do: call exes, invite them to reflect on our relationship, and include herein what they shared. My selfish ass waffled because I feared their depositions would seize some of the distance I'd managed between the deeds of my old self and how I live with myself. Because I suspicioned dredging deep hurts would null some if not most of the amends we'd made. Because I worried asking them to recount old traumas might damn well be yet another violence (maybe it is). But in the end, I resolved my dithering an assured punk move or perhaps another crime, messaged the women (five former partners) who, by my measure, suffered the greatest griefs in our time together, and invited them to share. Below, I include what, as a matter of indisputable truth, are victim statements. Figuring the least I could do is grant them the last word of this section. Knowing as well, though, that my voice framing their voices colors their account.

Way back when, during my age of infractions, my prospects were bound to school, church, the neighborhood. In my misdemeanor teenybopper period, one of my homeboys would drive a crew of us downtown in his dad's black Beamer and park by a high-traffic crosswalk, and we'd holler lame pickup lines till one or more of us copped digits or blarneyed some girl(s) into hanging with us past their-our curfew. Other times, we'd cut a late class, bus downtown to an all-girls high school, loiter the campus till they were dismissed, and see which ones we could charm into near-future fornicating. In my late teens into early twenties—simultaneous to when I began asserting my grown-ass-manness—sometimes solo-dolo, but more often with one or more of my homeboys in tow, I'd cruise a boulevard or park in a lot of a club, convenience store, mall in hopes of finding a woman who'd, in a short time or in time, yield to my young carnality. But sometimes that attraction moved beyond the superficial and, fewer times, the woman became my partner—though *my girl* or *my woman* is what I called them then.

My exes: One I met while I was idling outside a convenience store. She strolled out the door with another woman I knew, and the homeboy who was sitting shotgun beckoned them both to the car. To my surprise, she sauntered to my window, close enough for me to marvel at her winsome smile and hazel eyes. Soon enough she asked how old I was and I lied two years onto my age and told her twenty-one. That ex was a small woman, but within a few years I'd witness her heroic strength. One ex I first encountered in my mid-twenties while watching a summer hoop game. She sashayed into the gym dressed in all white to the gasps of me and the homeboy beside me. "Bro-bro, you see her?" he said, and nudged me. "Hell yeah," I said, and knew in a pulse I'd pursue her. As it turns out, she was the friend of a friend and that friend matchmaded us. For years she proved tenacious in securing our union. Over the years, she remained most critical of me, which is to say, she might well have seen me in the clearest light. One ex I met in my mid-twenties while awaiting entry into a nightclub. She and I had an amiable enough chat, but the truth is, she didn't arrest my attention till I got a good long (objectifying) gander at her figure. In the months that followed, I discovered how caring she was. I'd sometimes drive to her house, filthy and reeking of ink from working my part-time graveyard shift stacking papers, and she'd lay towels in the bathroom for me to shower and fix me a delectable full meal. One ex I met in my late twenties while in the front row of a New York comedy show. "If one of the comics asks," she joked, "we're married with a son." She was most stylish and the dark-dark I'd desired since I could remember desiring, but it was her kindness that drew us close. One ex I met when a homeboy brought her to my thirty-fifth birthday party. The party was held in the basement lounge of a West Village restaurant, but the music blared like it was a nightclub. "This is my boss _____," my homeboy announced above the bass. "And she reads books." She and I didn't chat much that night, bibliophilic talk or otherwise, nor did I have the occasion to get a long look at her, but I remember her wearing a long blue dress and her thick hair falling well past her bare shoulders. We met in the café of a bookstore on our first date—how fitting—and face-to-face in the light, I noticed the perfect slant of her nose, her fulgent smile, that she possessed a curiosity about the world that piqued mine too. On that bookstore date, she told me we were kismet—my first time hearing the word—which was in a sense prophetic given years later I proposed.

The lion's share of the women of my past are the same (so-called) race as me—which made it no less than reprehensible black-on-black crime. For most of my life, I've also favored not just black women but those of darker skin. My preference, I've tried to convince myself (knowing it might be a complex over my complexion manifesting itself), has been a raised fist against the narrow vision of beauty held aloft by the masses, which includes that of a majority of The Men I've known. While some men targeted women who suffer angst over an aspect of their appearance, I've favored women hankered for by The Men in my circles, the ones we blathered about in our watering holes. To persuade the devotion of a woman lusted after by many was to buoy my rep, and that promise was as much a part of whom I chose as the features I preferred.

Since there was high chance at some point I'd wrong her, I sought a woman who, by my judgment, valued forgiveness. But what I judged a pardon might've been a woman relying on revisionist accounts of my deeds because the last man hurt her and she couldn't afford to admit to herself, let alone someone else, that she'd been duped by like ploys. There was a time when I deluded myself that a younger woman wouldn't take me serious, so I was therefore relieved of honoring her expectations. However, the older I got, the less and less I wanted to engage with innocence, the more I hunted for women whose age I could argue made them half knowing. "A relationship is never one hand clapping," counseled a therapist I agreed to visit as an attempt to amend what was, in retrospect, a series of emotional crimes against a partner. In my twenties and thirties, I sought relationships with women who were close to a decade my senior, did so because I'd deceived myself that the wider our age gap, the less right they had to expect my devotion, and furthermore the better equipped they'd be to bear my misdeeds.

In hindsight, the heart of me hounding older women was believing them more able to foster the nurturing I craved, what now reveals itself as a search for surrogates, the want for maternal reparations. On the other hand, age withstanding, the women with whom I had the most volatile relationships, who metastasized the greatest dependency on me, who suffered the most egregious and-or numerous of my misdeeds, all had in common a flawed to no relationship whatsoever with their father. In retrospect, those women were also searching for surrogates, for a man to salve their wounds. How doomed were our high-risk unions: Them forever groping for reasons to stay. Me ever searching for reasons to leave.

But that's how I saw it, and as I said, a justice I must manage is letting them speak for themselves:

Statement One (via text)

Hey Mitch. How are you doing. I got your text messages and you know I have forgiven you for whatever has happened in the relationship we had in the past. So there isn't anything I have to say about it. But I have no problem with you telling your part in the relationship and what happened. I'm okay with that. Thank you for giving me the option to tell my part of the relationship.

Statement Two (via interview)

In the beginning I thought you were cool. For one, I was physically attracted to you. And your conversation was completely different from most guys I was dealing with at the time. You were the first person that I met that talked about hopes and dreams and future plans. Versus everyone else was thinking about the moment, being a rapper, what's going on today. You were always like, I want to write. I'm working on this novel. You were always focused, focused, focused. Or I guess semi-focused.

I knew your past, but I never saw you sell dope. You had your Oregonian job and were throwing parties on the side. When we first started talking, _____ was pregnant. My girl _____ saw her at Costco or Home Depot and told me about it, and I was like, what the fuck, and called you about it, and you said it was before me. I had known about her. You'd told me that _____ had found out about her and kicked you out the house. You were angry at that time. You were mad because you and _____ were trying to get pregnant and she couldn't.

In the beginning I was dealing with _____. I remember giving you my house keys, so you could come over and I wouldn't have to come downstairs to let you in. _____ called and said he was coming over, and I ended up having to tell him about you because you had my keys.

One of the first hurts was when we first started talking and you was fucking with some Asian chick, and you had a New Year's Eve party and you had _____ there and _____ there. I was hurt because you weren't even supposedly dealing with _____ and she was there and also because you weren't supposed to be fucking the Asian girl anymore. _____ kept giving me dirty looks.

A month or so later, we came back from All-Star weekend and you said you wanted to be in a relationship. But all that weekend you'd been with your ex. She'd spent the whole weekend in your hotel.

I remember _____ calling my phone once. She asked for you. I answered. She said, something, something, "Where's Mitchell?" And I woke you up and handed you the phone. "Here, it's for you," I said. I remember so much drama. She would call me looking for you. There was so many things that happened.

The timeline is hard. Wait, no, you definitely lied to me about the pregnancy. You withheld that. When I found out, I had to have been hurt. But it's one of those things I blocked out of my mind.

I often wonder what happened to me. When did I start caring? I used to be like, okay, you want to do that. Okay, you do you, and I'm gone do me. I don't know what happened to that girl. You fucked her up. Somebody did. There's a lot of stuff I haven't talked about when I wasn't angry or mentioned out loud.

We definitely had an abortion in that first year. I remember you promising me we would have a child. I remember you promising me we would do it and it would be different. You made all these promises. I 100 percent believed you. I think I held on to that for most of our relationship. You always promised once you got to New York things were going to be better. You promised we would have a family. You promised all those things. And you were believable. I had no reason to doubt you. That got me through a lot of stuff. The promises made me stick it out.

I wanted those things and I wanted those things with you. For one, I was already in love with you at that point. And who doesn't want to have a family and kids. Or maybe it was what I thought you wanted for us. I felt like you were heartbroken that you hadn't been able to do those things the way you wanted. And the feeling of me being able to give that to you and that you wanted those things made me feel like I was special and this was something we were going to do together.

I didn't give up on it until you had your son. After that you were like, I don't want any more kids, and I was like what?! What happened to the promise? I was like, Oh wow, I stuck it out with you all this time, went through all this bullshit, and now you have another kid, and you don't want to do it anymore? All right, that's fucked-up. Especially when I wasted all my good eggs. Had two abortions. And I did it because you weren't ready and we weren't ready and you had all those things you wanted to accomplish. And you get to New York and do all the things you wanted to do and still it's not the time. And I'd been like, okay, it's just not the time right now.

When you were in Portland, and you said you wanted to be in a relationship, I wasn't seeing anyone. No one came into the picture until after you left. You left and I couldn't get you on the phone anymore. Every time I called you'd be like, "Oh, I gotta do this for class" or "Oh, I'm gonna go meet my classmate," and oh this and oh that. You became very distant. And I was like these classmates must be really important. And the whole time, you were with _____. You were starting a whole other relationship. It was like after you left, you just kept dismissing me. I started talking to _____. You came home, and some chick told you I was talking to him, and you flipped out. I remember after that time, me and him didn't talk anymore. You and me went to Vegas that summer, and I moved to New York that November. You didn't want me to come. You begged me, told me don't. Told me there's no reason to come. But in my head, it was the only way we could work things out. If we were in separate states, it was never going to work out. And I hated New York. I came to visit and I didn't like it, but I was like, this is the only way. He promised this whole grand life and I'm going to have my whole grand life in New York. And I get here, and you had a whole other girlfriend.

When I got here, I found about _____. Either I called her or she called. I remember you told her that I was a friend from Portland that you were helping out. That I didn't have a place to stay. And it was like, wow, what a slap in the face. Like I'm this homeless person that you're helping out. And then after she knew who I was, she told me you went to her house and pleaded with her not to leave you. It didn't make any sense. But then, I guess it did because there were always Jersey train schedules at your house. And then whenever you two would go somewhere, she'd call my phone, so

I could hear you talking in the background. And then you'd come back and act like it wasn't nothing. Sometimes I didn't even say anything because you were going to lie anyway.

I remember times of going to your house and waiting for you to come home and you'd come home with somebody. And I'd just watch and call you later and let you deny it. One time I walked up on you. And the girl left and we went in your house and argued. I remember doing something with your ugly shoes. I think I threw a pair out. I remember _____ left a fur coat at your house and I took it.

Every time something happened, you'd come to my house the next day pleading and begging and telling me it wouldn't happen again. And I think it was just a cycle of me not wanting to see you hurt and saying, okay. And the whole shit would just happen all over again. And I think you were so used to if I say this, I can do whatever the fuck I want to do. Because it never stopped. It just kept happening. I remember reading a text and you had a date. And I showed up. I was mad that you were on the date, but I was even more mad that you had her drinking a drink that I'd told you about. And after that, you left the restaurant and you chased after her. And I remember thinking, I really don't mean shit to him. I remember blowing your phone up after that, like, are you serious? Are you really fucking serious? I don't think I heard from you until like the next day. I remember coming to your house one morning and you opened the door to go to work and you had a girl in your bed. And I started fighting with you outside the door, and she got up and got dressed and ran out. I didn't get to see who she was.

I wanted my happy ever after. Whenever you used to do something in Portland, that's what you'd always use. When I get to New York, we'll be together and have a family. You drilled it in my head. Maybe so much happened that I was numb to it, wasn't taking it in. Maybe I didn't have any self-worth. I kept believing it. I didn't walk away. I just kept taking it and taking it and taking it. Everybody hated you, but they had to deal with you.

I don't know why I stayed. No, I do know why I stayed. We were going to have this family and be together, and things were going to get better, and you loved me, and I loved you. It was just some bullshit you were going through and once you went through it, we were going to be happy in love.

I don't think we could've overcome it at that time. We just continued to throw shit in each other's face. Every time I got angry, I'd throw it in your face, but it felt like there was never a break. It was always something.

I think I'm a loving and caring person who will go out of my way for people that I care about. I did that a lot with you. I always made sure you were good before myself. Like I always made sure you ate. Even before I ate. Sometimes you'd want seconds, even before I ate, and I would give you what was left just because you were still hungry. It wasn't like we were struggling and it was no more food, but I would give you what was left and figure out something else to eat. I just always put you first. I'm happy when I know the people I love are happy. I think that's a good thing.

I think my weakness is never wanting to see the person that I love hurt. I think a lot of times when I did want to leave and I knew you were hurting, I'd take it back. I didn't want you to feel the pain I was feeling, so I'd stay so you wouldn't feel it. We all know what that pain feels like. And I wouldn't want someone to feel that pain. I don't think I ever wanted to pay you back. But I wanted to do stuff so I could justify in my head why I was staying. So I could be like, I did this, so it's okay. It's okay that I stay. It's okay if I take him back because I did this.

I thought that was love. But when you talk to other people they say love doesn't hurt. And I say to myself, well, I don't know. Did he really love me? Or do some people have different forms of love? Is love dysfunctional? Did I just get under his skin and he was confusing that with love?

I don't know that I learned anything, any life lessons. But I learned that I'm a sucka. You did a whole lot of stuff. I still stayed and came back. And stayed and came back. You'd have me in a party with all your exes and ignore me like I wasn't there. One time you left me in a spot and told me you'd be back, so you could go be with _____. I waited for like an hour and a half with my friends. Telling them, he's coming back. He's coming back. And you never did. I was a sucka for taking that shit. You bought me and _____ the same dress for Christmas one year and I saw her in the dress. I was like, that's my damn New Year's dress in a different color.

I don't hate you. I don't think you're a terrible person. I don't dislike you. I think you're a cool guy, I guess. I think you've always had issues with women. But I think sometimes I used that as an excuse for you as well. Your issues with your mom. Stuff we talked about before. Through all of our shit, you turned out to be good for other people. You were pretty selfish. But I don't think you're that selfish for you to have the relationships you've had. People have wanted to marry you. You've proposed to someone. You've had relationships. Something has worked out. I always knew I was going to make you better for someone else. I complained about things you weren't doing and you started doing them. And if things ever ended with us, you were going to do them for the next person. You cook now, don't you? That's because of me. You buy flowers. You probably let your woman walk through the door first. You weren't doing any of that before me. So essentially, I made you better for the next person.

I think all women are broken if they don't have a relationship with their father. Or if they didn't know their father. I didn't have a father figure. Well, I'm lying. My grandfather was in my life till he passed when I was in middle school. He was in my life but he wasn't with my grandmother. He had a whole other girlfriend with a side chick that we all knew about. I didn't have a father. I remember wanting to have a dad, someone to look up to. I think every girl wants to have a dad and be a daddy's girl. But then you get older and get into high school and you realize none of your friends got daddies either. Then it becomes like it's not a big deal anymore. This is just how it is. I never had anyone in my life to tell me this is what a man is. This is what you should look for in a man. This is how a man should treat you. I think those things were self-taught. Something I seen in public or on TV.

Me not knowing he's not good for you. He doesn't care about you. He's playing with you. I think if I had had a father, I would've known that, and I wouldn't have stayed and let you continue to play with my head. I think if I had a father, you wouldn't have did that to me. He would've had that talk with you, like, "Son, don't you be out here doing my daughter dirty." Or he would've whooped your ass.

If I knew everything that would happen, I'd tell my nineteen-year-old self, he is not going to be there. He's not good for you. Don't do it.

It's been eleven years. For the first six years, I didn't take anyone serious. I was still thinking things were going to work out between you and me. And I don't think you should hold on to anyone like that. I don't think it's healthy. Especially when I see you move on with your life. And then I'm sitting here like, what's wrong with me? Why can't I move on? Or if I do move on, I keep picking wrong and asking myself, why do I pick these types of guys?

Statement Three (via interview)

We met by chance. If the seating arrangement was any different, we wouldn't be sitting here today. And I remember saying to you, If the comedian asks if we're together tell him, Yes, we're married and we have one son.

And later you said I put voodoo on you. Our first date, you had on a Sean John velour sweat suit with Timberlands and I was hopping because I'd just had surgery on my toe. And you said, "Oh, I wish I could see you without that hop." I should've known from then it wasn't going to work out. The second date you said you couldn't wait for us to shower together. I drove you straight to the train station, thinking this dude just wants to have sex with me. It was really just sexual. There was no other attraction between us.

That first year, you were coming over. We'd go on dates. We'd go to the reggae club. We'd talk. Laugh a lot. I'd have dinner parties and you'd bring your friends over. We must've met in December 2003. We stopped seeing each other, and I saw you at the comedy club again, on a date with someone else. You walked over to me and said, "I can't stop thinking about you. You should give me another chance."

Was that game?

When _____ moved here from Portland, you told me about her, and I asked you if I should be worried and you said no. And then one time after you'd spent the weekend with me, I called you during the week, and she answered your phone. She said, "Oh, he's taking a shower. We just finished fuckin." I called you and called you back and you wouldn't answer your phone. And then I drove to New York, and I saw you walking near your house. And you got in the car and told me you wanted a break. And I told you, I don't do breaks. Either you want to fix it or not. And you said, "I don't know what I want," and got out the car. And I drove all the way back to Jersey bawling. And then you called me back and said, "I don't want to lose you."

That was more game.

Your indecision is what made me walk away. It was always some reason why we couldn't be together. And till today, that shit has me confused. Even now. I see how you are with your new relationships and you were never like that with me. And it's had me questioning myself. Like, is it something about me? Is it my complexion, because you say one thing and you do the opposite? Is it my education? One of the things I've seen with you over the years is that you're ambitious, goal driven. And anyone that's going to be in your life has to have some kind of status that you're proud of. And I think I never fit that. Maybe it was because I didn't have the education. I didn't fit what you think is perfect.

In the beginning I was in a relationship and you were just dating someone and you had benefits. Now that I'm looking back at it, I don't think it was a relationship. It was, she's here. She's willing to give me some. I'm going to take it. I don't think you ever fully committed to me. I think I was just there for whatever I allowed you to do.

You easily moved in with _____ and _____, and I'm like, what did I do wrong? But I realize, it wasn't me, and I've come to terms with that.

There's so many significant hurts. You took me to the abortion clinic, and after the procedure, you took me home and you got me something to eat. But then you left and my cousin came and stayed with me. Then I got pregnant again. One of the things I'll give you credit for is you came to all the doctor visits. You didn't miss any of those and then you were there for the birth. But then you went back to _____. And I ended up on the phone with her, and we argued. Then I got into an argument with your mom. That time you called me and cursed me out and told me I was dead to you, that you'd never speak to me again.

I live with that.

Then when he was three and a half, I don't know what you were going through, but you came and sat on the couch and said you wanted to give it a try, and you wanted to be a family. But you wouldn't move in. And now that I'm here by myself, I don't see how you could've moved in. It was like _____ owned the house, and I was living with her. She had so much say. And I would listen to her when she would tell me something and then dictate it to you. So, I can't put it all on you.

We had some fun times. But we had a roller coaster after getting back together. We were good for like a year or two, but you came back with the same things. You wanted to live in the city. You'd come over on the weekend. And I felt like I was pushing you. At one point it felt like an ultimatum. You used to always tell me, "The worst thing a woman can do to a man is give him an ultimatum."

I used to love the little stuff we had in common. We'd make plans about traveling. And we'd listen to songs, and you'd say a line reminded you of me. I wouldn't say being with you for the ten years on-and-off was horrible the whole time. There was a lot of good moments. And sometimes I wonder when it ended, why I took you back so quickly? Like didn't I learn anything.

Once I was in the car and dropped you and _____ at the barbershop, and you told me I had to listen to this song. And I don't know what happened, I'm not a phone searcher, but I went into your messages and saw the name _____. And I called her and we talked. And you called her and told her not to speak another word to me. Sometimes I sit and think about that.

I remember one year you were sending me pictures of brownstones and telling me I need to get my credit fixed. And I was like, Oh, we're going to finally do it. But it was gaming. And I was like, why would he do this? My question is, why when your relationships are failing do you come to me? I feel like you hate me. Like I'm a doormat.

The person I see you are today, I never dated him. _____ moved, uprooted her life. You showed her you are a man, a provider, secure in your profession. But when we were together, you weren't that person. So how could I—with a child and a business and house—how could I have uprooted everything and come to the city to live with you?

For the last year I haven't gone on your social media page because when you were with _____ I used to stalk it, and it would kill me, and I would cry. I'm like, what was it about her that made you want to show her off. I can't understand it. To this day, all my friends say we look good together. Even my pastor keeps saying, "Oh, you and Mitch are going to get back together." And I say, no, it's never going to happen. He's moved on.

I remember we went to Mexico and I felt like I looked my best and you didn't post any pics of us. And you said you didn't want to hurt _____'s feelings. Then you said that your relationship is something private you keep to yourself. Picture being in a relationship for years and hearing that and then seeing you in a relationship with these girls that don't look like me, and you're posting and posting. And I blamed me. I wasn't pretty enough. I wasn't light enough. I blamed me until I realized it wasn't me. That I had nothing to do with it. It was you.

Some days I get up and I think about stuff we went through, and I pray about it, like, why can't I shake this? I won't say I'm broken, but I say to myself, this guy can love, brag, feel good about his relationship, but I was his secret. I think _____ was the only friend who knew who I was.

You just couldn't commit. I remember you came to the salon that day with a ring and you said you wanted to do it. You said, "I'll pack my stuff and move over now." You never felt the need to move in at any time until I said I was completely done. That was one of my biggest fears. I said the day we have an argument, you'll throw it in my face that I forced you into this relationship. That I gave you an ultimatum. But that was the first time in the ten years of knowing you that I saw a little bit of fear in you over losing me. But it wasn't really losing me, it was losing the routine that you were used to. I think you were hurt. But you got over it quick. In three months you were in Anguilla with _____.

Everyone wants to know why I'm not dating. I won't say I'm scared. And it might be religious reasons why I'm celibate. It's more religious than anything, but another thing is I don't trust that I'll know when someone is spitting game. I tell myself that I'm too old to subject myself to that again. I don't think I can recover. So I just choose not to. Sometimes I think about you coming and telling me you're sorry.

One of the things you did that felt like the final nail: When I was about to go into surgery, you set up this thing like you were my savior. You said you wanted me to know before I went into surgery that you still loved me. And I was floating on air, like this is what I've been waiting for. We're going to have a family, and it's going to work, and we'll travel and _____ is doing good. I was like, I'm going to pay off my bills and sell the house and whatever he wants. And it was all a game. If I could hate you, I would have then. But I tell my mother, the sad thing about this is I still love Mitch. I never stopped. And I just feel like you never loved me—ever. I think you were attracted to me. You liked me sexually. But settle down and grow old with, I was never that person. I think part of your ambition is having the perfect partner.

I do have a lot of regrets. Not taking the ring. Also, taking advice from _____ that was against you. And I didn't stand up to it. She'd say you weren't a good person. She'd say, "He's not serious. Stand your ground." And I listened. Sometimes I ask myself was I perfect: no. Did I love you: yes. Could I have done more: I'm not sure. Should I have stuck it out: I'm not sure.

I'd tell my younger self, stop being so independent. Talk less, listen more. Don't look at things one-sided. There's a lot that you were saying that I wasn't hearing. Like when I was saying go take a summer job. Every summer I'd get some money and would give you a thousand dollars. But you said I wasn't supportive because I'd tell you to get a summer job. And you'd say, "What do you want me to do, flip burgers?" And I'd say, if that's what you have to do. You have two kids. You took that as me not believing in you. And I took that as you being selfish. Because there was no money. And maybe if I'd seen it through your eyes, I would've complained less. I don't know if I could've been more supportive. You felt like I wasn't there for you while you were writing the book. You knew your plan. How people see you now is how you saw yourself ten, fifteen years ago. But I didn't see it then.

I think you're damaged, broken. When you're happy you're kind, great.

But if you're mad, you can be mean, vicious. It's like there's two Mitchells. And I've met both. I think you would say stuff to hurt me, just so I couldn't hurt you.

I'm headstrong. I'm giving. I don't think I'm selfish. I'm independent, but maybe too independent. I have insecurities, but I pretend like I'm okay. Being with you and seeing your other relationships, and that nobody looks like me, it has me second-guessing myself.

My dad used to abuse the whole family. Physical, verbal, mental abuse. We were very poor, and I think a lot of the stuff that he did to us was because he couldn't do what a man was supposed to do. There was a time when my sister and brother had run away and my mother was in the US, and it was just him and me at home. One day, he came in the kitchen with a rope to beat me because he didn't like how I prepared his meal. And I took the meat cleaver to chop him up, and he looked at me and left the house. The next day I went to school carrying all the pills that were in the medicine cabinet with me, and when I got there, I swallowed them trying to kill myself. They found me, gave me charcoal, and pumped my stomach. The next time I saw my dad, he said, "You damn idiot. You should've died."

My dad was ruthless. I resented him for years because of the abuse. But he's not that person now. He's a great dad. Today I love my dad. Today we have a great relationship because I have an understanding of why he's the man he is now. I don't hold animosity against anyone. I can let go and move forward.

Statement Four (via text)

Hi - ok. I'll think about it.

Question: why are you still writing about this.

Ok, so your asking all of us who may or may not hv been broken to help? Just trying to understand cuz the irony feels really sad . . .

Statement Five (via text)

[Silence]

CRIME SCENE CHARACTERISTICS

Following an analysis of the *Physical Evidence* and *Victimology*, a criminal profiler moves on to determining the characteristics of the *Crime Scene*, defined as an area where a criminal act has taken place. The *Crime Scene Characteristics* are the distinguishing aspects of a *Crime Scene*, evidence born of an offender's behavioral decisions regarding the victim and location of the crime and the subsequent meaning of those decisions to the offender. *Crime Scene Characteristics* include *Location Type*, the kind of environment in which a crime scene exists, there are four general types: indoor crime scenes, vehicle crime scenes, outdoor crime scenes, underwater crime scenes. The *Point of Contact* is defined as the precise location where the offender first approached the victim and encompasses the primary, secondary, intermediate sites. The *Method of Approach*, the offender's strategy for getting close to a victim, includes surprise, con, and blitz. The means an offender uses to overpower a victim is called the *Method of Attack*. The *Methods of Control* are the means used to manipulate, regulate, restrain, subdue a victim during an offense and include control-oriented force, verbal threats, and unarticulated threats of force. Profilers consider *Weapons*: any item found in the *Crime Scene* or brought to it by the offender or victim for the purpose of administering force. The circumstances in which the victim submits to an offender's demands are termed *Victim Compliance*; however, a victim's acquiescence shouldn't be judged as consent. *Victim Resistance* is the means a victim uses to oppose a crime. Resistance can be physical, verbal, or sometimes passive. *Planning / Preparation* is defined as the extent to which the offender was prepared to commit the crime. *Precautionary Acts* are those an offender commits before, during, or after a crime to conceal their connection to a crime or the crime itself. They could involve an offender wearing a disguise, choosing a certain time of day to commit a crime, or removing items they think links them to a victim or crime. While Turvey's definition limits the *Crime Scene* to the specific location(s) where a prosecutable crime took place, in Scotia Hicks and Bruce Sales's *Criminal Profiling: Developing an Effective Science and Practice*, they argue for an expanded definition of a *Crime Scene*: "any location where evidence or information relevant to a crime scene will likely be found." In examining the serial *mala in se* offenses of Men on the Scale, that "relevant information" (again, this ain't me arguing for their-our-my forgiveness or an

acquittal of harms) should include the philosophies of the dominant thinkers as well as the offender's historical, cultural, and social exigencies—in
other words, the phenomena henceforth termed the *At-Large Crime Scene.*

Imagine Alcibiades in classical Athens envisioning himself as ruler of the
known world. How much would he have been inclined to challenge the pre-
vailing thought? What were the odds of dude picketing outside the Agora
for an end to slavery or women's suffrage? Picture him and Plato circled
around Socrates, their mentor exhorting, "Women will nevertheless be inferior in whatever they do." What were the chances of him conceding Socrates's concept of lateral virtue—if one possesses one virtue then one must
necessarily possess them all—given his status as an entitled, aristocratic
heartthrob, given his hella-sheer solipsism.

What to make of Casanova's exploits in light of that long eighteenth
century? How much of his committed libertinism was a middle finger to
believing in consensus or rightness or absolute truth? Should we ask if
he intended his swashbuckling as proof or disproof of the Kantian view
of Enlightenment as "man's emergence from his self-imposed nonage . . .
the inability to use one's own understanding without another's guidance"?
What if Venice's infamous son had lived in a world where "public outrages
against the holy religion" weren't impetus for a prison bid?

Though the hagiographers would prefer we not, picture JFK and tender interns Fiddle and Faddle splashing buck naked in the White House's
indoor pool. Then ask, how much of the president's incaution could be
chalked up to his unassailable bravery in World War II combat (were his
war heroics disproof of the Socratic notion of lateral virtue?) and the role
he later played in securing his beloved country from nuclear slaughter?
Would surviving those mortal threats and negotiating the dreads of the
Cold War cause him to feel destined or immortal? President Kennedy was
born in the age of modernity—how much of his future philandering was an
echo of Baudelaire's description of modernism as "the ephemeral, the fugitive, the contingent"? Did reaching adulthood in an America that was pre–
civil rights and second-wave feminism shape his vision of which groups
were worthy of the privileges and respect owed him?

Notable Men on the Scale aren't the only ones deserving of an *At-Large
Crime Scene* examination; so too are The Men whose roots don't reach to
Europe, whose biographies won't make the annuals, which includes The

Men of my era of which I'm most familiar. What questions should be asked of and about us?

––––––––––

Were we born as the fractional citizens of The Other America? Did our mothers fear, as did Margaret Burroughs, "What shall I tell my children who are black / Of what it means to be a captive in this dark skin / What shall I tell my dear one, fruit of my womb, / Of how beautiful they are when everywhere they turn / They are faced with abhorrence of everything that is black." Which of us black boys would be brainwashed to quest for girls and later women who fit standards that, generations prior, informed a test group of little black kids to choose this or that doll? How did the Cold War's long-lived threat shape our sense of conflict? Who, as a knee-high, beheld a dark-suited, slick-haired, stern-faced Nixon announcing, "America's public enemy number one in the United States is drug abuse. In order to fight and defeat this enemy it is necessary to wage a new, all-out offensive"? What became of those who, at the behest of their mothers, braved WIC (Women, Infants, and Children) lines for Tillamook cheese or powdered milk or white bread? What became of those who, thirty or forty years hence the New Deal, were bystanders to their mothers' slow wizening at the hands of the welfare state? Who witnessed their mothers attest to their fathers' absenteeism to keep their benefits? Picture one of those boys, years later, antsying in a metal fold-up chair while his mother, shouldering his infant brother, plies a dour-faced caseworker to increase her benefits. Whose Mom pledged most dire fidelity to Mr. Never-Was-Nor-Will-Be-Right? Ask who's sat unawares with cousins in their auntie's crib, heard the back door go BLAM! and police besiege the basement on what he couldn't have known then was an assured hunt for hard dope? We are a generation of men who lived through Reaganomics. Whose single mama falsified job search paperwork in the Reagan era of the largest tax cut in history and its harvest of record joblessness? If our fathers were the native sons of invisible men, were we neglected man-childs? Which boys appeased their lack with Composite Pops? Which ones fawned as hazel-eyed, fair-skinned Vanessa Williams—a woman whose features didn't reflect our mama's—became the first black woman to win Miss America and set evermore our standard for longing? Who watched their *Scarface* VHS on repeat, each time dreaming of equal coca-ine riches and escaping the ambush alive? Who laughed themselves to stomach cramps watching Eddie Murphy, leather-clad, in a stand-up com-

edy flick? Which ones minded Eddie's counsel in *Raw* that if a man made a
woman say, "wooo, oooh, oooh," she'd never leave him, not even for the trespass of her catching him in bed with somebody else. Who were our leaders?
What was our cause? Did we believe Jesse's sermon at the '88 Democratic
National Convention, "Suffering breeds character. Character breeds faith. In
the end, faith will not disappoint.... Keep hope alive"? What hope was to be
had for a people knee-deep in crack-bred suffering? What turned us ineffable, plagued our speech with "You know what I'm sayin," "You know what I
mean," "You understand," "You underdig," "You know"? When did we begin
obsessing over *real* niggahood, over keeping it real, keeping it funky, keeping it 100 or 1,000,000, and that's on everything we love, including God!?
We were born in the age of postmodernism. Was-is our hyperbolic need for
unassailable ethos the upshot of Nietzsche's claim in *Twilight of Idols* that
modernism dissolved the distinction between the "real" and the "apparent"?
Should we ask who peeped their young life portrayed in *Boyz n the Hood*
and *Menace II Society*? Or what it felt like to reach the end of adolescence
having lost a day-one patna or two to Clinton's "truth in sentencing" and
"three strikes"? Answer me this: Did either Bush ever love us? And if the
ancient Greeks had the lyre and Pythagorean harmonics, old Europe had
the piano and classical music, and early twentieth-century America had the
sax and nascent pop, what had we? And if other (patriarchal) periods had
Socrates, Kant, and Nietzsche, and the generations that preceded us had
Du Bois and Baldwin, who were our sages, prophets, philosophers?

Lucky me, I had the all-in-one of the 808, rap music, and East Oakland's
finest: Todd "Too $hort" Shaw. $hort released his *Born to Mack* cassette
tape in the summer of '87—a month before my twelfth birthday—and I
don't know how I got my hands on it, but I owned it. There I was in a bedroom in The House on Sixth, the door closed and locked, the volume on my
tape deck lowered to furtive, cassette spooling to my favorite song: "Dope
Fiend Beat." First the baseline, and a couple beats later, $hort screams,
"Biiiiiiitch!" a word that both begins, ends, and serves as a kind of chorus
for the tune. Between that first and last use of "Biiitch" occur thirty-three
other utterances of it. Believe you me, there were some first-rate curs-
ers around the neighborhood, but couldn't none of them even approach
$hort's "Biiiiiiitch!" In retrospect, $hort's "Biiiiiiitch!" contained a histo-
riography, a biography, a culture, an ethic. In the moment, nonetheless,

my non-prescient preadolescent self received it as straight salaciousness, the forbidden. And because I judged it so, I kept listening. Played the song, the whole tape—"Freaky Tales" was another favorite—again and again and again and again. . . .

One of those times, I forgot to lock the door, and Mom barged in, slammed a hand on her hip, and frowned all eyes. "Boy, just what the hell you think you listenin to?" she said, and confiscated the tape. The next week or the one thereafter, she sent me to fetch something from the trunk of the car and, lo and behold, there was my *Born to Mack* tape, begging me to reclaim it, which I did, and proceeded to indulge in countless circumspect listening sessions. Before long, I was whispering the lyrics right along with him: "Bitches on my mind / I can't hold back, now's the time / All you loud-mouth bitches talk too much / And you dick-teasin bitches never fuck . . . Motherfuck you, damn shit-head bitch . . ."

"Dope Fiend Beat" was crucial to the infractions of my *At-Large Crime Scene*. $hort's raps, which proved seminal, were the first I heard that seemed to celebrate cursing women, that in addition boasted remorselessness over abusing them. And I must've pondered whether he knew something I didn't about how to treat women. That summer, I was eleven going on too-old-to-be-a-virgin, and $hort spoke to my lechery, implied that when, at long last, I started doing the do, a woman's worth would be in her willingness to please me, and furthermore that one who couldn't or wouldn't submit to my desires deserved my ire. $hort's "Biiiiiiitch!" suggested there was joy in cursing women. But to be fair, it wasn't all of them, just the "loud-mouthed" and "dick-teasin" ones or, in other words, a woman who spoke up for herself and-or who wouldn't yield to my overzealous lust. It's easy, so easy now, to apprehend $hort's messages as pure misogyny but not so simple in those days. In those days, what I heard was $hort voicing my temporal fears, was him presenting vital counsel on how to distance myself—that space a form of preservation—from the corruption of my first love. That project took several years.

During which, the world kept right on twirling.

In 1992/93, I was a senior in high school and the second-best player on the hoop team—as a matter of absolute fact, we were a better team the season prior—with a pregame ritual of sitting in the bleachers blasting music on my Walkman. My favorite song at the time, a joint that I rewound till it was rote, till its chorus was a mantra, was Dr. Dre's "Bitches Ain't Shit," off what's now the certified quintuple-plus platinum album *The Chronic*.

Snoop proclaims even before the song's first baseline, "Bitches ain't shit but hoes and tricks." Then the beat comes on and he raps the chorus with what seems pure conviction: "Bitches ain't shit but hoes and tricks / Lick on these nuts and suck the dick / Gets the fuck out after you're done / And I hops in my ride to make a quick run." The song features Dre, Tha Dogg Pound, Snoop, and Jewell, each riffing about a "bitch," which in fairness is expanded to include Eazy-E, who was Dre's sworn nemesis at the time. But the verse that most moved me was Snoop's, in which he narrates a tale about a girl named Mandy May whom he loved but had been warned was no good. In Snoop's verse, he gets gaffled and has to spend six months in the county. He's released one hot sunny day, gets scooped by Dre and his homeboy the D.O.C., and they deliver the news that his beloved Mandy May was cheating while he was down. The D.O.C. drives Snoop to Mandy May's crib to confront her, and when he arrives, Dre passes him a strap. Snoop kicks in her door and finds none other than his little cousin Daz (of Tha Dogg Pound) having sex with her on the floor. Instead of busting, Snoop uncocks his pistol, admits he's heartbroken, affirms he's still loc'd, and curses Mandy May.

As much as any song, "Bitches Ain't Shit" shaped the misdemeanor era of my *At-Large Crime Scene*. Unlike $hort, Snoop and Dre et al. scorned *all* women, taxonomized them as "bitches" who were also either "hoes" or "tricks." Like $hort, they suggested a woman wasn't for loving but for pleasing my prurience—but unlike $hort, though, they went so far as to detail the acts. The song implied that sure disgrace awaited me if one or more of my homeboys witnessed (or caught wind of) me going weak over a woman. And since Snoop and Dre et al. painted all women as unprincipled, unfaithful, disloyal beings, that shame was imminent. Snoop's verse encouraged me to believe the most trusted safeguard against hurt was being "loc'd," which is to say tough, which is to say as close as I could get to unfeeling. Him finding Daz "fucking" his girl was warning that no matter how much I cared for a woman, no matter how high I regarded her, the next man could judge her close to worthless. Snoop uncocking his pistol upon catching his cousin and girl together served as counsel that there were cases in which even a main squeeze (oh, the hypocrisy) was little more than a body for passing around—advice preached on *Doggystyle*'s "Ain't No Fun"—and that a high measure of my manhood might be abiding another man, whether stranger, homeboy, or family, sleeping with a woman I claimed. Snoop was never a hero of mine or even my favorite rapper, but I suspected he knew more than me about besting trouble and so I heeded what I believed was his thesis: in the world that was becoming more and more of my world, absolute romantic apathy was a state of grace.

And of course, that world kept spinning.

Summer of '96—picture me rolling in my '86 Honda, my ride fresh from a hand car wash, after-market metallic blue paint and chrome five-star rims asparkle, windows lowered, Tupac's "Skandalouz," turning my trunk *BOOMbastic!* and my 6x9s and tweets all sorts of resonant. Pac, off top, announces his intent to rap about "scandalous hoes." Then, the world's most famous rapper—a sage to some, prophet to others—spends the next 4:09 bemoaning, critiquing, and defaming said "hoes," between a simple but most compelling hook: Nate Dogg crooning a refrain of "she's so scandalous." At one point, Pac raps, "You're lookin at a bitch who specialize in tellin lies . . . / Her face ain't never shed a tear through them scandalous eyes."

Pac's "Skandalouz" marks the transition to the felonious era of my *At-Large Crime Scene*. Pac most appealed to me then because like me, he was full of discord, naked contradictions. The same dude that had goaded me on "Dear Mama" to celebrate the strength of my single mother was now (it wasn't the first nor would it be his last paradoxical message) excoriating the shit out of somebody's young mother or daughter or sister. Pac like $hort singled out a certain type of woman: those who "specialize in tellin lies." And while I could argue that him pointing to a particular woman also implied a belief in the existence of truthful women or at least those who don't specialize in deceit, the message I received at the time was that women are wanton, duplicitous, conniving, and that I should therefore be suspicious of the whole damn gender. What I heard back then was Pac's description of a woman who "ain't never shed a tear," which implied a dry face could absolve me of whatever guilt I might feel over a trespass and-or that there was a chance I'd encounter a woman immune to hurt. What I didn't hear back then was word one of what might've turned them "scandalous" or Pac even approaching the argument that a woman deserves the same sexual freedom as him, me, the homies, or any man. Couldn't none of my favorite rappers nor me stand that truth.

Please, please, please don't mistake me mulling the influence of a few rap songs as me trying to use rap music as a scapegoat for my offenses. As I hope is apparent by now, there were myriad factors that shaped my troubled romantic relations. But there just ain't no gainsaying the impact of $hort, Snoop, Pac. As much as anyone else, they were my sophists. Their lyrics at one point foretold my life, at another point informed it, and for far too long reflected where and how I lived and what I lived for.

There's umpteen incidents from those long-lived days deserving of a *Crime Scene Reconstruction*, a term defined by Hicks and Sales as a process that "approaches the evidence by relating it to the behavioral information about a crime scene in the form of a timeline." In the interest of space, I decided to focus on one that, if it ain't the most incriminating, ranks high on the list.

It happened during my fool-headed early twenties, the period during which my emotional crimes had reached felonious, happened on a night when more than the usual number of usual suspects lounged around the house of one of my Big homies drinking brews and smoking chronic. Hours into the night, per custom, somebody declared we needed "chicks." On most nights, our expressed intent would've equaled dialing "old reliables" and persuading them to visit, but for some reason that night, it was almost a consensus that only new "chicks" would do. Ever eager to prove myself distinguished among those present, I volunteered for what was in effect a mission. My high school ace, ever down for the cause, offered to assist. With no further *Planning/Preparation*, me and my ace struck out in my Honda and, under a starry night, stalked up and down Killingsworth and Alberta; MLK and Broadway; past parks and bars; through gas stations and grocery store lots. We ended up in the parking lot of a convenience store on MLK—a place that had served as a *Point of Contact* several times. We weren't there but a hot second when we spied a pair of "chicks" pull up and stride into the store. "You see them?" I said. "Hell yeah," said my ace. "Them might be the ones." Our *Method of Approach* was neither blitz nor con or surprise, but my ace motioning them to the car once they swayed out of the store. Our convo, I disremember, but the outcome was either my ace—a patna gifted with an active and able mouthpiece—or me convinced them to follow us back to the house to "kick it." Here, I'll mention the women were black, about our age, and traveling with a preschooler. In minutes, my ace and me, beaming triumphant, swaggered through the front door of my Big homie's crib with the women and a little boy trailing us.

In what took longer but occurred, or so it seemed, in an instant, the house transformed into a *Primary Scene*: Someone led one woman downstairs; a handful of dudes tramping behind her. Someone led the other woman upstairs. The boy, meanwhile, sat on the living room couch digging hot food from a greasy-ass paper sack, and I, feeling most accountable for his present care, sat at the dining room table, a sentinel. Before long, though—this act in itself is another moral failing—I cautioned the boy to sit tight and padded into the basement. In that dank cellar, I heard dudes dirty-talking, the *SMACK! SMACK!* of skin on skin, loud slurping, and moans that sounded pornographic. Mere light grudged through a ground-level window, but it was enough to make out the woman bent over and fellating one guy while another guy pumped her from behind. Other guys chattered about who'd go next; in seconds, I decided I wouldn't be one of them. I'd like to credit my abstention to ethics, but in hindsight, that decision—and this speaks to my devolvement as a Man on the Scale—was less virtue or concern for the woman than it was reaping the pride of resisting what other dudes couldn't, feeling too supercilious for any spot other than first, and fearing the risk of catching a VD. Resolved, I plodded back upstairs, past the forlorn boy, to the second floor, where I found my ace and the other woman having sex in a bedroom. There's a blank now on what words we exchanged, if we exchanged any words at all; it could've been a look, a brief smirk, but whatever it was, I understood it as him offering me a turn with her, one I declined. Back on the first floor, I bumped into another homeboy who'd sworn off joining the crowd. We blathered about why; though neither of us, I suspect, admitted the whole truth. Meanwhile, the little boy slumped on the couch, silent, gazing into the grease-stained bag in his lap. Once my homeboy shuffled off, I sat down beside the boy. "Don't worry, little man. You gone be home before you know it," I said, patted a cushion, and wondered how cruel of a lie I'd told.

An offender's *Methods of Control* include physical force or the threat of it, but for me and The Men I know best, those tactics are off-limits. Period. That's our code, our principle, which is why, though I wasn't privy to the conversation that led one woman to engage in group sex and the other lie down with a stranger, I'm confident the methods used didn't include physical force or the threat of it, that whoever convinced them to do what they did believed himself or themselves of the utmost persuasiveness. On the other hand, in the case of the woman who ended up in the basement, for instance, anything short of us asking, "Would you like to go downstairs and have group sex with us until all parties agree to quit?" could be considered deceit. And I'm ashamed, pure shamed, to admit that it took an embarrassment of years after the fact for me to consider whether one of us coerced one or both of those women, for me to reason that anything short of a full disclosure and-or one of us speaking even the slightest falsehood, corrupts what I'd convinced myself was certain consent.

Turvey cautions against misapprehending *Victim Compliance* for consent. He contends it's incumbent upon the profiler to remember that a victim's responses to an offender are born of their history, experience, personality, and paradigms, that what might be extreme behavior for one might seem normal for another. He points out that certain victims might assent to an offender out of fear and-or to avoid further harm. He also explains that a victim might resist complying by means physical, verbal, or passive.

To my knowledge, neither victim that night resisted physically, verbally, or passively. Nonetheless their consent should still be questioned. Take the woman who ended up in the basement. She might've felt following my ace and me to the house was a tacit contract that constrained her to submit to whatever we asked once she got there. She might've judged the sheer number of us a silent threat to cede. Or maybe she smelled the 40s on our breath and the blunt smoke thickening the air and figured one or more of us was faded enough to get belligerent or even bellicose. Or was down for sex with one, two, or even a threesome, but, uncomfortable with voicing her limits, felt compelled to oblige the rest. It never occurred to me or else I straight eighty-sixed it from my mind, that she might've wanted to quit but believed she had no other option than to ply each one of them to satisfaction, and to furthermore convince them—whether true or not—that she was having a good time doing it. Compliance and consent are sometimes nebulous, and in circumstances like that night, I wasn't in a position to judge.

The whole scene was rife with ambiguities, true, but that little boy's victimhood is a point of absolute fact. It's tough to picture him in detail—or else pursuing undeserved grace, I've pushed his features out of mind—and yet for the rest of my days, there ain't no expunging the little elegies in his eyes nor the sad island-shaped stains on that paper sack. Beyond those images he remains with me as questions:

What, if anything, does he remember from that night? How many times had his mother made him an innocent witness? Would he recognize himself in my retelling? By my math, he's nearing thirty. And I wonder how he would now describe his and his mother's relationship. His relationship to women? Wonder if he has children—a daughter? If he has been neglected, abused, indoctrinated into a Man on the Scale? And if so, how much blame is his alone? Wonder of what profit and whose is weighing that blame?

Months, forever, that's how long I could spend mulling that night—trying to reconstruct it moment by moment, ruminating on the boy, considering the *At-Large Crime Scene*, deliberating on the long, long fallout—and still do it a marked injustice. And yet I haven't abandoned the project. And still, the hardest look is inward. One of the most disturbing aspects of that night is how it testifies to my predaciousness. It excuses me none that the women complied and left without complaint—it was my expressed hounding that introduced them to possible harm. What did it matter that I didn't penetrate either one? To abide what occurred (at no point did I chasten a single dude present, not even for the sake of the boy) I had to have convinced myself that the women—or rather "chicks"—didn't deserve my compassion, nor respect, nor protection. And those truths serve as further proof that I'd devolved from misdemeanors to felonies, that I'd sacrificed essential parts of what made me humane.

And for too long, I stood stock-still while the world revolved.

OFFENDER CHARACTERISTICS

Turvey explains that while criminal profiling can help establish the characteristics that distinguish an offender from the general population, it isn't a tool well suited for "individuating" offenders in and of itself. He asserts as well that deducing *Offender Characteristics* requires posing the right questions about offense-related behavior, first to define the characteristics, and second to determine which behavior serves as evidence of a particular trait.

Profilers have classified offenders into two distinct categories: *Organized* and *Disorganized*. The *Organized* offender leaves an orderly crime scene, one suggestive of cunning, planning, and forethought, as well as average-to-high intelligence, social competence, an ability to maintain control over his life. The *Disorganized* offender leaves a disordered crime scene, one that suggests, among other data, a lack of social competence, below-average intelligence, mental illness, a history of familial dysfunction, past abuse. It's important to note that some offenders demonstrate both *Organized* and *Disorganized* traits. Turvey, in fact, argues the *Organized/Disorganized* dichotomy oversimplifies, that most crimes present on the continuum between the two extremes. Psychologist David Canter divides offenders into *Marauders* or *Commuters* based on the spatial relationship between their crimes and what's termed an *Anchor Point*, a defined area of operation often rooted by an offender's home or the home of a relative or a job. A *Marauder* commits crimes bound by their *Anchor Point*. A *Commuter* travels a great distance from it. An offender's *MO* (*Modus Operandi* or *Method of Operation*) is a way of working, the actions needed to carry out a crime. An offender's *Signature* is a pattern of distinctive behaviors that are characteristic of and satisfy emotional and psychological needs. Profilers further divide the *Signature* into two parts. The *Signature Behaviors* are the acts unnecessary to committing the crime. The *Signature Aspect* is the theme satisfied by the offense. Those themes, experts argue, are suggestive of personality. In regards to their beliefs on personality, profilers can be grouped into two camps—those who believe the essence of personality is interior and stable across time and place, and those who believe personality is malleable and dependent on situation. Turvey defines *Motive* as the "emotional, psychological, and material needs that are satisfied by a behavior," and *Intent* as "the aim that guides behavior." Hicks and Sales argue that *Motive* requires *Intent*, that if an offender didn't intend to commit a crime, an inquiry into their *Motive* is close to if not moot. They furthermore hold that the opposite is also true: the presence of *Intent* implies a *Motive*—if an offender commits an act with purpose, it's probable there's a reason. The authors further divide *Motive* into two categories: *Expressive* or *Instrumental*. Per their rubric, *Instrumental Motives* are directed at some goal (financial gain, political advantage, eliminated foe) and *Expressive Motives* signal anger or another (jealousy, lust, revenge) chief emotion.

———

Men on the Scale prefer a girlfriend, partner, wife, a woman who affords them a sense of security, who comforts them, whose presence might limit their recklessness. The Men might perceive a partner as buoying their esteem, a ceaseless need given they live, even if unconscious of it, in a perpetual state of questionable worth. To address the ever-present hunch that they don't measure, The Men must hunt for a woman susceptible to their control. And crucial to the efficacy of that conquest is forging an as-close-to-as-possible one-sided bond. Tactics to establish that bond include over-the-top obsequiousness, grand proclamations, and extravagant gifts; they also might consist of wielding silence, withholding compliments, and treating a woman (best believe, her comfort is his antagonist) with blatant caprice.

The Men work most often as a *Marauder* since, while sex with a stranger elsewhere might profit them equal physical pleasure, seducing a woman acknowledged or, best, desired by those who live in and around their *Anchor Point* has a greater chance of shooting their rep into the statussphere, skirt-chasing they might experience as an existential need. Mozart's Giovanni tells his servant Leporello, "Leave the women alone? You're mad! You know that they are more necessary to me than the bread I eat! Than the air I breathe!" The Men might perceive a woman as a prospective mate but will resist believing as did Byron that they "cannot exist without some object of love." It's essential that The Men learn it's against their interest to be a keeper of hearts, that their endurance demands anesthetizing themselves to what the heart feels, their heart and the heart of any potential victim. A go-to MO of The Men is hit-em-and-leave-em, a fleeing crucial to forging what historian Chantal Thomas terms "the paradise of insouciance."

In her essay "Casanova: Inscriptions of Forgetting," Thomas describes that blissful state as absent the reflection that might yield wisdom. She calls it a "magical" state, one "without the threat of desire or rejection." That paradisiacal insouciance, I'd argue, also features a lack if not absence of remorse, which The Men work to achieve by cataloguing the traits they believe redeem them. Trumpets Mozart's Giovanni, "Love is much the same in any form. He who remains faithful to one is being cruel to others; I, who have an overabundance of sentiment, love them all. Since women cannot think clearly, they call my natural, kindly feelings betrayal." Giovanni's profession is all sorts of irrational, but on the flip, reasoning—what's apt to rack them with a head full of dissonance—can't be high on the list of goals for Men on the Scale. To avoid assured mental strife, The Men often resort to *Moral Rationalizing*, what, in his essay "The Moral Instinct," psychologist Steven Pinker describes as starting with a conclusion born of an unconscious emotion and working backward to justify it. In rationalizing, the act comes first, or said another way, rationalizing is ass-backward reasoning. The worst of The Men despise "true love" as defined by Frantz Fanon in *Black Skin, White Masks*: "wishing for others what one postulates for oneself." The worst of The Men are solipsistic, egotistic, narcissistic offenders who feel little to no need to so much as rationalize their crimes.

The most malicious Men on the Scale victimize without remorse ("Women are machines for suffering," Picasso once told a mistress), acts that confirm their lack of empathy, a word that wasn't even a part of the

American lexicon till the top of the twentieth century. Empathy has its roots in ancient Greece, evolving from the Greek *em* (into) and *pathos* (feeling), later *empatheia* (into feeling). Empathizing is the act of entering another's feelings, an action Men highest on the Scale go to great, great lengths to evade. The worst of The Men, too, pefer a girlfriend, partner, or wife and reap grand pleasure from flouting what they judge as her feckless need for their fidelity. A go-to *MO* of the worst of The Men is hit-em-and-leave-em-*felled*; plus memorialize the offenses with trophies (thong panties, texts, emails, videos, a Crown Royal bag of printed photos, old Polaroids, or a cubist portrait rendering a victim disfigured) to help normalize and-or aggrandize the deeds. Catch them and selfsame others boasting mementos and spinning accounts of their trespasses into creative nonfiction. Some of The Men, often the most injurious, are antisocial offenders who assume guises (loving, thoughtful, patient) to achieve their *Intent*. The most dangerous Men on the Scale possess average-to-high intelligence, are articulate, witty, funny, charming (trust all charm is at least in part a deception) but also intemperate, manipulative, deceitful, cunning.

In *The Ethics of Ambiguity*, the brilliant Simone de Beauvoir claims misfortune befalls man because he was once a child. But one could also argue that hardship bechances The Men from the natural fact of their being born at all, that apprehending their conduct demands tracking them back to birth. If that sounds Freudian, it's 'cause, as I see it, The Men are guided by Freud's pleasure principle, are egoists, are, in some cases, the most extreme cases, predators with an id unchecked by the superego.

Freud believed a full psyche emerges by preschool age, a view echoed in psychologist Grazyna Kochanska's "The Emergence and Development of Conscience in Toddlerhood and Early Childhood." Kochanska explains that the evolution of early human conscience begins at age three and matures to include the feelings associated with the consequences of our actions as well as the discomfort triggered by actual or considered wrongdoing, and that furthermore the processes shape the trajectories of adult conscience. Writes Kochanska, "Thus early childhood is a critical developmental context for future moral development."

While The Men might possess one of the moral excellences—the cardinal virtues of temperance, prudence, courage, and justice—they for damn sure live in defiance of others. Alcibiades was impeached for defiling sacred statues and parodying religious rites and, instead of accepting his sanction, renounced his country and defected to Sparta, whereupon he seduced the king of Sparta's wife into a public affair and even impregnated her. Some historians argue that Lord Byron liaisoned for years with his half sister and fathered a daughter by her. Biographers allege JFK cheated with interns in his and his wife's bed, splashed with a mistress in his personal tub, and turned White House lunchtimes into poolside sex fests. Suffice it to say, these archetypal Men on the Scale serve as credible evidence of a selective conscience or a depressed conscience, if not the unconscionable.

Psychoanalyst John Bowlby's attachment theory explains how such a conscience might form. Bowlby defines attachment as a "lasting psychological connectedness between human beings" and posits forming a strong relationship with at least one parent is vital to childhood development and serves as the prototype for all future social relationships. Bowlby's colleague Mary Ainsworth was essential to the theory's development. Ainsworth conducted studies in which she brought parents and infants into a lab, separated and reunited them, and studied their reactions. That research culminated in what Ainsworth termed *attachment behaviors*. Per Ainsworth, *secure infants* became upset upon a parent leaving but were comforted with ease when he or she returned. *Anxious-resistant* infants were colicky at separation, grew distressed in their parents' absence, were hard to placate even after the reunion, and sometimes behaved in ways suggestive of an intent to punish their parent. *Avoidant infants* showed little distress at separation and, when reunited, avoided contact with the parent. Given what I understand—or at least believe I do—of The Men, I suspect more than a fair share were once an *anxious-resistant* or *avoidant* infant. And yet, it's unwise, bordering on foolish, to believe that the character of early bonding is the end-all-be-all sure sign of who ends up on the Scale.

There's also a high chance that abandonment during the development of the psyche can set a child on the path to becoming a Man on the Scale. Casanova's mother abandoned him at a year old to the care of his grandmother, so she could chase acting stardom. Lord Byron's father ghosted when he was a toddler, leaving him to the care of an abusive schizophrenic mother. And attachment and abandonment ain't all. Trying to compensate for a physical ailment—though as I write this, I question whether it's crossing into the realm of excuses—might also doom a child to the Scale. Alcibiades owned a noticeable lisp. Casanova endured a host of ailments, including frequent nosebleeds. Lord Byron was born with a clubfoot and spent all his life self-conscious about it. JFK suffered from Addison's auto-immune disease and almost died from scarlet fever when he was two.

Inchoate childhood troubles might also manifest as what experts term maladaptive responses. Sometimes those responses become neurosis (i.e., a fear of helplessness, a compulsion to dominate, narcissism); defined as inner struggles and certain mental and physical disturbances, or as psychoanalyst Karen Horney puts it, strategies used to cope with interpersonal relationship anxieties that over time have taken on the appearance of needs. In her book *Self-Analysis*, Horney grouped those needs into three broad categories: Needs that move one toward others. Needs that move one away from others. Needs that move one against others. Or else or in addition to neurosis, childhood hurt might metastasize into a syndrome (abandoned child, attachment, pedestal/gutter) defined as a disease or disorder with a set of identifying features or symptoms. Or else or in addition to a syndrome, trauma suffered while young might result in a complex (ego, superiority, inferiority, Casanova, Don Juan), what Carl Jung described as archetypal behaviors that result from a "node" in the unconscious.

"How could they think women a recreation? / Or the repetition of bodies of steady interest?" writes poet Jack Gilbert in "Don Giovanni on His Way to Hell." And for the lion's share of The Men, both the simplest and most considered answer is this: their nurturing.

———————

Babies achieve long-term memory at three years old, and while my earliest recollections are from much later, I ain't heard a single story of someone abusing or neglecting me during the years I was developing my psyche. Mom claims I was a colicky baby whom she had to take long drives to mollify (to this day, a car, train, or plane ride works like a sedative); however, from all available evidence, I evinced a healthy attachment to her. The traumas, at least the ones I recall, didn't start till I was school age. Word is, I was precocious and perceptive, and I'm subject to believe that assessment since I reckoned from the time I hit the middle grades that it was my job to assume roles absented by the men in Mom's life, to atone for her heart hurts. At the same time, I loved the man who was then the source of most of them. There's little doubt that Big Chris—Dad—was nurturing me into a future Man on the Scale. There's less doubt that loving, to the extent that I did, a man who dealt my mother incalculable emotional violence proves a failure of empathy, attests that, despite what I've convinced myself, I've never entered her feelings for real, that her grief has remained, to some degree, a space I'm content to accept as cordoned.

Mom deserves credit galore—though this might be the patriarchy in me—for not turning her torment into an interminable parade of men. She chose the wrong partners—what might be the clearest sign of her self-image, of what anyone believes about themselves—but, by and large, she was steadfast in her commitment to those men. And that too was a cue for me. As it stands, the women with whom I've felt most connected have been the ones who've endured (accepted?) my greatest trespasses.

Sometimes I wonder if there's a tiny part of me that wants to punish women for some irredeemable wrong perpetrated against my young self. If there's a mood that dogged my late childhood and adolescence, it was the growing sense that whatever ailed my mother would also sentence me—and my little bros—to suffer. But I also wonder if mentioning my childhood is an attempt at plea bargaining. Like I've told my brothers, don't nobody care when we're grown about our tender-aged woes. We're either a law-abiding, respectable, productive adult or we ain't. For fact there've been plenty men, and I mean multitudes, who had childhoods far, far worse, who had no mother at all or a mother whose love couldn't be felt through her acute abuses, men who've evolved into loving, trusting, faithful, protective, encouraging (fill in the choice trait) caretakers of a single woman's heart. To complain too much or blame my pathology on blighted salad days is the move of an unassailable sucka—and if I haven't said it enough, I pride myself on being sucka's antithesis, and key to that objective has been keeping my head.

Freud compared the id and ego to a horse and rider. The horse provides the energy that propels them forward, but the rider guides the horse's movements. He pointed out that sometimes the rider loses control of the horse and finds himself along for the ride. From my teens into my early twenties (this long before I'd heard of the concept) I was wary of letting my id gallop away from me, was leery of letting pleasure drive my decisions. For as long as I've been grown, or at least as long as I believed I was grown, I've prided myself (which might be a delusion) on self-control, on aforethought, on the power to refuse the urges of my libido, have considered an out-of-control id the foible of a weaker being.

But I've also been guilty of egotism or, in the least, of being someone with an ego affronted with too great an ease. There've been times when I've struck solo to bar or club or function with the clear intent of persuading a woman into a one-night stand. The id had something to do with those missions, but it wasn't the crux of my motivation; that, almost always, was the need to satisfy my ego, to prove to myself that I was still capable, that I hadn't lost the power to, as we say, "make it happen." It was indeed power, one of the few I owned that could be quantified. It suits me right, though, that even in cases of mission completed I realized little pride and even less joy, if joy, in such cases, is attainable at all. It's justice, some might say that what replaced affirmation or its approximate was the sober wisdom that needing proof of my puissance was telltale *Evidence* of being some parts an invalid.

Freud might've judged my lack of satisfaction as evidence that my super-ego was doing one of its jobs, and while I've heard it warning me against this or that act, those admonitions, for the most part, have been whisper-ish. One such case was the time I found out that a woman I was seeing was also seeing a local NBA player—for reasons lucid to me, dude in the league was the pinnacle of someone to date for a young woman from the neigh-borhood—learned the info from a woman who professed to be the friend of the girl I was seeing. With the *Motives* of softening what felt like a blow to my suspect aplomb, gauging my dispassion, and discouraging the friend who fed me the intel from regarding me a sucka for love or, worse, a sucka for like, I persuaded that friend into sex. While the friend must've owned personal *Motive* and *Intent* for aiding and abetting an emotional crime, I did so *Intent* the news of what we'd done would reach the young woman I was seeing, which it did with swiftness, and exact stern chastening. It was premeditated, but I also rationalized that there were men who, in a similar instance, would've hunted for intel on the pro player and used it to slander him to the woman, others that might've gone histrionic and pleaded for the woman to cease seeing him, others who would've addressed the issue with threats or actual violence against the woman or the rival. However, accord-ing to my flawed ethics, none of those responses were keeping it player, that being the unofficial official writ on how to handle romantic interac-tions—and I, for one, needed constant proof that I could keep it player at all times, in all circumstances, at all costs. It all seemed so sensible then (most of what I did had a logic), though it's now clear illogic. And I mustn't for-sake mentioning that, in the end, I still felt affronted, foolish, less than, low.

At my core, I guess there's a need for love, affection, faith, endurance, which, not by coincidence, have also been qualities I find myself faltering to supply the right woman, a good woman, with consistent and equal devotion. Since I've displayed a long-term fear, if not resistance, to returning those gifts (yes, gifts) in kind, I've been guilty of fostering a coercive power over them.

The Men of my era called it "mackin" or "poppin it" or "shootin your shot" or "gettin at em" or "goin for what you know" or "hollerin" or "spittin," and meant approaching a woman. The *Disorganized* ones subscribe to the theory that hollering at several women guarantees them no fewer than one yes. For them it's a numbers game, an exercise in odds. But the *Disorganized* approach, with its dependence on chance, has never appealed to me, has seemed antithetical to the repertoire of a skilled seducer, hasn't squared with my belief that The Men—in those days, some dudes called them a boss-mack-player—must be keen, deliberate, deft. Playing the numbers was like getting rich on the lotto: all luck. The *Disorganized* method was also unappealing because it accrued equal if not more power to the woman, made what happened more a factor of her finding him attractive than his seduction. And couldn't no judge, jurists, or concerned person convince pathologized me otherwise: a Man on the Scale had no business whatsoever happening upon his romantic fortune; his portion should be the upshot of experience, assiduity, charisma, skills—*Organized*. That *Organized* offender discerned signals (a simper, a coquettish glance, a saunter too close to where he stood to be coincidence) and in that sense, each new contact was both premeditated and improvised.

In the poem "Don Giovanni on His Way to Hell," Jack Gilbert writes, ". . . to speak to her without habit / This I have done with my life, and am content." The more I read that verse, the more I judged it counsel. How couldn't I, when from my mid-twenties on I deemed habitual scripts the domain of average dudes and also-rans, when I'd decided my *Methods of Approach* was mega-weak up to dishonorable if it wasn't extemporaneous, that as Gilbert put it, I had to see a woman "in all her fresh particularity of difference." It's easier now to apprehend that what Gilbert suggests is inimical to the telos of The Men, that to divine a woman's particulars is inseparable from confirming her human.

As with all Men on the Scale, my *MO* included sex. But it wasn't sex for the sake of sex; it was sex for the sake of communion, and while it's true I could've established a bond without it, prime intimacy, which was the usual *Intent*, would be much less probable. Sex made a woman more susceptible to loving unreserved, to wishing upon a committed union, and the sincerity of her hope fueled me. But as it turned out again and again, it was a risk of high hazard for the woman, since one of my greatest fears was wagering a deep singular commitment. As a shield against what I perceived as almost assured precipice, I clung to the *MO* of hit-em-and-hold-em-*distant*.

In 1996, I was without question a marauding twenty-one-year-old Man on the Scale. That same year, Nas rapped on "Watch Dem Niggas" that he had no game, rather some women understood his story. His lyrics became one of my tenets, and thereafter I began sharing, with the women to whom I felt most connected, accounts about my childhood that, years before, I wouldn't have uttered to no-damn-body; a few times I did so, while nursing the fool's dream that I could overcome my trenchant fears and forge a true bond. The women, some of them, began to love me or believe they did (is there a difference?). In all of those cases, I perceived their love as largesse. However, it was never enough for one woman to love me. No. No. No. My sense of being unloved or misloved was much too chronic. To fill that void, I needed abundant love, copious love, love and care, love and healing, shape-shifting love, time-traveling love, a love that's more than love, a love that don't exist any-loving-where.

Since no amount of love could appease my need, I evolved what was in effect a *Signature*. The most obvious and persistent component of that *Signature* has been coercing a woman into leaving me rather than vice versa. Attachment-phobe that I've been, I've felt an unceasing need to foster unbreachable distance between me and any wager that exceeds a one-sided half-hearted half-headed long-term commitment. For so long, I judged commitment synonymous with dependence, dependence inseparable from letdown, and that disappointment not a matter of chance but timing and extent. Not a question of *if* it would happen but when it would happen and how much I'd suffer. To hedge against that dread, I'd keep a second, third, fourth woman in my precinct. And without fail, woman one would suspect me clandestine and quest for proof, and almost without fail, I'd furnish it. Most often, I'd deny the charges, be dogged in refuting them, unless, of course, they were flat-out incontestable. The fallout (as mentioned in "Evidence") would often include a woman reproaching me and-or weeping or punching or kicking or scratching me or some combo of physical sanction.

And at some point, points, I'd feel compunctious over the woman's naked hurt and cataract: weep proclamations of the greatest love of all; pledge absolute fealty; promise to protect, at all costs, her happiness; go voluminous on hugs and kisses and-or (if allowed) inspired sex; cop gifts I can't afford; plan dinners or getaways; agree (once) to see a therapist; delete contacts or pictures or videos; block numbers and-or call or text woman two or three or four and announce we'll be seeing each other none, never-no-more—atonement proffered, even if evanescent, with the utmost earnesty. Yes, I'd ply and ply the woman to stay, even though, more often than not, a part of me hoped she'd leave, and that her leaving would relieve me of the terror of being the one who left, would parole me from my self-adjudicated stretch.

Strange as I might sound, I disbelieved in giving up on a woman I cared for (it felt like quitting, like failing, like further proof of my flaws), and I cared for all of the ones I claimed as a partner. Those feelings, however, were insufficient in convincing me to stick it out. Next time, I'd console myself, if she didn't have the nerve to bounce—and she seldom did. And in spite of what I promised her or vowed to myself, I'd live for months or years in the interstices between absconding and staying put, fearful her leaving would afflict me with coldest loneliness, and that since I wasn't wise or loyal or caring enough, her staying was in effect a summons for future suffering. In time, sooner, I'd commit a *mala in se* so egregious, she'd have no choice but to cease our dealings lest she lose something unrecoverable. Once that happened, whether I was relieved or not, I'd feel unmoored, would fret over what to do without partner number one, and quickfast would run to the next woman who was time and again woman two or three.

Serial crimes.

On the subject of such philandering, my most philosophic homeboy once warned, "It's position not possession; not possession but position." His advice, as I construed it, means no one can possess another person, and that no one includes husbands and wives. It warns what a man or woman will or won't do is based more on proximity and access rather than control brought to bear by their partner. "Position not possession; not possession but position" is a safeguard, or so it purports, against the assured error of human beings.

The same philosophic homeboy that advised proximity over property once declared no woman is his; all women are his. He said it, I believe half in jest, but I nevertheless ended up adopting it as a credo, as part of my defense, as yet another pithy caution against authentic feeling. Claiming no woman as mine had the practical effect of mitigating serious and sometimes lethal strife with a man whose passions had turned him foe. None mine, all mine furthermore acquitted me of having to honor, please, protect a woman, a pardon that likewise hedged against the low feeling of failing at sincere attempts to meet her needs.

On the other hand, "all mine" announced no woman was off-limits, that on any given night or day, my romantic luck could change. In some cases, it ushered me as close to intrepid as I would get, swelled—albeit at the expense of women—my battered ego, encouraged me to believe I believed in myself and that that faith would yield a robber's haul.

These days, I read that ethos as damn near a slogan for the Don Juan syndrome, a disorder the writer Michele Novellino describes in her eponymous-titled essay as that of men who derive their esteem—a feeling of worth evermore out of reach—from seducing women.

For as long as I can remember, ambition has been the bedrock of my esteem, what's manifested as an insatiable need to succeed, best each milestone, and in most cases, earn acknowledgment for it. Be that as it may, I can also see how that desire could be interpreted as "the terror of insignificance, of remaining unrecognized by others," that criminologist Steve Hall (et al.) describes in *Criminal Identities and Consumer Culture*. The dread of being nameless and faceless to others, of living in most aspects anonymous, has goaded me again and again. Granted, witnessing women corroborate deep feelings for me, has, on occasion, made me feel as close as I might ever come to significant, I haven't shook with any constancy the feeling that I matter about a Planck in the wide world, that no matter what I achieve, it'll fade quick-fast-alacritous from the mind of others, that in the scheme of things, what I do don't count to the talliers, that the chance to enjoy the fullest measure of feeling seen, appreciated, and as my mama would say, mad-crazy-loved, is forever next—the next thing, the next time. It's quite possible that despite sincere efforts I've devolved into little more than an assemblage of complexes, neuroses, syndromes.

———————

Back when I was a love-letter-penning two-timing grade schooler or a lanky teen skirt-chasing as part of my post-varsity game ritual or an early twenty-something gallivanting in my ride with blasting rap music for a brain, I couldn't have imagined even an *almost* picture-book betrothing.

But there I was, the same year I'd turn forty, traveling with my beloved (for she was without a doubt loved) to her favorite city in the world for her birthday, which just so happens to be Valentine's Day. We flew out on a late afternoon from New York and landed in the City of Love a.m. local time on her Valentine's birthday.

We checked into our hotel and later that morning caught a cab, under a trinity-gray cloud-covered drizzle of a day, to Fondation Louis Vuitton. But weather be damned, spirited us snapped pictures outside the museum and marveled to each other about its architecture, about the green, green of the manicured grounds, about the LV sign above the threshold that resembled molten silver. In fact, our moods were so buoyant, neither one of us much complained about a queue that seemed to reach back across the Atlantic. Indeed, all was right in our universe as we chatted and held hands and inched toward the entrance. Once we made it inside, we decided to tour from the first floor up. We'd wander into an exhibit and snap pictures— can't remember what the rule was on photos, but we took them no matter—of each other near our favorite art. That day, she floated through the corridors and exhibits wearing a long down coat, jeans and sneakers, a scarf (her signature look), and a gray crewneck printed with a giant black heart. The heart on her sweatshirt seemed a portent, as all that morning, I'd been fingering the black velvet box in my pocket that encased her engagement ring—a brilliant stone that was much more than I could afford but that I bought hoping it would turn her ecstatic. When should I do it? I must've asked myself a dozen times, and each time, a spike in my pulse said, *Not here. Not now.* We climbed floors, read summaries of the installations, captured more choice photos, professed how awesome of a time we were having, flickery-eyed fawned over each other. Meanwhile, on the sly, I scouted for the perfect place (privacy being the chief criteria) to pop the question, rehearsed my lines, revised what I rehearsed, reminded myself on which finger I was supposed to place the ring.

In time, we reached the rooftop. We glided to the edge and stood wondering over the old cityscape beneath clouds turned to glowing shapes by the sun, over the people rambling below us, over each other, and while I must've appeared composed, had she lain a hand to my chest she might've felt the kick of a heart fleeing. There were a few dozen or so people on the rooftop, hunting vantage, wielding long selfie sticks for a perfect pose. *Can I do this?* I asked myself. *When, if not now? Where, if not here?* I asked, and fondled the black box for the billionth time.

We wandered into an empty space, and one last time, I scoped to see what roof-toppers, if any, had fixed us in their gaze. Secure that few to none had, I pulled the black box from my pocket, flipped it open, and proffered it. "_____, I love you. You make me happy. And I want to spend the rest of my life with you," I said, a botched version of what I'd rehearsed.

"Uh, are you asking me to marry you?" she said.

"Oh, shoot. Yeah. Yes, that's what I am asking," I said.

"Yes," she said. "Yes, I'll marry you," she said, and beamed, wide as the Seine is long.

Our whimsical day continued: we stood in the middle of the Avenue des Champs-Élysées, the ZOOM of traffic at our sides, and took photos that framed us in the Arc de Triomphe. We visited her friend's restaurant for dinner and feasted—me on a lamb shank big as a dinosaur leg—on Indian food, and she gushed to him about the proposal and flaunted the ring. "I just love it!" she said. "It's perfect." We strolled arm in arm from the restaurant to a park near the Eiffel Tower and took blurry pictures with the leviathan wrought iron twinkling behind us. We nightcapped at the Four Seasons Hotel George V, on the most extravagant cocktails I'd ever purchased in life. It all felt wonderful, wonderful, celestial—and for a moment I believed that I believed in her and us and me like hitherto I hadn't believed in no one or nothing.

But once we returned to New York and some of the stardust wore off, she indicted me on charges of why, on that rooftop, I hadn't kneeled. Pusillanimous as I am, I offered the punk-poor alibi of not wanting to get my knee dirty on the wet ground.

It was an inadmissible-ass excuse, without doubt, but also honest.

However, the most oathable truth is this: I forsook a bended knee because up to the second, I was fearful of a full commitment. And even in a moment that should've excluded all else in the world but us, I judged those certain careless strangers as potential eyewitnesses of my interior weakness rather than possible corroborators of my strength to love.

And in some cases, in this case, an apt sentence looks and feels just like that.

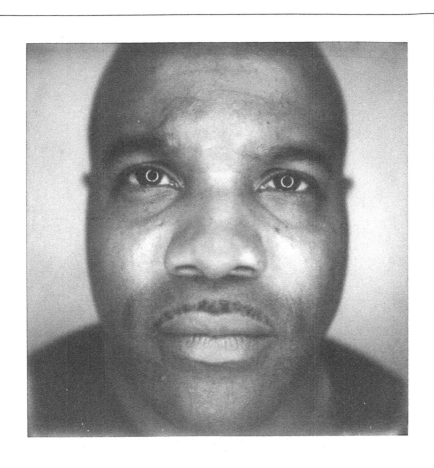

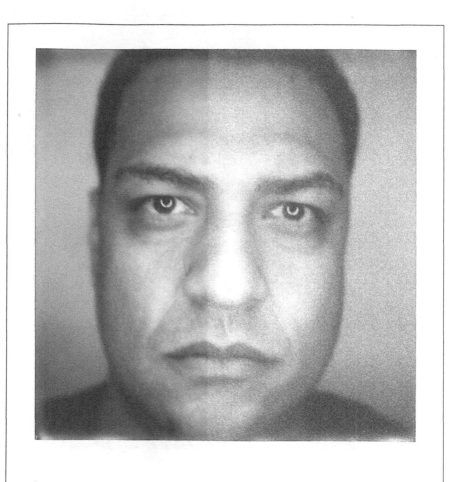

SURVIVOR FILE

You're a Catholic, no patriot, not even, but post a questionable decision to quit college your sophomore year, you find yourself "Sir-Yes-Sir'ing" at a naval base a couple of thousand miles from home. You're the yeoman of your company, which is naval parlance for an enlisted secretary who isn't allowed to carry a firearm. Some kind of sailor, you could say, but instead you treat your job with regard. One duty is assigning a fellow serviceman to, rifle-shouldered, plod back and forth in front of the barracks to protect it, or as you'll describe it years later, to *pretend* at guarding it. Two, three weeks into your yeomanhood, you botch the scheduling and, to cover the mistake, assign yourself to guard duty, and end up a rifleless marching sentinel until a superior happens upon you and asks, "Just what in the world you call yourself doing?" You try to acquit yourself of the blunder, but your superior nor nobody else is buying it. The somebodies that rule your natural life remand you from the San Diego training base to the psychiatric ward of the Oak Knoll Naval Hospital, and there you live among men who swear to voices babbling in their heads, who, in private, harm themselves, whose moonlight shrieking bullies through walls. You'll recall for the rest of your days the many instances of feeling critiqued, feeling more and more gaslit the longer you stayed, but won't recollect the particular tests or the questions they asked to appraise whether or not you're sane. Months into your stay, they order you before the evaluation board, a cadre of navy personnel charged with deciding your fortune. The board probes and probes and asks, as one of their last questions, what you'll do if discharged. "I'd go back to school," you say, say it with faux certainty because you can't fathom what else you'll do with your life, because you don't yet know that fatherhood and its demand of breadwinning is a little more than a year away, because if you stay in the ward, you just might become what they suspect you might be. The navy (thanks be to whom?) deems you unfit for military duty, grants you an honorable discharge, and furnishes a bus ticket. For want of any other clothes to wear, you don your uniform for the days-long Southeast-bound journey passing through a town with a billboard announcing it's "The Blackest Land for the Whitest People"—back to Jim Crow Montgomery, Alabama, a place that, months prior, was purgatory, but in this moment is welcomed respite.

SURVIVOR FILE

You've done it day for day—the whole stretch. Bid down to what's known behind the walls as a wake-up, which is why last night was otherworld when they called your name over the PA to carry your property down for prerelease—a call you've dreamed of for the more than six thousand days you were warned not to count. The morning of, you rise from your bunk, feeling afloat, feeling yourself watch yourself in slo-mo, drone through your morning routine. You swank to the chow hall for your last meal as an inmate and, while you're picking at the food, hear them call your name again (and for the last time?) over the PA followed by instructions for you to report to property. You bop down, see your boxes sitting on the counter, and grant yourself the brief succor of believing yourself at last at last at last on the verge of drawing your first free breath. You imagine the touch of your cheek against the cheeks of your great-niece and nephew, both waiting outside. You sign a series of exit papers, and beam reading the line that confirms you've fulfilled your sentence. "Been waitin for this a long, long time," you say, say it to the CO, yourself, the walls, to all the wide world. "Well, I got some bad news for you," the CO says. "There's a warrant for your arrest, and the sheriff'll be here in a few minutes." The CO produces the warrant and, as if on the warden's cue, a crew of stone-faced COs besiege you. You falter stupefied, but how could you be? How so, with a year and a half's worth of denied parole addresses, with the DOC headquarters having put your transfer to a minimum-security camp on indefinite hold. The troop of COs marches you to a cage and there you sit until the sheriff deputies arrive to transport you to the county jail. You find out soon enough that Washington State has remanded you into civil commitment (CC)—a power expanded by way of that state's Community Protection Act—which allows for the involuntary and indefinite commitment of violent sex offenders. You discover that the End of Sentence Review Committee had been screening you for months, a pre-release protocol for all sex offenders, and that your actuaries scored high enough for CC candidacy. Near the outset of your residence in the North Complex of the Special Commitment Center (SCC), you learn that damn near nobody wins their case. You're warned that since evaluators can devise countless impossible hurdles, and deem a resident deviant or deceit-ful for what seems infinity, men have died waiting to be set free. You spend a year being observed, taking interminable tests, watching men who've lost their trial stagger back to the complex weeping. You spend another year under observation and meanwhile preparing for trial, and though the proceedings are scheduled for a court in Snohomish County (a place known as three-quarters of a white man's land), you feel encouraged knowing you'll argue your case before a black judge, beside a pair of attorneys passionate about fighting CC. The trial lasts six weeks, and in those weeks, the state calls psychologists, old guards, experts, others. You will recall years later the moment one of those psychologists lies during his testimony and a CO who once supervised your pod scrambles to his feet to rebut. Your lawyers ask that same CO if he'd testify on your behalf and he agrees. Your dedicated defense duo also calls a nephew, your grown children, your ex-pastor, your AA sponsor. You slump from the trial each day hoping for divine favor while steeling against a verdict that precedent affirms is quite possible. Your lawyers present a passionate closing statement. The jury deliberates for two days, a span you read as promising since you've heard quick rulings seldom result in the respondent's favor. Then—judgment. The men and women who'll decide your fate shuffle into the jury box. The judge asks the foreman if the jury has reached a verdict. "Yes, Your Honor." The judge asks the foreman if the verdict is unanimous. "Yes, Your Honor. It is." Minding protocol that seems everlasting or at least long enough for a less faithful man to fall dead, the judge asks the foreman to step down and hand the verdict to the court clerk; the clerk hands it to the bailiff; the bailiff hands it to the judge; the judge peeks at the verdict and hands it back to the bailiff; the bailiff hands it back to the clerk; the judge announces a reading for the record. "We the jurors in Snohomish County find that the respondent does not fit the criteria for civil commitment." You hallelujah out of your seat, arms outstretched. "Praise God!" you say. "Oh, praise God." "Praise God!" you say. "Oooooooh, praise God!" The jury foreman drops to a knee and sobs. The bailiff tugs him to his feet. Other jurists whoop and cheer. The judge smacks his gavel, demands order in his court. He waits until the room quiets, calls your last name, announces that you're free to go. "Free to go? Free to go where?" you say. "Free to leave this courtroom," he says. "Wait," you say, and in the next breath ask the judge if he can send you back to the compound. "Are you serious?" he says, and informs you that he'll have your property boxed and sent to you. "Oh, no, sir, not my stuff," you say. "Them folks treated me bad for twenty years. I need to go get my stuff. I leave it to them, half of it'll be broken, the other half missin." The judge explains that he can't ship you back, that doing so would be considered confinement, and confinement at this point is a liability. The bailiff counters that allowing you to return isn't in fact against the law, that if they submit a transport order the SCC will pick you up the next day. The judge asks you how long you'll need. You've been down for almost twenty years by now, which is to say your sense of time is not his sense of time, which is to say, after all this time, what's time to you. "Um," you say. "How about a week?" The judge approves your request and you return to the SCC's North Complex, to gather the memories of almost half your days on earth, to bid farewells to men who may never pack and leave.

SURVIVOR FILE

You resolve the cure for your ailing young marriage is earning a secure living and, after considering options finite as a motherfucka, contact a local army recruitment office. The recruiter pitches enlistment as an experience that'll be tough, yes, but that'll arm you with rare skills, and in due time, a whole platoon of options in the civilian world. You go home and recount the spiel to your wife, and she encourages you, and though you've been no parts of a patriot for as long as you've known what one is, you sign US Army enlistment papers. Uncle Sam sends you straightaway to Fort Benning in Columbus and while basic training is much tougher than even the recruiter warned, you comfort yourself with dreams of solvency, of depositing your base pay, separation pay, cost-of-living pay—all told over two grand a month—into your and your wife's checking account, of earning the stable income that's eluded you since you've been grown—yeah, yeah, all of three years. They grant you exodus near the end of basic training. To prep, you troop over to the PX to buy gifts for your wife and family and while shopping notice your joint checking account is well below the balance it should be. You decide against questioning your wife over the loot and soon catch a flight back home. She swoops you, and the both of you, in the pithy bliss of reconciled distance, spend a few days in a hotel and a few days staying with a friend. Days after that, though, you uncover that unbeknown to you, your wife's been living in a different apartment with another friend and, per sense you won't heed for breach upon breach, has been cheating on you the whole time you were gone. *Well, what the fuck I'm doin all this for?* you chide yourself and, after a couplefew more internal monologues, choose against returning to the base. If finding a decent job was tough before you left, finding one AWOL with a federal warrant nears impossible. You persevere, and in time land a gig as a janitor through a temp agency. And wouldn't you know it, your carousing-ass wife returns. She moves into your mother's apartment with you, and (the nerve) before long begins criticizing your slight checks and living arrangements. Then you trudge home one morning from a graveyard shift and find that your wife has moved out. You call her but don't reach her, phone silence that lasts for days, that extends until you pack the rest of her things, drop them at her friend's house, and leave her a voice message sniping where she can find her shit. You keep working because what else can you do, and nurse the daft hope that reconciliation's within reason, a wish propped by a supervisor's promise to turn your temp job permanent. Before long, somebody from the temp agency calls and informs you there ain't no full-time job offer forthcoming because a sheriff just served you a no-contact order, that furthermore, you've worked your very last day for them and best march on down ASAP to collect your last check. You draft a homeboy to retrieve the check and the order, a document that alleges several instances of mental, physical, and emotional abuse against your wife, that mandates maintaining a strict distance from her. You know the allegations are BS, that the dates she listed for the physical abuse include dates that you were in basic training, but that's a defense you don't dare offer for fear of being exposed as AWOL. You somehow luck another gig and rent an apartment in downtown Portland. Your wife, surprise, surprise, returns. She appeals for marriage counseling (the gall) and you agree. On the first visit, however, she mentions the no-contact order and the therapist refuses to see you again. Bungled therapy be damned, she soon asks you to add her name to the lease. You hut-one hut-two to it, but when management runs a background check, they spy the order, and demand you vacate the unit. You find another place in Vancouver through a homeboy and save enough of your hella-meager checks to buy a hooptie from another homie. While you're driving that ride from a failed DEQ test, your wife riding shotgun, the police pull you over for bad brake lights. The officers run your names and peep the order and (damn, damn) your federal warrant. Sheesh— federal warrants must be a big-ass deal to police in the Couv cause another three cars screech up and turn your arrest into a turret-light siege. You're booked on a Friday night. So you worry over the specter of a hearing for the world's longest weekend. Monday, you find out that because of the federal warrant, the county won't make a judgment on the order, and because of the order, the army won't decide what they'll do about the warrant. You spend a week that feels as long as the Cold War in the county and (is this a surprise?) receive not visit-the-first from your dear wife. Meantime your skull rattles with questions. Meanwhile, your wife agrees to speak to your recruiter—the same grimy-ass dude who, while you were at basic training, tempted your wife into a weekend getaway trip to Fort Lewis—and he claims he can't do nothing to help. Two weeks later you appear before a judge. That judge notes that your no-contact order is set to expire in a week, and you explain (or is it plead?) that you and your wife have reunited under one roof and that you both want the order nulled. The judge finds this a reasonable claim but says he wants to hear from your wife and sets a date for her to appear in court. That date arrives, but your wife don't, and when your court-appointed lawyer calls her cell phone she claims she's too busy to show up and will call him back on her break. You nor the reasonable judge can reason her indifference, so you end up pleading guilty to a violation of your no-contact. The judge recommends seventeen weeks of diversion treatment, zero fines, and the consolation that, at some point, the conviction can be expunged. Hurt as you are about your wife, you feel relieved, though there's still the trouble of the federal warrant to resolve. Weeks later, the army sends word to the county to release you along with a mandate to appear at Fort Sill within seventy-two hours. The army foots a one-way bus ticket to Oklahoma City. You spend half of your first free day visiting family and board a Greyhound for the fifty-five-hour ride. Once you reach the fort, officers explain the possible outcomes of your charge: (1) You could be convicted of desertion, which, since it's wartime, carries a penalty punishable up to death; (2) You could be granted a general or dishonorable discharge; (3) You could be forced to reenlist and serve the rest of your duty. Weeks you wait for your turn to meet the base commander and learn your fate, and in those weeks, they task you with cleaning the barracks, scrubbing the latrine, disassembling army handbooks, clearing trash off the fields, sorting the recycling, hefting loads of garbage, cutting and edging the lawns, drudging hours on a tornado cleanup crew. Weeks, you live in barracks on the edge of the fort, wake early for the calisthenics, and eat your meals in a cafeteria cleared of officers in good standing. At last, judgment day arrives for you and about ten fellow failed recruits and you slug to a room governed by the fort commander and a committee of three. They ask you to explain the circumstances of your case and in the end mercy you a general discharge. You phone your ever magnanimous wife and ask her to buy your bus ticket home and (who's shocked?) she claims she's broke. You call your mother and grandfather and, thank goodness, they grubstake a ticket. Just your lousy luck, though, you lose that ticket (or was it stolen?) in Utah and replace it with what's left to your name save five bucks. With that last five, you buy a big bag of chips, a six-pack of off-brand pop, and two-for-a-dollar packs of cookies—provisions that must last the two days left on your trip. It's near midnight when you arrive at the bus depot in the Couv. Your caring wife was supposed to pick you up but (WOW! WOW!) ain't nowhere in sight nor reachable either when you call her phone, so you borrow a stranger's cell and ring a brother who swoops you and drives you to your apartment. Through a window you see the apartment's damn near empty and dark, so dark. You wait till you can't wait no more, then you bust a window and climb inside. You head straight for the fridge, swing it open, and—it's all but barren. You inspect the rest of the apartment including a second bedroom with sheets strewn over the bed and used condom wrappers littered about it. Your loving wife stumbles in hours later with a pair of dudes and a chick, all of whom reek of weed and liquor. You scream on frick and frack but don't own the energy or the heart to fight. Besides, your wife has gotten so high she worries her heart will stop. You spend the rest of the night comforting her and, against your sound judgment, praying for your marriage to resurrect. In days, you sign up for your mandated domestic violence treatment, you show the counselor your order of seventeen weeks, and he counters that the judge's verdict was just a recommendation, that Washington State law requires a year of treatment at minimum, that if he rules you in poor progress, he can prolong your term. You will spend not one but two years in the program, years that (is anyone out there shocked?) outlast what hopeful, faithful, foolish you believed would endure till death do you part.

SURVIVOR FILE

You wander into your mother's room with a Quran and a cross, ask her for menstrual blood, and when she refuses, march outside, shit in the Quran, smash the cross inside it, and bury the offering in her backyard. In time, you'll visit your first mental hospital, the period during which your mom visits and mourns your long thick nails, your wild hair and mustache, the drool spooling from your mouth; the stretch during which a psychiatrist diagnoses you schizoaffective. That first stay you throw your shit on the wall and try to smother a fellow patient and, per your doctor, hum days after as if unaware of what you've done. "Ma'am, I've been practicing mental health for twenty years," the doctor says. "And I've never seen anything like what your son goes through." Once you try to explain to your mother your episodes. "I know what happens," you say. "Somethin comes and gets me, and it does what it wants with me, and then it brings me back." Your mom implores you to take your meds and you argue they make you drowsy. She encourages you to ask for a lower dose. "But that won't stop the voices," you say. Once you ask her, "How you know I'm not normal? What make somethin wrong with me and not you? Which one of us has the problem—me or you?" Could it be that your illness is an inheritance? Of your thirty paternal siblings, what to make of more than a handful of them suffering serious mental health struggles? What to make of your young son's attempted suicide? One morning your mother leaves you in her house to attend a retreat for recovering addicts, and in her absence, you throw the dishes into the living room and the bathroom and the backyard and onto the front porch, unscrew the doors from their hinges and leave them wrong side up, disassemble the beds and stand the mattresses and frames against the walls, dismantle the bookshelves and nail them to other walls, snatch the drawers out of every dresser in every room, collect your mother's clothes and dump them in the bathtub, board the windows, remove the light fixtures, set a pot of coins boiling on the stove, set a pile of small bills afire in the backyard. Your mom returns and beholds the havoc. "Why, why, why, Son? Why?!" she keens, 9-1-1's the police, and snaps cell-phone photos of what you've wrought. "Why you takin pictures for?" you ask. "So you can tell your own story. You should videotape it, so it can have its own story. Pictures don't tell the right story." There's the time your son's mother leaves you to watch him and his siblings and you visit upon her home like destruction. She returns, eyes the wreckage, wails. "But I didn't do it," you say. Say it though all the children contend otherwise. There's the day, yet again, you mayhem your mother's house, and she, yet again, laments. "But how you know I did this?" you say. "How you know I did it, if you didn't see me do it?" There's the morning you stroll into your mother's bedroom holding a butcher knife and an orange and ask, "Do you feel threatened?" She sits up. "No, Son, actually I don't," she says. "But should I?" You suggest she go for a walk, proffer a wrinkled bill toward the cost of a motel. There's the time your mother returns from another retreat to find you living in her backyard with who-knows-what in a shopping cart. That same week, you knock on her door and ask for food or to use the bathroom and most of those times refuse to leave until she 9-1-1's. Once you find a plastic bat and bash your mother with it until she 9-1-1's once more. So many 9-1-1's. Calls where she implores police to come but not to shoot you and they say, "Miss, we can't promise you anything." Much less often, you phone them yourself and claim your mother has threatened you. There's the day you chase your mother out of her house and, when officers arrive, holler, "Y'ALL WANT ME? OKAY, I'LL COME OUT!" That day you plod out with your hands skyward, drop to your knees, and submit to cuffing. One night your mother summons officers, and they arrive six deep, find you sleeping, and against her adamant protest, Taser you many times over. Another time, you barricade yourself in your mother's house, force a standoff, and who-knows-how-long later, pace out the front door for your mother and officers gripping a rubber ball in one hand and a revolver in the other. That time police draw weapons and aim. "PUT DOWN THE GUN! PUT. THE GUN. DOWN!" they say, while your mother petitions them not to shoot you. There's the time you disappear for weeks and bop blithe as a newborn onto your mother's porch. "Where you been, Son? I been lookin for you everywhere," she says. "For what?" you say. "I ain't been missin. I been with me all week." Once, cinching a belt around the neck of a nephew, you drift past your mother toward her back door. She hysterics after you and seizes her grandchild. "Oh my God, Son, what're you doin?" she cries, before calling who she must. God's truth: it's tough, near hopeless, to believe the next thing that happens will be the last thing that happens, but if there's a blessing at all in your illness, it's the prospect that one near tomorrow you won't remember any of this.

PART 3

What have we endured?

Our repeated petitions answered only by repeated injury.
Curtailing the pursuit of life, liberty, and property.
Control of the labor of one man
for the benefit of another. Laws permitting,
even requiring us to suffer
instability, injustice, confusion,
disabilities and burdens,
a long train of abuses and usurpations,
absolute despotism.
A great Civil War.
Cruelty and perfidy—scarcely
paralleled in the most barbarous ages—
destroyed the lives of our people.

AMERICAN BLOOD

CALL 1

Here's rough copy of a call between Mom and me:

"Hey, Mom? What's good?" I said.

"Oh, it's goin," she said.

"Goin not so great by how you sound," I said.

"Well, I'm tired," she said. "Just came from donating, and oh Lord, it takes a lot out of you."

"Donating," I said. "You still donating. What for?"

"Why else, Mitchell? Because I need it," she said.

"No, you don't," I said. "How much do they pay you anyway? Matter fact, never mind. Whatever it is, I'll give it to you not to go."

"But that's not your place, Son," she said. "This is where I put myself, so I do what I have to, till I don't have to. You know what I say, we can do for a day what we can't do for forever."

"1 PINT, 3 LIVES"

As it turns out, my mama had been donating plasma for much more than a day. We're talking selling pints of her blood parts for near on decades. For those years, twice a week she'd catch a ride or take the bus or the light rail to a for-profit plasma center, a space built to resemble a hospital ward or medical clinic—cool walls, tiled floor, medical posters, workers in lab coats. She'd check in and submit to a process that consumed a couple of hours. Staff would query her about her health, check her vitals, send her to a room full of vinyl beds, clean her venipuncture site, tell her to pump her fist to help the extraction along, jab a sterilized needle in her median cubital vein, and suck a pint or so of whole blood out of her with a plasma-pheresis machine. That machine would separate her plasma by centrifuge and return her red blood cells, white blood cells, and platelets to her. Up

161

until a few years ago, the extraction was followed by the benevolence of pumping a saline solution back into her to help her recover, but in recent times, they'd have her drink water or Gatorade and wait ten or fifteen minutes, while meantime, they loaded her recompense (fifty or sixty bucks is the current market rate) on a prepaid debit card. After all that, Mom would slug off to destination X, which was often home, wherever home was that season, month, week since Uncle George, her middle brother, got her—or should I say *us*, cause we all felt it—kicked off Section 8.

It's wishful to claim my mama was duped, that she shuffled into that first center with the single virtuous intent that her blood was a gift to a person in need, that she expected no more in return than a Samaritan's joy. But I got to be straight with myself if no one else, and the real is, my mama ain't no Mother Teresa. Safe bet she wouldn't see heroics involved in losing her plassing innocence. Mom lost that riding the bus from her gig in the boonies to the downtown bus depot. Rides during which she kept seeing a billboard advertising the money to be made from anteing plasma. Let Mom tell it, this was around the time she was lightweight scheming on a way to make some extra loot without getting a second job. She says day after day after day after day she'd see the billboard and then one day decided to stop in and see what was what. Those first umpteen times she plassed for extra income, but at points—truth be told, more points than my racked mind can stand—her plassing has been her lone source of income. These days, Mom says she can't recall the name of the place she first plassed, claims that she ain't set foot in a center in months. She says her last time was at an outpost of an outfit named CSL Plasma.

Give my mama credit, please, for not getting down with a slouch business. CSL is, depending on whose word you take, either the first or second biggest player in the plasma protein therapies business. And best believe it's BIG business. I'm talking an annual $4B in 2008 (capital *B* as in *billion*) growing to $11B in 2014. CSL Plasma of Boca Raton, Florida, is a division of CSL Behring, a plasma protein biotherapies company out of King of Prussia, Pennsylvania. CSL Behring is a member of CSL Limited of Melbourne, Australia. The other major player is Baxter International, out of Deerfield, Illinois. The rest of the industry's big four, or what the FTC has called a "tight oligopoly," include Grifols of Spain, and Octapharma of Switzerland.

But it don't much matter which country the company calls home. If they do business in my mama's home country, they collect up to twice a week, more than any other first-world nation allows. Our proud nation stockpiles so much plasma, industry folks have taken to calling us the OPEC of the plasma business. But before the US was the OPEC of world plasma, before the industry amounted to capital-*B* billion-dollar big gross, the business of blood transfusion wasn't enterprise at all.

"IT'S NOT JUST BLOOD. IT'S LIQUID LIFE."

Blood banks didn't exist in the early part of the last century. Doctors instead transfused blood straight from the donor to the donee. Since the donor had to travel or hoof to that donee, the British began calling the program Donors on the Hoof, AKA Blood on the Hoof. In 1921, a man named Percy Lane Oliver of the London Red Cross organized the London Blood Transfusion Service—the first citywide panel of health-screened blood-doning volunteers. Five years later, Oliver's service received the backing of the British Red Cross Society and developed into the British Red Cross Transfusion Service, an organization that serviced the whole country.

In the US, researchers were studying blood in an attempt to comprehend how it changed under different conditions and how those changes affected its efficacy when used. In 1929, prominent New York hematologists founded the BTBA (Blood Transfusion Betterment Association) to supply reliable, tested donors on demand as well as funding to researchers. A decade later, September 1, 1939, Hitler's Third Reich invaded Poland and provoked World War II. The ensuing need for plasma in treating wounded Allied soldiers for shock, as morbid as it sounds, was a boon for blood bank research. The next year, 1940, the president of the burgeoning BTBA called a meeting of medical professionals, military leaders, and businesspersons. That collective agreed that, despite plasma collection being in the experimental stage, enough was known to justify an effort to amass large amounts, and also that testing America's competence in supplying plasma to the armed forces of our allies would be of service to the country's national defense.

That same year, Dr. Charles Richard Drew (the first black to earn a doctor of medical science degree from Columbia University) helped set up the first blood collection bank while working as a young resident at New York's Presbyterian Hospital. Dr. Drew, who would become known as the "Father of the Blood Bank," and his mentor went on to help launch the pilot program that became the first Red Cross Blood Donor Center of the World War II blood plasma program.

The initial centers in that program were, by and large, concerned with gathering and sending dried or liquid plasma, rather than whole blood, to Allied soldiers. From the get-go, the centers had trouble fulfilling demand, trouble, that is, until Japanese fighter planes sneak-attacked a US naval base and forced us into the war. The spike in donors post–Pearl Harbor makes perfect sense. Those wartime benefactors were fueled by a love of country, by the belief that responding to the Red Cross's pitch to aid wounded soldiers was a lofty form of patriotism. Unlike my mama, who acted over fears of finite ducats, the early donors gave of themselves with no prospect of pay. Or rather, their profit was the patriot's joy of supplying what might've been the most precious substance to soldiers fighting to preserve and propagate American ideals.

Facts: me and my mama ain't rapped one bit about American ideals nor patriotism; neither can I recall a single serious debate on politics. But since I'd goaded her into dialogues on her blood donating, I figured this was the chance—said, if not now, then when?

CALL 2

Another time, another call:

"So tell me, what's your idea of a patriot?" I said.

"Hmm. I'd say a patriot is someone who believes in their country, who's loyal to their country," Mom said. "A patriot is someone who, whether America is right or wrong, they ride with them. Someone who'd rather live in America than anywhere else. Come to think about it, a patriot is almost like being a mom."

"Almost like being a mom?" I said. "Okay, let me hear you explain this one."

"Because as a mom, sometimes you know your child is wrong, but you still stand by them. You stand with your child through the good and the bad until the final outcome," she said. "Some people see America as a mother. But what if it's the other way around? What if America is the child the patriot must protect?"

"Then I guess that means you're a patriot?" I said.

"Well, I wouldn't say that," Mom said. "But I will say donating is about the most patriotic thing I do. Cause even though I do it because I need the money, I've got to believe that what I give will be put to good use. Shoot, they can't pay you enough for no body fluids. That's priceless."

"BE A HERO. GIVE BLOOD."

Priceless—every damn part of my mama's blood—and don't no one forget it. For fact, it's both priceless and equal in biology to everybody else's on earth. But for some her blood was not, could not, and will never be equal to the twentieth-century compatriots who marched into those first Red Cross hubs during WWII.

For a great many those donors bestowed more than human blood.

They gave American blood.

American blood was born on March 5, 1770, on colonial Boston's State Street. American blood is made of what George Mason declared as man's natural rights: "enjoyment of life and liberty, with the means of acquiring and possessing property, and pursuing and obtaining happiness and safety." American blood is part of Thomas Jefferson et al.'s self-evident truths: "all [white] men were created equal" and owners of "inalienable rights." American blood is Walt Whitman's *America*: "Centre of equal daughters, equal sons, / All, all alike endear'd, grown, ungrown, young or old, / Strong, ample, fair, enduring, capable, rich, / Perennial with the Earth, with Freedom, Law and Love." It's John O'Sullivan defining the country's predestined quest for land. American blood is made of those beloved two-crusted apple pies invented by the Pennsylvania Dutch and ratted blankets stitched to quilts to keep out the cold. It's James Truslow Adams's defining a "dream of a land in which life should be better and richer and fuller for everyone, with opportunity for each according to ability or achievement." It's old and glorious and star-spangled. There are atoms of McCarthyism in American blood, as well as FDR professing, "The test of our progress is not whether we add more to the abundance of those who have much; it is whether we provide enough for those who have little." American blood, as JFK once did, asks "what you can do for your country."

But American blood seldom, if ever, asks, as writer Amy Hempel once did, "Aren't we all . . . somebody's harvest?"

For all her years as America's harvest, my mama, one of the Americans with little, ain't never supplied one drop of American blood. She could not.

To do so she would have to believe in the principles and guarantees of those Dunlap Broadsides, trust that her home is the center of equal sons and daughters. In order for Mom to bleed American blood, she would have to convince herself that what she calls "priceless" is valued in this great homeland of free and brave.

But most of all, to bleed true American blood, my mama would have to be white.

In what's a cold-blooded fact of our great nation's history, there was a point in time when my mama's mama and the adult Negroes of her era were banned from blood bank contributions. And check this: though he was a catalyst for blood donating and given prime opportunities by powerful white folks, not even the fair-skinned Dr. Drew was allowed to break that ban. The policy, of course, didn't sit well with the black press, the NAACP, and Negro sympathizers (tell me why, please, we seldom if ever call them empathizers?), so they took to protesting. Then in 1941 the Red Cross announced they'd accept black blood.

Accept it and segregate it.

I'll call that apartheid blood.

The era of apartheid blood collection aligned with the dying days of Jim Crow, which means pre–civil rights, which how I see it, ain't that long ago. But on the other hand, apartheid blood is based on ideals that form the bedrock of American patriotism. Patriotism, American patriotism, was the not-long-deferred dream of the Loyal Nine and Sons of Liberty, dreams that, we could argue, became, as my homeboys say, "official tissue," when those fifty-six men signed the Declaration of Independence. They risked, by virtue of that vow, beheading as punishment for dishonoring the crown, their financial health, their physical health, and the safety of their loved ones—outcomes that attest to their passionate commitment. But as historian Sarah J. Purcell points out in her book *Sealed with Blood*, American patriotism took hold in the revolution that ensued from that declaration. Dr. Joseph Warren was a surgeon, Harvard grad, and husband of an heiress, president of the Provincial Congress of Massachusetts, leader of the Sons of Liberty, a Masonic Grand Master, and a popular political speaker. Purcell argues that when Warren was shot in the face at the Battle of Bunker Hill, he became the first national war hero and great patriot.

Warren's death was commemorated and memorialized again and again with speeches, almanac entries, poems. And those tactics, while setting precedent for the kind of mythologizing men of means would receive, helped a newborn country define its vision of its most esteemed citizens: not only men who were willing to pay the highest price for the ideals of America but pedigreed white men who were willing sacrifice their lives.

Those men, over the ages, have proven themselves idealists who desire to build America's ethos. Those men have been moved to action on behalf of their homeland. They are territorial and proud to the point of hubris. The patriot, ripe for indoctrination, places high value on regarding the state over the self and believes one can die a myth if death occurs in service of country. Perfect countryman that he is, he hopes he'll bleed thick ichor from a war wound suffered defending his mighty flag. This nationalism has proliferated by symbols, photographs, speeches, news, fine art, fiction, subjective-ass history, et cetera, and since early cinema, via Hollywood's beloved war films.

Mom's quick to profess her hate of war flicks, to argue they glamorize blood and violence and suffering and for no worthwhile end that she can suss. Though I'm no blue blood and would never claim myself a dream-believing apple pie–eating quilt-making flag-waving "Star-Spangled Banner"–singing American, I will admit to indulging in a few World War II flicks and can imagine a scene like the one below—it of a sort I've never witnessed on-screen—about the madness of apartheid blood:

One proud member of the Old Breed, a Mississippian named Skip, is lying in a field hospital somewhere in the jungles of Guadalcanal with his fatigues cut open and a corpsman working to stanch his gushing gut. Outside the tent flying insects big as mammals, incessant rain, and cracks of lightning. Outside the tent, a gun-storm of Arisaka rifles and Brownings and M1 carbines and Springfields and grenades. Inside the tent, the sacred moans of one of Mississippi Skip's wounded comrades. A flustered doc checks Skip's systolic pressure, notes it's 100 and dropping, and sends a corpsman rushing for a bag of dried plasma. In what could be called a miracle, Mississippi Skip (Is there a home state more apt as a namesake?) musters the strength to ask if that package of dried plasma comes from nigger blood. The corpsman eyes the label and nods affirmative. Then, guts still hemorrhaging, Skip says, "Don't put that nigger blood in me. I'd rather die!" The doc attends Skip some more while the soldier blinks and gasps and cries for his mama. The moment before Mississippi Skip's eyes fall shut eternal, he murmurs, "God bless America."

"WEAR YOUR HEART
ON YOUR SLEEVE. GIVE BLOOD."

In his seminal book *The Elementary Forms of the Religious Life*, sociologist Émile Durkheim defines religion as "a unified system of beliefs and practices relative to sacred things . . . which unite into one single moral community called a church, all those who adhere to them." Durkheim asserts that all known religions feature one common characteristic, that is presupposition of all things real and ideal into two distinct classes: the *profane* and the *sacred*. He defines sacred things as those that are isolated and protected by powerful interdictions, and profane things as those that, according to those interdictions, must remain at a distance from their counterpart. Religious rites, he explains, act as the rules of conduct that prescribe how one should behave in the presence of sacred things.

Pew Research Center statistics affirm the United States is home to more Christians than any other country in the world. In a 2014 survey, 70.6 percent of American adults described themselves as Christians. The percentages for Jews, Muslims, Buddhists, and Hindus ran from a slight 1.9 percent to an even more scant 0.7 percent. That study also reported the number of nonreligious respondents at 22.8 percent.

One could argue, given the numbers, that America is a Christian nation. People have also argued that America owns a civil religion. Case in point, Dr. Carolyn Marvin and David W. Ingle, who write in *Blood Sacrifice and the Nation* that America's civil religion is patriotism. But if you ask me, the true American religion is neither Christianity nor patriotism. At the risk of sounding profane, America's true civil religion is whiteness. Whiteness is an identity or a race (for those still out here clinging to what's *been* debunked) but it's also a religion, a faith in which even atheists, agnostics, and religious "nones" can believe. And akin to other religions, kindred beliefs and practices have united its members into a church: The Church of Whiteness (henceforth called The Church). What that church deems most sacred is power, of course, which it has protected with multitudinous interdictions (the slave codes, Jim Crow, suffrage, mandatory minimums, excessive force, redlining . . . shall I go on?).

Marvin and Ingle also reason that violent blood sacrifice, in spite of challenging our ideas of civilized behavior, causes enduring groups to cohere. And if that's so, then answer me this: What group has coerced more material wealth in this land than The Church? And what group has unified The Church more than those coerced into a black race?

The stories of men like Joseph Warren, the country's first great patriot, making mortal and other sacrifices to secure the good fortune of their race, nation, church, are exalted (and I'll admit it's often righteous lauding). Because let The Church reverends preach it, there ain't no higher deed than an esteemed member of the flock consecrating his greatness by sacrificing American blood.

Since time immemorial "civilized" nations have sacrificed their young or old or poor or imprisoned, so much so that it has seemed decreed. The Incas sacrificed prisoners and children to the Gods. The Aztecs sacrificed captured rival tribesmen to the sun god. The Mesopotamians drove sharp pikes into the heads of palace attendants and handmaidens, so that they could serve their royals in the next life. The Etruscans offered the sick and low status among them in exchange for the eternal life of their ancestors . . . America has sent scores of Mississippi Skips for possible slaughter. This of course is a necessary element of building and protecting a prosperous nation. For those who fight and bleed American blood, there exists the prospect of gaining the bounties of Church membership upon their return. And should they be killed in combat, they can be comforted, if there is such succor in death, by the conviction that their actions have secured privileges for posterity, by the promise of being resurrected by The Church as a beatified patriot. But what about those who will never be one of the flock, who can't count on realizing equal rewards for their roles in America's wars?

On July 5, 1852, a spirited Frederick Douglass addressed a group of abolitionists gathered to commemorate the signing of the Declaration of Independence. Douglass stood at a lectern in Rochester's Corinthian Hall, his backcombed natural not yet graying. In his speech, he challenged not just his audience but his country:

> What, to the American slave, is your Fourth of July? I answer: a day that reveals to him, more than all other days in the year, the gross injustice and cruelty to which he is the constant victim. To him your celebration is a sham; your boasted liberty, an unholy license; your national greatness, swelling vanity; your sounds of rejoicing are empty and heartless; your denunciations of tyrants brass-fronted impudence; your shouts of liberty

and equality, hollow mockery; your prayers and hymns, your sermons and thanksgivings. With all your religious parade, and solemnity, are to him, mere bombast, fraud, deception, impiety, and hypocrisy—a thin veil to cover up crimes which would disgrace a nation of savages.

Douglass was dead-on about the white man's Fourth of July jubilees being a mockery to enslaved blacks, but his stance could also be construed as discounting the deeds of the heroic black men and women, handful that they were, who helped America break free from the crown. We could also use the Fourth as a chance to celebrate the strength of those few black soldiers, could cite it as proof that they, in their deeds, were patriots of the highest order, had shown an allegiance to America that those of European descent couldn't and won't ever reach. Those black Union assets were the ultimate patriots because they had to have understood there was no chance of them being granted access to what was at that point the more than 150-year-old Church of Whiteness. Unlike their runagate brethren, who fought for the redcoats under Lord Dunmore's decree that former slaves would receive freedom in victory, they couldn't even be assured that winning would free them of bondage, or effect redress for what heretofore had been *alienable* rights to life, liberty, and the pursuit of happiness. That consciousness, the constant torturous discord of fighting for a liberty that might've remained at large, is the nexus of what made those rare black Revolutionary War soldiers the paragons of American patriotism. No less than superpatriots.

———————

What follows is me envisaging Douglass summoned to present-time DC for a commemorative Fourth of July speech:

Picture him before a crowd of politicians, moguls, activists, (connected) concerned citizens, a cross-section of American poor folk including my mama. He saunters from behind the curtain looking 1850s clean in a tail-coat with a fresh white shirt gleaming under his double-breasted vest, not to mention fine long trousers and side-lace boots. He stands erect, relishing his applause, smooths his backcombed hoary Afro, and squints into the spotlight. "Mr. President, friends, and fellow citizens. He who could address this audience without a quailing sensation has stronger nerves than I have," he begins. He once again laments the legacy of Independence

Day, the effects of oppression, and the state of these degenerate times. He glides to the edge of the stage and casts his eyes to the blackness beyond the last row. "My business, if I have any here today, is with the present. The accepted time with God and his cause is the ever-living now," he says. So, I ask these years hence. What, I beg of you, what to the scions of slaves and this nation's poor, is American patriotism?

The obvious answer is not a damn thing! People as poor as my mama, poorer, never had no real action at life, liberty, and the pursuit of happiness. And if *patriotism* means even a smidge more than nothing to some of them, it means much, much less than it does to the heirs of those who were never disbarred from those nascent blood banks, whose life matter was never on the less-than side of apartheid blood, whose dried plasma Mississippi Skip would have never refused, and whose phenotype qualifies them for Church membership.

It's been more than seventy years since the "Father of the Blood Bank," and every other black being was banned from contributing blood. And the restriction on mixing the blood donations of blacks and whites was lifted in 1950. But, in essence, the billions business of blood donating has been built on another kind of apartheid: The Haves versus The Poor, Colored, Othered. Or those who are all three, like my mama, who twice a week slug into centers owned by CSL and the rest of the big four and ante 100 cc's of plasma for a measly-ass sixty bucks. Even if donors like Mom are encouraged by a belief they're supporting the welfare and prosperity of their country, they must contend, like those old superpatriots, with the bewildering dissonance that issues from believing in a republic that in numerous ways has forsaken them, from being compelled against their interests to foster the persistence of The Church, from being chosen again and again as a sacrifice to its God.

While the antagonist that unifies The Church has shifted over the centuries from blacks in chief to the poor and colored and othered, the practice of most often selecting the lowest ranks of The Church and those outside it as offerings has changed little. Sometimes the ceremonies occur in an alien land during a time of declared conflict. But often they happen at home, on streets that, for folks like my mama, have been anything but a sanctuary. For legions, their blood will be let one way or another and sometimes one way *and* the other whether they believe in America or not.

"EVERY TWO SECONDS
SOMEONE NEEDS BLOOD."

As proof, I offer this: one day in the late 1980s Mom got a call from Uncle George. He called frantic after returning from work to find his crib emptied, by his woman and her mother, he assumed, of almost every single thing of value. Mom drove the Interstate Bridge into Vancouver, with my infant brother Adrian, the youngest of her three sons, strapped in the backseat of her brown-and-tan Mercury Montego MX Brougham. Mom motored to her brother's assistance carrying on her person the $1,700 paycheck she'd earned from her job as a nurse's aide. Mom met her discomfited middle brother (Uncle George was an emotional sort) at his looted apartment and, when she couldn't console him, offered to help him locate his woman and the belongings he believed she pawned. They checked the nearest pawn-shop first and found a couple of his things, a discovery that inspired hours more of hunting for sign-the-second of a possession and-or sight-the-first of his woman. Meanwhile Mom, who was against lugging her infant boy in and out of a car, trailed Uncle George in her Montego, and in time began urging him to abandon his search. Unc wasn't hearing none of that, though, so Mom, in the end, had to leave him.

She arrived in Portland belated for bank hours but not mall hours, and since Mom's motto has been shop as soon as bucks touch her palm, she cruised to the check-cashing store and huffed inside with my baby brother wedged on her hip. The second she got inside, she peeped a pair of suspect dudes stealing glances at her. Mom, ever vigilant, requested the teller hand her the bills minus the custom of counting them aloud.

Mom carried my toddler brother and her uncounted bucks out of the check-cashing store and into her car—head swiveling the whole time to see if the furtive twosome or anyone else followed. She strapped my brother in his seat and stuffed the bills in her bra and socks and would've drove straight to the mall if she hadn't promised my great-uncle John, the last of Mama Edie and Bubba's adopted children, that she'd pick him up from a friend's place. That friend's place (major side-eye to this) was the infamous Mallory Court apartments. Mom pulled up to the complex, and given this was that prehistoric epoch before cell phones, she honked her horn and waited for my great-uncle to come jittering out of a building. He didn't. In the meanwhile, my baby brother fell asleep. Mom idled with no sign of

Great-Uncle John. She tarried until she was at risk of the mall closing, and since she wasn't about to forfeit a chance to blow a paycheck, she climbed out, locked my snoozing brother inside in his car seat, and hustled into the complex to find the address Great-Uncle John had given her.

Mom wasn't more than a few steps into the apartment's courtyard when somebody pushed her down and snatched at her purse. Feisty, she fought back. And that's when the dude started whooping on her something vicious. "HELP! HE'S ROBBING ME! HE'S ROBBING ME! SOMEBODY PLEASE HELP!" she wailed to the dozen or so witnesses, not one of whom intervened. The man beat and stomped and kicked Mom until she believed she would die, until she felt the lone way to stay alive was to play dead. So, dead she feigned until he stopped, until the crowd dispersed, until all she could hear was the thrum of her heart. She waited longer still before she got up and hobble-winced back to the car, with blood leaking from her head, face, and who knows where else. Thank God, Great-Uncle John was leaning against the Montego, a guardian of sorts over my slumbering baby brother.

The next time I saw my mother, which was either that night or the next morning, she was limping like she might need a bionic knee, painted with scrapes and bruises, and had a raw gash beneath her eye that should've been stitched but never was.

There are countless ways to be bloodletted in this republic, and I pray it doesn't happen again to Mom in the street, hope too that she's sold the last parts of her blood to a megacorp. But who knows, maybe one of Mom's pints spared a soldier in Iraq or Afghanistan, will aid a wounded Mississippi Skip in Syria. If Mom submits to plasmapheresis again, perhaps her blood parts will treat a burn victim or hemophiliac or kid with HIV. Maybe when it's time to give account in her church, our church, there will at least be that.

CALL 3

Another one of our calls:

"What else can you tell me about donating? I want to make sure I didn't miss nothin'," I said.

"Oh, I don't know, Mitchell," she said. "I think I've pretty much covered it. But if you really want to know, you'll go see for yourself."

"Me, donate? No way. I can't do that. I can't let them folks stick me. You know I'm scared to death of needles."

"So was I," Mom said. "But I guess that means you don't want to know that bad."

"That's not true," I said.

"Well," she said.

"BLOOD DOESN'T GROW ON TREES."

"Where's the best place for a CSL Plasma center?" tis the question I ask myself. Is it Lake Oswego, the richest neighborhood in my city? Or is it the Pearl District, in a renovated warehouse that costs the adjusted net worth of a founding father? Should it be in West Linn, where the median household income is near six figures? It makes sense to me to open a branch in one of those wonderlands, out where there's unassailable evidence of America the Beautiful, the virtues of American patriotism, out where reside the favored citizens who could bleed American blood. It seems sensible to put it right smack in a neighborhood where an appreciative congregant of The Church could wake up on a Saturday, don a flip-collared polo shirt and khakis, drive his weekend ride mere blocks, and ante a pint of plasma for dogma's sake.

Now there's a win-win-win if there ever was one.

Truth: the CSL my mama once frequented ain't nowhere near suburban life. It's located out on 162nd Avenue and Glisan—The Numbers.

One morning, I wheeled a rental car out there from Northeast. The first thing I peeped when I pulled into the lot was a cigarette outpost the size of a shack. The roof was decaled with cartooned cigarette packs and the words "SMOKE 4 LESS" in leviathan. Its walls were plastered with tobacco posters and price specials. The rest of the lot was near full with cars. A dented Jeep Cherokee. An old Chevy pickup with a U of O sticker in its back window. And more Saturns than I'd ever seen in a parking lot that didn't sell them. I circuited the lot, spied a man sitting against the building with his face pressed into his knees. Saw a pair of twenty-somethings strapped with backpacks skulking near the entrance of CSL—the guy tugging a mangy German shepherd; the woman dragging one of those dogs that don't never look grown—and keep right on past it. A dude I recognized from high school rolled through the lot in an old-school Oldsmobile with his trunk *BOOM-BLAPPING!*

The second I ducked inside the center, I was struck by the dread of being outed as an intruder, by the feeling that someone I knew would spy me and spread news of it on a neighborhood wire, and that that news would birth the rumor I'd fallen on hard times, or worse, dog me as a mandate to explain my motive. The room, in a stroke of good luck, was peopled with strangers: A frowning girl with her shirt hiked up over her belly. A slim guy wearing an oversized T-shirt, jeans from another era, and his socked feet crammed in slippers. An older dude donning a neon T-shirt and checkered shorts with his hair blown every-which-way. And damn near everybody looked as if surviving to next week wasn't foregone, a vision that made me wonder if Mom had ever slogged through the doors wearing her desperation in plain view. From what I hoped was an inconspicuous distance, I read posters and small placards hanging from the textured cream-colored walls. From behind a counter, worker bees in lab coats and rubber gloves dropped what resembled needles into metal trash cans lined with plastic. One of the workers nodded, what's up, and in an instant, I singled him out as someone who might assist.

That dude rambled up to the counter. He wore a white shirt with rolled sleeves and slicked dark hair, was about the only one of them not dressed like a chemist. "Can I help you?" he asked. "Yes," I said. "I was thinkin about donatin, but wanted to get some info first." Dude smiled, plucked a card from a counter display, handed it to me. The card read, "Giving has its rewards. Donate plasma. Save lives. Earn up to $200/mo.*"

Dude (why I failed to ask his name, who knows) suggested I read over a pamphlet. He also offered to explain.

"Sure," I said. "That'd be great."

"Well, first you'll need a valid ID," he said, and explained that I'd also need to bring a Social Security card or some other official doc with my SSN. He clarified that if my address wasn't current, I'd need to prove where I lived, with maybe a recent gas or light bill. Dude lectured: Plasma is in essence the water portion of my blood, and the other parts would be put back in me. "The water part gets extracted through a process called centrifugal, which whips it around at like sixty thousand times per second," he said. "Then after that happens, they ship it to one of their many warehouses, where the plasma sits for a year to make sure it's safe to use." He reported that with parts of the safe plasma, the company makes lifesaving medicines for hemophiliacs and burn victims and all kinds of other victims. "We aren't just a donor center," he bragged. "We're also a pharmaceutical company too." He informed me that I could donate twice a week, assured me the threshold was deemed safe by the FDA.

"What's cool is that, after you donate, we put the money on a debit card,"

he said. "So, you can get it on the spot." He followed his pitch with an anec-
dote about a time, while working at a post in Denver, he helped a twice-a-
week donor check his balance and discovered it was over three thousand
dollars! Dude claimed the donor announced he wouldn't be seeing him for
a while because he was using his balance for a trip. Dude went on to brag
that he'd been donating for years, even showed me an old needle scar near
a vein in his bicep, bore the pock the way a proud vet might flaunt a combat wound.

Straight-faced, he claimed there're seldom side effects from plassing,
that he could go hiking or backpacking right afterward. "But," he cautioned. "You might want to test it out a few times to see how you feel." He
handed me another legal-sized foldout. It read, "Donating Plasma Saves
and Improves Lives." The foldout showed a cheerful white boy, a smiling
black woman who appears close in age to Mom, and an older white man—
smart glasses, straight teeth, light scruff—of a sort who bleeds patriotic and
pays his tithes.

THE POSE

One of my least favorite of our live-for-now cribs was a run-down place off Killingsworth, a decrepit two-bedroom with a kitchen old as the Oregon Trail and shag carpet that no matter how many cleaning contraptions we rented from the grocery store, never ceased smelling too much of mildew.

One night, Dad and I were lying on a ratty blanket splayed over rank carpet, Dad meaning Christopher, Chris, Chrissy, Big Chris, Big Daddy Chris, Crisco, Pimpin Chris, Chris-Cross the Ho's Boss. The man had AKAs and BKAs. He was schooling me, spooling a new story or a refurbished version of an old one, a spin recounted with pimp verve and-or the beguile of a man whose very breath depended on being the object of a gaze, of turning even the wariest of listeners (to say nothing of a budding sycophant like me) into a zealous believer.

Dad got around to rapping about his time in the penitentiary, about being locked up with an infamous criminal (a claim I never once felt compelled to fact-check), about having to shank a fellow inmate for a violation of an inviolable prison code. He was gassing me on the kind of heroics that made me believe him more of a man than most if not all of the men in my life and because of this there I was, pre my growth spurt, with cherub cheeks, listening rapt as a motherfucka.

Dad spun a few prison tales and, for whatever reason, he shifted to philosophizing about the opposite sex. He bestowed me, at some point that night, with what he must've felt was the gift that would give in aeternum.

"Say, Cubcheck," he said. "When it comes to a female, you keep your head down and your palm up. You keep your head down and your palm up." The lights were off, and he got up in the semidark and mimed the pose more silhouette than all else. "You hear me, Cub? Keep it head down, palm up," he said.

Can't remember what he said beyond that, but it wasn't nowhere near as affecting as the bit of life advice I have come to call The Pose.

THE POSE

The Pose is handy as shit; scratch that, The Pose is vital as shit for any working pimp. Cause if he can't *check* his *ho* for all she's worth—her worth being what she can earn and-or scheme upon by any means save those that would leave her maimed or dead—then he may starve, then at the least he may fall short of what he believes he's most hustling for: money, a rep, esteem. The Pose is utile because it reminds the pimp of his prime motive and modus in one, which is no small thing. But it ain't all sweet. The Pose also bespeaks the psychic and emotional harm that happens to anyone who dares adopt it. Clamp your eyes and picture it. Can you see it coded in the posture, see how distant it is from a Buddhist bow or Christian genuflection or a Muslim in prostration; can you see how it fails to suggest deep respect or deference or greeting or grace or love? Yeah, you might clock a few bucks with it, but what my dad never let on was how The Pose with its bowed head and lowered gaze is also an act of shame, an acknowledgment of a pimp's role as a victimizer. It's an implicit warning for the pimp, cautions, Don't Look! Because looking at her or, worse, into her is to risk perceiving what makes her human—a job hazard if ever there was one. For it would take a rare brand of misanthrope to pimp on a human being. This is why for most pimps, though he might believe her an apple, a *ho* is never human. Nor a woman. Nor nowhere near a lady. No matter what or who she is elsewhere in the world (mother, aunt, sister, cousin, friend), for the pimp, the *ho* is but one thing: a conduit to electrifying his get-rich-or-else dream.

Us uninitiated shouldn't forsake the rest of The Pose, especially that outstretched palm. Or rather, the hand of need masquerading as a hand of demand—or vice versa. It's a pose too because the astute pimp knows in his naked heart that, in essence, he's never much more than a charming dependent, that if his pimp hand is outstretched for long with no recompense, his demand could morph to pleading and his pleading to begging. It's also a pose because he can't evade the overtruth that he's hurtling on a fuel-injected Cadillac ride to the poorhouse if his *bottom broad*—the one most committed to his cause—chooses a new pimp; and-or one or more of his *stable* falls disabled or sick; and-or turns contemplative, disgruntled, derelict; and-or fosters a friendship with a *renegade ho* who persuades her to follow suit, et cetera, et cetera, et cetera. And because precipice is always close at hand, there's zero room for a pimp's contrition. He must treat empathy for his *hos* as kryptonite, must figure a means to maintain prime distance between him and her. And many a pimp fosters this distance by abiding tenets and by learning and accepting and espousing pimp-centric scripts—one could call it a manifesto.

There are scores of retired or out-of-work or out-of-vogue pimps (a couple of my uncles among them) who've transitioned to full- or part-time preaching. Of those men, most, as most of the colored men of the cloth I know, turn their sermons into Bible knowledge challenges. But what if instead of God's word, the most gifted in-it-for-bread-and-meat-and-roof pimp-turned-preachers delivered their eager congregations the pimp's manifesto:

Picture one such rhetorician in the pulpit of a Baptist church suited and booted in a revived sharkskin suit, old reptile kicks, and just-out-of-pawn pinkie ring. Imagine stained-glass windows on all sides and some European's vision of Jesus looming large behind him and rows upon rows of pews decked with worn Bibles and hand fans printed with the face of MLK. Imagine the room teeming with acolytes—men with eyes and hearts wide open to revelation, inspiration, affirmation, dominion. The pimp-turned-apostle floats to the best-lit side of his pulpit. He pauses for effect and turns gleaming eyes toward a promised land. Mind the rules, he says. There ain't no love in pimpin, he says. When the game begins, friendship ends. Don't ever forget, the game is sold not told, he says. Trust nothin but the game, and don't black eye it, he says. Plan your work and work your plan. Keep it purse first and ass last, he says. Keep your *ho* in arrears. Don't turn down nothing but your collar, and keep your front up till you come up. He floats from one side of the pulpit to the other and slicks a Jheri curl receding at his temples and silvered on the sides. He gazes at the crowd and goes on. Pimp with your brain not with your balls, he says. Stay in high pursuit of a new prostitute. Don't chase em; replace em. Better a turnout than a burnout. Don't believe the hype. Pimp like you're ho-less. Get in a ho's head. Turn a new *ho* and play the new *ho* against the old *ho*. Don't never forget, pimp is what you do, not who you are. He struts onto the floor, loosens his tie, wipes sweat from his brow. He takes a breath and continues. Tell a ho, pimpin and hoin is the best thing goin. She's qualified to be satisfied. Let her know, it's choosin season, so choose a real pimp. He says, tell a *ho* to make her next move her best move. You don't need her; you want her. That it ain't a force thing, it's a choice thing. That your history is no mystery. She fucking with a pimp that's internationally known, nationally recognized, and locally accepted. He roams between the pews, touching the shoulders of his congregation. It's Gs up and *hos* down. Tell her to get it with lips, hips, and fingertips. That it's one team, one dream, and that teamwork makes the dream work. To stay ten toes down and it's greater later. The blasphemous minister clambers back onstage. He kisses his pinkie ring and makes the sign of the cross. My fellow pimps, go forth and tell all the *hos* this: Ask not what your pimp can do for you; ask what you can do for your pimp.

CULTURE FILE

My dad—Big Chris—would've got a chuckle out of my make-believe sermon. He was at the ass end of his pimp career when he told me about The Pose. Still, I'd seen it afford him, according to the unofficial pimp index, the best of times: settled monthly bills and pockets stuffed with fuck-off funds, Eldorados and Coupe de Villes on Trues & Vogues with fluffy white dice hanging from the rearview, gold nugget rings, watch, bracelets, Stacy Adams and alligator boots, designer European threads from the city's choice boutique. . . . But material wealth wasn't the nexus of why The Pose seemed so attractive to him, his patnas, his era. To fathom why that thinking, that life, attracted so many back then (please believe me when I tell you, pimps ain't born; they're forged) we must consider what shaped them. They were the native sons of invisible men, born around the time The Keepers ceased Emmett Till's life. Men who as boys heard grown folks harangue the white man martyring Medgar, Malcolm, and Martin and making a seraphim angel of Fred Hampton. As impressionable boys, they witnessed grown folks riot in Watts and Detroit, ogled news footage of Johnson signing JFK's Civil Rights Act into writ. That act all but nixed the rallying effect of an explicit foe but did little, in the immediate, to uplift them and theirs. For all their adolescence, Old Glory got trench-foot steel-toe stomped by Vietcong, a war that might've claimed an older brother or favorite uncle for reasons nebulous at best. As young bucks, they started believing the old heads' calls for solidarity were hella less pressing, sat passive while the Black Power and Black Arts movements burned to embers. They suffered a poverty most of them couldn't divine when the black intelligentsia and artists fled to Liberia, Ghana, Switzerland, France, and elsewhere. It wasn't no more dashikis and globe Afros for them; it was full-length chinchillas and processed hair.

Dad and his cohort were too cool, so hip, they revised the cool man's greeting from "What's happenin?" as in, "What's going on in your world?" to "What's up?" as in, "Tell me what's going good or don't say shit." Media made them the prime targets of pimp propaganda with books: Iceberg Slim's *Pimp*, Donald Goines's *Whoreson*, not to mention titles by less notable scribes. *Sweets and Other Stories*; *The Life: The Lore and Folk Poetry of the Black Hustler*; *Black Players: The Secret World of Black Pimps*; *Gentleman Pimp*; *Gentleman of Leisure: A Year in the Life of a Pimp*. Books, yes, but movies too: Check *Willie Dynamite*, *J.D.'s Revenge*, *Super Fly*, *The Mack*. Books and movies, sure, but music too: Curtis Mayfield's "Superfly," Andre Williams's "Cadillac Jack," Don Julian and the Larks' "Shorty the Pimp." Books, movies, and music, of course, but also comic champions: Redd Foxx, Dolemite, and Richard Pryor at their ribald best. Scores of them marveled at the televised pimp pageant that was Ali vs. Frazier, and later spent umpteen weekends woofing over the scorecards of a middleweight slug-out on *Wide World of Sports*, dreamed of posing ringside in Caesars Palace for Hagler vs. Hearns or Sugar Ray vs. The Hands of Stone. They came of age in the decades of unquestionable black predominance in the NFL and NBA, an era that plagued them with grandiose beyond-their-reach images of black riches. Picture Walt Frazier striding into MSG in a feather fedora and velvet suit, or Wilt the Stilt holding court with reporters in suspendered slacks, a silk muscle shirt, and gold chain. Theirs was a generation high-octane fueled off watching a decade of white folks flaunting excess on network TV: *Magnum, P.I.*; *Dynasty*; *Falcon Crest*; *Dallas*; *Lifestyles of the Rich and Famous*. I'm talking the moments before and right after Cosby dared pitch NBC Clair and Cliff et al.—AKA a functional black family. These men were born circa the same time as Michael Jackson and grieved their icon moonwalking away from his blackness in penny loafers and glitter socks. Dad and his cohort saw their kinfolk, friends, aceboons, associates get high or hooked or rich on powder coca-ine, pills, or heroin . . . And please oh please oh please, tell me who, tell me what would the confluence of those facts beget?

SCENE FROM THE SON OF A PIMP

Weekends my dad and uncles X, Y, and Z and his other patnas (uncles by association) would lounge in the second-floor living room of his mother's house—Grandma Nancy to me. Imagine a handful of young black men on cool factors of a zillion and cologne overload. Picture them sporting moisturized Jheri curls and velour sweat suits and oz's of gold jewelry. One of them would be charged with rolling Zig-Zag joints on a shoe box top while the others puffed and passed a previous rolled joint and, in arguing over whatever game or match was on the tube, touted an unimpeachable high sports IQ. Meanwhile, I'd sit among them, inhaling nosefuls (I've always loved the smell of weed) of what they called "killer," and tracking as best I could their banter. This was an easy task until the topic, as it always did, switched from sports to some aspect of grown folks' business, which at that time more often than it didn't concerned pimping. At that point, their speech would become almost impossible for me to interpret—reason being Dad and his patnas had invented a language indigenous to them, and maybe them alone, a specialized pimp speak that it took till I was grown to discover was a hybridized pig latin, a seemingly mystical tongue that sounded like this: "the gizzinaine, bizzinaine on the ninzzzaine up and pizzinained maine." Their chatter bewitched me to no end, catalyzed the childhood belief that Dad was a lowercase-g god. Dad's first acolyte was Uncle Z but those coded afternoon powwows were also a kind of prep school for me. "I'm surprised you ain't try your hand at the game," Uncle Z once said to me. "Cause we raised you to pimp."

WHITE SLAVES

One summer day, I was balling at Irving Park. This particular day there was a good-sized crowd. Dudes posted courtside in slouch-necked tees and tenny shoes, dudes wearing an old practice jersey with a headband and sweaty knee brace, next-on-the-court quartets circled on the sloped grass, loners lying in a spit of shade with their necks propped on an indoor-outdoor Spalding. This particular day there were girls scattered among us too, a girlfriend or two minding the water bottle or Gatorade of her sweaty unarmored knight; duos and trios of girls beneath the horse chestnut trees farther back; here and there, others who'd paired their tank tops and tight T-shirts with high-cut shorts; and still others dressed in sundresses and sandals. That picture-book afternoon a dude the whole neighborhood knew was a prime pimp (for the sake of what might be his freedom let's call him D) rolled his sun-colored Corvette right into the park and pulled up so close to the courts it was a dare for us to pay him small mind. D hopped out looking buffed and shined and downright nigger rich in a silk shirt and shorts with loafers and a royal ransom's worth of gold jewelry. He strutted over to the sideline, asked around for who had next game, and stood among us, the cynosure, chatting with a few idlers. Once his game arrived, he doffed his chains and gold Rolie, sauntered over, and asked me (why me is hard to call, but maybe he peeped my barefaced fawning) to hold them while he played.

D's gold had heft, and to keep it all the way funky, I felt honored to hold it. Can't remember how many games he played, but I do recall him impressing me and I'd bet other witnesses too—almost everyone present was a current or former high school or college hooper—with how well he balled in his loafers, with how agile, stylish, and graceful he was, with how he seemed to own the utmost aplomb. While I wouldn't go so far as saying he made me want to pimp, he for damn sure succeeded that day in making his life look appealing.

That summer and summers more, you'd see D high-beaming around town—a white girl sitting shotgun—in a pimp ride with custom rims and conspicuous Hawaii license plates. The plates I recognized as proof of his status as a cross-country, AKA an intercontinental, AKA a tall pimp, all denoting a man with the skill and moxie to work his trade all over the bubble. D was just the kind of audacious high-profile pimp that the Feds decades prior drafted a law to thwart.

Dudes like D, who send women (or worse, underaged girls) across state lines to sell sex for their profit face stern punishment: the United States White-Slave Traffic Act, AKA the Mann-Elkins Act, now best known as the Mann Act. The Progressive Era legislation can be traced to four key figures. The first was Clifford Roe, a former Chicago state attorney, who was partial to the incipient anti–white slavery movement (emphasis on *white*) and in the early 1900s was publicizing his prosecution of cases involving white women he believed had been forced into sex work. Another key figure was a seventeen-year-old girl named Sarah Joseph who was duped into working in a Chicago brothel. Joseph's case helped Roe stoke increasing public concern over white slavery (stress, again, on whiteness). The third key figure was Illinois representative James Robert Mann, who rushed his namesake bill on white slavery (key word: *white*) through Congress. And the last but no less vital figure was President William Taft, who, in 1910, signed into effect an act that criminalized "any person who shall knowingly transport or cause to be transported . . . any woman or girl for the purpose of prostitution or debauchery, or for any other immoral purpose . . ."

As you might've gathered, the rub was those social reformers didn't include black sex workers among those forced into the trade. But while the act didn't in specific cover black women or any other woman of color, federal prosecutors hesitated not charging black men (no matter their station) with offending it. Heavyweight champ Jack Johnson, who'd angered the masses by marrying a former white sex worker, was convicted of a White-Slave Act violation in 1913 for crossing state lines with another white woman. Rock pioneer Chuck Berry spent twenty months behind prison walls for his 1959 White-Slave Act conviction. And to be fair, notable whites were also charged: Frank Lloyd Wright and Charlie Chaplin among them.

Guessing most extant young pimps know little to not-a-damn-thing about the dawn of the Mann Act. Guessing too that they give .001 to .000 fucks about the British roots of the term *white slavery*. But a pimp needn't be a historian or etymologist to apprehend how the term insists on the great worth of white women, which of course is the prime worth of white men, and moreover that he reckon with the non-value of women of color, which is to say his minute worth to those "progressive" lawmakers. The White-Slave Act has been less about the protection of sex workers, or women's suffrage, or even feminism than it's been about punishing the men who compel those women. Though Taft, Mann, and the legislators who approved the bill had to have understood that not all those men belonged to the same race, they also had to have fathomed that any statute articulating the punishment of a pimp was directed at men who didn't look like them. In fact, Congressman Mann's namesake act, which now mandates a penalty of up to ten years in a federal prison and a quarter-million-dollar fine, should be read as a stern declaration of white men: Don't fuck with our women, apples or not!

Trust and believe, that decree has rung across the decades.

In 2010—a symbolic one hundred years after Taft signed the White-Slave Act into writ—the National Institute of Justice funded a study by the Urban Institute's Justice Policy Center that measured the size and structure of the UCSE (underground commercial sex economy). In 2014, Dr. Meredith Dank et al. of the Urban Institute authored a report of their findings titled, "Estimating the Size and Structure of the Underground Commercial Sex Economy in Eight Major US Cities." Chapter five of the report features data from seventy-three respondents, all of whom had been charged, convicted, and incarcerated for crimes related to compelling prostitution or earning proceeds by engaging in a business relationship with individuals who were paid by customers to have sex. Here's the profile of those "hidden economy" self-reporters: though 75 percent had graduated high school, attained a GED, completed some college coursework, or obtained a college degree—it seems even a pimp contains multitudes—85 percent of them were male, and 68 percent of them identified as African American. The report sharpens the common image of pimps being black men, a profile that fits the dudes featured in this 2014 FBI headline: "Ten Portland-Area Pimps Charged with Transporting Young Women to Hawaii and Other States for Prostitution."

It also describes America—a dude I met while doing time.

AMERICAN LIFE

To be exact, America and me (I'm using his handle for his and his family's sake) met while confined in Santiam Correctional Institution in Salem, Oregon. America wore his badge of shame (word behind the walls was the institution's logos were fluorescent-orange bull's-eyes on our chest, thigh, and back), a button-down with creases in his sleeves and shirttails tucked in his jeans, and kept his hair plaited in cornrows with sharp lines of scalp showing and a bald face save the thinnest of mustaches. He was an ex–high school track star and still owned sprinter's legs and body fat that might've dipped into the single digits. He was an above-average hooper with a lefty jumper that was money off our steel backboard. America was also a weight-pile wonder who schooled me on how to squat with good form and spotted me on heavy bench presses. But what most sticks in my mind about his physical presence was the way he floated around the yard. He had this way of air-walking, light-footed with a bit of high step, around the track, and when someone called, and there was always someone calling, he'd beam and cuff his hand and wave à la a beauty contestant. That wave seemed a symbol of cool that was far outside the reach of us recusants. By the time we met at Santiam, America had done calendars upon calendars inside. Word was he'd been down for pimping, though I'm quite sure I never asked him to confirm. On the other hand, I can affirm thinking how wondrous it was that America's time behind the walls seemed not to have darkened his spirit. In fact, what I recall was a man who was generous with his support, his smiles, and his wisdom.

We—the "we" being at least me—minded that insight because America was one of the few guys we saw reading a book who hadn't been transformed into a conspiracy theorist or Black Muslim or Christian evangelist. He wasn't the dude highsighting about a street résumé or posturing as the inmate with the biggest nuts. One-on-one, America would share his plans, which weren't specious post-parole schemes or a fallback plot for a hustle that had gone awry, but well-considered objectives that didn't include breaking a law. As a matter of fact, he seemed destined to prove what many of us many-a-night lay on our bunks and hoped and prayed was true: our Other American dream included do-overs.

It's fitting, I suppose, that the next time I saw America outside the walls was over a decade later on the Portland State University campus. Fitting too that that day I was fresh from filming an interview with my sentencing judge at the county courthouse. We were shooting B-roll footage for my documentary when I saw America shuffling out of a new PSU building, neat as ever, wearing a backpack slung over a shoulder, studious specs, and his hair shorn low. We wassup'd each other (he had the youthful face that's sometimes a parting gift for the long captive) and bumped shoulders, and I explained what I was up to, and he told me that he was studying business and was close to earning his bachelor's degree. He strutted off with a bounce amended since our time in Santiam. "That's the homie America," I told my camera guy. "We did time together. He's makin it happen now."

The next time I saw America was a year or so later. The details of place and most other context are hazy as shit, but from my lips to God's ears, when he told me he was all but done with his degree, I puffed the fuck up with a sense of shared triumph. My plan was to include news of America's ascent in this story, wanted it to speak to the chance for a man, even one as despised in the culture as a pimp, to transform his life, about the do-overness of an American dream. What I wanted was for people to read an authentic redemption story. In search of one, I hunted for America on Facebook.

America's profile page lists his government name and features him in a smiling profile pic. According to his *About* section, he's the owner of an investment company, studied Management and Leadership Finance at Portland State University, attended Benson Polytechnic High School (so did I), lives in Portland, Oregon, and hails from Portland, Oregon.

His timeline presents a high school photo of him and other high-cut-shorts-wearing teens on the Benson High track team, as well as grainy pictures of kids I assume are his nieces and nephews smiling at a birthday party. It displays several well wishes on his March 19 birthday, and him tagged in an October 22, 2012, note that I wrote titled "This Is What It Means to Say Portland." There's a note he posted on August 22, 2012, that reads, "As summer winds down, we should all take a piece of the sun and put it away. Then on a cloudy Oregon day we'll release it at the same time. I know, I'm not talking to all you people who get sun all the time. But you guys can save some for us and bring it. Lol." There's another of his notes dated August 21, 2012: "How's everybody doing today?" That note receives comments that include "just dandy" and "peachy keen" and "fine and blessed" and "getting better," to which America replies, "Now see if you can make it even 10x better." In a photo dated June 22, 2012, he poses in his cap and gown, cheesing for all the world, his arms swung around two smiling Asian women and a white guy; the picture is captioned, "My favorite team of all time." He wrote another note on June 19, 2012: "What an awesome week. Thanks all for your warm thoughts. I've seen grads and been one. Congrats to those I missed, to my classmates, and to my friends and family who had others graduate." America seems to have been in high spirits in 2012, as well he should've been. However, a lack of posts in 2013, as well as a post dated September 18, 2014, that reads, "your [sic] not forgotten keep your head up America, love u mane," led me to contact a couple of America's siblings (we were high school classmates) and inquire as to his whereabouts. His brother wrote back the next day: "He's in the Fed's in Sheridan."

The Feds? What? Noooooooooo! That was my first response. But I checked America's government in the Federal Bureau of Prisons inmate locator, and sure enough, there he was listed with a 2025 release date. My Google search found him named in an FBI press release dated August 21, 2013: "Interstate Sex Trafficker Sentenced to 15 Years in Federal Prison for Prostituting Adult and Minor Victims." Per the release, in late 2006 America was sex trafficking two adult women when he met a sixteen-year-old runaway in California and starting trafficking her too. It cites court documents describing America trafficking the women and girl in Arizona, New Mexico, and Texas, and then to Illinois, where in January of 2007 he was arrested and charged with, among other crimes, a Mann Act violation. The release also mentions that America served a 112-month sentence for a 1991 conviction of rape and sex trafficking two teenage girls.

It's tough for me to reconcile the man who counseled, mentored, and encouraged me during my personal nadir, with the man who victimized vulnerable women and, worse, underaged girls. And while I'm ever thankful for his generosity, and as I've written have victimized women in my own ways, I must acknowledge the potential harm he caused. Preying on a minor is wrong in every circumstance I can fathom, is not just behavior

I can't condone, but actions I must condemn. And America's past benevolence can't efface that fact.

America's story was supposed to point to the possibility of a pimp's redemption, of a strong-willed man's ability to move beyond the reach of his past. But instead, he's part of the data that suggest a pimp is seldom far from striking The Pose, that he'll remain head down, palm up in mind and spirit, and if an opportunity presents itself, in practice too, that once a pimp, pimping is forevermore an option.

UNCLE Z

Not pimping, which I imagine existed for nineties-era practitioners like America and D, seems never to have been a possibility for Dad's baby brother. Uncle Z, all these years later, speaks wistful as shit of how Dad used to buy his clothes for high school, of how when he considered dropping out, Dad warned him against it, gave him a Bible to build his reading and writing skills, and would test him because, as Dad put it, "pimps need to be smart." Uncle Z reminisces about the mornings Dad would wake him singing "Superfly," how Dad would stroll in from a night out and flash bankrolls of hundreds, of the moments Dad would pull him aside and school him on things like his *catch hand*—AKA the tools a pimp needs to claim and keep a woman's attention.

Uncle Z knocked his first "hooker" at fifteen, but was shook about sending her to work until Dad suggested he pair her with one of his veteran *ho*s. "She'll pick it up, just send her," said Dad. Uncle Z, with an obvious wistfulness, recalls more of Dad's early encouragement: "Say, blood, know this," Dad once told him. "The pimp god is always gone take care of a real pimp." And what a comfort Dad's counsel must have been during Uncle Z's years as a low-profile pimp, those nights when his *ho*s would leave for days or longer, the times when he had pimp pockets full of dust, those occasions when his *ho* had robbed the wrong trick and put his life in imminent risk. That a higher being would keep the faithful must've felt near providence. But what Dad failed to mention, my guess is because his life hadn't given him ample reason to believe, was that the pimp god and the *ho* god might not be kin, that no matter if they were, they often saw to the welfare of separate flocks.

AUNT ESSIE

Sometime in the early eighties, my paternal uncle Z saw my maternal great-aunt Essie—her name is unchanged and you'll soon know why—on the bus. Aunt Essie had a thick black Afro, a gap-toothed smile, and beautiful dark eyes behind wide glasses, or in Uncle Z's words, "She was fine as all outdoors." The two chatted and were so smitten with each other, that by the time they got off the bus, they'd set plans to catch it together on the regular. Uncle Z was a senior in high school at the time and Aunt Essie was a couple of years older than he with a young son. Not sure why—maybe the legend of the Jones boys' bad deeds had spread around the neighborhood or they had a sixth sense for impending woes—but when Uncle Z started calling the house for my aunt, my great-grands forbade it. We all know this story of how forbidden love becomes crucial love and my paternal uncle and maternal aunt were cliché in that sense. Uncle Z contends that in the budding days of their relationship, Aunt Essie informed him she wanted him to be her pimp, but that he refused at first because he considered her his woman. Uncle Z claims that Aunt Essie persisted, said her friends were doing it, and when he wouldn't relent, got to threatening him. "I'm going to do it anyway. It may as well be for you."

Let us not forget Uncle Z was a fledgling quotidian pimp who had been stargazing at brothers he believed had fast-laned to the rank of "high-profile" pimps. It's possible he may have felt that since Aunt Essie was so tenacious about *hoing*, his best bet was to keep her close at hand by obliging her. It's also quite likely that he recognized my aunt's beauty and adamant ambition and knew too that he had a moneymaker in his midst. They began their business local at first, but within months they—which included Essie's toddler boy—made the few-hours' drive up I-5 North for Seattle. This was sometime in '83. The triumvirate spent three or four months in Seattle, living itinerate in motels, though making dividends enough for it to be worthwhile for a span. But then the matrix of a serial killer targeting sex workers slowed business. Auntie stealing cash from a dangerous *john* and Uncle Z's scheduled court appearance prompted a posthaste return to The P. Uncle Z confirms that he, my aunt, and toddler cousin-brother returned home with his funds drained to critical, that he rented a motel room, and that he sent Aunt Essie out to work. One of those first nights out, my aunt mentioned to him that she'd seen a *john* from Seattle, and it worried her.

"You've been doin this long enough to know," Uncle Z said, and misgivings about the man aside, dropped her off on Union Ave. He and my cousin-brother motored back to the motel and, as they'd done several nights before, waited for Aunt Essie's return. They waited that night and the next, and since it was common for her to spend a night or two working, he didn't feel his chest tighten until a few days had passed. Anxious, Uncle Z, my cousin-brother in tow, struck out to search for my aunt, asking other pimps and *ho*s if they'd seen her.

No one had.

Uncle Z, shook now, called my mother and tried to get her to take my cousin-brother back to my great-grands' crib. My mother said she didn't want to be involved, though in significant ways she already was, so Uncle Z paid the room for as long as he could. Below I try to imagine Uncle's Z bind:

Half sick with worry about my aunt and also over his next dollar and forced into twenty-four-hour care of my four-year-old cousin-brother, Uncle Z spends nights punished wakeful by a headboard banging in the next room of a run-down motel that's no more than a *ho* hostel. He haggles with the motel manager the next a.m. over a rate that's too pricey no matter how cheap, and pays his contested bill in wrinkled bucks. Uncle Z feels his heart squeeze while my cousin-brother, dressed in onesie pajamas, whines for his mother or for food or for both. The next late morning, he straps his discontent charge into the front seat of his ride and zips to the closest grocery store. Donning daytime pimp threads, Uncle Z hunts the aisles for bargain grub with my cousin-brother jammed into the seat of a shopping cart. He returns to the motel at brunch hours, spreads a dingy towel over the bed, sits my cousin atop it, and watches him pick over a can of Vienna sausages and a sleeve of saltines, and wash it with swigs of juice from a gnawed sippy cup. Aunt Essie has left her clothes piled in a chair and falling out of a cheap suitcase, her heels strewn under a double bed. Scattered across the bathroom sink are her toothbrush and toiletries; makeup and a hairbrush filled with her dark strands, a half-full bottle of aspirin for the nights she staggers in from hours working the stroll with a heartbeat for a head. My cousin-brother drags Tonka trucks and choo-choo trains across a carpet he's stained with spills, which suffices as distraction until, after hours of play, he tosses his toys across the room. Uncle Z parks him in front of the tiny black-and-white TV and hopes for thrall. "Where Mama?" my cousin-brother grouses. "Hang tight, baby boy. Don't worry; she'll be back soon," he says, feeling less assured with each passing second. My cousin-brother grows inconsolable, and it occurs to Uncle Z that watching his bottom broad's son while she works is one thing, but that becoming his father or at the least his sole caregiver is something else entire. Uncle Z feels his breath catch over the premonition of serious criminal charges or worse penance. He pays his motel bill for a couple more days, and with another day's ledger due, an empty wallet, and options about nil, he decamps to his mother's house on Seventh Ave, which is but a few blocks from Johnny & Lennies—the convenience store where he last saw Essie. He Amber Alerts around the neighborhood for my aunt a few more times. No one's seen her. No one will.

This next scene might also be informed fiction, but it's a truth. One night, months after Essie's disappearance, my great-grands and I (special, since I'd been granted the beneficence of not just staying up past my bedtime but being allowed into their bedroom) were watching the late-night news when an anchor reported the story of a dead woman found naked in an embankment near Overlook Park. The anchor presented the news, shook his head, paused, and fixed his face into the most convincing concern. The next instant, for reasons unbeknown to me, I was struck by the feeling that dead woman was my aunt Essie.

Mom had been staying at Essie's apartment, on the hope that if she caught her aunt-sister creeping in to empty an emergency stash or grab clothes, she could convince her to stay. My brother Chris and I had been staying with my great-grands in The House on Sixth, in part to relieve Mom of parenting duties while she waited to ambush her aunt-sister but also to keep Essie's son occupied, distracted from the fact of his mother's absence. Aunt Essie had kept a room, or rather my great-grands had kept a room for her, in The House on Sixth, and left her effects unbothered inside it. Well, that ain't the whole truth. Sometimes, I stole inside the room and rummaged Aunt Essie's closet or drawers looking for clues. Sometimes I posted by the window and spied Union Ave—anxious to be the hero who spotted Aunt Essie when she tramped adagio down Mason Street for home.

The grown folks had kept secret from us kids the circumstances of Aunt Essie's absence, but I knew what I knew and that was this: my aunt had been gone and no one knew where. The news went off without me mentioning a word to my great-grands about what I suspected. And neither of them let on to me the extent of their foreboding.

The next morning or the one that followed, someone knocked at the front door. "Come, Sam, come," Mama Edie called, and cracked the curtain to the front door. Bubba, who was behemoth and most taciturn, plodded up behind his wife and hovered. Behind both my great-grands stood me, regarding a pair of uniformed officers.

"Sir. Ma'am," one said. "Sorry to trouble you. We're looking for the parents of Essie Jackson."

My great-grandfather laid a hand scuffed from gardening and handiwork on the shoulder of his wife, who wasn't much taller than five feet nothing but Hercules, Hercules to most of the known world.

"We're Essie's parents," she said.

"Sir. Ma'am. May we come inside?" one asked.

And here's where either my recall or fictive recollection fails, the part where my God-fearing great-grands, in an instant, wither into molehills of holy dust.

The following is an excerpt from a press release distributed by the Portland Police Bureau Cold Case unit:

On March 23, 1983, a citizen was walking along the western edge of Overlook Park at approximately 5 p.m., when he looked over the steep embankment between N Greeley Ave and the park when he discovered what appeared to be a woman's body. The police were called and discovered the victim, a 23-year-old African-American female, Essie Jackson, had been deceased for some time. An autopsy revealed that she died as the result of being strangled. Essie Jackson was the mother of a young child at the time of her death. It was reported that she was an active prostitute. Essie was last seen on Feb 12th at approximately 10:30 p.m. near the intersection of NE Union (now Martin Luther King Jr. Boulevard) and Failing Street.

For years, our family believed Essie was the victim of the Green River Killer, Gary Ridgeway, the most prolific American serial killer according to confirmed murder convictions (forty-eight). Essie was found miles outside Ridgeway's suspected area of operation but had been identified in numerous publications on his list of suspected victims. Having my aunt's name added to his list had afforded me a sense of closure. Over the years, having someone to accuse assuaged me, if for no other reason than it furnished a target for my ire. Seeing Aunt Essie's name listed among his victims made me believe, as macabre as it is, that she was part of official annals, and therefore wouldn't be forgotten; it also reminded me that my family and I weren't alone in mourning the tragic death of a loved one. And those meek consolations sustained me through the decades.

Those decades began on March 23, 1983. But on October 16, 2015, at 2:50 p.m. (EST), thirty-two years after Essie's death, I got this text from my cousin-brother: "I just got a call from a detective who said they arrested the guy who killed my mom and they are having a press conference at 3:00."

That day I found out that a man named Homer Lee Jackson (Hell nah, no relation) had been arrested and charged with murdering my aunt, two other women, and one teenage girl. Via news sites, I learned each of those women was black, and according to the state, each victim died of asphyxiation and had her breasts exposed and her pants either unzipped or unbuttoned or pulled down—a modus operandi that echoed Ridgeway.

Investigators found a bloodstain on the jeans of my aunt, but Homer Jackson was excluded from being a DNA contributor. Fingernail scrapings from Essie also failed to detect his DNA. However, police and court documents reveal that when Homer Jackson was shown several crime scene photos "which he studied very carefully," he made "inculpatory statements and admissions" and reportedly told detectives about the Overlook Park homicide, "See, I might have done that one." Homer Jackson's defense attorney has filed a motion disputing that admission: "Mr. Jackson, during his interrogation with police, never admitted to even knowing Essie Jackson," his motion states. "Let alone participating in any way in her death."

Homer Jackson has since pled not guilty to all twelve of the aggravated murder charges against him. At the time I write this, it has been twenty months since his arrest and we must wait months more for his trial. A guilty jury verdict, nonetheless, won't relieve my lingering doubts. Was it Jackson? Or Ridgeway? Or some other wicked being who hated sex workers?

The studies on sex work in just about every city in the civilized world attest that high percentages of sex workers have suffered childhood physical and mental abuse. And this applies to cities grand and small. The Council for Prostitution Alternatives (a Portland agency that offers support, shelter, health services, and education to sex workers) conducted a study of 123 former sex workers. The study discovered that 85 percent of them were the victims of incest, 90 percent had a history of physical abuse, and 98 percent had suffered emotional abuse. One need not be an expert to apprehend the link between a troubled home life and the troubling fact reported in journalist Victor Malarek's book *The Johns: Sex for Sale and the Men Who Buy It* that most girls enter the sex trade between the ages of twelve and fourteen. Since most entrants into the life are efflorescing girls, it's also no wonder to me (you?) that studies also confirm new sex workers are often runaways who lack the schooling or skills to subsist on their own. The girls enlist in the trade to escape abuse, but as is often the case, what one runs from one runs toward. Kaiser Permanente psychologist Melissa Farley conducted a study in which 475 mostly streetwalking sex workers from the United States, South Africa, Thailand, Turkey, and Zambia were interviewed. The results: 62 percent reported being raped, 73 percent reported being assaulted, and 68 percent reported being threatened with a weapon. As an outcome of those results, two-thirds of them suffered from posttraumatic stress disorder, depression, anxiety, irritability, insomnia, flashbacks, and nightmares. Can you conceive of that? Sex workers suffering PTSD on par with Vietnam vets.

Essie's tender years didn't presage a life of sex work. Mama Edie and Bubba had sufficient means to adopt three children, all of whom they reared with bounteous love. My great-grands adopted infant Essie (her biological parentage is Native American and black) from a family friend who raised foster kids. Mama Edie and Bubba sent their baby girl to Blessed Sacrament Catholic School from first through eighth grade, and, all the while, and for as long as they could compel her, to Sunday mass and Bible school. They bought The House on Sixth Ave, and made it a home inside of which it was all but impossible to feel poor. Once my great-grands discovered Essie evidenced what they judged as tomboy tendencies, they let her climb trees, taught her to build fires, and gave her the jobs of being Bubba's mini-helper in the garden and shoe-repair understudy. Essie's childhood was one of perennial family trips, of piling into a station wagon for journeys to Pocatello; Albany; Chicago; Montgomery; Detroit; Racine; Washington, DC—seeing the sites along the way and spending sleepy nights and days lounging around chain motels fitted with swimming pools. Essie's childhood featured rented cabins on Tillamook Beach, trips to Disney World and Disneyland. For high school, they enrolled her in Sisters of St. Mary of Oregon Valley Catholic School but consented to their baby girl, forever their baby girl, transferring to Andrew Jackson High School with her brothers for her junior and senior years.

Essie attended Portland Community College, which is where she was enrolled when she had her son, my cousin-brother, by a man no one I've known has ever seen. Essie claimed he was from the Middle East and had to return there—leaving Mama Edie, Bubba, and whomever else to infer he was Muslim and couldn't acknowledge an out-of-wedlock child. For certain, the story is porous, but there don't seem to have been much questioning on the specifics of Essie and his dealings. For their part, my great-grands, as they always had, as they would until they passed, cupped their hands under needful kin, an act that must've given Essie comfort.

God knows, for as long as they lived and breathed, Mama Edie and Bubba never let a member of their tribe struggle alone.

There are details that can be shared outside that tribe. But there are also particulars one would be hard-pressed to get one of us to breathe outside a confessional. What Mama Edie and Bubba and other grown folk kept quiet was the concern that my aunt had been deflowered in grade school, was furthermore promiscuous, and was a closeted heavy drinker by high school. Whether those suspicions were true or not, there had to have been more to foretell Essie's eventual choices.

Mama Edie was given to speaking in tongues and owned a Bible whose annotations alone might've secured a spot in third heaven. And though Bubba wasn't a proselytizer, he was devout in his Christian ethics. Given their leanings, it's possible that the couple considered their adoptions as a form of missionary work. It's also feasible that Essie would've comprehended that mission, that she could've viewed sex work as a way to test the faith and intent of her caretakers, to gauge just how much they were willing to suffer to prove their love, as a potent means of confirming that the parents who chose her were as Panglossian as they portended.

Know this. Know this now and until: not a single letter of what's written above is meant to malign my aunt. My intent is to pursue why she chose sex work. And while the question of why might persist, knowing more of what happened is helpful, which is why I pushed my mother to share this story:

My great-uncle Ezekiel—no name change for Uncle Zeke; he's saucy like that—heard about Essie's sex work in Seattle and told my great-grands, who in turn sent word through their son that they needed to meet with Essie ASAP. Before long, Essie and Uncle Z blustered up to The House on Sixth, in Uncle Z's Caddy. They hopped out and marched up the steps onto the porch. Mama Edie and Bubba greeted them at the door and invited them inside. The parents paused in the living room, asked their daughter if they could speak to her in private. "This my man," Essie said. "Whatever you got to say to me, say it in front of him." Essie, Uncle Z, Mama Edie, Bubba, Uncle Zeke, and my mother shambled into the dining room. The mahogany dining table, the palatial chandelier, the cabinet of fine china suggested this: parents with the means to provide such a home for their child should be spared of these woes.

Bubba and Mama Edie assumed the heads of the table—the matriarch and patriarch in a show of strength and accord. Essie and Uncle Z roosted beside each other, and Great-Uncle Zeke and Mom hunkered opposite the star-crossed couple. My great-grandmother cast a disconsolate eye at Uncle Z, informed him and Essie that she'd heard news that "hurt her heart," that wounded her all the more because "we didn't raise you like this." Mama Edie quoted a Bible verse or two, reminded Essie of the morals she and Bubba instilled in her, reasserted her high-high hopes for her daughter. She confirmed that while she and Bubba raised Essie to believe she could be anything, her current career was never among those choices. She encouraged Essie to return to school, promised to pay every copper cent of what it cost. She told Essie that if she didn't want to reenroll, she and Bubba would pay her rent until she found a job. "Please, Essie, please. Whatever you want to do, we'll pay for it," she said.

Essie pushed away from the table and huffed to her feet feeling maybe as large as she ever had, maybe as large as she ever would. She glared at her adoptive parents, one first and then the other. She grabbed Uncle Z's hand and clenched it with might. "I'm doin what I want to do," she said. "And you can't stop me!"

ESSIE POSTSCRIPTUM

There's a glut of provisions in The Pose to turn a pimp apathetic, to protect him from being crushed by the death of one of his *hos*, but there ain't no provision to shield a living, feeling human from contrition over what happened to my aunt. The pimp's sorry maxims will never succeed in turning a *ho* into an object; in fact, they do more of the opposite—remind him how much self-delusion it takes to deny a *ho*'s humanity. And let no man, no woman, forsake the fact of my aunt's humanity, forget that there's no measure to the respect and compassion she's due. Not one of us has the right to define Essie in chief by what happened that day in The House on Sixth or during her brief stint on the streets. And bet not no one lose sight of this unequivocal truth: Essie Carie Jackson was a most beloved aunt, cousin, sister, daughter, mother.

BY BLOOD

Dad, Uncles X,Y, Z—all men connected to me by something other than blood—nurtured in me an appreciation of pimps, of pimping; however, my relation to the profession is also by paternal blood, among them my paternal uncle Henry (no pseudonym for him; he'd without question want it that way), AKA Stateside Hank—a man of multifarious hustles.

Some time ago, Brother A (the same brother who years before involved me in the predicament that almost canceled my move East) emailed me a YouTube video featuring Uncle Henry titled "Stateside Production 2." The UGK (featuring Outkast) song "International Player's Anthem" provides background music while opening credits scroll to a prompt encouraging curious viewers to send an email to this address: ask_arealpimp@ yahoo.com. The video cuts to Uncle Henry posturing on a park bench in an oversized green T-shirt that reads "The Gift is Recovery," a pair of never-will-gleam-again white shorts, and a gold-colored watch. "Welcome back to Pimpin 101," he announces. "As promised, I'm gone give you information about all the facets of the game. Now what I want to do is cover how important it is to have pimp tools. Pimp tools are your car, your gift of gab, your clothes, your apartment or your house."

For the next 3:42 of the choppy video, my uncle espouses wisdom on the pitfalls of *gorilla pimping*; i.e., the iron-fisted tactics he terms "mis-pimping." Unc asks, "How you gone beat a motherfucka up so bad where she can't go to work and that's your livin?" He goes on to explain, "One thing about pimpin, when it's good it's good. And most pimps live good day-to-day. Cause we don't know what's comin to us tomorrow." Uncle Henry brags, "I got more game than Parker Brothers and I'll tailor-make a game for a motherfucka." Unc keeps right on proselytizing till the end credits roll, a monologue that encourages viewers to be on the lookout for his books *Stuck on Stupid* and *Booker and Me*, that reminds them of his close-to-indelible email address.

The first time my brother sent me the video we had a hardy mutual laugh over it; however, the megatruth is this: Uncle Henry's manifesto ain't no joke to me. There's too much desperation in it for me to be ha-haing over it—the shaky camerawork, the choppy edit, Unc trying his damnedest to be seen as he poses in all that nondescriptness. There's Unc fidgeting and cranking his jaw in the manner of long-term addicts I've seen, not to mention the absence of anything approaching the bejewelment of his acme—the man without question had a heyday—and the lack of a pimp's fine threads. In the video, those luxuriances have been replaced by a worn T-shirt screen printed with recovery lingo.

What I witness is my blood kin and our shared fortunes.

On "The World Is Filled," off his classic album *Life After Death,* the Notorious BIG boasts that he's a pimp "by blood, not relation." Biggie's few bars have, on more than an occasion, caused me to wonder what to make of those who claim The Pose is always an instance of this or that, that you either come to it by way of adjacency or nurturing, or else it's in your DNA. Biggie nor no one else I know has accounted for the influence of nurture *and* nature, for the impact of a Big Chris *and* an Uncle Henry, for what it means to reckon with the truth of how and where they intersect.

That truth was tested one night when a girlfriend and I were in a gentlemen's club deep in Northeast. Strip-club hopping is a pastime or what passes for a decent date or else prime comp for the plethora of sports bars in a contest of choicest spot to grab a bargain steak or burger and brew. If you've seen one of these places, all the rest are all but redundant. This one like the others was bathed in fractal colors, with a platformed DJ booth pushed in a dank corner and stages the shape of half worlds with thick poles as an axis. Solemn-faced women, with bills flapping from their bikinis, hunted between tables for a paying lap dance. Meanwhile, a cheery tattooed bartender chatted up the heavy drinkers perched at his counter. Other patrons waited expectant in seats edged near a stage clutching a fistful of what I gathered was too much of their bill money meted out in singles.

While my date and I sipped Heinekens and waited on a plate of bioengineered chicken wings, an unremarkable stripper climbed on our stage and writhed and stomped and twirled and sought our eyes. If I'd been there alone, I would've picked a seat farther from the stage, cast my eyes low, and kept most if not all of my hella-hard-as-fuck-to-come-by cash pocketed, but I couldn't do that on a date without being deemed cheap or, worse, broke, so I tipped. Tipped as the dancers came and went and my date and I murdered our jumbo wings. My date and I had to have managed a dialogue, though I couldn't say about what, that is until a few green bottles into the night, when she touched my arm and turned to me, her face ever serious. "You know, I'd do this for you," she said.

"You'd do what?" I said.

"I'd do that for you," she said, and motioned at the girl. "And you could have it. I'd give you what I make."

This happened a year or so after I came home from my short-before-you-hit-the-door prison bid, which meant I was in college scratching by on a Pell Grant, high-interest school loans, and a part-time gig stacking newspapers. This at the time when there was many a month I couldn't afford my high-risk car insurance and was in ChexSystems for bounced checks that I couldn't repay. In other words, another income stream would've been welcomed, shit, was downright crucial.

The particular moment is hazy now, but I had to have done something for effect, slammed a bottle or jerked my head or both. "What?!" I said. "No the fuck you won't. And don't ever let me hear you say no shit like that again."

It's also worth mentioning that I was smitten, so smitten, with her. She was fresh out of her twenties, straight pulchritudinous, and blessed with a body scores of other women chase with the aid of needles and knives.

As I said, I could've used the bread, and she for-damn-sure could've earned it.

On the other hand, I couldn't ignore the times I'd wandered all by my lonesome into a strip club and felt my gaze as a trespass against a dancer's intimate parts. On the contrary, my date's offer was a no-go on account of how few times I'd managed to set aside the sympathy of imagining a dancer in the worlds outside her work. Negatory too because I couldn't bear the chance of another man seeing her bare, and not just unclothed but exposed to his discerning. But maybe my resistance was less about my virtue or her protection. Maybe I was so resolute against it because, wrong as it was, there was a part of me that believed her physical gifts were mine to possess—mine and mine alone. Or else it all came down to a truth I could never admit to Dad or my uncles: by virtue of one being out-and-out reliant on a woman for bread and meat, I'd resolved the pimp a lower caste.

In that sense Big Chris—Dad—Uncles X, Y, Z, Uncle Henry, and the like succeeded in turning my pure parts into what I believed was the antithesis of a pimp, into instead, a dude who'd sit in a strip club and, in effect, *trick* bucks he couldn't spare rather than coerce (or even accept an offer of aid) a woman out of every copper cent of her capital.

But I was wrong. A pimp and a *trick* aren't antagonistic; they're partners; they're often men honoring unspoken pledges of support. Though neither would be apt to admit it, their linked desires consign them as codependent. And while, yes, madams exist and, yes, some women work sans a pimp, the lion's share of sex workers are women compelled by men for the pleasure of men.

One night in the mid-nineties, I had just come from hitting a lick and was driving backstreets to the house where I lived with my then girlfriend and her two kids when I saw a woman flouncing down the block dressed as if she were advertising. Any other night, I would've shook my head and kept my foot on the gas, but that night I crawled slow beside her and stopped and she flitted to my driver's-side window. Don't know what she said, but it couldn't have been much more than what most of them say: some version of "How can I be of service?" Let me clarify that I was not of want for sex, stress that my live-in girlfriend was blocks away and that there were a handful of women who, truth be told, would oblige me for nothing more than a phone call. But for reasons only God or his sworn nemesis might know, I swung my door open and motioned her inside.

Her face—I can't picture it, but I do recall that she reeked of a cheap fragrance, outdoors, and the odor I recognized from my curb-serving and dope house days. I'd posted in my fair share of those dope houses by then, had seen more than a few women wander in broke and broken and barter with me or some other dope dealer from crown to tippy toe for as little as an off-white shard. Up to then, I'd abstained, had refused to indulge not because I lived ever absent the urge but because I couldn't abide the judgment I foresaw, and also because I was bent, even then, on guarding the qualities I believed made me distinct from other hustlers. But most of all, each of those women were corporeal reminders of my mother and the harms that, any given night, she might face elsewhere. And since, in a like circumstance, some peccant-ass dude unsparing my mother would've killed me dead, dead, I needed God to receive my abstinence as a convincing appeal for reciprocal favor.

But that night was not nights prior. For one: there was the comfort of being in my neighborhood. For two: there were zero witnesses. For three: I'd had plenty days to day-by-day resign myself to the idea of my mother's commitment to the substance that had become her spouse. There I sat in my car with a stranger ready to ply me for all I'd pay. We drove a few blocks—my nerves aspark, her smelling like she smelled—and found a parking lot in the back of an abandoned building, and she fellated me to stubborn displeasurable spasms. Her payment, I don't recall. Hell, I couldn't say for sure whether I paid in cash or product. But I won't soon forget watching her stagger off into the dark and feeling sorrow, for her and me, feeling my dignity sink to a shameful new low.

AMERICAN PIMPS

As far as I could see, the subjects of the Hughes brothers' documentary *American Pimp* affect an industrial-strength shamelessness. The film was released in 1999, and there was abundant blathering in my circles about one of the cast members: a pimp named Charm from Portland. Charm's pimp-ish debut near the opening of the film is him cruising Waikiki, Hawaii, at night in an S500 Benz replete with a fluffy faux-mink steering-wheel cover, him donning a red sport coat, black T-shirt, gold medallion, and Rolex. "When I was in the fifth grade, I had three white bitches bringing me candy every day by the bags," Charm brags. "And here I am years later getting money out a bitch's ass. But it wasn't no candy. This time it's for some major money." Spoiler: Charm is not a round character in the film, is not shown devolved or pensive or contrite like many of the other pimps. As a matter of fact, of all of them he seems to be the most blithe of the lot, the one enjoy-ing, if such a thing exists for a pimp, an actual charmed life. The film shows him decked in a gleaming polo shirt, slacks, and spectator golf shoes while he tees it up with well-to-do white men. The film, too, shows him parroting Silky the pimp's claim of "making more money than the president." Pimp-tastic Charm cruises Waikiki's Kalakaua Avenue, one of the world's most famous *ho strolls*, in his Benz, explaining the landscape and beaming as he declares himself human just like the doctors and lawyers and Harvard grads and pro athletes who share his love of golf. Professes Charm, "You can close your eyes and spin around and just pick a state, right, and ask them about Charm, and they gone tell you, 'aw, [he's a] magnificent pimp.'"

Charm, and his pimpificence, was choice barbershop fodder for months after that film. It was as if he'd become some sort of prince among us, the us being not just pimps and hustlers but whoever else dreamed of more than seemed their lot. He was a kind of royal because his transcontinental daring was something most of us couldn't envision with our local minds and timid hearts. It mattered less that the man was more so despised by the masses; he made us proud in ways those foreign to us, squares especially, couldn't apprehend. If there was a consistent knock on Charm's film debut, it was that his S-Class's "Charm-1" vanity plate was registered to the damn Aloha State rather than Oregon.

It's easy for the uninitiated and detached to cast aspersions in the abso-lute against Charm and the pimp-or-die hustler's living head down, palm up off the proceeds of a misguided woman's womb. The Pose is absolutely a troubling pathology, but I reason it's also coded in our DNA—the "our" being America's—a land of free, and brave, and rich. If The Pose is at its crux coercing labor without fair, if a cent, of remuneration, then the concept is as old as the institution on which this country was built. Centuries of American history later, The Pose helped fuel our assent to industrial supremacy. Who could argue against The Pose featuring in the BIG business practices of the gilded-era monopolists who, on quests to conquer the universe, corrupted government, throttled competitors, coerced stock markets, and exploited as much of God's green earth as mortals could. Where's the argument against The Pose, for all epochs, figuring into our politics?

Before we absolve ourselves of the sins of our corporate forbearers, deem ourselves remote from the greed quotient of politicians and avaricious entrepreneurs, consider the ways each of us might assume The Pose or have it wreaked against us. Assuming The Pose is stiffing a friend on a loan or shirking, by any means, a summons for jury duty. The Pose is suffering negligible harm in a fender bender but spending max rehab time in pursuit of the heftiest settlement check. Best believe Terry Williams (O Terry, wherefore art thou?) was head down and palm up when, while I was bidding my biddy prison sentence, he duped me out of a home deed and more than 30K of real estate profit.

QUESTIONS & ANSWERS

Back when we lived in The House on Sixth, my evangelistic great-grandmother worked hard to counter The Pose and any other "devil's work." But try as she might on her watch, she couldn't keep me from glimpsing it when in the presence of my dad and uncles. Shit, in those days, beholding it live was no more than a hop-skip away from her house. On many an afternoon, I'd bop out of Martin Luther King Jr. elementary school, a crushed dollar or copper and silver burning a hole in my pocket, and head straight for Johnny & Lennies—the convenience store outside of which Aunt Essie was last seen alive. The store was a few blocks down a hill from school, and I'd truck the whole way singing pop songs or composing love notes for my crushes. Before I knew it, from a distance that was both intimate and an unapproachable breach, I'd see wan women posted near the store's brick wall, some of them wisps in tiny skirts and stilettos and tops that bared skin. The scene was sometimes enough to give me pause, but never enough to keep me from ambling inside and working all manner of new math wonders on my candy-purchasing assets. Every so often, one of the women would wander in and I'd get a closer look. These decades later, I can't recollect a particular face but my impression of the ones I saw up close is of rose-colored cheeks and lips and eyes smoked blue and thick strips of store-bought lashes. Whether I saw one at an intimate distance or not, I'd yawn out the store with, best case, more than I could afford of sweets. Those women were beguiling strangers at most, relieved for me of their roles as cousins, aunts, sisters, granddaughters, daughters, mothers.

Of the decade and more that Big Chris and Mom were an item—the era of me being awed by pig latin pimpspeak; witnessing uncles I revered return from Hawaii wearing the finest threads; spending dozens of afternoons riding shotgun in Dad's Caddy while, unbeknown to me, he checked his *hos*; the seasons before and after Dad advised me to keep my "head down and palm up"—I swear for God, it never once dawned on me that my mother might've been a sex worker. Chalk it up to flawed thinking or the most willfullest ignorance or self-preservation or me needing to believe that them being a couple meant he loved her and that a man who loves his woman wouldn't dare compel her. Whatever it was, I now know it was foolish for me to never have conceived of it as possible. But sheeit, that instance of foolishness don't rank nowhere near the top of my list.

Blame the timing of my belated acknowledgment on Uncle X, who in varying explicitness suggested his brother, BKA Dad, LKA pimpin Chris and Chris-Cross the Ho's Boss, once pimped my mother.

For days, I carried what I suspected was a truth about my mother. Days, I anguished over whether to confide that unconfirmed data to someone I trusted—or go right to the source. A couplefew nights or more, I dithered on whether to ask her about it and meanwhile began questioning Uncle X's integrity—he a man who once hawked schemes for a living. In the end, I asked myself what would he have to gain by lying to me, which left me conflicted again about the zillion-dollar question: to ask or not ask Mom, and also what would I do if she confirmed? As in, would I be able stand it? As in, would I share what I learned with my brothers? As in, would writing about what I discovered be an irredeemable abuse of a never-should-be-violated code?

But at last, I texted my mother and told her I needed to interview her for something I was writing on Dad. She said sure. She always says sure cause Lillie's brave like that. But me, I'm part punk, so I postponed it for almost a week. The day I called, I did so hours after the time we arranged because—well, I already said why.

All by my lonely, I sat in an apartment with the blinds shut and the lights off and my cell phone on speaker.

"So, how'd you and Dad meet?" I asked.

And Mom said, ". . ."

"What were some of your most memorable moments?" I asked.

Mom said, ". . ."

"How'd you describe Dad?" I asked.

". . . ," she said.

That light questioning went on for a good half hour, me half listening the whole time, while working full-time to muster the courage I'd need to ask *the* question.

"Umm, there's something that, uhhhhh, that I never knew?" I said.

"What's that?" she said.

"Well, uh. Well, um, uh, one of my uncles said that, um, uh, he said that you used to work for Dad, that he sent you to work," I said, and flinched like she could punch me across the miles.

"No," Mom said, with calm that, for a moment, allayed my dread. "No. They always thought that I was, but I wasn't. Okay, look. You remember that time we went to Canada? Well, your dad was supposed to be turning me out," she said, and laughed—Mom's forced mirth a frequent reflex to admitting something tough.

Mom revealed that Uncle X's *ho* was supposed to be turning her out during what I'd believed till that moment of our conversation was no more than an exciting family vacation to Vancouver, BC. Mom claimed that Dad sent her out a couple of times with Uncle X's woman but that each time, she devised an excuse and waited in a restaurant while Uncle X's woman went to work. "So," she says. "I'd come home and tell your dad that I didn't have any money and I didn't have any money and I didn't have any money." Mom explained that Uncle X's *ho* didn't like to work bachelor parties, so she began scheduling Mom in her place, and because Dad thought dancing was close enough to sex work, he believed he could turn her out. Mom assured me her "just dancing" was legal, that the men always knew the rules, that there was no touching and "absolutely no sex."

She let a long caesura prop her last claim. But it wasn't nor could it have been silence enough.

"So, yes, Son, I used to be a dancer," she said. "I'm going to tell you that."

FAST TEN, SLOW TWENTY

UNC, WHERE ART THOU?

What the fuck we gone do now? That was the question top of mind that summer of '93, a summer we—the "we" being me and the brother who, again, out of love I'm calling Brother A—were the newest alumni of Jefferson High School, known as the School of Champions and, so it seemed at that time, a school of fledgling dope dealers. What we gonna do? The most attractive answer was make some loot, make some major loot if we could, and with that goal in mind we'd gotten our hands on a few ounces of powder or what we hoped was powder coca-ine since as neophytes neither of us could be sure it was. Neither of us knew how to cook it either, which was no low hurdle. We needed a tutor, needed a tutor quick, fast, with the hurry up, but our options were hella finite because both of us were sans a Rolodex of dudes who knew how to chef. Because directory or not, we couldn't just call up any dude. Because we needed somebody who wasn't an outright competitor, whom we believed we could trust, who was down for a tutorial, and who wouldn't tax our light pockets too tough for the tutelage. We mused candidates. We resolved our safest bet was to recruit one of our kith, and who better, or so we believed, than Uncle Henry. Uncle Henry, our ex-pimp, ex–drug kingpin of an elder. Uncle Henry, who had long ago fallen from the glories of his Stateside Hank days, had a legend that remained aloft in our impressionable minds. (Again, no pseudonym for my uncle, and trust me when I tell you, he prefers it that way.)

Knowing we needed Henry Jerrel Johnson was one thing. Finding him, he of itinerate tendencies, well, that was a whole other situation. We searched around Northeast for him in my un-air-conditioned and uninsured '82 Oldsmobile Cutlass with the ambivalent starter. Seemed like we hunted for Uncle Henry for a week, driving from one cousin's or uncle and aunt's place to the next and asking if they'd seen him or had any clue as to his whereabouts. One cousin or uncle or aunt sending us to the next place he wasn't.

We found him at long last at his brother Jesse's apartment, which was just a block or so from Jefferson High. Brother A and me hopped out my hooptie and scrambled up to Uncle Jesse's crib. Uncle Henry answered and let us in and asked us what was up and we told him. He said he could show us how to chef, could hip us on how to sell it too. He bragged that in the blink of an eye he could shepherd us to making more scratch than we'd know how to spend, promised sage mentorship for the nominal fee— whether he'd sell it or smoke it we didn't dare ask—of a few pieces of our dope. We obliged of course. We were green, but not so naive we thought we could negotiate.

Maybe Unc sent us to a corner store to fetch baking soda and plastic baggies; maybe he had supplies on hand. Whatever the case, Uncle Jesse's crib was dank and decked with furniture he might've had since his and Uncle Henry's heyday, and soon enough, Brother A and me were sitting around a rickety kitchen table while Uncle Jesse sat across from us in a worn recliner snoring loud as an appliance, and Uncle Henry as best he could schooled us on how to rock our powder, a recipe, by the way, that I wouldn't pick up for a good long while. He cooked it over a stove, and meanwhile warned us against stretching our dope because by his measure, the better product always won. The rest of what he said while hovering that pot remains hazy, but I'll remember until I'm dust the sound of the water boiling and the dope's fragrance. Unc finished and pinched his payment and set us to the task of cutting and packaging our product. We might have had a scale. We might've eyeballed it. In either case, we got it packaged and got our mess cleaned up and followed Uncle Henry across Albina Avenue to a house that wasn't exactly a dope house, but it wasn't exactly not one either. We sat on the porch and watched cars scroll by beneath a benevolent sun, our pockets weighted with blond pebbles tied off in baggies, our breasts nursing the silent hope that a lick would show and we could commence clocking the double-up profit we so craved. Sometime that afternoon Uncle Henry got to sermonizing. "Take all money," he said. "I don't care if somebody come up to you trying to buy a five piece and all they got is a paper sack full of nickels. If them nickels add up to five dollars, you take it." Unc hopped off the porch and stood before us in his shirt and slacks, a little sweat donning his brow, his hook nose flaring. "Look here, nephews," he said. "The fast ten beats the slow twenty. You understand? While you waiting around all day for twenty bucks, you coulda made ten bucks umpteen times. And them tens add up, trust me. The fast ten beats the slow twenty every time. Every. Time."

Unc didn't ask us what we thought about his dictum, delivered it as if there was no superior guidance to be had in all of the known world. Not that it mattered much. With Brother A and me being about as credulous as they come, with us knowing not much more than nothing at all about hustling. But we knew better than to pay Unc's advice no never mind. Both Brother A and me had heard beaucoup stories about our uncle, had furthermore got our hands on a profile that ran in the April 1977 edition of *Oregon Times Magazine*, a story titled "Superman in Solitary: Oregon's Biggest Dope Dealer Tells All." Writer Mark Christensen detailed Uncle Henry's ascent from a petty criminal to a mediocre pimp to, at one point, "Oregon's largest volume heroin dealer." Christensen described pictures Unc sent him to verify his lore: pictures of a two-tone purple house in the suburbs, a picture of him sporting a twenty-two-carat diamond pinkie ring while posed beside a fellow legendary dope dealer, a picture of his Rolls-Royce replete with bar and telephone, a picture of his Lincoln sedans, a picture of his Ferrari, a picture of him at the wheel of a race car scripted with his name across the doors, pictures of him with his airplane (yeah, you read it right: a motherfucking airplane!). Christensen also included Uncle Henry's claim that for a couple of years in the 1970s he was making thirty-two thousand dollars a week selling heroin. Christensen, in his story, seemed loath to disbelieve Unc's legend. Decades later, I, for one, could ill afford to judge it anything but true.

The profile noted how my uncle was the third child of my grandmother's nine children, how he used to tag along with her when she traveled out to the burbs to clean houses or babysit. Christensen explained that by the time Uncle Henry was a junior at our shared high school alma mater, he had twice been sent to reform school for stealing cars. It chronicled his evolution from teenage master car thief, to pimping (the man at one point even pimped his wife), to boosting, to selling Ritlins, to pimping again, to selling dope. What the article didn't mention but that Uncle Henry boasted to me many years later, in one of the rare times I got him on the phone, was that his first hustle was back in childhood, back when he had a strong stuttering problem and did so poor in school that several family members believed him "retarded." He said his mother—the paternal grandparent I wouldn't meet till I was in middle school—was among those who believed him dim, which is why he'd spent time at his grandmother's, which doubled as a whorehouse. He said that his job was to escort the *john*s to their rooms, and that afterward the *ho* would tell her *john* he had to tip Uncle Henry.

"And he don't want no dimes, nickels, or quarters. He wants a silver dollar or a dollar bill," she'd scold. Uncle Henry said that, after the *john* tipped him, he'd wait at the door while the *ho* asked her *john* if he'd brought a condom, and if the *john* hadn't, she would inform him that they cost a dollar and that Uncle Henry would fetch one for him. He said he'd run downstairs and pay his grandmother fifty cents for a condom and keep a fifty-cent profit for himself. Uncle Henry told me about the day he came home and saw his mother on the porch of the house crying to a landlord who was threatening to evict her because she was months behind on her rent. "D-d-d-d-don't cry, M-m-mama. I'll, I'll, I'll p-p-p-pay it," he stuttered, ran to his room, dug through the sock he kept stuffed with the loot he'd made at the whorehouse, and returned with the arrears in hand.

THE DAWN

It's easy to claim adolescent Uncle Henry a hustler. But adolescent Uncle Henry was *not* a hustler. The case could be made that prepubescent Uncle Henry was little more in those days than his grandmama's worker bee, little more than a child being tossed around by the winds of circumstance. It could be claimed my uncle in those days was at most a precocious boy evincing the promise of future hustlehood. And even if we grant that he was hustling at the time, he still wouldn't qualify. People who hustle are plentiful where I come from, but being a hustler is more than hustling. Bona fide hustlers are a rare, rare breed.

Hustle, metathesized from the Dutch *hutselen*, which means "to shake, to toss," entered American usage in the 1680s by way of hustle-cap, a game of pitch and toss in which coins are shaken in a cap. By 1840s America, *hustle* had evolved to mean "to get in a quick, illegal manner." It took a few more decades for *hustle* to transform from a verb to a noun, from what one does to who one is—an evolution that makes perfect sense to me given the heed of the old heads: "Don't talk about it; be about it." Per the etymologists, *hustler*, as in "one energetic in business," entered mainstream usage—I'd bet the bank, certified hustlers were using it well before the squares—around 1884.

In the forty-odd years between *hustle* the verb and *hustler* the noun, old Abe begrudged an un–United States what might be its most historic event: the emancipation of four million slaves. As well during *hustle*'s etymological metamorphosis, one of America's most famous former slaves was a featured speaker at the Centennial anniversary of the Pennsylvania Society for Promoting the Abolition of Slavery. During his speech that April of 1875, the great Frederick Douglass declared this:

> The world has never seen any people turned loose to such destitution as were the four million Negro slaves of the South. The old roof was pulled down over their heads, before they could make for themselves a shelter. They were free; free to hunger, free to the winds and rains of heaven; free to the pitiless wrath of the enraged master's hand. They were without roofs to cover them, or bread to eat, or land to cultivate, and as a consequence died in such numbers as to awaken the hope of their enemies that they would soon disappear. We gave them freedom and famine at the same time.

Douglass's dialectic is a bridge to this theory: the treacherous conditions (the hunger, homelessness, joblessness, lawlessness) that those four million manumitted humans faced compelled the first hustlers into being—those for whom the word was both who they were *and* what they did. Those first-generation hustlers had been born in bondage, but believe me when I tell you, Reconstruction begot them.

And who, it's worth asking, was the pioneer of the pioneers? Well, that's a damn good question for which I can offer no sure answer. But, alas, I can imagine:

> Marster and missus gathered us round da big house porch. Marster sayed, youalls ain't niggers no mo. Sayed, I can't whip you no mo. Yous just as free as I am. Marster sayed dat and us all commence to such rejoicin and hootin as you neva heard in all a yo days. Marster and missus jest watch. Den Marster told us we could stay on. Telled us he give us the woods land and half a what we made on it. Telled us we could clear it and work it or starve. Plenty stayed cause dey ain't know where to of went, but I sayed old Marster, I's take my foot in my hand and leave. Sayed, I neva been free and I's gon try it. Sayed I's goin away and by my work and the help of the Lord survive somehow. Set off next couplefew sunups from then, on foot, budget slung cross my shoulder, dusty cap cocked. Member so well how the roads was full of folks walkin long and ridin ox-wagon. Most knowed not where dey was goin. Jest dat dey gon see about somethin else somewheres else. Miles on dem roads, sun beatin down, budget gettin more heavy, no

vittles. Jest grazin and a gulp of water down by a crik or stream when I could find one. Sunup, sun down till I's sittin roadside dirty and tuckered out and a old marster come up and telled if I work for him, when his crops come in, he pay me five bushels of corn, five gallons of molasses, hammeat. Meantime cover all my vittles. Sayed dat old marster, was a right kindly offer, sure nuff, but dey say since the freedom come I's might earn a little change with dese first-class hands. Dat ole marster looked about to curse me to low names but he studied a mite and offer $10 a month till the crops came. Reckon I get on like dat, one plantation or a other, for a year or so fore I reached up north. But up north wasn't no ole marsters hirin out, wasn't no work for first-class blacksmithin hands such as mines nor no negro hands atall. Wasn't no bureau for freed mens anywheres near us. Up north learnt might quick liberty wasn't nothin lest I had somethin to live on and a place to lay my head. Wasn't fore long till I knowed I had to find a other way. Till I knowed I had to make a way or else.

Prior to Lincoln's executive order granting freedom to my fictional slave and the four million flesh-and-blood bodies that'd been enslaved in the Confederate states, their lives were treated as no more than a conduit for the budding American dream. Those persons were, as I've said, no more than subjects whose toil would earn them more toil, nothing resembling a prosperous life, no higher station, no station at all; and those facts are why, though there ain't no official date, I'm calling September 22, 1863, the born-on date of the place I shall call The Other America.

It's true that Jackson's Indian Removal Act and the creation of reservations—without question, major projects of othering—both occurred before Lincoln's decree. However (and this is in no way meant as dismissive of a pogrom), the natives were never assimilated into America the Beautiful; they were instead antagonistic to it, conquered by it, and pushed, by and large, to spaces outside of it. On the other hand, the millions of manumitted men, women, and children, themselves human capital, were never not an integral part of the white world's wealth. As a result, Lincoln's decree presented an unprecedented challenge to America the Beautiful, which is to say to that white world's way of life. And over the angst of sharing their space; the terror of yielding their power; the threat of competing for resources; the dread of conceding that their logic was specious and their morals corrupt, whites forged The Other America.

Since then it's also been called the Jim Crow South, the ghetto, the slum, the North Side, the South Side, the East Side, the West Side, the North-east Side; it's been called the hood, the block, the curb, the trap, the numbers; it might be more well-known as the Appalachias (yes, it includes poor whites) or Brownsville or South Central or Skid Row. But no matter what it's called, it features substandard living and hella-sundry tactics to stunt legitimate means of building wealth. And fast ten, slow twenty is nothing if not a dictum to best those conditions, to shirk certain fiscal oppression.

THE EPOCHS

We are the posterity of those ambitious, industrious, assiduous freedmen determined to fight that injustice. And by "we," I mean my cohorts and me, the generation of babies born-and-raised in the seventies and eighties whose lives were transformed by an unprecedented phenomenological portent. We being the first generation of crack dealers who were the children of crack addicts. We, who were pseudo-neo-overseers, our hustles doing the master's work of oppressing our own. We transmogrified our peoples into crackheads and base heads and dope heads and dope fiends, into nonbeings we called strawberry or a smoker or tweeker, into inanimates called a cluck or a hype or a lick, into whom we on occasion referenced with a pronoun but seldom if ever by a given name. We couldn't afford proper names, the exorbitant price of acknowledging an addict who had parents and grandparents, that they too might've been a parent, that in the least, their lives included people dear to them who worried over their weight and whether they laughed or cried, who anguished over their absences. We felt behooved to evade those facts, to foster as much distance as we could from the truth that those whose slaughter we were aiding-and-abetting deserved better, much, much better, than us.

It's tough to call whether I deserved better than Uncle Henry in my life those summers ago. He was something of a boon after high school, the same summer that, Division I hoop dreams dashed, I registered at Clark CC across the bridge in Washington State. The campus was a short drive from my high school and a short time on foot from my mama's crib: the two-bedroom, one-bathroom apartment where I slept on a twin bed pushed under a drafttastic first-floor window that faced a parking lot and, on more nights than not, was flooded with somebody's headlights. Me balling at the juco (junior college) had much to do with why that summer

I copped the soft with the five-hundred-dollar scholarship I won from a local club, hunted Uncle Henry, and spent the whole summer chasing fast tens. Because what else was I supposed to do, wait on a Pell Grant and high-percent federal loans that wouldn't, under a circumstance I could envision, come close to financing all the material shit I hungered? The plan was to cop a sack and serve love till I earned consistent clientele in Vancouver, so I wouldn't be forced to wheel back into Portland for a buck, an action that, despite the short distance and high unlikelihood, put me at risk of an interstate trafficking charge. The come-up: one cluck knew another, one dope boy who needed double-up knew another, and by the end of the first quarter of school (or was it the second?) I was buying ounces of hard and delighting at the number of customers who rang my pager and-or blowup cell on the regular. Before I knew it, I was hitting licks between classes and after classes; before practices and after practices; mornings, late nights, weekends. Before long, my hustling was an imperative, so much so that when I broke my foot and wore a cast, I either drove with my one good leg or asked my girlfriend to chauffeur me. In no time, I was dropping loot on Mom's rent, buying groceries when the fridge ebbed close to bare, and blessing my brothers with lunch money and pocket scratch. In a little more time—okay, some testing months—I was bopping around on an average day with a grand or two in my pocket, as a weak defense against feeling poor. That year or so I lived with my mom and brothers (Lillie and her three boys till wheels fall off) in what we called V.W. or the Couv, I stashed my dope or my loot or both inside a pillowcase or a shoe box or in the pockets of clothes hanging in the closet. Sometimes I'd recount the dope, deduce a few pills missing, and suspect Mom of pinching them. But not a one of those sometimes did I ask if she had. It was cowardice, no doubt, but also it didn't take long to convince myself that such was a price of what I believed I'd become: no less than a part-time, three-quarter-hearted hustler.

These years later, I'm less sure, or rather much more suspicious of whether I was ever even a hustler at all.

DEFINITION OF A HUSTLER

The hustler is not—with heavy emphasis on the *not*—a scrambler. A scrambler is reactionary, impulsive, myopic. A scrambler is never not living moment to moment, never not losing days to the near-constant motion of dodging one unmerciful outcome after the next, never not chasing funds insufficient in sustaining them. If a scrambler births a plan at all to clock those funds, it's a petty get-rich-never scheme like duping kids out of their back-to-school shopping money in three-card monte or selling loosies outside a mini-mart or collecting cans for refund or boosting soaps and lotions to hawk at barbershops and salons. Since to boot, most scramblers live in constant debt, a come-up ain't even in their realm of actualities. See a scrambler on the street and make the mistake of asking, what it do? "Doin bad out here, boss," they might say. "Let me hold somethin."

The hustler is also not—emphasis on the *not*—a mere survivalist. The chief concern of a survivalist is subsisting from one period to the next—be it a day, a week, a month. The survivalist is so consumed with that subsisting that they never mature a vision that might transform their circumstance or at least alter it in some significant way. Know a survivalist by their nearsighted-ass half hustles: indefinite curb-serving, burgling apartments for petty shit, spending interminable seasons selling nickel, dime, and twenty sacks of bunk weed. The survivalist also lacks discipline, which accounts for why the lion's share of the ones I've known also fight a vice: wasting whole days placing bets on the wrong greyhound or squandering their re-up funds on 4-5-6 games in the gambling shack or drinking double shots of that hard shit from open to close of an after-hours. On occasion what thwarts a survivalist (this was me; oh, was this me) is the need to feel and look the part of a hustler before, if ever, reaching that rare status, a fault that leads to them blowing the ends they need for a true come-up on gear and kicks, on customized car you-name-it, on bejeweling themselves and other highsightin tools. One brand of survivalist is an old head who either ignored or was ignorant of the omen that his hustle had burned out and-or who couldn't adapt to the latest praxis: think a bad-check passer who never mastered credit fraud; think a seventies heroin dealer who missed the bounty of ready rock. See a survivalist on the street, ask what's up, and they're liable to say, "Maintaining." In the worst of times, that maintaining looks a lot like scrambling. In the best of times, it's tough to tell a survivalist from an authentic hustler.

The real live hustler is—emphasis on *is*—at heart a transcendentalist, by which I mean at some point they gaze out at the world borne upon them and see beyond the moment, beyond the day, beyond the week, beyond the month, by which I mean they envision a future in which they've transcended their station. Hustlers, ever optimistic, ever ambitious, see themselves as the catalyst for that transcendence, though I don't know one who'd use a word like *transcendence*, it being the diction of squares. The come-up, getting to it, making a way when there was no way—that's what a hustler says, and there's no higher feeling than that ascent, than that time in their maturation that most demands acuity, prudence, discretion, discipline, thrift. Hustlers, the ones that persist, mind doctrine meant to keep them alive, out of prison, prospering. Hustlers treat their underworld business as if it's aboveboard. For a true hustler, there can be no such thing as half hustling. The true hustler strategizes, intuits when to forsake the short term for long term, learns the rules of their enterprise, studies those who, previous, plied the same hustle. Wise hustlers heed the detriment of making decisions under duress and therefore keep their emotions in check. But one can't avoid mistakes—a hustler knows that. Those mistakes cost—a hustler concedes that too. No L should go unpunished is a hustler's mandate. Wise hustlers will affirm there ain't no thriving without a prime plug or faithful clientele, will attest simple subsisting shouldn't ever be in question. True hustlers own a safe stacked with surfeit, a house and-or condo with obscene square footage, GIA-certified bedazzlements, garments priced downright offensive. Experienced hustlers see the efficacy in recruiting and mentoring aspirants (franchisees, if you will), be they younger or just less seasoned. Munificent hustlers warn their mentees, foolish is the perennial apprentice—AKA a long-term small-time survivalist—that, after a certain point, if they ain't came up, the come-up ain't in them.

Unc was my first mentor for sure, but he wasn't, however, my lone cicerone.

S.L. wasn't the first dude who sold me dope. But he was the first I can recall who sold me an ounce—ounces! We'd meet in his apartment or in a grocery store parking lot or on occasion outside of wherever he happened to be at the time. The times we met in his crib, he'd weigh my purchase in plain sight, assure me I was getting all the grams I paid for. There was never a time I suspected him of selling me dope cut with acetone or cooked with airholes or weighed wet—all ploys of less ethical dudes. Word was S.L. was plugged with some Mexicans, a claim I was loath to believe given the small-to-medium business he and I did, though as long as he stayed in pocket and on the up-and-up I wasn't about to investigate. S.L.'s plug ranked low on my list of concerns until, months into our business, he confided that he thought someone was watching him, that sometimes he'd shuffle circumspect out of his apartment in the morning and see vans parked nearby, until soon after that when he said he suspected a helicopter of following him, and we began meeting instead in underground parking lots. S.L. was no kingpin, so it was hard for me to believe that the FBI would spend the time and resources necessary to put him under surveillance. It seemed too fantastical for real life, but it proved sure enough actual when his girlfriend called me one night and said that the Feds had picked up S.L. It was S.L. who learned me that in due time, the law would come for all of us, the law of the land or the law of the streets—and most times both.

D.M. was-is the Big homie. He was the one who taught me how to chef, which at first meant convincing me that I needed to learn. D.M. wasn't my regular connect for long but was someone with whom I felt comfortable doing business. Near what unbeknown to us would be the end of our business dealings, D.M. invited me to go in with him and a clique of more committed and moneyed dope dealers, a group who, for the love of bulk discounts, had been piecing their cash together, caravanning to California, and transacting dozens of kilos at a time. He assured me that if I ponied up with them, I'd see a significant price drop, which of course meant being able to cop more dope for my dollar, which also, of course, held the promise of increasing and quickening my profits. His pitch had me counting all the loot I could make and the flossy shit I could buy with it, had me dreaming of gallivanting around the city with my head cocked off the pride of reaching a higher echelon. But I could never quite convince myself to ignore the risks involved in road-tripping with them (it would've been big boy interstate trafficking, not no minor jaunt across the Interstate Bridge), and I also couldn't persuade myself to risk sending thousands of what would've been uninsured dollars along without me. As attractive as D.M.'s offer was, it was a deeper engagement than I could stand, one that reminded me once again that I had to know my limits.

J.Y. was a certified local legend, a conspicuous drug dealer who, at that time, had never done serious time for selling dope. He was also rumored to have fathered twenty kids. Yeah, you read it right: 2-0! One of those kids was a son by my girlfriend at the time, a woman who, per a source, he was given to reminding was better off with him. Our tacit or expressed or just perceived antagonism made me hesitant to reach out, and I might not ever have done so, had I not spent time with him the summer my girlfriend and her (and his) son were in a deadly car accident, the same summer a citywide dope drought and my dwindling funds filled me with what seemed a rare new dread. Shook over inching near insolvency, I hit J.Y.'s line and, no lie, rejoiced a little bit when he said swing through. He owned a deli in

Northeast, and would sometimes transact in it during off hours. That first time I went to see him, I intended to buy a quarter kilo (or maybe 4.5 oz's), not a negligible amount by local standards but neither a grand purchase. J.Y.'s right-hand man South Central opened the door and nodded me to where J.Y. stood behind the counter wearing slacks and a tucked polo and a gold Rolex. J.Y. led me into the basement and, after cursory chitchat, in his slow drawl, he asked what I was looking for, and I told him. He reached in the duffel bag at his feet, scooped a duct-taped package, and handed it to me—my very first brick. He told me to keep the loot I'd brought and pay him off top from what I made. He never asked whether I could sell it (I question whether it mattered to him), and I never mentioned how I toddled out of his deli damn near stupefied over being indebted for more bread than I'd been at any point in life. With J.Y. fronting me, I bought frippery, a fancy ride, and a house; on the other hand, I also became a target, which is to say, our business imparted me a most precious lesson: in drug dealing, every gift is cursed.

THE AMERICAN WAY

While fast ten, slow twenty is a worthwhile lesson for a would-be hustler, it also reminds us our hustle is often fleeting, fleeting. It persuades us to favor impulse and treat patience as a handicap. It indoctrinates us to judge hard labor anathema, to deem those who work nine-to-fives as suckers, lames, squares. In practice, it exposes us to the jeopardy of contact with more customers. Fast ten, slow twenty is a dictum that breeds recklessness in damn near every other aspect of our life.

But ye unanointed jurists, be forewarned: it's wise to adjourn judgment.

Fast ten, slow twenty is a boon for those who, for seasons, have ducked and dodged holiday dinners at our grandmama's house for fear of being forced to admit to a brother or sister or uncle or aunt or first, second, third cousin that we're short on the funky few dollars we borrowed back who-knows-when. Fast ten, slow twenty is grace when we've known the shame of running into a homeboy on the street and having to admit we ain't got a buck of the much dollars we borrowed yesteryear, that we won't have nary a red cent of the debt till next payday soonest or, if we're jobless, until our woman's welfare check or our SSI check or our disability benefits or—praise, praise—our refund or settlement check hits the mailbox. It's appealing to the hilt after umpteen odysseys to an unemployment office to scout job after job after job after job, every one of which asks for a high school diploma when our school days ceased in tenth grade and the most we can offer is an alternative school GED or a certificate from a trade program or Job Corps. It beguiles like little else when we've been bumming rides from friends and-or fare dodging on the light rail or bus or suffering the soul-stomp of hoofing blocks in a city where the rain falls for what sometimes seems ceaseless. Soon not hustling seems less an option; soon enough, we're boxed, or believe ourselves so, into trying our damnedest to wrest a life from the want bequeathed us—into chasing dinero, stacks, bands, bankrolls, C-notes, cake, cheddar, ducats, cheese, chips, scratch, feddy, dough, skrilla, large, green, guap, paper, cabbage, fritos, spinach, lettuce, moolah, bread, dividends, into following neo-apostles who preach, Cash Rules Everything Around Me; Get it how you live; Get it from the curb, favor not them slow twenties over fast tens.

And for those who succeed—the dream: a gold presidential Rolex, a her-ringbone thick as a wrist, a Jesus pendant the size of Jesus, chains made of diamond solitaires, wrists stacked with Gucci link bracelets, a mega-carat pinkie ring. Stunna shades and silks and furs and reptilian kicks, and wool fedoras and cashmere sweaters and velvet sweats and bespoke suits and belts, wallets and luggage made of monogrammed canvas. Plus illuming around our city in an old school customized in chameleon paint or a Cadil-lac on Trues & Vogues or a Benz, Beamer, or Acura on deep-dish chrome or a Range Rover with TVs in the seats and a fifth wheel or a Lexus with the premium package and a sunroof or a drop-top Porsche or Jaguar, or for our get-money heroes, a Lamborghini or Ferrari buffed bright as a summer solstice. And furthermore flaunting our abundant liquid worth on dice, dominoes, or spades bets.

We believe fast ten, slow twenty will lift us off our knees, turn our mea-gerness into a muchness. Listen—and hear it imploring us to get all we can while we can cause ain't a spicule more promised to none of us, because should we endure, soon, sooner, The Keepers or their instruments come to seize what we've earned by the scant means begrudged us, arrive intent on repossessing our fresh freedom.

If, that is, we ever had freedom to begin.

Liberation is at the heart of philosopher Paulo Freire's essay "The 'Bank-ing' Concept of Education." In it, Freire defines the "banking" concept as a pedagogy in which knowledge is a gift from those who consider themselves knowledgeable to those who they consider to know nothing. He explains that the teacher (what he calls a narrating subject) fills the student (who he calls a patient listening object) with information and the student's job is to record, memorize, and recall that information. Freire argues that this kind of teaching transforms students into receiving objects, discourages them from thinking, and promotes the static dichotomous roles of teacher-of-student and student-of-teacher. He contends it also submerges the consciousness and creates students that are dehumanized, a major concern given his beliefs that one's greatest aim should be becoming more human, that authentic liberation is the process of one acting upon the world. He claims the "banking" concept interposes such evolution, that it fosters oppression.

In the mid-nineties, fast ten, slow twenty seemed like a maxim to aid in me eking out a snatch of autonomy. But these years later, despite its potential yield, I see it for what it inevitably, invariably, indubitably becomes: yet another pedagogy to keep us adherents oppressed. Fast twenty is, in the end, a tool of the oppressor, not the oppressed, because it goads us into perceiving customers as little more than units of capital, dupes us into believing, despite ample oppositional evidence, that the promise of short-term riches could be worth the almost assured endless consequence; fast ten, slow twenty is, after all, oppressive because, for a hustler to realize its greatest reward, he must sacrifice what Freire argues is a life's mission.

Brother A told me a story that testifies to the long injuriousness of fast ten, slow twenty. He said he was driving and saw Uncle Henry tramping down MLK. That he cracked his window and hollered and Unc waved him to the side of the road. "Nephew, nephew, so glad I ran into you," Unc said. "My car just broke down. Say, spot your unc a twenty so I can have it towed." Brother A said he gave Unc a once-over. "Twenty bucks? Since when does all it cost is twenty bucks for a tow?" he said. "Since now," Unc said, and claimed he had a hookup. Brother A patted his pockets, bared his palms, shrugged. "Aw, come on now, Nephew," said Unc. But Brother A wasn't having no parts of acquiescing. "Well, damn then," Unc said. "At least let me get ten."

Fast ten, slow twenty is an economic theory of us disenfranchised. At its nexus, it supposes the economy (read: American capitalism) is rigged against us and that the fate of our liberation is seizing fiscal sovereignty from The Keepers and their instruments. There's little doubt to me that

Uncle Henry, S.L., D.M., and J.Y. all considered themselves capitalists, believed themselves entrepreneurs following a doctrine not much different from the millionaires and billionaires who white-market enterprise their way onto the *Forbes* list, or the handful of rappers who harvest from their expertise in hustling a livelihood replete with the spoils of new Negro ascendance. The case has been made elsewhere and often that the crux of the difference between the moguls that the mainstream media lauds and men like my old associates and mentors has been the systemic exclusion of the latter from legal means of building wealth. But I wonder if that logic could withstand the critique of the man noted as the father of capitalism? In *Wealth of Nations*, Adam Smith describes the invisible hand that guides man's natural tendency toward self-interest:

> He generally, indeed, neither intends to promote the public interest, nor knows how much he is promoting it. By preferring the support of domestic to that of foreign industry, he intends only his own security; and by directing that industry in such a manner as its produce may be of the greatest value, he intends only his own gain, and he is in this, as in many other cases, led by an invisible hand to promote an end which was no part of his intention. . . . By pursuing his own interest, he frequently promotes that of the society more effectually than when he really intends to promote it.

Smith argues that if a businessperson pursues "enlightened self-interests"—an enlightenment that includes thinking long-term, thriftiness, and saving—the spur of the invisible hand will yield unimaginable wealth. Smith uses as example a butcher who provides meat based on the motivation of profit, not good-heartedness. He explains that the butcher recognizes that if he sells bad meat, he won't attract repeat business, and thus won't earn profit; therefore, it's in the butcher's enlightened self-interest to sell good meat at a price customers are willing to pay so both he and his customers benefit from each sale.

The way I see it, Smith's "enlightened self-interests" could also be seen as concern for the interest of others—AKA being humane—or in other words, a canny way of his advocating for integrity and compassion in business. Now I've known dope dealers, my mentors among them, who've practiced thrift and saving. Have known those who seem to have made long-term business plans. However, I've known few who've preserved "enlightened" self-interest for a sustained period. Despite what they might believe—the "they" including Uncle Henry, my old mentors, dope dealer John Doe from a hood near you—a drug dealer can't be one of Smith's ideal capitalists. Because at some point their hustle will demand forsaking an enlightened business model, will necessitate treating another human as other than human, will charge them with passing moral tests.

About those tests—one of my first was a night in the mid-nineties when I got a call for a lick that would best what, at the time, was an average transaction. Since the dude I was serving gave me an address just a few blocks from where I stayed, I hoofed it. The house I believed was the right house was located on a dark block, set back on a hill, and had a steep flight of concrete steps to reach the yard, and a path and another set of steps to reach the front porch. From the base of the first set of steps, I stood squinting up at an address hidden in shadow, wondering what I'd say to whoever answered the door if it turned out I was at the wrong place. In what occurs to me now as a dummy move, I dug the dope from my pocket and fisted it as I stuttered up that first flight, stopped, looked to one side and the other, and tried to peer into the house through a crack in the front window's curtains.

It happened so fast—somebody darted up the stairs behind me, jabbed what I believed was a pistol in my back, and said, "Drop it!" Slow, real slow, I opened my palm and felt him snatch the dope. He kept the pistol punched in my spine a little longer—a message—and didn't need to warn me where not to look. *Survive!* Once he was gone, I dropped to a knee and waited for my heart to quiet its complaint. The dude whom I was supposed to be serving called me moments after and asked where I was and what was taking so long. He, at best, feigned surprise when I told him I'd been licked, but since I couldn't prove he'd set me up, and wasn't sure I was prepared for what confirming his hand in it would oblige, I decided not to press. That night I slunk home, counted and re-counted my stash, and brooded over what I'd done wrong, what I'd do different the next time.

Those tests—there were more.

The last one of that sort occurred after I'd paroled, after I'd put the kaput on slanging that hard shit in favor of working a part-time square and peddling a little bud. One day an old hoop teammate—we shared acquaintances and a couple of friends—called me up for a half pound. He was not a usual customer, and half-pound licks were hard to come by. Suffice to say, I was hyped, so hyped that no sooner than we agreed on the price, I started planning what I'd do with the bread if he started copping regular, got to imagining him and-or dudes with equal means as conduits for the second coming of a come-up—though this time, so I reasoned, the money would serve the worthy purpose of financing my exodus East for grad school.

Courting the solace of a public space and its witnesses (not that I didn't trust him, but forreal, forreal who could I trust?), I arranged to meet him at the Lloyd Center mall on the bridge above the ice skating rink. He arrived a couple of minutes late wearing an oversized T-shirt and baseball cap tugged low. "You got that with you?" he asked. "Yeah," I said, told him we needed to find a place to make the exchange and suggested my car, which was parked out in the lot. He slugged out behind me and we climbed in my Lexus. Once inside, I pulled the weed from my sleeve, handed it to him, and asked, more as affirmation than question, if he had the bread on him. He sat quiet for long enough to unsettle me and torqued his face to menacing. "There ain't no money," he said. "What? Nah. You can't be serious," I said. He drew a deuce-deuce from his waist, jammed the barrel into my ribs, and asked if I wanted to die. "Aw, come on, bro. Not this," I said. In an instant, I wondered if his gun was loaded, if I could survive a .22 bullet at close range, if he had the nerve to shoot me in a surveilled lot, if getting licked yet again was also foreboding—plus, what I was losing in cash and pride. *Survive!* He opened the door, eased out of the car, and sauntered across the lot and into the mall. When I couldn't see him anymore, I banged my fist on the wheel and head against the seat, saying, FUCK! FUCK! FUCK!

Soon thereafter, I confessed the robbery to ballistic-tending Brother A. He was quick, as I suspected, to remind me of what I knew, that if I let another dude take something from me with no consequence, it would happen again—and again, that I was well past due on delivering vengeance.

Strapped, we drove to where we believed dude lived, parked nearby, and waited for him to appear on the porch—coming, going, no matter. We lurked for what could've been hours or an eon, and in that waiting, I mused possible perils: shooting and murdering dude; shooting and wounding him; shooting and missing him; shooting haphazard at the house and hitting an innocent. Biding till the ambush, I mused which way I'd speed from the scene, *if* I'd get away from the scene, what shape dude's retaliation might take if it happened that he lived, imagined police arresting me and having to explain to close kin why I was headed back to penitentiary, this time for major time, imagined decades in a prison too distant for regular visits, imagined my conscience dogging me unending, eternal. In the end, I realized, even as exasperated as I was with being a mark, I couldn't yet (and might not ever) summon what it took to kill.

WHERE ART THOU?: THE SEQUEL

Unc, those years ago, never mentioned—should I interpret his failure as charity or malevolence? Neither? Both?—nothing about murder. For whatever reason, he never broached the myriad ways employing his maxim would lead to our misfortune. But an equal truth is all we—Brother A, me, whoever—had to do was pay even loose attention to his life to glean what becomes of a lifetime full-hearted full-minded hustler.

Henry Jerrell Johnson is itinerate as ever, which I know because for more than a year I tried to track him down for an interview: calling up his oldest son to query his latest cell number. Calling Brother A to inquire about possible sightings. Flying home and tracking Unc to this or that place he wasn't. Obtaining a different cell phone number from another cousin and leaving him a message. Having him call me but end it quick on account of his prepaid minutes being low. He promised to call back. He never did. Calling him to learn his latest cell phone number "isn't accepting calls." Calling Uncle Phillip (his closest brother) to ask if he'd seen or heard from him.

"Oh, you lookin for Henry?" said Uncle Phillip. "Well, I wish I would've known that. He just left from round here a bit ago. But I tell you what, Nephew," said Uncle Phillip. "Swing on by tomorrow and I'll take you around to where he stay. He don't live far from here." The next day I phoned Uncle Phillip to take him up on his offer. He was busy, but recited Uncle Henry's address, described the house, and said if I skedaddled, I had action at catching my elusive-ass kith at home. Uncle Phillip's description of his brother's house, as it turns out, was insufficient in prepping me for what I witnessed when I parked across the street from it. Uncle Henry's crib was a weathered pink one-story with a winding wooden wheelchair ramp and a rusted boat trailer in a yard that was half grass, half mud. Check it, I'd spent all that time hunting for Unc, and still for a radio tune or two, I debated whether to get out or get ghost, whether the chance, at last, to rap in person with my uncle was worth the upset of observing his living conditions up close. Determined, I got out and huffed up a little incline of a driveway past a flip-lid mobile garbage can teeming with trash. Raw pity for my uncle formed a shape in me, as I stood at the door—a feeling that enlarged when a young shirtless dude with an untamed fro sprouting under a baseball cap answered and cracked the door wide enough for me to glimpse a cluttered living room, a girl standing in a near shadow, and a do-rag-clad heftier young dude squatting in the seat of an assisted walker. "Henry here?" I asked, and hoped I hadn't, in an instance of irony, landed at the doorstep of a dope house. In a slow slog of seconds, I imagined how the rest of the house looked, wondered how Uncle Henry maintained himself in what, at a glance, was squalor, wondered if what I was witnessing was part of the life that had beckoned me. "Henry," said the bare-chested dude, said it like he'd never heard my uncle's name in life or else so fast he'd judged me the police. "Yeah, Henry," I said. "He my uncle." "Nah, Henry ain't here," he said, his quick offense just as naked as his chest. The chances of tracking Uncle Henry shrank to almost nil. But then the girl stepped out of the shadows.

"You his nephew?" she said.

"Yeah, his nephew," I said, and told her my name.

"Ooooh, you're Mitchell," she said, as if she'd heard of me, although I wasn't about to ask.

"Yeah," I said. "Mitchell."

"Oh, okay," she said. "Well I'll tell him you came by."

Brother A called me months later and told me someone found Uncle Henry unconscious in that same house, and that he was in the hospital on life support. Damn, Unc OD'd, I thought, and whispered a prayer for him. The next time I checked on Unc, Brother A said the doctors were unsure of how much brain damage he'd suffered and that, since Uncle Henry's wife claimed he'd told her he didn't want to live as a "vegetable," the family was debating whether to pull the plug. The next time I checked on Unc, Brother A said that they wouldn't be pulling the plug because he'd moved his toes. *The man's got some kind of will,* I thought. Brother A and I chatted again, and he told me he'd gone to check on Unc and found him recuperating into too much of his old self.

That visit Uncle Henry sat up in his hospital bed. "Say, Nephew, I got some firewood and alternators for sale," he said.

"Yeah, that's cool, Unc, but I don't need an alternator or firewood," said Brother A.

Said Unc, "Aw, come on now, Nephew. Why don't you take it off my hands. I'll cut you a deal!"

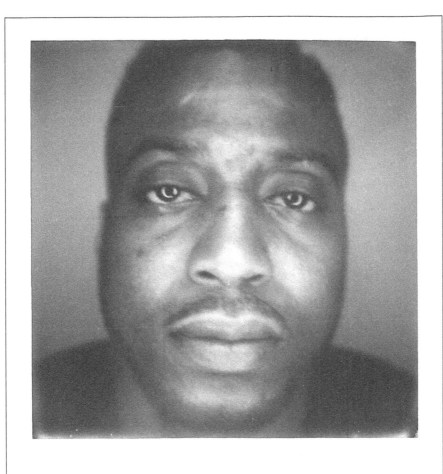

SURVIVOR FILE

Your eyes have seen a glory, witnessed a teammate with a forty-two-inch vertical, a first step quick as a sling pass, and a work ethic as strong as your faith. The summer heading into your junior year, which is his redshirt freshman year, your NBA-bound teammate has a stroke. The stroke shakes him of course, not to mention the rest of the team. But he's from Watts, has bested gangs, a kind of poor alien to you and, also like you, is covered in the blood of Jesus, so the stroke, and an MD's prognosis that he may never play again, is but another defender over which he must leap. The doctors prescribe him blood thinners, clear him to play before fall workouts begin, and his clearance has the whole squad weighing whether he's the key to winning the conference, to making it to the Big Dance. The season begins and (*Hurray! Hurray!*) the first few games, he flashes the talent that made him an all-state blue-chip prep. Covet not thy teammate's talent: it's just a matter of time before the coach inserts him into the starting lineup with you, before he's a team star, till he's earned a spot among the premier players in the conference, the nation, and what better place to serve notice of his approaching ascendance than his hometown. The team flies to LA to play USC and UCLA (it's the most anticipated road trip of the season) and the coaches assign him and you as road-trip roommates. On Wednesday, as if it was written, your road-trip roommate's high school retires his jersey. That night you flout the curfew blathering about whether Cali or Oregon breeds the best hoopers, about how fresh you'll both look for games in new haircuts, about how he wants to play well in his hometown, about his long dream of suiting up in the purple and gold. The next night, your road-trip roommate scores thirteen points, albeit in an almost-twenty-point thrashing at the hands of USC. The squad's still pumped though, because Saturday's the day. Saturday you face powerhouse UCLA at the pavilion. Friday night, the two of you once again prattle well past curfew. The next morning, you wake to a January day made of Californian sunshine. You and a few teammates decide to spend your per diem on breakfast from a nearby fast-food joint, but your road-trip roommate declines, says he wants to sit in the hot tub to loosen up and relax. Later that morning, the team boards a bus headed for the shootaround, and your road-trip roommate is nowhere to be seen. You'll learn that your road-trip roommate (the great hope of a team, a school, a family, a city) had his second stroke stepping out of that hot tub, but head to the shootaround knowing no more than that he's been involved in a medical emergency. You return from the shootaround, your nerves a full-court press, and learn your road-trip roommate has been placed on life support. The team plays spirited in what would've been his first game as starter but loses to the Bruins in OT. You catch the flight back to school feeling more melancholic than you have in life. Before practice the next evening, the trainer calls a team meeting and announces your road-trip roommate's family pulled him from life support. For months, you'll question your faith—a first—and stumble around campus feeling a malaise you thought reserved for nonbelievers. For months what-ifs and whys dog you. *What if you'd warned him against hot-tubbing? What if he had the stroke because you kept him up all night? Why'd the MDs clear him to play if there was a risk he could die?* You question whether you should keep hooping. If your league dream is worth the risk. If God's plan for you is also a short life. You seek counsel from your mother, spiritual mentor, and girlfriend. You search scripture after scripture and find little to appease your grief. Earlier in your long mourning, the Blazers' billionaire owner lends his jet so the team can attend your road-trip roommate's LA homegoing—a service that packs a multitude into his high school gym. You serve as a pallbearer, on a balmy winter afternoon, help lay your road-trip roommate's vessel to eternal rest in an Inglewood cemetery that overlooks the arena of his beloved purple and gold.

SURVIVOR FILE

You and your roomie are headed to a club when he mentions he left his girlfriend-ho in your apartment, the same girl, months back, you threatened with stern consequence should she step so much as another toe in your crib. "Oh. Hell nah!" you pipe, and double back to evict her. You find the girlfriend-ho in your living room, and it don't take no toxicologist to know she's hella faded. You ask her to leave with a deference she don't deserve, and true to your sense of her nature, she curses you, spits it's her boyfriend-pimp's house, and she "ain't got to go nowhere, motherfucka." You find calm—a feat given your irascibleness and the three triple-stacks of ecstasy and quarter ounce of weed in your system, not to mention the half gallon of Hennessy you and your roomie been chugging since the moon showed face. "Okay, this the last time I'm gone ask you nicely," you say. You stomp out to the car, and she troops out behind you menacing. You climb in the driver's seat—a seat you must occupy since your roomie's L is suspended—and the girlfriend-ho slams herself into the backseat and keeps right on jabbering. "Bro, can you quiet her the fuck down," you plead to your roomie. "She's blowin my high." He laughs—bold. The girlfriend-ho proceeds to call you a "Faggot!" Says, "You ain't shit. I'll beat your punk ass." You whip around to shush her and she socks you in the face, and for a second, tops, you weigh the dread of a PV (your probation officer hands them out like prizes) against your instinct. "What! Who you callin a faggot, bitch?!" you bristle, bound out of the car, throw her door wide, and snatch her onto the pavement by her hair. "I got your faggot," you say, and punch and kick and stomp her till you judge her good and injured. You stand and spit, "You got one more time to hit me. And I'm really gone whoop your ass." She huffs and huffs and charges you once more. She swings. You swing. You *BLAP!* her jaw. She *OOMPHS!* your gut. And the two of you go blow for blow till your roomie jumps out of the car and says, "Bro, bro, chill, you're bleedin." You swipe your nose, but don't see no blood on your finger. "No, look," he says, and points. You drop your head, see the chest of your shirt's stained scarlet. "Oh, a bitch stabbin me now," you say, and rush her again, but your roomie wedges between you. "Bro, stop," he says. "You need to check on that shit." You stomp into your crib, your roomie trailing, inspect the wound, and change your shirt. You suck the blunt a couple of times and tilt more Henny, cause why not. Your roomie (a gang-member-dope-dealer-pimp) implores you to shuttle his girlfriend-ho home before the police show. But you say, "Ain't no way that bitch gettin in the car with me." He asks again, this time assuring he "won't ask you to do nothin else." Something in his voice persuades, and you speed the free-way, and drop the girlfriend-ho at her apartment. "Well, what now?" you say, and touch the wound, believing it little more than a surface cut. "Fuck it, let's pop it," your roomie says, and you wheel to a gas station and post in its parking lot with others who think loitering at gas stations in the wee hours is a fine idea. You smoke another blunt to a roach and down the last of the Henny. You bend a few more corners in Northeast, wander until you begin to feel nauseous. "I need to go home," you tell your roomie. "Matter fact, I'm pickin up my boyfriend so he can make sure I'm straight." You swoop your boyfriend and mash back to your and your roomie's crib, to the scene of what would've been a crime had it been reported. Your boy-friend begs you to eat, and you manage a few mouthfuls of cold spaghetti before feeling your stomach clench. You totter into your room and lie down, and though you feel blood leaking from your wound, you swear off a doc-tor. Because you're uninsured. Because you're on probation with an arrest record as long as medical intake papers. Overnight, though, you feel weaker by the minute, and the next morning, resolve to schlep alone to the near-est hospital. The hospital measures your blood loss at a pint but informs you they can't attend you further for lack of a trauma unit. That hospital ambulances you to one across town, and lo and behold, Portland's finest are among your receiving crew. The police want to know who did it. But in the meantime, your gang-member-dope-dealer-pimp roomie has sent hella texts threatening your life should you hazard snitching on his girlfriend-ho. In your hospital room, the officers grant you a phone call to your mom, but one explains his slant of the circumstances before putting you on the line. "You better tell them who did it," your mom warns. "And let them folks do whatever they need to do to fix you." You can do no such thing and know it. A doctor shoos the officers outside the room and sticks something in your wound to gauge its depth. You kick him with the full force of your wizened strength, but he shakes off the blow and orders you into surgery— now! What you recall of the operation is seeing an all-over black-black, witnessing what you'll swear is the gleaming grandeur of heaven's gates, and pleading, "Please Lord, no. It's not my time." The next moment, you lie loopy in a hospital bed with the doctor leaning over you. He briefs you that by the time you arrived, you'd lost two pints of blood, and that during surgery, your heart stopped, and he almost lost you. "Thank you, thank you, thank you. Thank you so much for bringin me back," you drowse. But the doctor refuses credit, explains that you revived minutes after the stoppage. "You know what, in spite of whatever I do in life, I'm very religious," you explain. "And I believe that it wasn't nothin but the grace of God that brought me back." He grins, shakes his head, touches your shoulder. "No, sir, not God," he says. "It was the high volume of ecstasy in your system that saved your life."

SURVIVOR FILE

These were the hip-slick-cool years that you sold the cocaine and your older brother the heroin and both of you lived in his curious-colored house out in the suburbs. You could claim this was the consequence of somebody burgling TVs and guns out of that house, might argue it began days after the heist, when you drop by the pad of a patna who buys your coke and see your Trinitron TV in it. You ask him where he copped the TV and he discloses he bought it from a white boy who you also sell dope. Your friend admits the white boy furthermore sold him a gun, which, as it turns out, was also stolen from your house. "Well, ain't this a bitch," you say. You file a neighborhood APB on the white boy and obtain an address out in Southeast. You recruit your ace-boon-coon and a younger brother, hop in your ride armed with pistols and a shotgun, and wheel out to Southeast with half your hardening heart set on killing him. Soon your hodgepodge crew of hit men reach the address and, strapped, march onto the front porch. The house is lit and you can see people loafing inside it, see what looks like a family, not a one of whom resembles the white boy. It don't take long to glean you've been fed a bunk address, for your slapdash crew to scramble stealth off the porch and into your ride, for you to wheel back into Northeast, woofing the whole way about what you'll do if-when you find the thieving-ass peckerwood. You cruise by the jumping night spot and, wouldn't you know it, spy the white boy's car with him in it. You creep on the white boy, threaten him out of his car, glare with your pistol drawn. You'll be thankful years later for the whisper in your spirit that won't let you kill him, but in the moment, you watch the white boy jerk as if to grab a gun and your ace-boon-coon ram him through the front window of the nearest building. While the two of them tussle, you wonder what next, what next. No such ambivalence in your brother, though, who takes one long step closer and busts several shots through the window. By luck or grace or sinner's faith, the shots miss your ace-boon-coon but hit the white boy in the arm (or was it the leg?). You'll be mighty, mighty thankful years later that the white boy didn't die and that nobody involved the police. Because you believe with all of your softened heart that killing a white boy would have been the end of your freedom, which is to say the end of any life you could stand. . . . Or could it have been when you were living on the fumes of hip-slick-cool? That time, in the throes of your addiction, you schlep into a dope house with umpteen days' worth of dirty clothes stuffed in a duffel bag and spend days (or was it an eon?) puffing rocks with one of your old ace-boons and reminiscing on the years when you wanted nothing more than to pull a Cadillac with automatic shut-off lights off the showroom floor, back when there was little more important than laying claim to women galore, back when you dreamed of traveling to big places, owning a big house on a hill. You shamble into the bathroom to piss and find a toilet bowl chocked with shit and toilet paper. You pinch your next breath, hold it, hold it, and power piss. You quick-wash your hands and, ain't this a bitch, see shit smeared all over the towel when you reach to dry them. Fast as a beam up, you feel every bit of what you've become. You slump out of the bathroom into the room where your old ace-boon sits fondling his pipe. "That's it for me, man," you say. "I ain't usin no more." You grab your duffel and lumber out the door, don't stop till you reach your sister's house, the same sister who's miracled two years clean. She answers, peers at you, steps aside. "Sis, I don't wanna do this no more," you say. "I know you know how to do it. What should I do?" Your sister throws up a hand, whisks into another room, returns carrying towels. "Here," she says. "The first thing you need to do is take a bath."

SURVIVOR FILE

You bury your roommate's father the day before, a funeral you also helped plan and, as consequence, have suffered a string of restive nights. The night before, you sent the teenage brother in your temporary charge to visit your mother, who was fresh out of another drug rehab. Tonight, you switch off your cell phone's ringer and for the first time in too long, woo hours approaching a full night's sleep. As soon as you wake, you check your log and see a million missed calls from your mother's phone. You try her back a few times, and when she doesn't pick up, you throw on clothes and haste out the door. Outside, you see your older brother sprinting toward you. "Go to Mom's," he huffs. "Go now!" You scram to your car, screech out of the lot, and—with your older brother tearing behind you—gun it to your mother's place. You rush inside, see your younger brother crouched in the living room. "What happened?" you ask. And silence. "What happened?" you ask, and he murmurs that when he went in to say hi, he found his mom—your mom—slumped by the closet, cold to his touch, her eyes fixed wide. You stagger into your mother's room and find her hunched between the bed and closet with a sheet of paper crumpled in her hand. You call her name a few times, call it in faux disbelief, because the moment you see her you know. You hover, feeling at once a vast sadness and something close to relief. You stoop and pick the paper out of her hand and discover it's the certificate from the drug program. You were hopeful this was her last rehab but have learned better than to let those hopes aloft. How could you, when you've been ruing her failed rehabs for years? When just a couple of months ago, she was charged with a pair of DUIs? The neighbors will report they heard your little brother shouting his mother's—your mother's—name, then keening, and called 9-1-1. Officers arrive within minutes of you entering her room. They inspect the apartment in a rush, rule against it being a crime scene, and request a medical examiner. Your little brother drifts outside and you tramp out after him and ask if your mother—his mother—left at any point the previous night. He admits she drove a friend to the grocery store. You wander into another room and phone your sister in California. She's driving, so you advise her to pull over and call you back ASAP. You phone your uncle with the news. He shrieks, cries he's on his way, and ends the call. Your older brother leads your little brother to the side of the house while men in uniforms carry out your mother, but you, eyes damp-ening, track the grim transport. Weeks from now, the coroner's report will rule your mother's death a heroin OD, will note as well, that the amount of dope in her system shouldn't have killed her. But today, you search her room and find her stash, check her call logs and notice her dealer's name from a previous failed intervention. You break outside, shout the dealer's name, and plead-order the cops to arrest him. But the cops balk they don't have enough evidence to "harass" the dealer, much less toss him in jail. Later that night, you phone the dealer. Say, "You fuckin piece of shit. Your poison finally killed my mom." Say, "Cocksucker, I wish you were dead. I wish I could do it myself." Say, "But you just wait."

PART 4

How do we proceed?

Let facts be submitted to a candid
world: If we wish to triumph, we must
fight. Give [us] liberty.
The battle is not to the strong alone,
but the vigilant, the passionate, the brave.
Resolve [our] treasured dead shall not
have died in vain. United by public
and private faith, in the people by the people
for the people, by dawn's early light,
we pledge to each other
our lives,
our fortunes,
and our sacred honor.

SURVIVAL MATH

This happened on one of those rare radiant days bequeathed to my sullen gray city by the god of good weather. On that particular summer day, I was cruising down MLK Boulevard when I peeped an older cousin—out of love and deference I'll call him Cousin S (for strife)—wearing all red everything and sitting atop the rear deck of a drop-top old school. The driver of the old school pulled into the same lot as me, and I climbed out of my ride and sauntered over to where he parked. Cousin S, who since the late eighties has claimed Campanella Park Piru (a Compton Blood set), hopped off his convertible perch and swanked so we were vis-à-vis. Traffic whizzed along the boulevard, and there we stood: he a flaming-red bull's-eye for a strapped irascible Crip, and me close enough to be a bulleted bystander. "Damn, Fam. You sure is flamed up. Ain't you worried?" I said, wary of offending him, since there are blood relations and relations owed to color, and he and I owned between us what is sometimes the least meaningful of the two. Cousin S made a face and gestured. "Aw, Blood," he said. "I been bangin seventeen years. I don't give a fuck!"

COLORS

The Crips-and-Bloods as we know them started circa 1969—the same year Douglas Dollarhide became the first black mayor of a major city in California—when South Central High School students named Raymond Washington, Stanley "Tookie" Williams, and Craig Munson founded a gang named the Baby Avenues to protect themselves from other area gangs. Soon, the members started referring to themselves as "Cribs." In time, members began calling themselves crips, did so, so goes the legend, because Raymond admired cane-strutting pimps in blaxploitation flicks. Canes along with the pimpish black leather coats Raymond also admired became part of the Crips uniform. According to OG Crib-Crip Raymond "Dhanifu" Cook, members, at the behest of Raymond, would travel to an affluent neighborhood to "requisition" materials from its residents and return said materials to the hood. The victims of the seizures would describe their attackers as looking like cripples or "Crips."

The Crips evolved into the Eastside Crips and the Westside Crips, and later the Compton Crips, and in addition to the requisite requisitioning, the sets would arrange "rumbles" with foes. The fights were hand-to-hand at first, which lionized founder Raymond favored, but intensified to include the use of bats, chains, and knives. Rival gangs emerged in the early 1970s (at a time when Compton was over 90 percent black) to protect themselves from the Crips. Per urban legend, Raymond, Tookie, and some other Crips jumped Sylvester "Puddin" Scott and Vincent Owens of Centennial High School. At the end of the brawl, one of those rivals screamed, "Don't mess with nobody from Piru Street!" Posthaste, those Centennial High homeboys founded the Piru Street Boys and claimed a turf around Compton's West Piru Street. The Pirus forged an initial alliance with some Crip sets but soon turned nemesis on account of a beef with the Compton Crips. Then in the early 1970s, Piru sets and their allies held a meeting that birthed an anti-Crip alliance: the Bloods.

Crips-and-Bloods proliferated in the late 1970s in feudalized South Central LA, claiming turf and more turf. To mark themselves in battle, the groups chose colors: the Crips, the blue of LA's Washington Preparatory High School, and the Bloods, the red of Centennial High School. The Crips-and-Bloods (much credit due to the matchmaking future kingpin Freeway Rick) upped their role in drug trafficking in the 1980s, establishing rock houses state to state and spreading the culture of gangbanging to, among other places, my dear city, which, not by coincidence, is when their violence grew more and more lethal.

TO LIVE?

On one visit to my beloved Rose City, I ended up at a shindig. In truth, I should've known what kind of function it was by the clique of dudes gathered at the entrance, all of them flamed up and reeking of blunts; should've been further clued when, no sooner than I'd taken a few steps inside, I heard a dude warn, "Blood, that's on everything, that nigga don't want it with me!" God knows, I should've minded my smarter self and left bullet-speed, but call me nostalgic, because almost twenty years hence from my last ballistic threat, I instead shuffled to the bar, ordered a glass of red wine (granted, curious drink choice), and dawdled, drink in hand, wearing nerd glasses and pants a tad too snug for the set. The scene featured plenty of short skirts and plain-view tattoos, an ephemeral fisticuff or two, and no few goons stalking the crowd with a wicked scowl and their chests poked out. Sometime during the night, one such dude bumped me so hard it could've only been a taunt, and slugged off like the dead and jailed of my yester-years. The culprit left me napkin-dabbing the spilled wine from my sleeve, tracking his route, and figuring an equation.

Before and since that brush, I've understood those computations as crucial to my survival. The word *survive* is derived from the Latin word *supervivere*, meaning "live beyond, live longer than," from *super*, meaning "in addition," and *vivere*, meaning "to live." Since the mid-fifteenth century, *survive* has meant "to outlive, continued in existence after the death of another." Other extant definitions include "to continue to live or exist, especially in spite of danger or hardship. To continue or exist in spite of (an accident or ordeal). To remain alive after the death of (a particular person). To manage to keep going in difficult circumstances."

Freedom or bondage. Harm or health. Life or death. These are common equations in the provinces of Crips-and-Bloods. And I call that algebra survival math.

STRIPES

French philosopher Ernest Renan delivered "What Is a Nation" as an address at the Sorbonne in 1882. The lecture addresses French nationalism after the country's Revolution, and is now considered a seminal text on the modern concept of nationalism. In it, Renan asserts, "a nation is a soul, and a spiritual principle," two elements he claims are one and the same and fostered by a group possessing in common a rich legacy of memories, as well as the present consent to live together and invest in the heritage the group was bestowed by its ancestors. Renan argues that a nation, like an individual, is the outcome of a long past of efforts and sacrifices and devotions, and that the national idea rests upon the social capital of the glorified past heroics of its forbearers. He proposes that the essential conditions of being a people (nation) are sharing those common past glories, as well as the will to continue them into the present. Members of a nation (I'll call them nationalists) love in proportion to the sacrifices that they've committed and the troubles suffered. Renan contends mutual suffering is essential because it unites a group more than joy, and that since collective grief demands of its members a duty to common effort, periods of mourning are worth more to a nation's memory than its triumphs. Towards the end of his essay, Renan argues a nation is "a great solidarity constituted by the feeling of sacrifices made and those that one is still disposed to make."

Renan's explication of nationalism echoes Nenad Miščević's "Nationalism" entry in the Stanford Encyclopedia of Philosophy. Miščević writes that nationalism is most often used to describe two phenomena: "the attitude that members of a nation have when they care about their national identity, and the actions that a member of a nation takes when seeking to achieve (or sustain) self-determination." He explains that a national identity is often defined in terms of common origin, ethnicity, or cultural ties, that a nation can exist as an ethnic or cultural community (ethno-nation), and that what most coheres that group is language and customs. Miščević argues that a nation successful in achieving dominion over its domestic and international affairs becomes a nation-state, and that if-when that transition occurs, the loyalties of its group members become "civic."

Crips-and-Bloods are gangs without doubt, but given Renan's and Miščević's descriptions, they also qualify as nations—Red and Blue. Their members (nationalists) unite over a sense of a shared destiny, over having to forge and protect their identity, over a sense of mutual suffering. "I took my position within my set seriously. And every day I put that uniform on. And every day I went to work," reports Kershaun "Lil Monster" Scott in the documentary *Inside Bloods and Crips: LA Gangs*. As did the members of previous ethno-nations, Red-and-Blue nationalists evolve customs and a group language. As did nation-states before them, they guard their boundaries with blood. Recounts Scott, "The ultimate goal was to create as many funerals as you possibly can." But for all the embodied elements of a nationhood, even the most ambitious Crips-and-Bloods must concede that achieving sovereign statehood is a hopeless cause. In a speech titled "The Other America," Dr. MLK describes America the Beautiful as a place "overflowing with the milk of prosperity and the honey of opportunity . . . the habitat of millions of people who have food for and material necessities for their bodies; and culture and education for their minds; and freedom and human dignity for their spirits." The nationalists know good and damn well, America the Beautiful has condemned them as exiles, transmuted their bodies into grist for its wealth, forsaken even their most cautious hopes—and those immutable truths are the nexus of their bond— what again and again fuels deeds that are often unfathomable everywhere outside their domain.

THOU SHALT NOT

One morning my girlfriend's daughter burst into the room where her mother and I slept, yelling, "Somebody's trying to kick in the back door! Somebody's trying to kick in the back door!" Her voice jolted me out of bed and into the closet where I kept my pistol. The pistol wasn't where I put it, but shit, shit, I kept rooting the closet, ransacked that joint for seconds that equaled a couple of lifetimes before conceding it wasn't in there. Then I hunted the dresser hoping someone (God, me, a ghost) misplaced it. And still—nothing. Convinced I wouldn't find it—cognizance that occurred in no more than a few whirring pulses—I broke downstairs, stood near the back door as whoever was outside *KA-BRACK! KA-BRACK! KA-BRACKED!* it, and panicked over how I'd protect my girlfriend along with her shrieking daughter and son should they bust it down. It never occurred to me to call 9-1-1, but thanks be to the sweet baby Jesus for the white man's audacity ("caucasacity") my neighbor shouted he was calling the police from a window, and the crew of would-be home invaders got scarce. A day or so later, I went to visit J.Y. to cop a package and mentioned the incident. "Yep— Yep—I heard about that," he said. J.Y. informed me that word on the street was a Crip named Stitches—a dude I'd bet breath had once partnered with another dude to jack me for almost a half kilo— and his boys were to blame, that rumor had it, I kept fifty grand and several kilos in the house. Neither of those claims were true; however, I was sure Stitches et al. wouldn't have believed me had they *BLAMMED!* their way inside. In J.Y.'s deli, I began to compute: What were the chances of Stitches or one of his patnas attempting a redo of the heist? What were the odds of them kidnapping my girlfriend or one of her kids and ransoming them for cash and-or dope I didn't have? Was it wise to buy another strap? Should I draft some down-to-ride homeboys, hunt Stitches, and—? What was the likelihood of me catching a murder case, of me or somebody I love ending up dead?

Not none of my math was abstract.

———————

Such was the warlike era of pistols and pathos and misguided ethos and what seemed very little logos that began in my city sometime around the late 1980s, right after the seminal gang movie *Colors* hit our dare-to-show-a-black-flick theater. Ours was a generation fueled by N.W.A., who made gangster rap a marvel, and later found a passionate spokesman in rap idol Tupac, a dude whose ambivalent music both uplifted us—the "us" being the young, black, and disenfranchised—as well as persuaded us to accept Thug Life as a way of life.

And while it might seem senseless to some, it's a way of life grounded in trenchant doctrine.

Miščević's entry cites the political scientist Russell Hardin's rational choice theory, another concept that sheds insight on the decades beef between Crips-and-Bloods: "If an individual has no reason to trust someone, it is reasonable for that individual to take precautions against the other. If both sides take precautions, however, each will tend to see the other as increasingly inimical. It then becomes rational to start treating others as an enemy. Mere suspicion can thus lead by small, individually rational steps to a situation of conflict." Miščević also postulates that a nationalist picture of morality is aligned with the theory of political realism, defined as the view "morality ends at the boundaries of the nation-state; beyond there is nothing but anarchy." While the average nationalist won't believe anarchy exists everywhere outside their turf, I'd argue most perceive the demand of minding, above all others, the morals that exist inside it.

As for me, I never gangbanged or claimed myself a thug; never pledged a set or scrapped over a color; never stabbed someone or shot bullets into a car or house window; never hired a gun boy to revenge my affronted ego or drug deal gone bad or even an attempted home invasion. But given, however, my career as small-time-part-time dope dealer, that ethic often felt puredee foolish.

———————

One summer dawn, I was hightailing out the house of a young woman who lived on a notorious street in Northeast, when from a block or so away, I noticed a dude bicycling toward me in an all-black getup replete with a black wool cap. The biker wheeled down the hill, and meantime, I frisked my pockets for my keys and couldn't find them. Closer, I saw that the dude on the bike was Stitches, somebody I hadn't seen since before he and his boys tried to boot into my crib. Stitches wheeled to an arm's length and leaped off his bike.

"I heard you was lookin for me!" he spit, confirming he'd heard that someone had told me about his scheme, a fact that by our code (more on the code later) circumscribed us to beefing. Before I could answer, he yanked a pistol from his waist, aimed it at my bony chest, and seethed at me with what I had reason to believe were the empty eyes of a man who'd do damn near anything. "Cuz, is you lookin for me?" he said.

I looked one way, then the other, saw not a single potential witness in sight. At that time, I'd heard rumors of Stitches smoking sherm sticks (the blunts laced with PCP that were all the rage among the most violent nationalists), about him shooting people about as easy as he breathed. Secreted in my locked car was a loaded 9mm—but what good would it do me now?

Survive.

"Nah," I said, shook my head and dropped my eyes. "Nah."

"Yeah," he said, his voice cranked, his pistol steady. "Yeah, that's what I thought. Cause I'm a real killer!" He slammed his pistol into his waistband, snatched his bike off its side, hopped on it, and pedaled off. Dude didn't even bother to look back.

Stitches, or Stitches Loc, wasn't, as we say, fat-mouthing. As a matter of fact, he'd become a paragon of what criminologist John Dilulio christened a *superpredator* (a term later propagandized by the Clintons).

If I told you his government name, what you'd find, if you cared to search, is that he's now serving life sentences in a maximum-security prison for two murders: one that sent him to prison about a year after our confrontation, and one he committed while inside a prison. And here's another telling detail: both victims were his former friends. In fact, he and I could've been friends. Just a couple years prior, we were skinny bare-lipped teens who attended the same high school, palavered in a home economics class, and shared what I believed were genuine laughs. In those days, he was but embarking on life as an active nationalist. His side: blue.

Crips vs. Bloods. Bloods vs. Crips. Crips sets vs. Crips sets. Bloods sets vs. Bloods sets. Crips-and-Bloods vs. the hustlers. Friends killing friends.

Kith on occasion killing each other. And everyone else trying their loyal best not to get wounded—or worse.

In the jurisdiction that birthed Crips-and-Bloods, the statute for murder—maybe the most famous in all the land—is CA Penal Code 187: "the unlawful killing of a human being, or fetus, with malice aforethought." The penal code for murder in my home state is ORS (Oregon Revised Statutes) 163.115 and can be summed as an intentional homicide by a person acting either alone or with one or more persons who commits or attempts to commit a specific crime (the particular crimes shall not be listed), and in the furtherance of that crime, or during flight from it, the person, or another participant if there are any, causes the death of a person other than an accomplice. Or by abuse when a person, recklessly under circumstances manifesting extreme indifference to the value of human life, causes the death of a child under fourteen years of age or a dependent person.

While nationalists are subject to the extant state and federal penal codes, the ones I know operate with ethics closer to the laws of the Old Testament. In umpteen Bible study classes and family devotions, I'd be challenged to recite the Ten Commandments and would list "Thou shalt not kill" as the sixth one. But of recent, I learned that Bible scholars contend a more accurate meaning of what God inscribed on that stone tablet for Moses is "Thou shalt not murder." The Hebrew word often interpreted as "kill" is *rasah*, and scholars have argued a more exact translation of that word is "the intentional, premeditated killing of another person with malice." That translation, though, also suggests there are conditions in which one is justified in killing. In biblical times that justification was God's word. Among the nationalist, it's a particular set of principles.

"I'm a real killer," declared Stitches.

"He's a killer," or "He got a body," or "He got stripes," I've heard whispered about an infamous nationalist or über-dangerous non-affiliate. And I imagine at some point the whispers became an urge at the man's back.

The most malevolent of those men owned a raison d'être nada and handle that let you know what they were about: Stitches, Pistol, Menace, Grease. They anesthetized from wake-up and flaunted yield-colored sclera and scorched lips. They owned mug shots aplenty and weren't worried about boxes—coffins nor cells. They flaunted knife and-or bullet wounds and wore hats slung low and sported tattoo tears on their cheeks and affiliations and RIPs on their necks and arms and bruises on their knuckles and didn't bother cleaning the grime under their jagged nails. But most notable might've been their languor—as hurry implies a kind of hope—and how they moved through the world, by which I mean how, size aside, they claimed a preponderance of physical and psychic space, claimed it and dared someone to breach it. Double dared them, so they could show them what they were made of. Or rather what they were made for: living outside of peace and prayer and morals and any attempt to soften their slow-ticking tragic hearts. On the other hand, in dominions where grave penalties exist for offending the codes (soon come, words on those codes), the deeds of nationalists and select others were seldom judged as unjust; which might also account for why the killers among us weren't out-and-out outcasts, were often respected, in some circles exalted, and, dare I say, loved for what they did.

But a murderer is something else. A murderer's homicide is divorced from both the state-statute notion of justice *and* the principles we've ordained off the books. A murderer's deeds accrue no respect or status, inspire no empathy, earn no love. Wouldn't nobody I know whisper "he's a murderer" with reverence. And because we can't divine his motive, his means, nor his intended ends—keys to safeguarding ourselves from him—a murderer is just as much of an anathema to us as he is to those who live outside our bounds.

———

One of my high school hustles was cutting hair. For a time, I'd cut dudes in the school bathroom, but after our top-flight school security got to busting me mid-cut, making me sweep the hair, and threatening stiff sanctions, I started barbering in the basement of my grandfather's house, or in other words, in my bedroom. Larry was a school associate and fellow athlete, so I didn't think twice about lacing him (he wore a box, one of my specialties) when he asked me for a cut the first time. He met me at my house and followed me into my bedroom barbershop. We jabbered a bit, and by the time I finished his do, I'd concluded Larry was a much more amiable dude than he seemed at school. He paid me and I showed him to the front door, and saw my grandfather rambling up the front path. He stopped to greet us. "Dad, this is Larry. Larry, this my granddad," I said. Granddad and Larry shook hands, and Larry moseyed across the street to his car and left. No sooner had Larry pulled off than Grandad asked about him, and

I explained that he went to Jeff and played football. He was also a Crip, a little tidbit I omitted. Granddad shook his head. "Boy oh boy, I don't know, Mitchell," he said. "Something ain't right about that boy. I tell you something just ain't right about that boy." It was the first and last time Granddad made such a statement about someone I'd brought to the house, and maybe my granddad got a little soothsayer in him, because months later his comment seemed psychic.

That summer, a man—for legal reasons I'll call him G.C.—had his brother hire hit men to kill his wife. Per court records, the brother approached a young dude about the "hit" and he agreed to do it. The brother then met with the hit man to plan the murder, showed him photos of the woman he was supposed to kill, and asked him if he was still down. He was. The brother informed the hit man that he wanted the murder to look like a robbery and that he shouldn't shoot his sister-in-law in the head because her husband (his brother) wanted an open casket. The next day, the brother picked up the would-be hit man and called his older brother: the man who wanted his wife dead. The husband informed his younger brother that his wife had gone to church and therefore the hit had to be postponed. The conspirators agreed to wait till the next day. The next morning the brother picked up the hired hit man, but this time lent him his car with instructions to kill his sister-in-law and return it to him afterward. However, instead of setting to his task at once, the hit man cruised around visiting friends, wrecked the car, and injured himself. Days later, the injured hit man called the brother and asked if he still needed someone to kill his sister-in-law and the brother said he had it handled. As it turns out, the brother had hired, for the grand sum of one thousand dollars (yes, that's all they believed an innocent life was worth), Larry and another dude I'll call R.S. to carry out the hit.

On the day of the murder, July 30, 1993, the husband called his wife at the Head Start day-care center where she worked and told her he was coming to take her to lunch. Almost timed to that phone call, Larry and R.S., both masked, stormed the building screaming, "WHERE'S THE MONEY! WHERE'RE THE PURSES!" One gunman broke for the doorway of the wife's office and shot her through the wrist, cheek, and arm and three times in the back. The other gunman stormed into the second office and demanded money from the wife's coworker. Before they left, not a single stolen dollar between them, one of them shot another woman in the lung. It didn't take long for the police to discover the plot and names of the shooters. Larry, who was fingered as the gunman who killed the wife, fled town. He ended up in Birmingham, Alabama, where he was killed two years later in an unrelated crime.

Whether Larry was a killer or murderer (for the official record, I don't condone either but believe he's the latter), he is without doubt an example of the incalculable costs of adhering to an ethos that normalizes, and in many cases, excuses mortal violence.

Many cities have been hit harder stat-wise by what could be described as nationalistic terror, but in the case of my dear city, those numbers mislead. As I said, blacks have equaled a negligible 3 to 5 percent of Portland's populace for decades, with most of us clustered in two quadrants. And a significant upshot for us was this: when someone was robbed or stabbed or shot or beat or killed, when someone hired hit men to murder his wife, there was a chance we knew the assailant and the victim and almost a sure bet that we were no more than a third-person removed from both. For all of us, our communion was such that in aftermaths our allegiance was oft confused. Our intimacies were such that our outcomes often felt preordained.

And yet here I am with a pulse, free of the penal system, making a life three thousand miles from home.

How, I've asked myself, how did I avoid the fate of a hash mark in the city's criminal homicide tally?

There were practical ways born of what I claim as common sense, e.g., I concluded that, in the midst of conflict, it was unwise to aggravate a pistol-bearing foe, e.g., I worked hard to keep someone nudging me in a club or an after-hours or a gambling shack from inciting me to blows, e.g., I avoided consorting with women I knew dated nationalists and-or Janus-faced hustlers, e.g., after Stitches and crew tried to bust down our door, I urged my girlfriend to move to a suburb and kept our address private from everyone but a few family members and my closest friends.

But what also kept me alive was apprehending the paradigm shift among us, that the time of fighting a fair one (a one-on-one fight with no weapons) was all but out the window. It was realizing that, while other dudes were risking life and soul to defend their sense of honor, I needed (call it punkish if you like) nuanced forms of courage. It was minding the immutable truth that, on numerous occasions, the most gallant thing I could do was *no* thing at all.

Those are some deeds and tenets that kept me alive.

But what, I've asked myself, has kept me from killing?

The answer can be found in the code (see, I promised I'd get back to it), which is some unquantifiable matrix: sense of right, sense of wrong, sense of worth, family, fame, faith, stature, ownership, allegiance, love, lust, legacy, justice, grace, trust, strength, esteem, freedom, family, hope, pride, pride, pride.

To *continue to live or exist in spite of danger or hardship*, we must discern the almost incalculable ways that code could be breached, to wit, the circumstances under which we had been or would be violated. If someone spoke ill of our name, fought us, tried to rob or robbed us, harmed a loved one . . . we'd been violated. If we wore the wrong color at the wrong time or wandered onto the wrong street on the wrong turf, we could be counted in breach. If we flirted with the wrong girl, had sex with the wrong girl, scorned a dude in jest, associated with the wrong dude in good faith, shaded the wrong thug, nudged the wrong fool with nary a sorry, nudged the right fool with too meek of an amends, sold dope to somebody's customer, shorted a customer, dispensed too much product for what a customer paid, sold prime product, secured a better plug; if we highsighted or flashed our wares among the right rogues, or gambled and lost too much, or gambled and won too much, if we were accused of the high crime of tattling to the fuzz . . . we might be considered in offense and punished. And per the paradox of the code: whosoever, for whatever reason, harmed us should be assailed in return, a penalty that should be swift, stern, symbolic, that should be a message to the near future, a warning, a declaration. And according to the justice of the land, that declaration could or should be lethal.

So why am I not a killer when by that code once, twice, thrice or more I would've been just in the act? To begin, I didn't, like so many of my peers, nationalists and others, rely on atomic toughness, take up arms as panacea, resort to bullets proving my tensile strength.

And also, since I planned to one day cease and desist my days as an irresolute hustler, I was careful to avoid doing business that would dictate a future of dire distress. Why else? Well, I could cite the collective counsel of my elders or God, and though each has played a role, the crux of why I'm not a killer has less if at all to do with a higher power or morals or mercy or fear or the legacy of my forefathers or the belief that nothing but chaos exists outside my borders; in fact, it has little to do with any calculus save the simplest survival math: I have yet to meet a man whose life is worth more than mine.

———————

Cousin S is the oldest son of Uncle Henry and, like his father, proves one helluva dude to track down. For a year, more, I'd call family members for his number, only to find out that number was disconnected or message him on social media and receive a tardy cryptic reply. Once or twice he left me a number to a prepaid cell phone on which he hadn't loaded enough minutes to use. But one trip back in 2016, I caught his line and explained that I wanted to interview him. He agreed, gave me directions to where he lived in The Numbers, and since I wasn't about to let him shake me again, I told him I'd drive out to his house pronto. "Fam, don't leave. I'm gone call you soon as I get off on your exit," I said, and he agreed to stay put. True to my word, I pulled off the exit he gave me and rang his cell. "Yo, I'm out here, fam. What's the address to your crib again?" Cousin S said he wasn't at his crib anymore but at a convenience store close by, and I could swoop him from there, which I did.

He climbed in my rental and right off announced we wouldn't be heading to his house but rather the crib of one of his patna's. "We bout to throw somethin on the grill," he said, and sounded as excited as I was suspicious. He directed me a few blocks from the store to his patna's place. We pulled into the driveway and a toddler darted out of the house trailed by a fat unleashed rottweiler. For a hot second, I considered inventing an excuse to leave, but abandoned the idea after weighing the potential of another months-long goose chase for Cousin S. I tamped my fright of dogs and schlepped inside the house where I encountered two dudes, neither of whom I recognized, lounging on a couch in T-shirts and shorts. As introduction, Cousin S announced the dudes were OGs and told me their street names, though I forgot the names almost as soon as they hit my ears. He bopped out to the patio to man a tiny grill, leaving me in the living room with the OGs, whose handles I couldn't recall. Soon, the OGs began swapping sentimental stories about old home invasions and carjackings, the one time that one of them stole a neighbor's car system because he heard that neighbor playing his music too loud. "The nigga shoulda knew better," he said. And while I wondered whether I should've left my iPad and watch in the car, it was also not lost on me that, in an alternate life, the OGs could've been my heroes or at least counsel. Someone turned on the stereo and the conversation segued to the argument that old-school West Coast rap is the hardest, and these new-booty rappers is "soft as cotton." The OGs rolled a blunt and passed it. Cousin S shuffled back into the living room with a pint of Hennessy and asked who wanted to hit it. The OGs partook, and Cousin S recounted a couple of tales of his own while the Henn made circuits. The diapered toddler tottered into the kitchen, an older kid trailing him, and hunted for something in the cupboards. The rottweiler (was that drool?) haunted not far behind them. Since it's never taken much for me to imagine extremes, I pictured the neo-cattle-herding canine going rabid on us all.

Whew! It didn't. My cousin loafed outside to man the grill. He left the patio door cracked and the barbecue smoke bullied inside. The OGs transitioned into critiquing E-40's and Pac's hood integrity, and although I had an opinion, I resolved against my usual pugnaciousness. One of them offered me a hit of the blunt but I said no thanks. In time, another dude arrived, a nationalist—his color, of course, red—who went to high school with me. The OGs and the new dude sent the blunt on more ambits, gulping Henn all the while. Then Cousin S unsheathed a bottle of neon rotgut wine from a paper sack, and asked, "Who wanna hit this?" with his voice on the verge of slurring. *Pssssssssssssssss!*—that's the hissing my hope for an interview made as I watched my cousin swill. And yet I was steadfast because sometimes, many times, I'm stupid-stubborn like that.

Cousin S stepped out to take some meat off the grill, bragging while he did it about his skills. He marched back into the kitchen with a plate of meat. He answered a call on his cell, roamed into the living room, and lowered the music. "Yeah, I ain't gone be home for second," he explained. "I'm at my patna's house, so just bring em over here." Cousin S recited the address. "Yeah, I'm gone be here," he confirmed, and ended the call. He announced the caller was his daughter, that she was bringing his grandson to the house. He paused and tipped his bright potion. "Man, that little nigga can throw them thangs," said Cousin S, more, I guessed, for the OGs than me. "All you got to do is slap him."

"Damn, fam," I said. "How old's your grandson?"

"Aw, man. The little nigga only two," he said. "But he gone be ready. He can go."

REVISION

Where to start? The day of the lone arrest of my life, I cooked dope in my then girlfriend's house, a blatant disregard of her wishes. By an act of Arm & Hammer legerdemain, on this occasion, I cooked a near double-digit gram surfeit of crack—my first time getting extra too; how's that for ironic? I boiled it, cut it, bagged it, and cleaned up, then bounced out of the house. Per routine at the time, I stashed the sack of rocks under my seat and my pistol under the dash of my '86 Honda. Common sense says I should've headed straight for the suburban apartment where I stored my dope, but on the contrary, my sense-deficient self cruised to a rec center gym to hoop with my homeboys. We balled a couple hours, and afterward, I for-damn-sure should've ferried my dope to the suburbs, but my silly ass instead drove to swoop my other girlfriend. We weren't more than a few blocks from that pickup when the cops pulled behind me. They followed for a block or so and hit me with flashers the first turn I made. "Don't worry, don't worry," I told myself first and her second. Said it because I had a license and valid insurance and knew how to speak assimilated Negro English. Said it because I'd been pulled over riding dirty on occasion and had gone free. So I rolled my window down with that false peace, and no sooner than I said, "Officer, may I ask why you—" I heard his partner say "HE'S GOT A GUN!" from the passenger side.

Now I'd made those sense-deficient silly-ass moves, but I didn't so much as twitch before the white men with guns and badges barked, "EVERYONE PUT YOUR HANDS WHERE I CAN SEE THEM!" It was dark; it was raining; I was wearing an ever-obfuscating puffy black coat, and real talk, if those officers were having a bad day, had the wrong bias or a nervous *digitus secundus manus*, I could've ended up the kind of headline that makes a mother keen. They didn't shoot (hallelujah!), but what they did was order me out my ride, handcuff us both, stuff us in the backseat of their patrol car, and conduct the avid search that bore the 9mm Smith & Wesson under the dash and the sandwich bag of crack hidden under my seat, a baggie laden with those extra grams I mentioned a second ago, which seems now to have been foreshadowing.

255

"Look. What. We. Found. Here!" said the cop, and slo-mo raised the tumid baggie to twitching streetlight.

That was March. In June, His Honor Henry Kantor sentenced me, on the Class B felony of distribution of a controlled substance, to a place that was both inconceivable and foreordained. It was a super-sad-face moment for me and mines, but on the other hand, granted it was uncommon for a first offense, if Judge Kantor, say, had one of those days, was overwhelmed with his caseload, or just wanted to send a message of less-than-zero tolerance, he could've punished me with a maximum of ten years, in which case if I mattered enough, which I didn't, I could've ended up this super-sorrowful-sad-face headline:

DOPE-DEALING SCHOLARSHIP STUDENT
LANDS TEN-YEAR PRISON SENTENCE

Instead, I served a sixteen-month sentence first in Mill Creek and then Santiam correctional institutions. My last few months at Santiam, I scribbled on loose-leaf paper the first paragraphs of what I would hope-pledge-dream-school-cry-will-pray into a novel. Muscled-up off countless push-ups and pull-ups (how cliché), I paroled on July 8, 1998, and whether I realized it then or not—and for the most part I didn't—I began to revise.

Revision isn't editing or proofing. Editing is finding minor problems. It's addressing those minor problems with easy fixes such as deleting a word or sentence or copying and pasting a paragraph elsewhere. Proofing is seeing the work as static. Proofing is correction; it's fixing a comma splice or a misspelled word or faulty subject/verb agreement—AKA applying the rules of convention.

But revision is something else. Revision might include editing or proofing but will always move beyond both. Revision is seeing the work in progress. Revision is seeing the work in context. Revision is recognizing the parts of a text and how they work to form a whole. It's seeing what could and should and shouldn't be there and conceiving of ways to make it so. Revision is discovering what's right and imagining how to make it more right. It's pursuing a new way of seeing and being. Revision is a philosophy, revision is a chance to transform.

Thank God, I've learned to revise my work. Thank God, the angels, the saints, and a few heathens I've been given chances to revise my life.

In *Christian and Oriental Philosophy of Art*, philosopher A. K. Coomaraswamy contends, "The artist is not a special kind of man, but every man who is not an artist in some field, every man without a vocation, is an idler . . . No man has a right to any social status who is not an artist." The premise that every man should be an artist made me wonder if it's possible to apply the skills for revising the page to revising a life, and if that revision or *re*visioning could transform what someone had misperceived or forecasted as their fate.

SECOND GANG MEMBER
DIES AT APARTMENT 43

A gunman fired one shot and killed an 18-year-old man Saturday afternoon at the Towne Plaza Apartments. Kevan Hai Miller died at the scene with a gunshot wound to the chest.

Kev and me met freshman year during daily-doubles football practice. That season he was a starting star safety and I was a frail second-string defensive back. Kev was the one who talked courage into me when I didn't want no part of our Heads Up drills. He was also one of the first teammates to slap my shoulder pads when I serendipitied an interception during our last game of the season. Off the field, Kev was a bona fide math savant who had an easy smile and a voice that made you lean in to hear him. The set Kev claimed was a mystery to me, but most days he wore creased Dickies, Nike Cortez, a symbolic fitted cap with no bend in the brim, and beaucoup red—a virtual uniform that let you know he was an aspiring or affiliated or official nationalist. Kev was down with gangster symbolism, for sure, though it never ceased seeming to me that the homie was playing dress-up.

My last memory of Kev alive was the summer after we graduated from high school. We were in my basement bedroom, and I was flaunting the low-grade weed I'd bought from who-knows-who, when my might've-been-clairvoyant grandmother crept down on us. Me, I was stunned into a gape-mouthed stupor, but Kev copped to it swift: "It's mine, Mrs. Jackson. It's mine." My grandmother stabbed a finger toward the door, ordered, "You leave now. Leave right now and don't ever come back!"

Kev's banishment mattered little. He was murdered that December.

SCHOOL DAYS

These days I teach writing to grads and undergrads who range from middle-class to affluent and who, for the most part, know as much about dope dealing and gangbanging as I know about, say, European boarding schools. Their lack of awareness isn't something we discuss but something I intuit from their writing, their comments in class, our one-on-ones during office hours, the bits of conversations I earhustle on campus.

Imagine me standing at the head of a classroom seated with the young living versions of my dead friends. In this vision, I'd beam a presentation onto the board and spread notes across a lectern. "The word *essay* comes from the French word *essai*, which translates to 'to try' or 'attempt,'" I'd begin, and add that the godfather of the form Michel (Mr. What-Do-I-Know?) de Montaigne named his opus *Essais* because he understood the primal need for revision. As proof, I'd point to the fact that Montaigne wrote, published, and reworked his "attempts" for over two decades. If I peeped at least an inkling of interest, I'd make the case that whether or not they believe themselves artists, they should consider themselves essayists, practitioners ever working to sharpen their ideas. And if they cottoned to it, I'd pitch considering themselves the essay itself, would argue that they are, we all are, in effect trial runs.

How to Revise: Step 1

Ain't no way I'd dismiss class without stressing revision is a process, without explaining that the first stage of that process is assessing the *Content*. "It's the stage where we ask questions," I'd tell them. "When we ask, who's our audience? What's our purpose? What's our argument(s)? Who and-or what supports our claims?"

One-on-one, I'd try to convince Kev that there's another way of seeing, would point to what the critic Edmund Wilson asserts in *The Wound and the Bow*: "The conception of superior strength is inseparable from disability," or in other words, our wound is our bow. Whether Kev knew it or not, and I presume he didn't, his disability was his difference. Those of us who bothered looking could see it in the way he authored himself for the world, in the way he played down his exceptional brain, how he was seldom vocal in a group. To ply him to see the strength in his difference, I'd confess how, the whole time he'd known me and the years before, I was ashamed to admit to anyone how helpless I felt during what I'd come to understand as my mother's first marriage. I'd confess how, even after I summoned the courage to call myself a writer out loud, to pursue it for-serious, for fear I'd be judged, I dodged setting down what was too close to that wound. I'd concede to Kev that for a long while (all the while?) my work suffered because of it. Before he left, I'd explain how, along the way, I realized what once terrified me could be a resource, that exposing what I feared on the page strengthened my work, strengthened me. The over-grown-ass-man I profess myself can't help but wonder how it would've turned out for Kev had he been convinced to embrace rather than flee what set him apart, had been persuaded that his greatest fear or shame or doubt could one day become his gift.

MAN, 20, FATALLY
SHOT OUTSIDE CLUB

A 20-year-old Portland man was shot and killed early Thursday after arguing with a man outside a nude dance club in Northeast Portland.

Lil Anthony and me knew each other from almost the womb. As it happens, our mamas were so tight when we were young that, from infants, we considered each other cousins. One of my earliest memories of Lil Anthony—he was only a couple years my junior but seemed younger—was when he and I were in grade school and staying over our auntie's house. In those days, Lil Anthony had an outie belly button, and I used to tease him about it something vicious. That particular day, I duped him into submitting to the crackpot theory (not sure where it came from) that we could "fix" it by taping it down with a coin. And damn, damn, he looked dour as I don't know what when it didn't work.

The last time I saw Lil Anthony alive was the June day Judge Kantor sentenced me to time behind the walls. Bailiffs too carefree for the moment marched me out of the courtroom and onto an elevator and up to a top floor in the courthouse and off the elevator into a gloomtastic room that housed a holding cell. Most of that tour, I kept my wet eyes lowered—wasn't no fronting as a Man of Maraging Steel—but I perked at the sound of what I believed was Lil Anthony's voice: "Cousin, cousin. I heard you was comin'," he said, from inside a cell. Lil Anthony had been a committed blue-flag nationalist since his tweens, one known as the Lil Smurf to a beloved OG Crip named Big Smurf. Both Smurfs had been on the eight-person list of Crips indicted on RICO (Oregon Racketeer Influenced and Corrupt Organizations Act) crimes earlier that year. Lil Anthony announced he was headed to court to seek bail on his charge. "And if they give it to me, I'm gone," he said, and flashed a smile that brightened, however brief, my mood.

A judge gave him bail.

Someone posted that bail in September.

And he was gone—as in gone, gone forever gone, by early October.

How to Revise: Step 2

Picture me back in the classroom, the lecture projected on the screen, the young homies slouched in their desks but otherwise attentive. "Revision is process," I'd remind them. "And the second stage of that process is *Organization*." This is the stage where we ask ourselves if we chose the right structure for the content, if we've ordered our ideas for prime effect, when we critique whether we've created strong links between those ideas.

In *Killingsworth*, the biographical documentary on Lil Anthony's life, a then deputy district attorney reports, "He [Anthony] was public enemy number one in the gang world because of how active he was . . . the Gang Enforcement Team thought he was responsible for half the shootings out there—either he was doing them or he was the target of them." The adult me wishes I could pull Lil Anthony's collar and persuade him into believing, with the same wholeheartedness that he gangbanged, that another way of life was within his reach. To sway my cousin, I'd present the advice the writer Barry Hannah once offered a room of Bennington College writing students: "Be a master such as you have." In an attempt to win him over, I'd admit that I admired how, all things considered—his mother's addiction, whatever beef he had on the streets—he never seemed in low spirits, how even though he was younger than me, I looked to him as a measure of what could be endured. To urge my cousin, I'd concede how acute I've felt my dearths as a writer, would explain how minor I feel compared (despite a sage mentor chiding me "Never compare") to writers who boast childhoods as voracious readers, who learned Latin in grade school, who studied abroad as biddy brainiacs, who received a Rhodes Scholarship or fought on the front lines in Iraq, or spent a year at Yale on a postdoc or a season doing missionary work in the DR Congo. Before we parted, I'd admit that a fear that dogs me on and on is that my deficiences will be laid bare in what I write, that it's hard, if not impossible, to shake the feeling that I won't ever overcome my lack. But I'd also tell him how there's profit in a childhood like his or mine, would cite the preachers and pimps and hustlers I loved and loathed as a youngin having informed my writing voice, would point to how that voice, which some have praised, has given me reason to believe, if not that I belong, then that I can challenge most exclusions.

The way I see it, Lil Anthony had much to master. He owned a smile that was full of charm but seemed earnest, that made grown folks fawn, that won him grace for damn near any trouble he might've caused. And check it: as an ambitious and industrious but nonetheless slight middle schooler, he'd stack phone books in the seat of a hooptie, crane over its steering wheel, and tour around Northeast. On top of that, he was unassailably, unimpeachably, unremittingly brave, was seen swaggering around neighborhoods (albeit wearing a bulletproof vest) while there was a rumored hit ordered on him. With such as he had, Lil Anthony could've been whatever he wanted—a CEO, an engineer, a mailman, a writer, a mighty-fine motivational speaker—and I wish I could've seeded him with that faith, that I could've convinced him that pursuing mastery of his gifts may've altered a future that he felt predestined.

VICTIMS IN EAST VANCOUVER
DOUBLE HOMICIDE ID'D

The victims in Sunday's double homicide in east Vancouver have both been identified as Portland area men. Allen J. Collins, 37, died of gunshot wounds to the head and neck, and Jason D. Benton, 42, died of multiple gunshot wounds.

Jason, Kev, and me were members of the undefeated (GO TECHMEN!) 1989/90 Benson High School freshman football team. In fact, my earliest and most indelible memories of Jason are of him intrepid, dashing here, there, everywhere on the field. Our freshman season, he was the unques-tionable defensive star of our team, a linebacker whose hits, even in those days, sounded like high-speed car wrecks. It appeared to me then that Jason was either at or near the height of strength, passion, and ferocity for a four-teen-year-old boy. Our sophomore year—while I abandoned all notions of a football career—Jason became a starting linebacker on the varsity football team. Catch Jason in the weight room bench-pressing trillions for reps or on the field sprinting around cones or in the lunchroom declaring he'd one day hit the field for the Huskies (University of Washington). Jason, like a couple of dudes on the team, also was a nascent nationalist. His color: red. On game days though, he and the rest of the team paraded the school in their orange-blue-and-white football jerseys. Even now, more than twenty-five years later, I can see him strutting around the halls, barrel-chested, hair shorn low.

One of the highlights of my high school years was attending the Friday Night Lights games in the Civic Stadium. This was an occasion to wear my freshest gear, lounge in the stands with the popular girls and my patnas, and awe at the triumphs of Jason et al. The stadium lights gave the games a sense of grandeur, and, as a result, Jason's star blazed. Every other play, he was turning some dude's hope for the end zone into what I imagined was the sound of semis colliding, a feat honored by the announcer calling, "Benton on the tackle."

From sophomore season on, Jason, known as a defensive specialist, lob-bied his coach to let him run the ball, and he got his chance his senior year. Ultimately and grievously, Jason suffered a high-ankle sprain when, during a preseason practice drill, a teammate fell on him. Jason sat out regular-season games, and was much more human than superteen when he returned. His team didn't make it to the state championship as they'd hoped that year, nor did Jason play well in his last game. Dejected about his injury, his season, and the now near-impossible dream of suiting up for the Huskies, he shifted his passion for football into gangbanging and earned the handle Ogre.

On the up-and-up: Jason wasn't my patna. We didn't keep in contact beyond high school, but we had plenty of mutual friends, and I'd hear tales about him, some rumors, some truths, I suspect, most of which confirmed he was fast becoming a notorious nationalist. I can't recall the last time I saw him in person, but we followed each other on social media, and I'd browse pictures he'd post of him and his girlfriend, some with loving cap-tions, and, from a distance, would wish him and her well.

How to Revise: Step 3

"And the third stage of revision is *Expression*," I'd continue. "This is where we start to consider our voice or, in other words, our personality on the page." I'd explain that this is the part of the process where we make more pointed choices about the *way* we say what we need to say. That includes diction and syntax, which rhetorical tools to use, where we ponder other choices connected to style. "Expression," I'd say, "is where we work to become, in what we write, more of who we believe ourselves."

It seems obvious now that Jason lost a vital part of his will to persist in high school. The grown me wishes I could travel back to those days and share with him what Vladimir Nabokov writes in *Speak, Memory*: "I have rewritten, often several times, every word I have ever published. My pencils outlast their erasers." Nabokov's pronouncement speaks to the process of revising on the whole, of try, try, trying to achieve eloquence, of how tough it is to chase eloquence. It also stresses the need for an indefatigable work ethic, which Jason, without doubt, owned back at Benson. Also contained in the statement is the urging to endure, to will one's self between narrowing gaps of opportunity, over obstacles, beyond boundaries, which, above all, demands holding fast to hope.

Had the old me had a chance to reach the young Jason, I'd confide how, for a couple of years, I had a mentor whose advice I treated as gospel. Would admit how, when I worked up the courage to send that mentor the novel manuscript I'd been revising for over a decade, he sent me a quick postcard reply that was the ultimate eraser: "Throw it all out!" To be sure I hadn't misread his hand, I called him, and the mentor confirmed his advice. While I sat on my couch and listened to him explain why my life's work was of little worth, I felt more than a few tears dribble down my cheeks. For a day or so, I considered tossing the novel, giving up altogether, and doing I-don't-know-what from there. I'd ask Jason if that echoed his feelings at the end of his senior season and, if he said yes, would disclose that, the next day or one soon-come, I resolved to keep revising until I had a novel, until I'd achieved what at one point was my longest dream deferred.

Had Jason kept his spirits through the crucible of that ankle sprain, I have little doubt he could've played, if not for UW, then some other D1 school, and that that experience would've changed the trajectory of his life. With a full recovery Jason was headed for Sunday-afternoon marvels, and an astonished announcer whooping, "Benton on the solo stop."

WANNABE NOVELIST
SEEKS BENEFACTORS

That was my *actual* headline. They ran it right before I moved to New York for grad school. This was a couple of years after I paroled, and I was amped about the chance I'd received to *re*-envision my life. At the time they ran the story, though, no small part of my public self was that of an ex–dope dealer, one who could still be seen bending corners in my money-green Lexus, or in a club decked in repeat-print Versace jeans, gleaming Air Force Ones, and a fresh-from-the-swap-meet paper-white tee, never to be worn twice. For those reasons and more, "seeking benefactors" had me feeling downright ignominious, like a beggar, a lowlife, worse. But in retrospect, my *actual* headline was key to grasping (though it took over a decade) another important aspect of revision: the need for collaboration.

At every stage of my evolution as a writer (shit, my growth as a human being), there have been a host of folks asking questions of me; critiquing and encouraging and inspiring me; agreeing to serve as a soundboard for ideas that weren't nowhere near fleshed; challenging me to rethink or reimagine whole drafts; hipping me to models of prose, poems, drama; sharing histories and theories . . . And the list of indispensables has included partners, family, mentors, writers, professors, editors, friends who write, friends who don't. And that collective beneficence has made me question, beyond these words, what must I do to aid someone in need of revision? How might I, or anyone who cares (you?), help another human avoid a death sentence or a life sentence or a so-much-of-their-life-there's-not-much-life-left sentence? How could we—me and you, that is—foster the next Kevan or Lil Anthony or young Jason, seeing themselves in context, seeing their lives in progress, discovering what's right about themselves and imagining ways to make it more right?

How to Revise: Step 4

"The last stage of revision is *Mechanics and Format*," I'd tell the fellas. "And it's the least sexy part." I'd explain to them that this stage involves checking things like grammar and misspellings and punctuation errors and omitted words. It's also the stage where we format the work, depending on discipline, where we follow the conventions of the MLA (Modern Language Association) or the APA (American Psychological Association) or the youngest of the big three, *The Chicago Manual of Style.*

Near the end of our time together, I'd mention "The Art of Editing No. 1," a *Paris Review* profile of legendary editor Bob Gottlieb. In it, several authors cite anecdotes and advice from Gottlieb. One of those authors is the world treasure Toni Morrison. "Endings I always know, because that's always what the book is about," she explains. "The problem is getting there. I used to have these really awful beginnings—never really beginnings, they were starts—and Bob always caught them."

Morrison spoke in reference to fiction, but let me tell it, gleaning the differences between a start and a beginning is crucial to revising one's self. Starts are beholden in some respect to time. Beginnings are a harvest of timing. A start might be static. But beginning will happen in medias res, in the midst of something crucial. "There are false starts but no false beginnings," I'd say. "Beginnings are what evolve after a start."

To close, I'd relate one last story about revision. This one about handing in my novel at last, after eleven, twelve, thirteen (my heart had to stop counting) or more years of revising it. I'd begin it during the mid-May week when my "final pass" draft was due, a week that featured a Friday flight to Atlanta to chaperone my daughter's field day. That week I would teach from morning to night, drag home on the train, scarf takeout or a quick-cooked meal, edit, proof, and in some cases, more cases than corroborate good sense, revise my "last pass" pages till right before the sun rose. Then shower. Then dress. Then bolt. Repeat, repeat, and so on.

Thursday rolled around and I was clinging to the hot thin hope that I could meet what my editor confirmed as my capital-D Drop-Dead due date, AKA the one that, if missed, would mean a pub date pushed to what might as well be Nevuary, not to mention a gang of more fallout. Proactive me worked a deal to have my girlfriend messenger the pages to the publisher that Friday, which seemed well within the realm of mortal possibilities until that Thursday, when I gloomed at the clock on my computer and the stack of unread manuscript pages and understood, as if a wise scribe had whispered it in my ear, that there was no way and no how in the heavens or the known universe I'd finish before my flight. That prophecy prompted me to email my editor—I'll call her K.B.—and ask if there was even an infinitesimal chance I could deliver the pages to her on Monday. No! K.B. wrote. She needed the manuscript by close of business Friday at 5:00 p.m. And not a second after! K.B.'s mandate sent me in the small hours huffing the few blocks from my girlfriend's apartment to a college where I taught. Once there, I convinced a wary security guard that I had to get into my office for an emergency, blustered upstairs, and prayed the last thirty pages out of a fickle-ass printer.

There was just enough time after that to grab my bag and cab to the airport and, delirious, so damn delirious, board my flight. Maybe I edited a page or a paragraph on the flight. Maybe I didn't. What I can tell you is my brain wasn't broadcasting right. What I can tell you is my daughter's mother drove me from the airport to our daughter's school. Once I got there, a woman informed me that my job would be manning a field day station where kids tried to balance golf balls on spoons with a hand behind their backs: Golf Ball Boxing. For what felt like eons, I stood, in spirit and body if not mind, in Southern spring heat, and when at last the games ended, I broke for the car, grabbed those last twenty or so pages, and scratched what felt like the most important words I would ever write in this life or the afterlife. In truth, what I did was more editing and proofing than revising, but, let the church say amen, I finished my business just about the time field day ended and we—the "we" being my daughter, her mother, and dematerializing me—set out on a mission to find the nearest print-copy outpost.

Per Google intelligence, the closest one might as well have been in Alabama. I'm talking miles. We trekked those miles, though, and once there, abided the albatrosses of being forced to buy a flash drive damn near priced like a hard drive, submitted to an impossible line for the computers, suffered a test-tastic log-on, waited on the slowest copy-center worker on planet earth to problem solve the center's baby ENIAC computer failing to find my thumb drive, braved an Internet connection the speed of human evolution (this all happened; my word is my bond), but, in the end, I was able to let my daughter hit send on my "final pass" pages seconds before the capital-D fall-out-and-die Deadline.

She and I walked out, her smiling, me with my chest loosening.

"We did it," I said.

"Yes, we did, Dad," she said, and looped her arm in mine. "Does this mean you're done?"

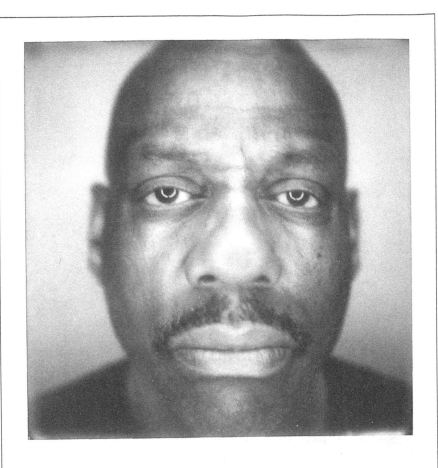

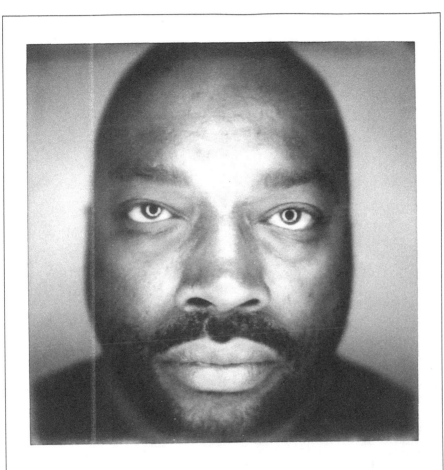

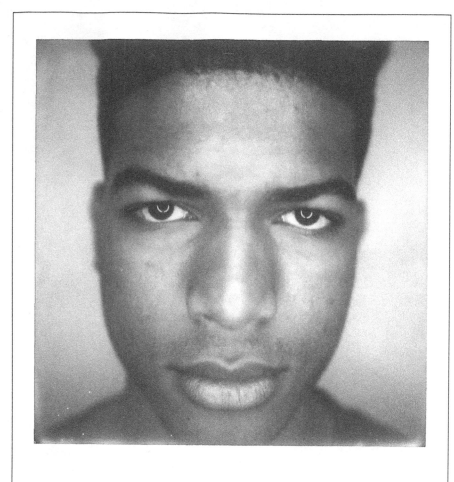

SURVIVOR FILE

Your day, so you bide at the crib for your ex to arrive daughter in tow. She don't. And you hit her line from minutes after she was due till it's clear she won't show nor answer, at which point you ring your attorney (who also happens to be the homie) and curse a fusillade. "Chill, bro, chill," he says. "We knew she'd fuck up and do something crazy cause that's what she does." You trust your homeboy-lawyer, which is to say, you're subject to accepting his counsel, and that night, console yourself that this silly shit'll be over in a day or two. The next morning, someone raps your front door and rouses you out the bed. That someone is a woman who announces she's a CPS (Child Protective Services) worker. The CPS woman informs you that some one filed a report claiming you abused your daughter. "What! Aw, hell nah, that's some bullshit!" you say. You check yourself the next instant, apologize for cursing, ask her to hold, and dial your homeboy-lawyer. Your homeboy-lawyer advises you to let the woman search the apartment and to be sure to tour your daughter's room. You heed and, post the CPS woman's probing, sit with her and your new fiancée in your hella-spare living room. The woman asks if there was a situation where you spanked your daughter. "Yeah, there was," you say. "I told her to go to bed and she started cryin and kickin the walls. So, I warned her once. Warned her twice. Warned her a third time. And after that there's consequences." You tell the woman that you found one of your daughter's belts and, as she bicycle-kicked, slapped her on the leg with it a couple times and ordered her to sleep. You explain that your daughter woke up the next morning her usual chipper self and, per her routine, skippety-skipped off to school with her cousin. "Well," the CPS woman says, "your story sounds consistent with what your daughter told us." She reveals that your daughter said she was kicking while you spanked her and on accident kneed herself in the lip. "Oh shit," you say. "I didn't know nothin bout no busted lip. Why didn't her mama call me? She could've just called me." The CPS woman confirms that your daughter said you didn't know about her busted lip and that it doesn't appear to be any abuse, but adds that she's mandated to keep the case open for thirty days. She assures you when the thirty days expire, she'll close the case, and adds she won't need to meet with you again. You question whether your daughter can come home, and she clarifies she doesn't regulate whether a child can return to a residence, that the decision is in the jurisdiction of the courts. "As a general rule," she says, "we'd rather the child be returned to the accused parent, so we can observe the kid and the parent together and see how they interact." You complain you haven't seen your daughter in days, and the CPS woman stresses she has no bearing on the absence. You call your homeboy-lawyer the second the CPS woman leaves, and he assures you he's doing all he can to find your daughter. You believe him, but that don't stop a week from passing, another week, that don't stop weeks and weeks from slogging by without a word from your ex or her answering a single one of your calls—vexation that demands a blunt. One day you tramp down the street to cop some chronic and see your cousin (the one who dates your ex's sister) lounging in a car in front of the weed man's house. "What up, fam?" you say. "What up?" he says. You mount the steps, and midway your cousin announces the weed man's gone. "Damn, fam, I need some chronic," you say. "A nigga out here stressed." Your cousin proposes selling you a sack, even pitches driving you back to your crib and blowing a blunt with you. And he ain't got to offer twice. He rolls to your complex and the two of you hotbox in the parking lot. "Yo, your ex still out in Baltimore?" he asks, between pulls. "Baltimore?" you say. "She ain't in no Baltimore. She ain't sposed to be in no Baltimore." You ask if he's sure, and he confirms. You explain to him (what good's an explanation?) that the courts said since there's no custody resolution, neither you nor your ex can transport your daughter more than forty miles outside the city limits. Your cousin reports he's heard where your ex is from his girl, even volunteers to call her on speakerphone to confirm. "Yeah," you say. "Do that for me, fam." He calls his girl, chitchats for a few, then prods, "I thought you said your sister went to Baltimore. How's that when I just seen her at the bus stop." His girl's voice notches an octave. "You ain't seen my sister at no bus stop," she says. "My sister's in Maryland. I'm sure of that," she says. "And that's fucked up what she did, taking that baby away from her daddy like that. I'd hate to be him." Her words turn you combustible. You jump out and flame across the parking lot for your apartment, smashing your homeboy-lawyer's digits into your cell. He answers before you reach the front door. "Well, at least we have a target now," he says, with what seems an inexplicable calm. "At least we have somewhere to search." You're due in court weeks from now, and you half hope that your ex don't show so you can broadcast what she's done. Your court date arrives, and you attend with your homeboy-lawyer, your parents, and one of your sisters. Your ex don't show, but her mama and lawyer do, and that lawyer requests to speak at the start of the proceedings. "Your Honor, I'd like to resign," she says. "I don't want to be a part of this case anymore." Your homeboy-lawyer objects; the attorney is your lone point of contact with your ex, and therefore she should be ordered to stay on so you and he can serve her papers. The judge overrules the objection, which feels like the abuse they accused you of, and at once you dread having lost the one person you could hold accountable for your ex's actions. You reel to some dark terminus till (did he just say what you thought he said?!) the judge awards you full custody of your daughter, not a default, which could be protested, but a judgment—as in final, as in you won! Once you were charged with domestic violence, what in truth might be a paternal inheritance, and now here you are granted full custody of your daughter. Though your six-year-old could be anywhere, for a moment your heart floats somewhere among the city's ever-gray clouds. Following the verdict, you spend endless hours calling all possible leads and task your sleuthhound sister with hunting online. Meanwhile, your ex changes her number but begins calling you private with your daughter on the phone. "Daddy, come get me," she cries. "Tell me where you are," you say. "I know you might get in trouble. But tell Daddy where you are, whatever city, and I'll be there tomorrow." Months pass, holidays, and your daughter calls balling about a barren Christmas. You try to imagine how she must feel being shuffled from one house to the next, from a cousin to a friend, and your woes seem ceaseless until, Allahu Akbar, your snoopficient sister finds your daughter's school in Maryland. You contact the school and the judge who presided over your custody case and apply for the order that you can take to Maryland to prove your custody. Weeks later (each second is its own anguish) you receive the paperwork you need. Your homeboy-lawyer advises you to send someone else to retrieve your daughter, warns that you might see your ex and rage. Per his counsel, you arrange to send your dad as an emissary to fetch your daughter from school, head straight to the airport, and fly back the same day. You coordinate the pickup with the school and spend a fitful night chastening yourself against too much hope. And how prophetic, the school calls that next day to inform you your daughter was unenrolled two weeks prior. Again, you beat back the creeping panic that you may never see your daughter again. In time, your ex calls from another private number with your daughter on the line. "Where are you?" you ask, and your daughter reveals her mother has moved them to Phoenix. You ask to speak to your ex. "This shit ain't right," you say. "Just let her come home. Please, please, just let her come home." Sometimes, your ex calls and sobs that she and your daughter are near destitute and in need, and though it's almost impossible to support someone who's abducted your child, you send money with the hope it secures your daughter, that it ushers you one step closer to a reunion. Inshallah, the life of roaming place to place and living hand-to-mouth will wear your ex into acquiescing. You keep plying your ex to let you buy your daughter a ticket, and one time, to your shock, she agrees, concedes with the caveat you wait a couple of weeks. Those weeks pass and, to your immense gratitude, your ex calls and gives the go-ahead, so long as you foot her cab fare to and from the airport. You buy your daughter an unaccompanied minor ticket with the quickness and send your ex her transport ransom. You also buy the most expensive computer tablet you can and download it with dozens of games. You ride with your sleuth-fabulous sister to the airport well ahead of your daughter's flight. The two of you blow chronic in the parking lot, dawdle into an airport bar, and drink too many rounds for the occasion. You stride to the gate reminiscing on what it's taken to get here, how it's been almost a year since your daughter refused bedtime and bicycle-kicked herself a busted lip. Your daughter's flight lands at last. One passenger files out of the Jetway, then another, another, another . . . and Mashallah, an attendant escorts your daughter into view. She spots her aunt first and bolts for her but stops short, turns to you, and squeals, "Daddy! Daddy!" You swoop your precious six-year-old off her feet (she's bigger than you foresaw), squeeze her tight enough to feel her heart, and dapple her face with infinite kisses. Years from now you'll remember this moment as one of the happiest of your life, but in the moment, worry over what the time and distance may have birthed between you lives beneath your joy.

SURVIVOR FILE

You meet her at a club one night: no beauty queen, but cute. This cutie is the friend of a friend, and the friend mentions several times that night that she's told him she wants you to pay her notice. You do so for the rest of the night, and sure enough, you and she get busy for the first time later that week in the office of the furniture store where she works. It will never exceed much more than sex to you, a setup that suits you fine as a man who's in the separation phase of a divorce. You advance to alacritous barebacking after she assures you she and her ex-husband, both in the throes of drug addiction, had tried to conceive many times and couldn't. You boast, half in jest, about your virility, but keep right on raw-dogging. Months later, the two of you attend a New Year's party at her sister and rich brother-in-law's house. Minutes into the new year, you shake the carousing and spin your BMW to a black-black field not far from the party. Unbeknown to you, in that car, in that field, she conceives. Between the time she knows and the time you find out, she begins to ask how you feel about her, suggests she'd like more from you than you're willing to give. You see her much less often, then find out that she moved to a hick town hours away from Portland. One day she calls and alleges she's pregnant. "By who?" you say. "By you," she says. "What? Wait. But how's this even possible?" you say, and with your next breath demand a paternity test. You take that test once the baby is born, though it seems a formality after one of your daughter's first pictures attests your DNA. You begin paying child support. You visit your daughter on the rare occasions she stays with an aunt who lives in your area, and one of those times, you introduce your oldest daughter to her. You hear through a friend that her mother has rekindled with the white man of her dreams. Next, you hear that she and that dreamy white man married. That husband calls you and announces he wants to adopt your daughter, that he and his wife would like for you to surrender your parental rights. "No way. I'm not givin up any rights!" you shout. Later, you receive a letter in the mail requesting your presence at a weekday court date in the hick town where your daughter, her mother, and her exalted stepdad live. You're scheduled to work, so you blow off the date, flout it without so much as a phone call or email to the court or your daughter's mother. You believe the worst consequence of your no-show and no response would be a rescheduled court date. How could anything worse happen when you've made your position clear, when you've never abused or harmed your daughter, when you've been paying your child support all the while? You learn the extent of your wrongheadedness when you call to check on your child support and a clerk explains that you needn't make any more payments because your daughter's been adopted. "What?" you say. "How?" You'll find out later all your parental rights have been usurped, which includes visitation. For weeks, you'll feel dazed by the judgment, puny, impotent. For years, you won't see your daughter. But once, you and your oldest daughter travel to watch her high school track meet. In the school's parking lot, you instruct your eldest not to tell her sister you're present. That afternoon, you cheer your daughter from a seat high in the stands, imagine hurdling onto the field at the finish of her races, and swooping her into your arms. However, you do no such thing; in fact, you leave the meet without speaking a word to her. Your daughter is in college now, and you can't count all the times you've wanted to call or write her, to profess your love for her, your vast sadness at not knowing her; you want to do all of these things, though, as yet, haven't attempted a single one.

SURVIVOR FILE

You're a junior high superjock who believes the rules at most half apply to you, and therefore swank into the locker room insouciant as shit about your lateness. Dressing down, you hear the coach holler your last name. "You're late," he says. "You're running a jaunt." You scope the room, eye teammates in various stages of undressing, and decline the honor. "You're running the jaunt or you won't be on this team," the coach says. "Fuck that," you say. "I ain't runnin." You snatch off your pads, slam yourself back into your clothes, boom your locker shut, and stomp outside and into the stands, where you try to console yourself with the prospect that, though a reprimand is damn near assured, the coach is certain to let you back on the team. Practice ends and you bop out of the bleachers to the edge of the field, where you dap your boys as they slog off. In the midst of this, the coach marches over to you. "I told you you're off the team. Get your shit and go!" he says, blitzing your pride. "Fuck you!" you say. The coach yells, "Fuck you! You ain't gonna be shit, just like your brother." And why oh why oh why in all the world did he say that? You call him a "Faggot!" A "Punk muthafucka!" You say, "Don't say shit about my brother!" and berserk for him, but one of your boys catches a handful of your shirt. "Chill, bro, chill. It ain't worth it. Just leave," he says. "Yeah. Get the hell outta here!" the coach taunts, and turns what was a blitz into a siege. "FUCK YOU! FUCK YOU! My brother just got out, and me and him gone come up here and fuck you up!" you say. "On everything I love, we gon come back up here and fuck your punkass up!" Your boys urge you off the field and around to the front of the school, where you wait with your adolescent heart doing high knee kicks. One of the first boys out of the school is a kid who ain't a friend but who also ain't heretofore been an enemy. "Why you quit? That was some bitch shit," the kid says, and summons the whisper of your father's gospel: *Son, you wanna solve a problem quick, sock a motherfucka in his jaw.* You smash your chest to the kid's chest. "Bitch. Who you callin a bitch?" you say. "You's a bitch. We can scrap right here, right now." The coach's daughter sends you a look from her ambit of friends and you grant the kid a pass. You menace minutes longer outside the school and head home to the apartment you share with your mother and the brother your punkass coach damned as a forever also-ran. You don't mention a word about the trouble to your mom. Instead, you count all the times you've seen fracas at school, the times students have been caught carrying a knife on campus, the number of squabbles you've witnessed between the Mexicans and the Russians, between the Red Cobra Bloods and the Carson Block. You wake the next morning and catch the bus to school wondering if your spat with the coach is enough to earn your nth suspension. You assume your usual post outside the school with your crew and spy the kid whose jaw you almost cracked. You approach him and apologize and he accepts and the both of you laugh off your brief friction, a moment abridged when a school security guard marches over stern-faced and asks if he can see your bag. "Yeah, sure," you say. "What's up?" The guard handles your bag as if it's crime evidence and commands you to follow him inside, where you feel eyes everywhere tracking your steps. "What's goin on?" you ask. The guard orders you seated in the principal's waiting area, carries your backpack off to who-knows-where. Meanwhile, the bell sounds for first period. Meanwhile, the Pledge of Allegiance echoes in the halls. Meanwhile, not a soul in the office charities you a single word. The guard, belated, escorts you into the office, and the principal—he of rust-colored hair, glass eye, and bush mustache—offers you the chance to explain your side. You admit that you lost your temper but that you intend to apologize to your coach. "Did you threaten to shoot him?" he asks. "What? I never said nothin about shootin nobody," you say. The principal reports the coach is distraught and concerned for his and his daughter's safety. You argue again that you never mentioned shooting nobody, but concede to threatening to involve your oldest brother. "Well, unfortunately," the principal says, "we heard otherwise. We heard that you threatened to bring a gun and shoot him and we must treat that threat with the utmost seriousness." Years from now the weight of this moment will be clearer—most of all, how it's mere months after a mass school shooting in Thurston, which is a town too close to ignore as elsewhere. The principal announces that you're expelled. "But wait," you say. "Security didn't find no gun." He shakes his head. "But wait," you say, and petition once more for him to reconsider. "Okay, okay," you say, and, having seen other expelled students allowed to return, ask what's the length of your expulsion. You appeal for the principal to call your mother, which he does, but he can't reach her. You request he call your oldest brother, which he refuses because you've implicated him in the clash. A school cop appears at the door to escort you off the premises. You bound out of your seat and smash your back against a wall. "Nah, nah," you say. "I ain't goin to jail!" The cop frowns. "Please, Son, don't make this worse," he says. You accuse the coach of lying again, reiterate the fact no one found a gun, appeal once more for someone to call your mom. "I can't go to jail," you screech, duck, and dodge around the office, squeeze your eyes against tears, and feel your pulse dancing a Super Bowl shuffle. You skirt school security and the officer till struck still by the futility of actual escape. You let the cop cuff you. He reads you your rights (a first despite assorted juvenile woes) and leads you slumping out of the school feeling each step as part of your fortune. The cop loads you into the car with care. On the way, he asks if you're hungry, promises to feed you just as soon as you reach the jail, offers further encouragements while you weep. You're booked, mug-shotted, finger-smudged, led to a holding cell, and left to sulk. It's Friday and, per the protocol, if they can't reach your mom by X o'clock, you'll spend the weekend in custody. You brood the tests you might face over such a weekend but (call it grace) your worry is cut short when they reach your mother before the deadline. You explain to her what happened on the way home and feel both comforted and confused by her calm. No school for you until your expulsion hearing in a couple of weeks, and in that time, the local paper runs a story on the incident. In that time, the parent of one of your homeboys forbids him from kicking it with you. In those weeks, other friends foster fresh distance. You begin to wonder if you're the boy in your behavior file, if the expulsion is an omen. You wallow in this ambivalence until your court date arrives, a proceeding you attend with no one but your haughty mother. The two of you sit opposite a school district worker and your ruddy, glass-eyed ex-principal. They pull your file, papers thick as fingers you've jammed in hoop games, a record that includes the time you tried to spit on a teacher, the time you threw a crayon at another, the time you slapped a kid in class, the countless fights, the in-school suspensions, the out-of-school suspensions. You gawk at the file and reassess your chances of escaping this latest entry. The judge upholds your expulsion, bans you from attending any school in the district; in fact bars you from attending even the popular alternative school. The judge, as a matter of fact, mandates you to attend a brand-new alternative school. You arrive at that school the first day and discover your classroom is a trailer parked on a pebbled lot. You soon learn your classmates include boys in their late teens who binge on cheap vodka, a white dude forever on his penultimate chance, Mexicans chasing a passing

GED score, classmates who float into the trailer-classroom high as the cost of dreams, others who smoke Marlboros and pinner joints on breaks, girls who cut and run from home to join meth-smoking marathons with grown men, bully-prone gang members. You're the youngest in a trailer-classroom of eighteen-, nineteen-, twenty-year-old pseudostudents but discover your age don't exempt you from the rule that requires all students to attend group night with their parents. Your mom runs late the first night of group, and while you sit taciturn, you witness a girl curse her mother to low names, another parent lament having not seen their son in weeks. The group leader asks you to introduce yourself and explain why you're in the school. You hesitate but admit the expulsion. She asks if you threatened to shoot the coach, and you deny it. "Well, you're here," she says. "So that means something." You concede but add, "Yeah, but I don't got problems like them." One of your classmates pipes, "Ooooh, look what we have here. The dude who don't got problems like the rest of us. What, you better than us?" You giant out of your seat—hear your father's scripture on blast: *Son, sock this motherfucka in his jaw!* You say, "What you say, punk? I'll whoop yo ass!" He sparks erect and glares. "What? What?" you say. "We can go outside and get the ones right now." The group leader pleads against blows, and in pulses, pulses, pulses her will prevails. She waits for quiet, or as close to it as the room will cede, and turns to you: "Now I see," she says. "Now I think I know why you're here." But it will be many years of defeats before you can see what she sees.

SURVIVOR FILE

You ask your mom for movie-ticket money and maybe even a popcorn; for a couple bucks to hang with your buds; for a check to cover registration or the sports fee or the student ID fee; for cash to purchase the C package of school pictures and, all year, she snaps, "We don't have it." Then one day after school, you bop home and see a white sheet taped to your front door, the words "Eviction Notice" in boldface. You snatch the sheet off the door, gape at the small print, teeter inside the apartment, and wait. Thinking, *Why didn't she tell me how bad it was?* Thinking, *Why didn't she call my dad or grandpa for help?* Thinking, *Where will we go?* Your mom schleps in from work, and you hand her the notice. "EVICTION! WHAT? NO!" she says. She tramps into her bedroom and calls somebody, and you can hear her pleading with whomever it is. She stomps out of the room, eyes smudged black, and confirms you'll have to move. You have a few weeks, and each day she doesn't find an apartment is another day for you to anguish over if you'll end up homeless. Close to the deadline, she reports she found a cheaper apartment in, of all places, a complex across the street from the one you must leave. Your mom can't afford a moving truck, much less movers, so she and you alone load TVs, tables, couches, shelves, dressers, clothes, the megatons of junk she hoards, etc., in her raggedy Rover, jaunt it to the new complex, and unload it all. With each trip, you feel your arms and legs losing strength, begin to feel aches in your back, fire in your palms, breath gusting out of you, but you're determined to finish because you must, because it's your destiny to discover not just the limits of what you can heft but how much weight you can bear.

EPILOGUE

Dear Justice,

Do you remember our final father-daughter dance? What I remember is being excited about seeing beautiful you with your hair done up in your new dress and shoes, about the chance to watch your smile turn electric, about seeing you as close as you (or I) come to carefree. What I also remember is being on tenterhooks about traveling to the dance because, months prior, I'd overbooked my schedule. What I recall is sitting on a train to New Haven, checking the hour-to-hour winter forecast minute after minute, and feeling my nerves kick off a crusade in me. Which is to say, I was struck with the need for faith. The timing was gonna be tough minus weather issues, but with a snowstorm predicted to start a half hour before my departure, the odds of making it to ATL edged close to the precipice. And what, in all the world, could've mended me missing our last father-daughter dance? What, on God's earth, could've softened another hurt from me?

The weather was at fault, yes, but the most truth is, this was yet another time when my need to feel of consequence was the heart of an issue. One of the organizers of a Yale Law School conference had invited me to speak, and I can't lie, it seemed like an accomplishment, like a deed that years from then would continue to swell me with pride. On top of that, the dude who invited me said, per his unofficial research, that I'd be the first novelist to speak at the conference, which made it feel that much closer, as close as I'm allowed, to august. Though it's easier now to diagnose it as a stone-cold case of solipsism, I also imagined, an assumption that was a suspect reversal of our roles, that you'd be proud of me as well. That you might brag to your friends that your dad had been invited to speak at an Ivy.

The itinerary was almost impossible from the jump, but I accepted the invite, said yes before your school announced the exact date of the dance, and remained committed even after I discovered they were scheduled for the same day. That date was a Saturday, which also meant unless I forsook

283

my scheduled time with your brother—what I've been adverse to doing—
he would have to travel with me. Maybe I suffer from self-deception, but
I'd somehow convinced myself that speaking at Yale was of some benefit
to your little brother too, that it would make both of my children stand
tall—he from witnessing it, you from the chance to brag to your junior
high friends. For this chance, I recruited your uncle to come with us so
he could escort your little brother back to Jersey while I dashed to a small
Connecticut airport to reach you.

That plan was to read-speak-hightail back to the hotel, speed-change
into my suit (as you know, we had a precedent of father-daughter dance
flyness to uphold), get your brother situated, remind your uncle of the
instructions for escorting him back home, and hop a cab for the fifty-odd-
minute drive from New Haven to Hartford. If all occurred according to
plan, I'd make it to the airport with enough time to rush through security
and board my flight.

But there was that forecast: if your great-great-grandmother was alive,
she would've seen the devil in it. There was also the devilish prospect of
me boarding the plane only to sit on the apron for the limit of the DOT
weather rules. Anguish over those prospects blustered around my brain
as the seconds ticked off in my temples and *BOOM! BOOM! BOOM!*ed
in my chest, and meanwhile my cabdriver Sunday drove the highway
on a Saturday. We were minutes into his slow-motion locomoting when
the first snowflakes alighted on the windshield and drizzled toward the
wipers. "Is that snow?" I asked him, knowing good and well what it
was. *No, God, no, God. You can't!* I said to myself, and the next instant
imagined a universe in which I didn't make the dance, in which you sat
expectant on the living room couch in your new dress, in which after
waiting, waiting, waiting, waiting the limits of your teenage patience, your
mother had to wipe your tears and invent an excuse to console away my
absence.

The driver crept along the highway, the snow falling abundant, while
I obsessed over checking my phone, terrified I'd see a message that
announced a delay. We might've reached the airport within the hour;
it might've taken an age. Can't recall now how many people were in
the security line, because however few it was, my trip through TSA
seemed an eternity. Then there I was, hard-sole slip-sliding my way to
my gate. The windows near the gate overlooked the apron, and I could
see the flakes flurrying out of the sky—a portent. *Oh no! Oh no! They're*

gonna delay this flight! I thought. *Oh, please, God, no!* The next second I theorized how long of a delay I could afford before there were chances zip, zilch, none of us reaching the dance before it ended. "Oh, God," I exclaimed again (and you know that ain't even how I talk), and began to invent alibis, a story that would absolve me of what I knew in a deep true place would be an irredeemable blow. To you. To me.

While I waited at the gate, gaping out the window, the snowflakes grew big as the corsage I still hoped to pin to your dress. What else could I do but call, once again, on God, and hope. That hope being a form of faith, that faith being, as I understand it, "the assurance of things hoped for, the conviction of things unseen," being, as well, a belief in a power that can control what we can't. For most of my life, I've considered faith too fickle and, because of that, have avoided depending on it as much as I could, have worked hard, harder, to dictate my fortune. That day, holding fast to faith seemed about all I could do given the weather. On the other hand, for you, sitting almost a thousand miles away, it should not have been needed at all. Me being present for your dance, or for any moment you deem important in your life, should be a given. A child should never be required to need faith in a parent. Nah, that's an abstract. You should've never been compelled to need faith in *me.* You should've been able, without question, to count on my presence at each and every thing that's been important to you, on me being available when you've needed to talk, on me encouraging you in times of doubt. There should've never been a time when you were in want for something essential—be it love, protection, or new school clothes. And here's a hard truth, one that's not so much a dressing for a wound or amends but a statement of empirical fact: the ways I've required you to have faith in me have been nothing short of failing you.

Those thoughts came to me later. That day, I couldn't think much beyond the celestial favor I'd need to make it to Hartsfield in time for us to promenade hand in hand into our last father-daughter dance. To my colossal relief, the counter person announced on-time boarding, though there remained the terror of air traffic control grounding us at the last minute. The number of actual passengers that boarded the plane escapes me, but if it was one, it was a million, billion, quadrillion. They closed the cabin doors and the pilot broadcast he was going to do his best to get us out on time, an announcement that was more like prophecy given the snow boulders tumbling out the sky and the umpteen-member ground crew scrambling around the apron. But we did, hallelujah, back out of the gate and taxi for the runway. It was then that I texted your mother that I'd make it, said another prayer, and squeezed the armrest till the wheels lifted, and we rumbled up into white.

Sometime during that flight, and often since, I've replayed moments from previous dances, how your mother would take dozens of pictures of us (you bemoaning most of them) before we left. How we began the custom of snapping flicks of our shoes once we arrived. How we'd critique the outfits of other dads. How you and your friends would circle and do some curious-named new dance (y'all ATaliens are serious about your boogying) that I hadn't seen in life. But my favorite moments were the two or three slow dances, the times when you'd lay your head on my chest, put your hand in my hand, and let me lead, when I'd ask if you were having a good time, and your answer was always a convincing "yes." Those dances were ours and ours alone, moments I felt the blessings of fatherhood, twinklings in which I wished whatever distance had been birthed between us could be shrunk, annulled.

I'd made all the previous dances, which meant you trusted me to show up for the final one. Which is how it should've been, should be. You should've never been expected to do any more than trust me. If faith is the belief that an unseeable higher being will grant us favor, trust is a firm belief in the character and integrity and moral fitness of another human. While faith needs no logical proof, trust cannot exist without it. This is why faith is the domain of God, but our trust should exist in the dominion of man, why your trust of me should be supported by my words *and* deeds. What I mean is if someone loves you—no one is exempt from this law, and that no one includes me—they should persuade you to trust them by showing up when you need them, honoring their word to you, treating you with compassion, offering candor when it's called for. And though I've fallen short of earning your full trust, I hope it heartens you that I'll work and work and work for it.

By grace (what else could it have been?) the pilots landed at Hartsfield on time. Soon as I got off, I broke into a slip-slide wing-tip weave for The Plane Train to baggage claim and outside, where I witnessed your mother (can't remember feeling so pleased and relieved at once) pulling up curbside. You were your usual nonchalant self in the front seat, but I needed a hug from you for passing my self-made gauntlet. I tossed my bag in the trunk and hopped in. "Sheesh, you wouldn't believe what it took to get here," I said, wiped my brow, and set to the task of knotting my skinny tie into a just-so single Windsor while your mother sped to the school, which, we know, means she drove her normal speed. Do you remember the picture your mother took of us on the front steps of the school? Well, I do. It's one I revisit, think, *Look at us, look at us*, and give thanks for what was no minor miracle.

For fact, August 19, 2001, was a *major* miracle in my life. In retelling it, though, it's best to begin August 18, 2001, AKA, the night before you were born. That Saturday night my boys and me (we've called ourselves the 833 Crew since the days of me sporting a texturized low-top fade) had pieced up to throw a boat party on the *Portland Spirit*. This was our annual shindig, what each summer had been a highlight, and to tell the truth, I was psyched about it (don't you know it, even before father-daughter dances, I loved an excuse to get fresh). The crew had spent weeks meeting to discuss the party, had spent nights as duos and trios standing outside of clubs handing out flyers and-or slogging through parking lots to slip them under windshields; we'd spent hella time texting everyone in our address books who we thought maybe-might-probably-would buy a presale ticket or pay a surcharged cover at the door. For sure we needed a healthy crowd to turn a profit, but maybe even more so I wanted and needed to feel that I mattered that night, and that need was the crux of why I scraped up the cash to invest, knowing full well that my share of max profit wouldn't have equaled much more than the few hundred bucks I spent on my all-white linen. So it went, I showed up early and offered to help load supplies and began schlepping boxes back and forth while trying to preserve my fresh. On one of my trips to pick up this or that, one of the boat's staff stopped me and asked for my ID and when I showed it to him (it had expired on my birthday a few days before), he barred me from reboarding.

"But I already been on there," I said.

"But I'm one of the ones throwing the party," I said.

"But my ID *just* expired," I said.

"Well, let me to talk to someone else?" I said.

"Well, let me to talk to who's in charge," I said, until I was vis-à-vis with the captain, and the captain warned that if I boarded the boat, he wouldn't let it leave the dock. Since I wasn't about to ruin the party for everyone else, I skulked to my green Lexus with the rip in the seat—the car I would drive to pick you up just two days old from the hospital—with my pre-party glee pressed out of me and my head sunk.

But that's not the end of the story, not the point of what I wanted to tell you: I wanted to get at what was symbolic about it for me, by which I mean an object or action that takes on a significance greater than its literal meaning. These years hence, I'm convinced that being denied that night was a symbol, was, as far as I can see, prime evidence of something I perceived as a missed opportunity instead heralding an immeasurable blessing. Because you and I have never lived in the same house, I've always felt the need to amplify our always insufficient time together, to will it into symbols, totems, amulets you could carry with you when I wasn't there, and that I too could carry. In some sense, it's a project fated for failure, and although I realize that, Justice, it was never not rooted in this absolute truth: IloveyouIloveyouIloveyouIloveyouIloveyouIloveyouIloveyouIloveyouIlove youIloveyou.

There's strength and utility in perceiving the literal world for what it is. You will need it many times, so cultivate it. But also ask yourself if-when it benefits you to look beyond the apparent. Sometimes the answer will affirm your choice to live in the concrete world, and it alone. Still, I wish you'll one day become fluent in symbol, in transmuting the corporeal, what we can touch, into the symbolic. To do that takes imagination, which too will serve you well. To survive our world, the one brought to bear on me, and the one I've been instrumental in bringing to bear on you, you'll need to divine metaphor—comparisons between dissimilar things—but also be able to make it. Both the seeing and the making are crucial, not just to your survival, but to your material and spiritual well-being. And believe me, I wish you all the wealth in this world.

The night of August 18, 2001, I believed myself poorer for missing the boat party. However, I abandoned that thought the moment—this a couple hours later—your mother called and told me her water had broken. My recall is mostly shot about the drive to your mom's duplex and the few miles' trip to Good Samaritan hospital. But here's what I've gathered: I drove not my Lexus but your mom's Mazda 626, and your brothers—who must've been off-the-charts nervous—rode in the backseat. Your mom complained of feeling every pebble and dip in the road. I was speeding, which also meant that I could've been pulled over and cited for an expired license or worse. Sign-of-the-cross we made it without incident to Good Sam. They checked us into a birthing center room that was dim and wide and too close to quiet to leave my nerves settled. A nurse helped prop your mother in a bed and your brothers hovered close by, but me, instead of, as I should have been, holding your mother's hand and offering all conceivable comfort, I sat in a reclining chair that may as well have been on the moon.

Shameful, shameful, but in truth, I bucked up to the moment and past it at the thought of guiding another human, you, safe through the world, and though I couldn't see it clear while your mother labored, the crux of my resistance was this: because my innocence had been usurped when I was just a boy, I was convinced that my chief parental concern was serving as an impeccable guard over yours, and that that unfailing vigilance would be a duty for which I was ill-equipped.

Innocence. It's our birthright. It's the grace of not knowing and not having to know. If we're lucky, I guess, we carry it into our teens. But the rub on innocence is the longer we live, the less right we have to claim it. Soon enough, and in my case, premature, the world sieges upon it. Wrongheaded it might be, but wanting to protect you from the world is why I've supported sending you to all these parochial schools, why to this day when we're riding, I'll change a station if I hear cursing or some other language I deem explicit, why I still try with might not to curse in your presence, why I've leaned conservative in the clothes I buy for you, why even though you're old enough to own a license, I'm hesitant to watch a rated-R movie with you. It's why for years I made the mistake of calling you Princess, which was, I now glean, me stunting or, worse, restricting your efflorescence.

But let me say this: I've never intended, and thank the Lord you aren't, for you to be ignorant. If innocence is a charm of childhood, ignorance is a bane of maturity.

This might sound like a sermon, and as a rule I'm against preaching (well, for the most part), but how else to stress what I believe. Ignorance requires us to ignore history and our experience, demands we cease questioning what we don't know, and encourages us to be static in a world that keeps right on spinning against stagnation. Ignorance is what happens when we try to preserve innocence in the face of living, when we refuse evidence that we are meant to evolve. Ignorance isn't anyone's birthright; it's the willful wrongheaded attempt to time travel back to infancy, to birth.

The night you were born, not much about the hours between when we arrived and early the next morning offers itself to me; as a matter of fact, it's hazy until 4:16 a.m., which is the minute when, with my heart cranked, breath arrested, and a feeling of freefall, I watched your mother push tiny marvelous you headfirst into the world, when I watched you, Justice Serene Jackson, arrive. The next fact remains a heart-hurt to rule heart-hurts but is also just penance for the way I behaved: your oldest brother—not me—cut your umbilical cord. The doctor, moments later, invited me to hold you. "But she's so small," I said, and felt, in an instant, embarrassed at betraying how darn scared I was. The doctor stabbed her eyes at me, turned, and huffed off. She whisked back over to me with tiny you swaddled. "Here," she said. "She's bigger now."

Here you are—bigger, matured—intellectually, emotionally, spiritually. Here I am—hoping, hoping, one day you'll see that I, too, have grown. And while I've been less than worthy at times (one time is too many) of your trust, I intend to earn it: by honoring my word, tending your lows, and listening—all aims that will also evolve. Before I go, let me leave you with this, dearest daughter of mine, all the while and forevermore-always-everlasting, I've loved you limitless.

Dad

ACKNOWLEDGMENTS

As I see it, my list of acknowledgments is destined for incompleteness. Let me tell it, the task of listing all the folks responsible for this book is no less than listing all the people who played a role in my reaching this point in life. And that's impossible, impossible. Still, I'd be all sorts of remiss if I didn't at least attempt to single out those crucial to the conception, drafting, and revising of what became this book. For sure this work wouldn't be what it is without my mother: Lillie Jackson. She was my chief resource—her memory is miraculous—and showed again and again a willingness, a great courage, to bare herself inside out. Mad, crazy love for eternity, Mom. Huge thank-yous to Uncles X (RIP), Y, and Z for sharing parts of their stories with me, for keeping it 100 about things that weren't flattering, for revealing more of Big Chris—forever Dad—to me. Thanks to the family members who shared their survival stories (and all of those who also participated in the film). Let the record show, your resilience inspires me. Deep gratitude to the former partners who allowed me to interview them—what you did was compassionate and brave—and who served as a resource in other ways. Shout-out to all the other family and friends who answered my queries by call or a text. Gooood lookin to my 833 patnas who never ceased serving as unofficial interview subjects and my personal history historians. Thanks to the folks who helped me produce *Survival Files: A Lyric Film*, especially Todd Strickland and Ime Etuk. Thank you to the members of my Open City workshop for reading many drafts of parts of this book and offering critical feedback: Robb, KKP, Carrie, Treska, Diana, Joe. Thanks to Dawn Raffel for your editorial insight. Deep thanks to Bob Quillin and Vanessa for your magnanimousness, for being amazing humans. Thank you to the institutions who've supported me: the Lannan Foundation, the Whiting Foundation, TED, NYFA, the Ford Foundation, the good folks at the Baton Rouge Area Foundation who administer the Ernest J. Gaines Award for Literary Excellence, the Hurston/Wright Foundation, and Self Enhancement, Inc. Thank you to New York University and in particular my former dean, Fred Schwarzbach, and current dean, Julie Mostov. Immense thanks to my agent, Jin Auh, for all her guidance and encouragement and advocacy. Jin, I can't tell you how much I lean on your calm and confidence, how so often after our chats I feel poised to win. Thanks to Nan Graham for your support and encouragement. There isn't a person in publishing whom I respect more, which is to say, it's an honor to work with you. Thanks as well to my Scribner team: Susan, Roz, Brian, Colin, Kara, Jaya, Ashley, Rosie, Sally— and all the others whose names I don't know who were instrumental in making this an actual book. And of course, of course, of everyone at Scribner, I owe the deepest gratitude to my editor (friend, ally) Kathy Belden. Eternal thanks, KB, for your guidance and patience and belief and unwavering support. It was a long journey and I couldn't have asked for a better cicerone. Thanks to my beloved partner, Safiya, for inspiring me with your brilliance and for your support and encouragement and understanding and patience and belief and critique—even when that critique was critical, I knew it was for the good of the work. Thanks to my city: Portland, Oregon; P-Town; The NEP. Count me always and forevermore your native son.

NOTES

13 "Men, women, children [dis]united": The word *cento* is derived from the Latin word for "patchwork." The cento (or collage poem) is a poetic form made up of lines from other poems. Poets often mix their own lines into the poem, but a true cento is composed entirely of lines from other sources. Early examples can be found in the work of Homer and Virgil. The centos for parts "1," "2," "3," and "4" were composed of the following source texts: the Declaration of Independence, the Gettysburg Address, the "Give Me Liberty or Give Me Death" speech, *Notes on the State of Virginia*, "The Star-Spangled Banner," the Monroe Doctrine, Chief Justice Roger B. Taney's majority opinion in *Dred Scott v. Sandford*, Associate Justice Henry Billings Brown's majority opinion in *Plessy v. Ferguson*, "The Federalist Papers 10," the Constitution, the Pledge of Allegiance, the Emancipation Proclamation.

EXODUS

18 "'Please, Officer, please'": The police ended up taking me back into the living room, where they had Brother A on the couch. Brother A kept up the belligerence, bellowing about his rights, demanding to see the warrant. "Look," one of the officers said. "We got a lot of discretion on who goes to jail today and who doesn't." Brother A spouted some more and one of the officers kicked him in the shin and told him to shut up. "Did you see that, Mitchell?" Brother A said. But by then I might as well have taken a vow of monastic silence. Guess which one of us left the apartment that day in cuffs and which one didn't?

18 "'Gooooo down, Moses / Waaaay'": Tell me what *can't* you tell about someone by knowing their favorite hymn?

18 ". . . MLK asks for volunteers": This is not the beginning of activism for Mama Edie or her sisters. Word is they used to troop door-to-rural-Alabamian-door encouraging blacks to vote. To boot, the legend is that her older sister Essie once posted bail for MLK Jr., and that her sister Eliza worked as a part-time custodian of the now historic Jackson-Community House.

19 "Mama Edie's enterprising mother": Alabama State was the fruit of the Article XIV, S256, of the 1901 Alabama constitution that stated "separate schools shall be provided for white and colored children, and no child of either race shall be permitted to attend a school of the other race." During Reconstruction, Northern white missionaries worked with black church leaders to found the Lincoln Normal School at Marion in 1867, an established date that makes it the oldest state-sponsored liberal arts institution for the higher education of blacks in the country. Translation: it's one of the old-

est HBCUs. The school, which offered its first class in Montgomery in 1887, has, over the years, undergone beaucoup name changes: State Teachers College. Alabama State College for Negroes. Alabama State College. Alabama State University.

20 "They also became active members": Mama Edie was a proud member of the Oregon Association of Colored Women's Clubs.

22 ". . . the infamous era of American history": According to the Tuskegee Institute, 4,730 lynchings were perpetrated between 1882 and 1951, 3,437 of which were of black people. It was less common, of course, but let this record show that while folks, too, were lynched.

23 ". . . black folks transformed": A number of historians argue that one of the upshots of the civil rights movement was a weakening of what bound blacks into a nation.

COMPOSITE POPS

26 ". . . there are aspects of being": Sincere gratitude due to advocates who've been fighting for gender equality. By male and female, I mean cisgendered male and female—the Latin prefix *cis* means "on the same side"—i.e., men and women whose gender identity is aligned with the gender they were assigned by birth.

26 ". . . long before Obama made it a project": Obama (B.O.) is the latest exemplar of a president whose life confirms the efficaciousness of a composite. A total of twelve presidents were either abandoned or lost their biological fathers when they were young. It's damn near folklore now, how Barack Hussein Obama Sr. had bounced on his wife and B.O. by the time his son was a toddler, how B.O.'s mother spent time in Seattle, remarried in Hawaii, and took young B.O. to live with her new husband in Indonesia. How circa the time B.O. hit fifth grade, his mother sent him back to Hawaii to live with her parents. One of B.O.'s composites thereafter was his maternal grandfather, Stanley Dunham (co-parenting props also due to Dunham's wife, Madelyn), the man who assumed the role of B.O.'s primary caretaker until he went off to college. Stanley was also the one who introduced B.O. to the man who just might own the title of Most Controversial of all presidential composites: a libertine, ex-journalist, poet, and communist associate named Frank Marshall Davis, a man whose lore grew during B.O.'s first campaign, when conspiracy theorists claimed Davis was his biological father. The truth as confirmed by B.O. in his memoir wasn't paternity but the truth that Davis helped shape B.O.'s views on racial identity, race relations, and social justice. Davis was a part of B.O.'s life but for a handful of years, but I'm calling him a composite on account of his impact. Though this may be a stretch (then again, so was a black man being elected the leader of the free world), remnants of Davis's radical thought can be found in the socialist-leaning legislature that is Obamacare. George Washington (G.W.) lost his father, Augustine (Augustine's people called him Gus), when he was eleven. From that point, G.W.'s older half brother Lawrence Washington became his surrogate father. Answer me this: What would America look like if G.W. hadn't followed Lawrence into the military and politics (Lawrence fought in the War of Jenkins' Ear and was later elected to Virginia's House of Burgesses)? Lawrence christened the Mount Vernon estate (or should we call it a plantation?) and G.W. paid homage to his beloved older brother when he possessed it outright by hanging a portrait of him— the lone one in the room—in his study. G.W. and B.O. are notable as the first and last, but the list between them includes Thomas Jefferson (T.J.), who lost his father at thir-

teen and found a mentor in philosophy professor William Small when he entered the College of William & Mary a few years later. Smith fostered in T.J. a great admiration for diverse disciplines and also a love of enlightenment thinkers. He also introduced T.J. to politician and law professor George Wythe—the man who became T.J.'s unofficial political and cultural mentor—AKA as much a composite as any man was for the future president. How amazing it must've been for philomathic young T.J. to sit around a supper table discussing politics and culture with Small, Wythe, and a governor. How fortunate T.J. was to have been given the chance to later study law (there were no law schools in colonial America) with Wythe and have an apprenticeship that included history, philosophy, and ethics. If you're looking for the lasting influence of T.J.'s composite, you need look no further than the ideals and language of the most important document in American history. The list of presidents who built composites also includes Gerald Ford (G.F.)—born Leslie King Jr.—whose mother, Dorothy, divorced his biological father, Leslie King Sr., on the grounds of "extreme cruelty" when her son was five months old. G.F.'s biological father was the son of millionaire businessman Charles Henry King, but that didn't stop him from bolting out of state (so much for broke pockets as impetus for a deadbeat dad) and, as rumor had it, colluding with his father to skirt alimony and child support judgments. Lucky for baby G.F. that Dorothy met Gerald Ford Sr. a couple of years later. Ford Sr. became a successful businessman and was a church vestryman, a Mason, and later a local politician. He married Dorothy, adopted her young son, christened him a junior, and was, in G.F.'s words, "kind, fair, and firm." Ford Sr. and Dorothy had three more boys together and never mentioned that Ford Sr. was not G.F.'s biological father. G.F. didn't find that out until his biological father popped up at his high school job. But years and years later, in a letter he dictated from the Oval Office, one can see how that visit did little to sway G.F.: "I loved and was guided in life by the only father I ever had—Gerald R. Ford Sr. There was never any longing on my part to seek family outside of the one in which I was raised with such love, tenderness, and happiness."

28   "Those years I lived": When Essie was murdered, my cousin-brother went to live with my great-grandparents for a time, but when he hit the first grade, he moved in with my granddad and lived with him until he became a legal adult. My granddad parenting him is yet another hash mark in the ledger of why he deserves my love, respect, and honor.

28   ". . . he had to slap spit from me": The backstory—this occurred after I'd been caught occasions with naked to half-naked girls in my basement bedroom. The scene—my granddad's house sits beside an alley, and there's a park bench at the opening of the alley. The action—this particular day my granddad came home early from work and spotted me posted on a park bench whispering who-knows-what into the ear of a girl whose name I can't name now for nothing but whose face I will never forget. She and I had not dared into the house, so I was miffed when Granddad parked his Buick in the alley, hopped out, and furied over. "Hey, Dad, this is—" and before I could finish, he barked, "What did I tell you?! What did I tell you about this?!" and slapped the pow! of fireworks out my cheek. He breathed over me for a moment or two and moseyed to his idling ride and pulled into the garage. It took an infinite crawl of seconds for me to courage up and face the girl. "Hm, I think you should go," I said. She, still agog, nodded, rose, and started up the alley. The. End. The credits—these years later I realize it was a testament to how much I love my granddad that it never dawned on me to curse him under my breath or mull packing and leaving like my dunderheaded ass had

somewhere to go. And I'm almost sure I never snuck another girl into the basement either—which spells "mission accomplished" for Sam Jackson Jr., excuse me, for Dad.

MATRIMONY

33 "But trust, at its nexus": Go ask the Igbo of Nigeria, ask Chinua Achebe, ask John Edgar Wideman: all stories are true.

34 ". . . the woman who matters": In 1985 US cocaine users reached 5.7 million, what was at that point the apex.

35 ". . . the Catholic Church's Great Council": The Fourth Lateran Council of 1215 (canon 51): "Whence, following in the footsteps of our predecessors, we absolutely forbid clandestine marriages; and we forbid also that a priest presume to witness such. Wherefore, extending to other localities generally the particular custom that prevails in some, we decree that when marriages are to be contracted they must be announced publicly in the churches by the priests during a suitable and fixed time, so that if legitimate impediments exist, they may be made known."

39 "Blandon was a direct associate": Blandon and Meneses were funding the Contras in their home country. This after Congress defunded the operation—a key factor in the Iran-Contra scandal.

40 ". . . '[God] put him down [on earth]'": In 1996 "Freeway" Ricky Ross was sentenced to life imprisonment for his part in a 100-kilo cocaine deal. Following several appeals, he won a sentence reduction, and was released September 29, 2009.

45 "'Just give me somethin, please'": Though there is not an accurate figure for relapse because it requires self-reporting by those who are, in their choices, unreliable, figures from the several sources I checked ranged from 75 to 95 percent.

46 "In fact, the idea of marrying": Marriage for reasons other than a civic duty and-or social responsibility didn't begin to change until the Protestant Reformation of the sixteenth century that rejected the dogma that clerics maintain celibacy and therefore couldn't marry. The next significant revision of the institution occurred in the seventeenth and eighteenth centuries, when the enlightenment thinkers of Western Europe and America began pioneering the idea that life's greatest goal is the pursuit of happiness. While this "enlightenment" didn't hasten a lovestruck world, it began causing would-be spouses to believe that marriage should satisfy more of a person's psychological and social needs and furthermore one's needs for intimacy and affection. Once the industrial revolution came along and with it the booming economies of industrialized nations, it expanded the middle class and made it easier for men to be less concerned over how they'd support a wife and less deterred by the reproach of parentals.

APPLES

74 "One could argue": The spurious concept of whiteness has been critiqued, debunked, rebuffed, lamented upon by many an adroit *Homo sapiens*, though none more sagacious or eloquent, I'd argue, than the Big homie of my literary dreams: James Arthur Baldwin. Baldwin might've been most succinct in his critique of whiteness in "On Being 'White' . . . and Other Lies," the essay wherein he calls whiteness a "moral choice" and argues, "America became white—the people who, as they claim, 'settled'

the country became white—because of the necessity of denying the Black presence, and justifying the Black subjugation." Other keen minds have since echoed the brilliant Big homie's idea that racism created race as we now comprehend it, and not, as the uninitiated might think, the other way around, evincing a logic that as far as I'm concerned is un-fuck-with-able. In that same essay Baldwin also claims, "It bears terrifying witness to what happened to everyone who got here, and paid the price of the ticket. The price was to become 'white.' No one was white before he/she came to America. It took generations, and a vast amount of coercion, before this became a white country." For a good long while, I accepted with nary a critique the stance that whiteness was born in America. Easy to do since it satisfied my less-learned-than-I-would-like perspective, easier averse as I am to heresy against my heroes. Or else I wanted to claim whiteness for us—the us being Americans—as paradoxical as it seems, wanted to believe there was power in us and us alone possessing it, and therefore coerced myself into accepting Baldwin's claim that none of the seventeenth-century Europeans who disembarked on the shores of the colonies believed in whiteness, that none of them were white or in-the-midst-of-becoming-white before they took up planting apple seeds, guzzling cider, and buying Africans. But here I must ask, what if I've been wrong or at best myopic in hypothesizing the evolution of the so-called white race? Though elements of the apple precede the idea of a white race, for damn sure, apples would not exist without it. The idea of race hadn't even been invented in antiquity, but the seeds of what became the illusion of whiteness are present in the Greeks naming, and in effect othering, the Scythians and Celts as barbarians who lived at far reaches from their empire. The white race wouldn't exist if scholars like Hippocrates hadn't hypothesized that human variations were owed to the climate in which the people lived, that his Greeks were beautiful beings who possessed a temperament that suited them conquering and dominating other peoples. The Greco-Roman empire advanced the tradition, refined the nomenclature of the barbarians they encountered in their quests to conquer the known world from Celts alone into Celts, Gauls, and Germani, and then re-enlarged them later into one large group called Galatics. The whole white race ought to sing paeans to Constantine, the Roman emperor who issued the Edict of Milan, set out converting his kingdom to Christianity, in part by commissioning huge basilicas adorned with Christian symbols. Under the rule of the Christians' great patron, Roman Catholic artists began producing paintings and sculptures that portrayed Christ, Mary, the apostles, and other Christian figures as fair-skinned and light-haired, as bearded and blue-eyed, as other than the brown-hued, dark-haired, Semitic-featured people that they were in real life, images that've proliferated for millennia. Though we could trace whiteness back to antiquity and the advent of Christianity, trace it through the Dark Ages and its attendant rampant slave trading, trace it through Britain becoming world-class slavers, I believe what Baldwin meant was that the advent of the white race as we perceive it in these United(?) States began when British pirates captured a Portuguese slave ship and delivered "20 and odd" African (from what is now Angola and DR Congo) souls to the Jamestown colony of British North America to join the European convicts, young vagrants, and indentured servants in bondage. Those unfree Africans and unfortunate Europeans were soon subjected to the ideals of men like Massachusetts Bay Colony governor John Winthrop, who believed, "God Almighty in His most holy and wise providence hath so disposed of the condition of mankind as in all times some must be rich, some poor; some high and eminent power and dignity; others mean and in subjection." A crucial moment in the evolution of the white race occurred in 1662, which was the year the Virginia House of Burgesses passed *Partus Sequitur Ventrem*, or *Partus* for short, a doctrine meant to perpetuate slavery sine die, and therefore the supreme status of incipient whiteness, a legal principle that, unlike the British common law, which linked the status of a child to its father, decrees "all children born in this country shall be held bond or free only according to the condition of the mother." In the decades to follow, along with those lifetime indentured slaves, more and more of the on-the-road-to-white souls forced into servitude in the North American colonies were convicts, numbers that spiked after Parliament flexed on colonies refusing penal ships in their ports by passing the Transportation Act of 1718. We could argue the most significant moment in the evolution of the white race occurred thirteen years prior to the crown's act, when the Virginia House of Burgesses passed the series of laws that became the slave codes, in effect defining the treatment of the explicit nemesis of the efflorescing white race, which was the burgeoning black race: "All servants imported and brought into the Country . . . who were not Christians in their native Country . . . shall be accounted and be slaves. All Negro, mulatto and Indian slaves within this dominion . . . shall be held to be real estate. If any slave resists his master . . . correcting such slave, and shall happen to be killed in such correction . . . the master shall be free of all punishment . . . as if such accident never happened." Meanwhile, across the pond, European scientists were working themselves into mad taxonomists, almost as if they needed to invent the logic to justify their compulsion to oppress. Many of them classified races into two classes: the ugly brutish Africans and Asians and the beautiful Europeans—or said another way, white folks and others. Then Huguenot Sir Jean Chardin came along and published a two-volume account of his voyages titled *The Travels of Sir John Chardin into Persia and the East Indies 1673–1679*. Chardin wrote about the countenances he encountered in the famed Caucasus Mountains region, praising the blood of Georgians as the most beautiful in the world, proclaiming them "angelic," with women endowed with "graces not to be seen any other place." Chardin's descriptions helped poise apples as the epitome of human beauty, a rank supported by German art historian Johann Joachim Winckelmann. Winckelmann, often touted as the father of art history, claimed Greek art was the greatest of all eras, in his *History of Ancient Art* idealized Apollo Belvedere as the embodiment of human beauty, and added that Apollo's white exterior made him all the more sublime; it was Winckelmann who, in spite of his lightweight hatetrocity of art depicting women, romanticized the Roman copies of Greek art as the paragon of beauty. In 1792, the statue of Apollo also featured in another notable moment in the evolution of the white race; that year Dutch illustrator and professor Petrus Camper sketched a facial chart that presented the facial angles of an orangutan, a Negro, a Kalmuck (Mongolian), a European, and Apollo. Camper, who intended the chart for artists, also meant to highlight the parity of humans, but it was where Camper placed the subjects—the Negro's proximity to the orangutan and the European's distance from that orangutan and closeness to Apollo—that ended up trumping all other elements for those progenitors of whiteness then known as African slave traders, a proximity that for decades would yoke the Negro to the orangutan and, oh yes, would help forge the bonds between whiteness and beauty, between whiteness and holiness. Race scientists all over the world boarded the physiognomy bandwagon, arguing that outer appearance, the skull and face in specific, correlated to one's worth and character. Scores of scientists produced taxon after taxon, categories that were often part of studies named with damn near interminable titles—*An Account of the*

Regular Gradation in Man, and in Different Animals and Vegetables; and from the For-mer to the Latter. Or: *On the Natural Variety of Mankind.* Or: *Essays on Physiognomy Designed to Promote the Knowledge and Love of Mankind,* texts that turned human beauty into scientific racial trait, that posited the idea of polygenesis or, more to the point, that the white man's origin was separate from their lessers. That origin was introduced by renowned German polymath—and owner of the world's most envied skull collection—Johann Friedrich Blumenbach, who published *On the Natural Vari-eties of Mankind,* which, despite opposing polygenesis and the idea that humans had evolved from an intermediate species, also defined four varieties of humans based on region: (1) people from Europe; (2) people from Asia to the Ganges and some parts of North America; (3) people from Africa; (4) people from North America. Blumenbach published his chart in 1776, which is of course the same year that Jefferson and brain trust declared independence from the British Crown, which is also the same year Scot-tish philosopher Adam Smith published *An Inquiry into the Nature and Cause of the Wealth of Nations* and argued as noted much earlier that man's natural tendency toward self-interest and a free market would create a nation with universal wealth— AKA the birth of the economic system that has ruled the white man's land. The found-ing fathers of this white man's land had little to no issue expressing their belief that it should remain theirs. Ben Franklin in 1751 made a case for his vision in *Observations Concerning the Increase of Mankind, Peopling of Countries, etc.,* in which he writes, "The number of purely white people in the World is proportionably very small. . . . I could wish their numbers were increased. And while we are, as I may call it, scouring our planet, by clearing America of woods, and so making this side of our globe reflect a brighter light to the eyes of inhabitants in Mars or Venus, why should we in the sight of superior beings, darken its people? Why increase the sons of Africa, by planting them in America, where we have so fair an opportunity, by excluding all Blacks and tawneys, of increasing the lovely white and red?" Thirty-six years later (1787) found-ing father John Jay emphasized the hope for a homogeneous white race in "The Fed-eralist Papers 2," writing, "Providence has been pleased to give this one connected country to one united people, a people descended from the same ancestors, speaking the same language, professing the same religion, attached to the same principles of government, very similar in their manners and customs." The year after Jay published his papers, founding father John Dickinson also made his case for the one team, one dreamness of the white race, asking in *Letters of Fabius,* "Was there ever a confederacy of republics united as these states are, or in which the people were so drawn together by religion, blood, language, manner, customs." Best believe that by "people" Dickin-son meant white. Trust and believe whiteness was on the mind of founding father Thomas Jefferson when he addressed a request for information about his beloved birthplace with *Notes on the State of Virginia,* the racist treatise in which he narrowed the view of whiteness by arguing that white Americans—to his mind the only Americans—were English and of liberated Anglo-Saxon ancestry. Jefferson's oft noted for his abolition-mindedness, but let this record show that he also argued that "when freed, he [the Negro] is to be removed beyond the reach of mixture." Without ques-tion, the Constitutional Convention of 1787 was a momentous moment in the evolu-tion and empowerment of the white race, a gathering during which South Carolinian delegates Charles Pinckney and Pierce Butler pitched their colleagues—not a one of whom dissented—to add the amendment that federalized recapturing fugitive slaves, during which, in drafting the Constitution, future Supreme Court Justice James Wilson persuaded his fellow delegates to accept for the purpose of voting electorates that the black man was three-fifths of a human, which, per my twenty-first-century eyes, was an attempt to legalize the white race into the realm of the deified. That divine white race also decreed in its Constitution that it would quantify its power every ten years. It began that decennial counting in 1790, and true to its telos, named but a single race in its initial classifications: Free white males under sixteen. Free white males aged sixteen years and upward. Number of free white females. Number of other free people. Number of slaves. Let this record show that the census has never not included white as a race, has never not defined an ever-changing Other. The year of the first census the free white men who ruled the new republic passed the first Naturalization Act of 1790, which ruled only "free white persons" of good character could become citizens. Not to be outshined by American white men and their politics, the celebrated European racist Blumenbach made history again in 1795 with the third edition of *On the Natural Variety of Mankind* when—concerned, à la his contemporaries, with hue and beauty, he ranked skin color, placing white skin in the number one slot and black skin in the last slot. He also christened those belonging to the first group the *Caucasian Variety* and idealized them as having "Colour white, cheeks rosy; hair brown or chestnut-colored; head subglobular; face oval, straight, its parts moderately defined, forehead smooth, nose narrow, slightly hooked, mouth small. The primary teeth placed perpendicularly to each jaw; the lips (especially the lower one) moderately open, the chin full and rounded. In general, that kind of appearance which according to our opinion of symmetry, we consider most handsome and becoming." And just like that, the beautiful master race had its name. The Caucasian Americans, or should we say white Americans, marched into the nineteenth century enlarging and critiquing and varying their identity, fretting over what to make of the poor and uncivilized among them, of the effects that climate had on skin color, of who were their rightful forefathers, all of which was of course about who among them could be granted the privilege of entry. Some whites tout the Free Soil movement—free soil, free speech, free labor, free men—of the 1840s, which banned slavery from territories acquired after the Mexican-American War, including my home state, as a magnanimous moment in the evolution of whiteness, claim it as proof that abolitionist-minded idealists were intent on fighting the broadening hegemony of whiteness. But there are others, count me among them, who are inclined to believe that the movement had less to do with challenging the preeminence of the white race or protecting the downtrodden from oppression, a stance lent credence by Democratic senator David Wilmot, who persuaded his all-white congressional colleagues to pass his Wilmot Proviso—he was fond of calling it the "white man's proviso"—with the grandiloquence of a tried-and-true white-privilege preservationist: "The negro race already occupy [sic] enough of this fair continent; let us keep what remains for ourselves and for our children." Ain't the evolution of the white race relentless? Let me count among part of its relentlessness that Dred and Harriet Scott lost their lawsuit for freedom against Missouri, and Chief Justice Roger Taney writing in his (cento source material) note: "They [negroes] had for more than a century before been regarded as beings of an inferior order, and altogether unfit to associate with the white race, either in social or political relations; and so far inferior, that they had no rights which the white man was bound to respect." A group of abolitionist-minded white men gathered in a schoolhouse and birthed what became the Republican party, a Grand New Party that in a few years propelled the future emancipator of the slaves to the highest office in the land. However, in the senatorial Great Debates of 1858 old Lincoln declared his belief in the inferiority of the race he begrudged manumission or, in other words, in the superiority of his beloved white race. "I am not nor ever have been in favor of making voters or jurors of Negros, nor of qualifying them to hold office, nor to intermarry with white people. And I will say in addition to this that there is a physical difference between the white and black races which I believe will forever forbid the two races living together on terms of social and political equality." Even in the midst of the deadliest war fought on American terra firma, a war fought, as we know, over slavery, but a war never not in favor of whiteness and the mind-set that there could be no egalitarian coexistence between blacks and whites in America, Lincoln supported the pro-planter Corwin Amendment and was so ambivalent about abolition that, in an early draft of his Emancipation Proclamation, he threatened to liberate only those slaves living in rebelling states, in essence proposing the legal preservation of what might've been the most crucial element of whiteness. Though Lincoln as president of the disunited states was in 1862 the first to invite freedmen to the White House, he let them know America was still the white man's land: "There is an unwillingness on the part of our people, harsh as it may be, for you free colored people to remain with us." Men who believed like Lincoln founded the American Colonization Society to "rid our country of a useless and pernicious, if not dangerous portion of the population," a group that realized years of distinguished membership, established the West African colony of Liberia, and for the better part of a century sent as many freed slaves there as they could. The next year, wartime whiteness received an early Christmas gift in the form of a pamphlet that satirized unions that had been outlawed in Massachusetts, Pennsylvania, and all the Southern colonies since before the Constitution. The anonymous author (an anonymous letter sent to a London paper would expose coauthorship) of *Miscegenation: The Theory of the Blending of the Races, Applied to the American White Man and Negro* explained that he'd invented the word *miscegenation* from the Latin roots *miscere*, meaning "to mix," and *genus*, meaning "race," and intended the term to describe the practice of an American white and a black birthing a mongrel baby into the world. Someone forgot to tell the Supreme Court the pamphlet was a hoax; for twenty years hence the justices set the legal precedent banning interracial marriages in *Pace v. Alabama*. But I'm getting ahead of myself; let me get back to the historic moment of white solidarity that followed General Lee marching into the Appomattox Court House and offering the formal surrender of his Confederates, that is, when Union army soldiers tended their starved and wounded former foes. Whiteness and the supreme nature of the white race was fortified in April of 1865, when no sooner than the war ended, John Wilkes Booth shot Lincoln, and no sooner than he assumed the presidency, Andrew Johnson nixed Lincoln's "ten percent plan," which offered amnesty to any rebel who swore fealty to the United States and granted former rebel states the chance to form a new government once 10 percent of their 1860 registered voters vowed an oath of allegiance to the new united (?) nation. Johnson proved a boon for white planters reclaiming power when, under his reign, the Southern states began adopting more and more ingenious tactics of black subjugation, AKA the systemic privileging of whiteness that codified into the black codes writ that kept the nemesis of whiteness, a people then rejoicing over the Fourteenth Amendment, from bearing arms, voting, being a politician, being hired for a job that paid anywhere near a living wage—statutes that ordered if those freedmen were caught "wandering or strolling about in idleness" they could be locked in the county jail, sentenced to chain-gang work, and forced right back into the indentured servitude of an evil-ass fascist of a planter. Another notable moment in the evolution of the white race occurred in 1876 when the Republican nominee Rutherford Hayes sent his people to meet in secret with moderate Democrats—some of whom were still seething over their surrender, its jeopardy to their livelihood, and their status as supreme beings of the universe—to negotiate an agreement in which he'd order federal troops out of the South if the Democrats agreed not to block his election, a compromise that would have the effect of luring the former rebel states of Florida, Louisiana, and South Carolina back into the Union. Hayes hinted at his intentions in his acceptance speech for the Republican nomination: "It will be practicable to promote, by the influence of all legitimate agencies of the general government, the efforts of the people of those States, to obtain for themselves the blessings of honest and capable *local* [italics mine] government." True to his words, he goaded a vainglorious moment in the history of the white race when a couplefew months later, he ordered the Union army out of the South and put the effectual kaput on the contentious era of Reconstruction, which in effect ushered in the acme of The Keepers, which is to say the era when Confederate-hearted deep-South radicals—most of whom sprang up after the war—began propagandizing, threatening, colluding, terrorizing, and murdering to protect and honor the great white race. True, the Ku Klux Klan became the most infamous, but there were others (more on this in the note on The Keepers). The whole white race, including the I'm-white-and-therefore-American and the I-accept-my-role-as-the-purest-and-fairest-apple, must acknowledge the year 1877, which, per recent records, was the year The Keepers inaugurated the practice of American lynching. The supreme white race marched into the twentieth century terrorizing and worrying over its purity, a conundrum Edward Ross sought to address in "The Causes of Racial Superiority," the essay where he coined the term *race suicide* and claims "There is no bloodshed, no violence, no assault of the race that waxes upon the race that wanes. The higher race quietly and unmurmuringly eliminates itself rather than endure individually the bitter competition it has failed to ward off from itself by collective action." That higher race was damn sure buttressed the year Homer Adolph Plessy flouted Louisiana's law of "equal but separate accommodations for the white and colored races" by refusing to sit in a Jim Crow train car and Judge John H. Ferguson and the Supreme Court judged Plessy's defiance unprotected by the white man's law—excuse me, the Constitution. Whites all over who held the superior character of their whiteness close to their tiny little racist hearts were flummoxed a day in 1905 when twice-elected president Teddy Roosevelt delivered a progressive speech on race, proclaiming, "We of to-day, in dealing with all our fellow-citizens, white or colored, North or South, should strive to show just the qualities that Lincoln showed—his steadfastness in striving after the right and his infinite patience and forbearance with those who saw that right less clearly than he did; his earnest endeavor to do what was best." The president further confounded his race when he argued for striving to "secure each man, whatever his color, equality of opportunity, equality of treatment before the law. As a people striving to shape our actions in accordance with the great law of righteousness we cannot afford to take part in or be indifferent to oppression or maltreatment of any man who, against crushing disadvantages, has by his own industry, energy, self-respect, and perseverance struggled upward to a position which would entitle him to the respect of his fellows, if only his skin were of a different hue." Though progressive he may have been, Roosevelt was also a man of his time (this time, all time?), and took care to reassert the white man's domain: "If in any community level of intelligence, morality, and thrift among the colored men can be raised, it is, humanly speaking, sure that the same level among the whites will be raised to an even higher degree." The same year the white man swooned over Thomas Dixon Jr.'s *The Clansman: An Historical Romance of the Ku Klux Klan*—a novel that became the play *The Clansman* that became the film *Birth of a Nation*, all of which inspired terrortastic-minded Atlantans to revive that "invisible empire of the South." Meanwhile Danish geneticist Wilhelm Johannsen in his heredity research conceived the pillars of whiteness known as the genotype-phenotype distinction. Johannsen coined *gene* as a unit of heredity, a genotype as person's genetic traits, and a phenotype as their observable physical traits, concepts that stressed the white-black binary and upheld the myth of white beauty being the most handsome and pulchritudinous of all. But not all whites were beautiful creatures shaped like Greek gods with skin the pallor of Roman sculptures. Some were degenerates who didn't meet the minimum measures of whiteness, who were singled out with slurs or demeaned with the catchall of Poor White Trash, who threatened to corrupt the pure-bread super race, a race that by then was riding high off the recent achievement of becoming the world's economic (emphasis on *economic*) superpower. To protect against outsiders corrupting the race, legislators passed the Immigration Act of 1917. So much for "Give me your tired, your poor, your huddled masses yearning to breathe free, the wretched refuse of your teeming shore." The white race, to safeguard itself from those huddled masses, subjected them to an IQ test and tests for diseases and defects, to questions that confirmed whether they were a bigamist or a communist or an anarchist in practice. Those immigrants who answered wrong or failed a particular test, by federal law, could be sent right back where they came from, which is to say ferried a great distance from the master race of America. The year 1924 must be counted as a stupendous year in the annuals of the white race. That year Virginia, which as we know was a great bastion of whiteness, voted into existence the Virginia Racial Integrity Act, which set the precedent for voiding *Partus* and begot the one-drop rule, AKA the invisible-blackness or traceable-amount or hypodescent or one-black-ancestor rule, a writ that also outlawed marriage between a white person and any *Homo sapiens* with one drop of nonwhite blood, as well as requiring that every person born in Virginia be noted either white or colored and which also legalized the sterilization of unfortunate degenerate residents of state institutions. That same year poor Carrie Buck, who was impregnated by a rapist and committed as a teen by her foster parents to the Virginia State Colony for Epileptics and Feebleminded, became the test case for state-sponsored sterilization. "Feebleminded" Carrie was forever marked by Associate Justice Oliver Wendell Holmes's egregious *Buck v. Bell* majority opinion: "It is better for all the world, if instead of waiting to execute degenerate offspring for crime or to let them starve for their imbecility, society can prevent those who are manifestly unfit from continuing their kind . . . Three generations of imbeciles are enough." That same year—1924—in the infamous annals of the white race, Hitler penned *Mein Kampf* while locked in prison, a manifesto in which the Austrian demagogue praised the American white race as the world's paragon: "But in North America the Teutonic Elements, which has kept its racial American content and will remain master of it as long as that element does not fall a victim to the habit of adultering its blood." Hitler paid further homage to the land of the free, brave, and racist by arguing that miscegenation produced two deleterious effects: the lowering of the superior race and a physical and mental degradation that would lead to weakening of the superior race's "vital sap." That same year—

1924—Congress moved to protect its vital sap by passing the Immigration Act, which limited immigration from any one country to 2 percent of the number of people from that country living in America as of the 1890 census. The white race was anti-imbecile and, as it had been for epochs, anti-Jew. Bigoted industrialist Henry Ford authorized shipping hundreds of thousands of anti-Semitic *Dearborn Independents* inside his Model Ts, dispatches in which the gazillionaire berated God's chosen people as the world's foremost problem, accused them of being the instigators of World War I, bemoaned them being accepted as immigrants in his country, into his glorious white race. That white race, of course, became synonymous with Americans. Favored American citizens were deserving of the American dream as defined by James Truslow Adams: ". . . that dream of a land in which life should be better and richer and fuller for everyone, with opportunity for each according to ability or achievement." The big white house and white fence became essential markers of that American dream. Those favored Americans enjoyed the means to obtain dreamy white homes with major thanks due to FHA (Federal Housing Administration) chief economist Homer Hoyt, who in 1934 wrote *One Hundred Years of Land Values in Chicago: The Relationship of the Growth of Chicago to the Rise of Its Land Values, 1830–1933*, a dissertation that ranked races and nationalities by order of their "desirability" to receive a mortgage loan—the pinnacle of desirability was granted to the oft aggrandized Anglo-Saxons and the nadir of desirableness was foisted upon the Mexicans and Negroes. Hoyt and the HOLC (Home Owners' Loan Corporation) coded neighborhoods as "green," "white," "blue," "yellow," and "red," with "green" neighborhoods reserved for the beloved Anglo-Saxon well-to-do Protestants and the "red" neighborhoods, as in red-lined, denoting the hoods fit for blacks and Mexicans—their religion, schooling, and wealth be damned. The Europeans once again proved instrumental in reaffirming the exclusivity of whiteness when in 1935 British eugenicists Julian Sorell Huxley and A. C. Haddon published *We Europeans: A Survey of Racial Problems* and advanced the term *ethnic* into *ethnic group*: "Nowhere does a human group now exist which corresponds closely to a systematic sub-species in animals. . . . For existing populations, the noncommittal term ethnic group should be used." Not to be out-taxoned, American sociologist W. Lloyd Warner and later David Riesman evolved the term *ethnicity* to, in essence, include new groups entering the honorific white race, though, in an ironic turn, it has come to define all but the white race. Whiteness was at the nexus of the United Nations' UNESCO branch's decision to charge, in 1949, a collective of the world's foremost anthropologists and sociologists to "study and collect scientific materials concerning questions of race; to give wide diffusion to the scientific information collected; to prepare an educational campaign based on this information." The next year those UNESCO experts issued what could've been a watershed in whiteness: "Scientists have reached general agreement in recognizing that mankind is one: that all men belong to the species, *Homo sapiens*. . . . This means that the likenesses among men are far greater than their differences. . . . A race, from the biological standpoint, may therefore be defined as one of the group of populations constituting the species *Homo sapiens*." Hopeful as that pronouncement could've been for nonwhites, the collective of doyens also echoed their taxon-happy predecessors by decreeing three major divisions of mankind: the Mongoloid, the Negroid, the Caucasoid. The evolution of the white race, or Americans, has never ceased being political. As proof, I cite the time scores of Southern whites ceased supporting the Democrats in protest of JFK and later President Johnson's endorsement of the civil rights movement. Johnson, per lore, rued, "There goes the South for a generation," when he signed the Civil Rights Act, a premonition that Richard Nixon exploited to the utmost using the "Southern strategy": his party appealing to just enough of the concerns of racist white Southerners to win their vote, a scheme that—as the egregious, grievous extant tenure of a superfool named Trump attests—has kept the South aligned with elephants ever since. More evidence of the white race asserting their exclusiveness occurred in 1966 when sociologist William Petersen published "Success Story, Japanese-American Style" and coined the term *model minority* to praise what was in effect the degree to which Asians had manifested the values, mores, and financial success of the master race. Far as I can see, there hasn't been much in the way of evolution of the concept of the white race since the radical 1960s. More so whites working against the fate of being drafted into the low ranks of ethnics; more so the fierce protection of their interests, their existence, with policy and more subversive policy, with propaganda, symbols, pedagogy, art, subversion, violence, sundry displays of homicidal might. The white man, *the* true American, has defended his whiteness at high cost and offered the rest of us—the lessers, ethnics, minorities, others (pick one)—on occasion a wispy gesture as atonement, a discarded janissary for us to punish as weak appeasement.

85   "But ask me if there are men": Let me be clear: not all white men are The Keepers. In truth, few are, but The Keepers, like the apple, are an essential element of the white race. Because The Keepers forever believe in that whiteness, they therefore believe in blackness and othering. They were staunch anti-miscegenationists and ardent proponents of the one-drop rule, but habitually fornicated with women they othered, which is why, though they're loath to admit it, there's the strong chance there's ethnic blood in their veins. The Keepers might be descendants of those fifty thousand convicts sent from Britain to the North American colonies, but they also favor revisionist history when it suits them, so maybe they ain't. The Keepers have believed as Governor Samuel D. McEnery once pronounced, "God Almighty has himself drawn the color line." There's a strong chance they were a pro-planter Democrat, applauded those who conspired to end Reconstruction, and decades later were an anti–civil rights Republican. The Keepers, at some point, have made enemies of Republicans, Democrats, Native Americans, Christians, Jews, the Irish, the Germans, the Slavs, the Russians, the Asians, the Indians, the poor, the ailing, and but of course the blacks. They've been staunch segregationist in all its eras and xenophobes of the highest order. They were pro the Fugitive Slave Act and the three-fifths compromise. Pro *Partus Sequitur Ventrem*. Pro the Virginia law of hereditary slavery and the Virginia Racial Integrity Act and the Naturalization Acts of 1790 and 1795. Pro the Chinese Exclusion Act and the Johnson-Reed Act. Pro the Immigration Reform and Control Act and the Immigration and Naturalization Act of 1965, pro Executive Order 13769. They were proud proponents of the Immigration Restriction League, and as far as these days, ask one about the Minuteman Project and watch his pale face alight. The Keepers were once disposed to painting their pale faces black and satirizing themselves a Jim Crow or a Zip Coon or an Uncle Tom or a Buck, and less seldom an Uncle Sam. They believe that evermore the rightful place of black folks is a new Congo Square: an arena, a stadium, a stage, a screen, a track or field, a court—venues to perform for his amusement. At the time I write this, it's clear quintessential versions of The Keepers work in Congress, the courts, the White House. The most menacing members of the rank are devout and candid in their bigotries, do the dirty work of whiteness: the antagonizing, intimidating, oppressing, terrorizing, for they are not above perfidy, not afraid of being viewed as violent or

duplicitous or base. The Keepers were once phrenology-loving eugenicists and seldom admit that they're an ethnic no matter what DNA attests. These days, peep The Keepers flying a Confederate flag and binge-watching *The Dukes of Hazzard* box set on Independence Day or cheering news clips of a certain elephant-vetted, orange-faced, xenophobic, debt-dodging, double-talking, polemical, unfit fool in chief. Sometimes, The Keepers rant onstage about niggers and call it comedy. Sometimes, The Keepers carry tiki torches and chant "All Lives Matter." Other times they wax nostalgic about the good old days, by which they mean the antebellum South. The Keepers are liable to claim no state history is more grand than Virginia's, a land they view as a legendary wellspring of racial animus. Global-minded members were grieved to hear of the end of British Raj and apartheid. The most punkish among The Keepers are masters of subversion and microaggressions and send bold disciples to do their work, those whom henceforth I shall call their instruments. Instruments of The Keepers perpetuate their oppression but often without realizing the prime benefits of whiteness. The new age "death by persons unknown" is The Keepers—or their instruments—again and again and again and again, perpetrating and investigating and vindicating themselves of murdering the descendants of AfricanNegroidNegroColoredMulattoQuadroonOctoroonSacatraGriffeMarabonMetifMeameloucQuarteronSang-MêléBlackAfricanAmericanMinorityPersonofColor—AKA the folks I call my folks, who, though try a few might, could never enter the ranks of The Keepers. The Keepers make infamous headlines. Like a pair in Jasper who offered a ride to one of my folks, drove him to a field, beat and pissed on him, chained him to a pickup truck, dragged him until a culvert severed his head and arm from the rest of him, dumped his mutilated body parts in front of a church, then cruised over to a local barbecue. These days deeds of The Keepers or their instruments become high-profile videos and sound clips, macabre transgressions that are shared like the lynching photos once hawked in five-and-dimes. The dispatches issue from Ferguson and Staten Island and Sanford and Baltimore and Montgomery and North Charleston and Chicago and New York City and Tulsa . . . and the white man's Eden I call home. Portland, where officers stopped a car carrying a trio of black folks, one of whom was a young mother of two, for failure to stop at a stop sign, and in that pretext stop discovered the driver had a warrant. The young woman who was in the passenger seat jumped to the driver's seat and attempted a getaway. Then an officer, behaving in this instance as The Keepers or an instrument, tried to yank her out the car by a wig, tried to Taser her, tried to pepper spray her, and unsuccessful in all attempts, smashed a gun to her head and ordered her to kill the engine. That woman shifted the car into drive and The Keepers and-or an instrument (you decide) shot a bullet into her hip, snatched her out the car, cuffed her, and left her lying on the street untended while he claimed she was "faking" unconsciousness, while unbeknown to him that bullet shuttled up her ribs and ended her life—a death disallowed a public inquest by the mayor and DA. In my hometown, officers profiled a young black man driving a car that "didn't belong in the neighborhood" and pulled him over for failure to signal twenty to thirty feet before he turned into a grocery store parking lot. So claims the officer's report, he asked to see a driver's license and insurance, and the guy said he didn't have one. The officer asked for the driver's ID and he mumbled something they couldn't hear. One officer asked the driver to produce his ID and opened his driver's-side door. The driver ignored orders to place his hands on top of his head and tussled a bit with police inside his car. Per the report, police (were they working as The Keepers or their instrument?) shot three bullets and a Taser at once and killed the driver, left him dead with almost twelve grams of crack in his mouth and about a gram each of crack and weed in his pocket, but no weapon to be found. Back home, The Keepers or an instrument arrived at the scene of a hotel room where a young black man, cranked on PCP and meth, was thrashing a three-year-old boy. They ordered him to stop several times and, when he wouldn't, shot four bullets into him, shot them while he held the toddler in his arms. Home—where in another low-profile incident, a crew of officers arrived one evening at an apartment complex where a young black guy was holed in a unit threatening suicide over the death of his brother earlier that day. One crew staked out the parking lot of the complex, armed with an AR-15, a beanbag shotgun, and a police dog. One of the other officers texted the guy. "We need to know if you intend to hurt yourself," he texted. "I'm truly sorry about your brother. Can you promise me you won't hurt yourself." The officer then called and convinced the guy to surrender. He came outside, and with his hands locked behind his head, shuffled backward to the roar of armed cops—men who would claim themselves unaware of the texts—shouting commands and dogs barking. One officer commanded him to walk backward and put his hands straight up in the air, and when he didn't comply (or couldn't hear them) he shot the guy in the ass with the beanbag and, so fast, fired another five rounds to bring him down. But the rounds didn't bring him down. Instead, the guy reached for where the beanbags hit his back and scrambled for cover. That's when one officer (in this instance The Keepers or at least their instrument) sighted him from behind a squad car and shot a bullet into his low back that took out enough "vital structures" to kill him, and meanwhile another sicced a police dog that bit him on his calf and shin. . . . Is there any wonder why The Keepers' defense of his privilege and power has turned riotous? The Red Summer, the Harlem riots, the East St. Louis race riot, the Atlanta riot, the Newark riots, the Pulaski riot, the Tulsa race riot, the Chicago race riot, the Perry race riot, the Meridian race riot, the Rosewood Massacre, the Watts riots, the LA riots, the Ferguson riots, the less famous Albina riots that occurred in my city, and on and on. Some would claim the ranks of The Keepers have been restricted to the bold members who've pledged allegiance to groups like the Ku Klux Klan, the Constitutional Union Guards, the Order of the White Rose, the Order of the Star-Spangled Banner, the Order of United American Mechanics, the Knights of the Golden Circle, the Knights of the White Camelia, the Heroes of America, the Men of Justice, the White Brotherhood, the White League, the Red Shirts. But group membership or not, The Keepers are at base supremacists, those who must believe in the white race and the black race and othering and apples because without them, there ain't no him.

THE SCALE

143   "And in some cases": Alcibiades was living in exile with a mistress when assassins surrounded his most meager crib and set it on fire. Then when he dashed outside, sword drawn, they shot him dead with javelins and arrows. In Mozart's *Don Giovanni*, per Giovanni's invite, the animated statue showed up at his door. Giovanni gave the statue his hand to consummate an agreement, and the statue seized it and demanded repentance for his rakish transgressions. Giovanni refused and sank to hell while a chorus of demons condemned him. Casanova wrote his famous tome while working as a librarian in Bohemia and died almost destitute, feeling what I

imagine was the gloom of insignificance. Picasso died in his home of heart failure and fluid in his lungs and uttered his last coherent words to his doctor: "You are not wrong to be married," he said. "It's useful." Historians report that JFK tore his groin cavorting poolside with mistresses, and the injury forced him to wear a stricter back brace. Because of the brace's strictness, when Lee Harvey Oswald's first bullet struck JFK, it was impossible for him to bend in reflex, making him an upright target for the last and fatal bullet.

AMERICAN BLOOD

161 "... and suck a pint or so": Plasmapheresis comes from the ancient Greek word *apo*, which means "from" and the Greek work *hairein*, which means "take," which formed the Greek work *aphaeresis*. This combined with the word *plasma*, which comes from, you guessed it, the ancient Greek word *plasma*, which English speakers have interpreted to mean "something formed."

162 "... they loaded her recompense": CSL charges a fee for using a card loaded, in actual fact, with blood funds. Now ain't that cold.

162 "... since Uncle George": Mom hasn't had a steady place to live since the housing folks found out Uncle George was living there and kicked her—us—off Section 8. It was a mournful event. We—or at least I as the eldest—knew of my mother's waiting for years for Section 8, so much so that when her number got called at last, it was as if we'd won the Megabucks. You need not be a US housing scholar to know of the Housing and Community Development Act of 1974, AKA legislation that created the Section 8 assistance my mother coveted, a term that has become damn near synonymous with poor blacks, but not so fast with the racial stereotyping. The Housing Act of 1974 has its genesis in one of the last major acts of FDR's New Deal: the Housing Act of 1937, AKA the Wagner-Steagall Act, which in practice was a program that provided housing assistance for poor-to-working-class white folk.

162 "... I'm talking an annual $4B": In 2013 CSL made a deal to pay $64 million to escape an antitrust class action lawsuit brought by hospitals that claimed they took part in a conspiracy to hike prices on their plasma-derived therapies. Check this out, the Plasma Protein Therapeutics Association was their codefendant. It's little wonder why Judge Joan B. Gottschall called the industry "ripe for collusion."

162 "... they collect up to twice": This allowance for a higher frequency of donating is protected by the FDA and blood shield laws, and encouraged despite the fact that, among other dangers, it might cause severe dehydration, fatigue, numbness, seizures, and hypocalcemia.

164 "Or rather, their profit": That most precious substance is made up of four main parts: Red blood cells (AKA erythrocytes), whose job it is to carry oxygen throughout the body. White blood cells (AKA leukocytes), whose job it is to fight infection. Platelets, whose job it is to help the blood clot by protecting against easy bleeding. Plasma, the liquid part of our blood whose job it is to carry blood cells, waste, nutrients, hormones, and other important substances. Plasma, which comprises 55 percent of whole human blood, is its largest component. It's the yellowish-to-clear-colored part of blood. Plasma itself consists of 90 percent water but also contains salt, enzymes, and proteins—albumin, immunoglobulin, fibrinogen, etc.—and other antibodies.

165 "But American blood seldom": It used to be that the harvest was American inmates.

See the documentary *Factor 8*, which makes the case that for decades, prison officials of the Cummins Unit prison in Grady, Arkansas, ran an illegal plasma center inside the prison and sold blood tainted with hepatitis and HIV from its inmates to a Canadian blood launderer who resold it worldwide. That despicable racket led to thousands of hepatitis and HIV infections.

166 "In what's a cold-blooded fact": Those to blame for the law banning black blood donations claimed the British would be offended if we sent it to them.

166 "They risked, by virtue": The revolutionists needed high persuasion since the population of the colonies was 1.3 million, 500,000 of whom were loyalist to the crown.

166 "Purcell argues that": If this ain't precociousness, you tell me what is: according to lore, Warren enrolled in Harvard at the age of fourteen and by twenty-two was the youngest doctor in Boston, with patients that included Samuel Adams, John Hancock, and both John Adams and son John Quincy Adams.

168 "People have also argued": Sociologist Robert N. Bellah is credited with defining the current concept of civil religion, arguing in his 1967 article "Civil Religion in America" that it should be viewed as common elements of religious orientation that the great majority of Americans share, as expressed in beliefs, symbols, and rituals.

169 "Since time immemorial": There are ample definitions of *civilization* but I'm rocking with Philip H. Bagby's, which is "the culture of the city." What you won't find, or at least what I couldn't find, was a culture that deemed the human sacrifice of its rich and powerful and noble as acceptable practice.

170 "Douglass was dead-on": Peter Salem fought at the Battles of Bunker Hill and Concord and is credited with firing the shot that killed British major John Pitcairn. Artillery man Austin Dabney wounded hundreds of redcoats and was believed to have been the lone black soldier to fight in Battle Creek. For Dabney's role in the war, Georgia looked out in a major way, paying his master seventy pounds to emancipate him *and* giving him fifty acres. William Lee, who, as George Washington's slave, bodyguard, and ace-boon fought in every battle our first president did, and later became the first black person to live in the White House. The valiant Nancy Hart, while her husband was away, would dress up as a feeble-minded man and wander into British camps to collect intel for the Union. Nancy's a legend for holding six British soldiers (she killed one and wounded another) at gunpoint for killing her turkey and trying to punk her into cooking it for them. James Armistead, touted as America's first double agent, gained the trust of British generals, including that famous turncoat Benedict Arnold, in his work as a Union spy.

170 ". . . they couldn't even be assured": No matter if some of those black superpatriots were promised freedom and a small few were even granted that freedom, they couldn't have been certain about this while they fought. It wouldn't have been the first time whites had duped the folks I call my folks.

172 "Mom, ever vigilant": Mom tells me this info as if she believes there was some kind of plot to rob her. But I don't believe her. The men don't seem to have followed her nor to have known her next destination.

172 "That friend's place": The Mallory Courts were infamous for drugs and gangs and violence back then. There are numerous rumors/reports of shootings, stabbings, assaults, and robberies in the complex. The crux of what anyone needs to know about the Mallory Courts can be summed up by a 2014 Facebook post about them credited to a woman named Julia Nabors. "You never want to live there," she writes.

173 "The next time I saw": It's been more than thirty years or so since that beating at

Mallory Courts and I can still see the scar under Mom's eye, showing faint, so faint, through all manner of makeup.

174   "'BLOOD DOESN'T GROW ON TREES'": In case you're wondering, each of the section headings is the actual slogan of a blood donation advertisement.

174   "Truth: the CSL my mama": Hell no, you won't find a plasma center in the suburbs or anywhere else where the American dream thrives. They put plasma centers in the same places they put liquor stores and dialysis centers and the check-cashing store.

THE POSE

177   ". . . Dad meaning Christopher": Also Known As. You don't know a true hustler without an AKA. Word to everything, you don't know an ex-half-hustler who longed for an AKA more than me. And while I'm on the subject, *AKA* ain't just about names; it also means *this* is also called *that*, the this and that being younameit. Better Known As. Used to hear the OGs use this one. It, in essence, means the same thing as *AKA*, though a real slickster, à la my dad, might have an AKA and a BKA.

177   "'You hear me, Cub?'": Big Chris (Dad) nicknamed me Cubcheck, which was a misnomer of the surname of former, and longtime, Lakers general manager Mitch Kupchak. Since my dad not only mangled the name but also, like almost every other new Negro I know, loved to shorten even a nickname as close as possible to monosyllabic, he soon clipped it to "Cub." Cub or Cubcheck was the only one of my nicknames that wasn't ephemeral. Come to think of it, maybe it's part of the reason why I loved Big Chris so. *Nomen est omen.* There was always something in me that felt I needed to escape ordinariness. It took time to learn that a nickname of any import must be earned (Plato, Suleiman the Magnificent, Ivan the Great, Richard the Lionhearted, Attila the Hun, Wild Bill Hickok, Che Guevara, John Africa, shit—Tupac), that a name worthy of remembrance had to be christened by deed. Big sad-face for me it didn't happen or rather hasn't happened. But please, let me keep my hope alive.

180   ". . . no more dashikis and globe Afros": I'd be smooth out of pocket for glossing my Jheri days. My Jheri was mean. Okay, I'm frontin. My Jheri was extra medium, but it wasn't for lack of want. I made sure it stayed activated and out of the sun as much as I could. Even snuck and wore my shower cap (a common practice of the old heads back then) mornings to school so it would look Hawaiian Silky fresh when I got to class and snatched it off and pulled a single wimp curl down in the front à la Michael Joseph Jackson. Yeah, I can almost hear you snickering while you read, but don't knock the Jheri. If you were subject to the black man's kink you either had a Jheri curl or wanted one or knew someone who did or all of the above. And let me end with this factoid: the Jheri curl—which I'm betting processed not one silky strand on the head of one white man anywhere on earth—was invented by one Mr. Jheri Redding.

181   "Media made them the prime targets": Susan Hall and Bob Adelman documented the life of a New York City pimp named Silky for a year. The result was the book *Gentleman of Leisure.* Silky is an underworld celebrity for declaring, "The term is *pimp*, but I don't use it. I'm a professional gentleman of leisure. And I make more money than the president."

183   ". . . President William Taft": The White-Slave Act also included 50k to help expand what was then the fledgling Bureau of Investigations into the force we now know as the FBI.

184   "Guessing most extant": The term *white slavery* was first applied to English female fac-

tory workers in the industrial age but was soon co-opted to describe girls who were abducted and forced into sex slavery. British anti-prostitution crusader W. T. Stead brought broad attention to the issue in 1885 when he published "The Maiden Tribute of Modern Babylon," a series in which he focused on the abduction, sale, and rape of British virgins, and in which he detailed his purchase of a thirteen-year-old girl.

188   ". . . a pimp is seldom far": America was arrested in 2007. We saw each other circa 2010/11. He was sentenced in 2013. That means that when I saw him on campus, he was in the midst of fighting a federal indictment (he accepted a plea deal of fifteen years, which means that at that time he was likely facing much more time). It also means while he was earning his degree, he had hovering over him the specter of calendars upon calendars behind the walls. That makes me wonder about the genuineness of his smile in a profile pic dated September of 2011. It makes me question whether the cheer in other photos is false. And what about those affirmations, aphorisms, encouragements? Were they emblems of America's generous spirit or ploys to persuade a judge for mercy come sentencing time? It is possible they could have been both? What was his outlook during what had to have been long study sessions with his "best team ever"? Did he confess that soon after they donned their caps and gowns, he was headed for prison? Is the feat of earning a bachelor's degree annulled by his verdict? Or does the fact that he finished despite the prospect of prison make his degree that much more impressive? Did America imagine E-Lit Investments as a legitimate business with a chance to endure? Or was its founding just another means of exhorting those who would dictate his fate? I found an article on America in the *Chicago Tribune*. Its headline reads "VICTIM CONFRONTS PIMP AT SENTENCING." The article focuses on the girl who testified at his sentencing hearing. "I just don't think what he did was right," she says. "It's disgusting to do that to a little kid." The article goes on to detail much of what appeared in the FBI press release but also references America's sentencing statement, one in which he made a tearful apology to his victims and also lauded his work as a volunteer youth football coach. "I am embarrassed to be known as a person who did these things," America said at sentencing. "I pray that the scars I have caused on these women will one day recede into as small a place as possible." Is America so wicked that he's undeserving of grace? Should you (the you being the good folks with eyes on these words) and I refuse him forgiveness? What does it bespeak of me and my nature that I've called him a friend? Does his inexcusable lack of compassion for women outside prison null his kindness to me inside it? Is his speech at trial and the fifteen years he'll serve just penance for his crimes? And if not, what would be? Are we all worthy, or nah?

188   " 'The pimp god is always' ": Per Uncle Z, Dad dispensed Rumiesque advice: "Don't wear all that loud shit and let everybody in your business; we get pimpish after dark. Don't trust a *ho* cause she can look up at you longer than you can look down at her. Figure out whether you got a 10k *ho*, a 20k *ho*, or a 50k *ho* cause not everybody's a 100k *ho*, and you'll waste plenty time tryin to check 100k out what's only worth 20k." Uncle Z, attest to Dad's sense of humor—think Rumi meets Richard Pryor. "Pimps don't fart; they pass gas," Dad would joke. "Pimps don't stink; they have an odor. Pimps don't get mad; they get upset. Two things you never chase after are a *ho* or a bus; they both run about every fifteen minutes." Per Uncle Z's recall, Dad was a comedian and Lombardi-level motivator: "Make your pimp flavor success and nothing less. Keep it pimpin and more pimpin. To pimp is your destiny; it's what we do best."

189   "Aunt Essie had a thick": Essie was my maternal great-grandparents' adopted daughter.

She was three years younger than my mother, so they and everyone else considered themselves sisters.

189   "They began their business local": It was standard practice for a pimp to watch his *ho's* child while she went out to work for him. Though it seems an obvious obligation now, it was one I hadn't considered until I began writing.

193   "'Mr. Jackson, during his interrogation'": Closure—I want it. But my aunt's specific case appears to be the weakest of all four cases against Homer Jackson. There is no DNA evidence linking him to the crime. Plus, he told detectives he takes medication for schizophrenia, so how much can anyone trust his word? "I may have done them, but I don't recollect," he claimed during interrogation. "That's as good as I can do. I may have, but I don't remember."

196   "She grabbed Uncle Z's hand": Sure enough, every tongue must confess: my mama didn't describe the physical details of how Essie replied, only what she said. But I couldn't fathom it any other way. Aunt Essie would've needed to do something that made her feel bold. She would've needed to feel the potency of rising above her parents, would've wanted to borrow Uncle Z's strength. Therefore, I added in the physical details. And not for theater, for truth.

196   "'And you can't stop me!'": My great-grandparents assured Essie that if she changed her mind, their offers still stood. Essie and Uncle Z blustered out the house. My mother was the lone person to follow them out. Mom says she snatched—praying she would mind the fear of losing previous fights—her aunt-sister by a loose top and swung her around. "You ain't about to be hoing," Mom said. "Every time I see you on the street, I'm gon whoop your ass." Essie paused a beat before she climbed inside and she and Uncle Z skirted off. Now, I could've added the last bit into the main text, but felt "And you can't stop me" was the most honest way to cut that section. That declaration is the locus of scene. There is Essie, as every child must, declaring independence from her parents. My mother confronting Essie outside The House on Sixth amounts to a denouement, was included as much to characterize my mother as to highlight the futility of the family's effort that day. Mom never got a chance to hop out on Union Ave and whoop Essie's ass for hoing. Matter fact, she never got the chance to see her aunt-sister alive again.

196   "Essie Carie Jackson was": Dear Fam: I could've called. Should've called to vet the section. But didn't call in favor of this punk-ass note. Need you to know that I mean you no harm, that I mean for no one in our family, but especially not you, to suffer, want you to know that there isn't a fraction of a percent of me that meant in any way, shape, or form to demean your mother's life. No lie, I was so worried about that possibility that I considered leaving her out of the essay altogether. In the end, though, I didn't see how I could if I were going to tell my truth, and what I lay down is always at best my truth, couldn't fathom it if the mission was to make sense of that time. I'm not pitching for handclaps, but it ain't easy writing about folks you love and about the loved ones of folks you love. There's often a decision between protecting whom you love and protecting the integrity of what you set out to do. This is your story, no doubt, but we share at least part of it, and though mine can't compare, you weren't alone in your grief. I could go on, but will end with this: if what I wrote births even the least bit of rift between us, know I'll make every effort to mend it. Love, Your Bro—AKA (no matter what granddad says) the funniest Jackson.

202   "... Terry Williams (O Terry, wherefore art thou?)": Somebody help me find this dude. It's damn near twenty years after the fact, and I'm still sick about the con.

202   "On many an afternoon, I'd bop out": Union Avenue became Martin Luther King Jr.
Boulevard. Today there are more than nine hundred streets nationwide that bear Dr.
King's name, an awesome fact, but what's not so awesome is the fact that in the four
decades since Dr. King was honored with a federal holiday, many of the streets have
become locales for urban blight. Professor Derek Alderman, who has studied the cultural and political impact of such streets, argues that streets named for Dr. King are
being "racially profiled." Now, I'm no conspiracy theorist, but if I was, you can bet
I'd argue there's a collective effort of city planners nationwide to besmirch the man's
legacy.

FAST TEN, SLOW TWENTY

207   "It chronicled his evolution": In the article Uncle Henry explains about his then wife,
"If a whore wants to whore, she's going to whore, no matter what, and I didn't want
anyone pimping my wife beside me."

208   " 'Don't talk about it' ": *Hustle* in 1891 evolved to include "to sell goods aggressively"
and "pushing activity; activity in the interest of success." By the 1960s, *hustle* was used
in the sense of a swindle.

212   ". . . I was buying ounces": In the late nineties, I used to cop blowup cell phones from
Fat Fred. Fred would sell me a Nextel and tell me I could make all the calls I wanted for
three or four months. But a couple times, my cell quit working (blew up) in less than
a week. Those times I'd have to hunt Fred and haggle for a refund or another cell.

217   "And furthermore flaunting our abundant liquid worth": We called it *flossing*. And
it, too, would get you licked. Stories hit the neighborhood wire of dudes who'd don
masks, besiege an after-hours, pistols drawn, order everybody to strip to their underwear and throw their clothes in a pile, and plunder the cash, jewels, and other valu-
ables. Yep, fast ten, slow twenty, lives in the blackened heart of every misanthrope
who commences robbing hustlers as they come up, every bank robber, the nefarious
others who feature take, take, take, who favor the biggest, quickest lick no matter the
risk.

221   "In the end, I realized": Sometimes I question whether the dudes who robbed me
deserve to live.

SURVIVAL MATH

241   "Cousin S, who since the late eighties": The Nellas are a Piru set in Compton. Its found-
ers named the set after Roy Campanella Park, which is in the heart of their turf. Roy
Campanella was a Hall of Fame Negro League and Major League Baseball star whose
career was cut short when he was, as a member of the Brooklyn Dodgers, paralyzed
in a car accident. Campanella died in 1993. I wonder what he'd think about being the
namesake of a Blood set.

241   "The Crips-and-Bloods": The first LA gang murder occurred in 1972 when the Crips
beat a dude named Robert Bilal to death over his leather coat.

243   "The lecture addresses French nationalism": Renan argued that race and linguistic
groups shouldn't be considered analogous to that of existing peoples (nations), nor
should a religion or a community of interest.

244   ". . . a national identity is often defined": Miščević contends there are several nation-states but there are also nations that are not fully sovereign states. He cites as examples the Jews and the Armenians and the Kurds.

245   ". . . my neighbor shouted": My girlfriend's brother, a teen who was living with us at the time, had, unbeknown to me of course, found my strap and sold it. But since I would've shot through the door had I had it that morning (can you imagine the fallout?), I've since judged his theft a blessing.

245   ". . . a Crip named Stitches": In 1994, the Portland Police rounded up fifteen members of two Blood sets—the Woodlawn Park Bloods and Loc'd Out Pirus—and charged them under the Oregon Racketeer Influenced and Corrupt Organization Act, claiming they were members of a criminal enterprise. Those nationalists, most of whom were close in age to me, were sentenced to between eighteen months and thirty-nine years. The police did the same thing with eight Kerby Blocc Crips in 1997, though two of them were killed (one of whom was Lil Anthony) before they resolved their charges.

247   ". . . paragon of what criminologist": In 1995, Dilulio was invited to the White House to speak about juvenile crime. Dilulio claimed America's urban neighborhoods were teeming with "kids who have absolutely no respect for human life and no sense of the future who maimed or killed on impulse without any intelligible motive." He described kids who place zero value on the lives of victims they "reflexively dehumanize." He argued that they were capable of committing the most heinous acts of physical violence for the most trivial reasons and that for as long as their youthful energies held out, they would do what came "naturally," which is murder, rape, rob, assault; and burglarize, deal dope, and get high.

247   "And here's another telling": On August 23, 1997, Stitches hosted a going-to-prison "gangsta" party at his mama's house. One of the partygoers was a Crip whom Stitches deemed a snitch for testifying in a murder trial. The two started squabbling. Then Stitches, feeling himself losing, got his gun, shot the dude in the chest, and, while he was on his hands and knees, shot him another three times. Stitches declined the chance to speak at his trial. "There has been a complete and utter lack of remorse on the part of the defendant in this case," bemoaned the DA.

248   "The Hebrew word often interpreted": In the Old Testament, there was a difference between the two types of homicide, murder with premeditation and homicide. Malice separates biblical "murder" from "killing." One who killed without enmity was granted sanctuary in the City of Refuge. Some scholars argue that *rasah* was a reference to the killing (whether premeditated or accidental) of someone in the covenant community—only God had the right to terminate a cleric's life—and that murder was an abrogation of his power. *Rasah* didn't cover killing in war or capital punishment.

251   "Many cities have been hit": The FBI's National Gang Intelligence Center (NGIC) published "National Gang Threat Assessment: Emerging Trends" in 2011. The report asserts, "Gang recruitment of active duty military personnel constitutes a significant criminal threat to the US military." It states that almost all major street gangs—including the Crips-and-Bloods—have been identified in both domestic and international military locations. It confirms that gangs are most prevalent in the army, the army reserves, and the national guard but pervasive in all the branches across all ranks (though most common among junior ranks). The report explains that some gang members (nationalists) scheme entry by misreporting criminal convictions, or falsifying documents, or concealing tattoos that mark their affiliations. The report lists reasons for them enlisting, and among those reasons are the following: escap-

ing their environment, gaining access to drugs or weapons, learning combat tactics like urban warfare, and avoiding a jail or prison sentence. The report also noted that military training is apt to result in more organized, sophisticated, and lethal gangs ready to apply their skills against law enforcement officers and rivals and also to share their expertise with civilian comrades. The report cited incidents—drive-by shootings, assaults, robberies, drug distribution, et cetera—involving active-duty military personnel, and also noted how gang members target the children of enlisted personnel for recruitment. The authors of the report point out that deployments have also helped expand the reach of gangs overseas to countries including Afghanistan, Germany, Italy, Japan, and South Korea, that, in effect, gangbangin done gone international. In related news, the army—go figure—disputed the FBI's report, characterizing the threat of gang activity in their ranks as low.

REVISION

255   "Where to start?": It's still all sorts of inexcusable, but my girlfriend nor her kids were in the house while I cooked dope. For me, for always, there has to be a line.

Mitchell S. Jackson's debut novel won the Ernest J. Gaines Award for Literary Excellence. His honors include a Whiting Award and fellowships from the Cullman Center at the New York Public Library, TED, the Lannan Foundation, the Ford Foundation, PEN, New York Foundation for the Arts, and the Center for Fiction. His writing has appeared in the *New Yorker*, *Harpers Magazine*, the *New York Times Book Review*, the *Paris Review*, the *Guardian*, the *Washington Post*, and elsewhere. He is an assistant professor of creative writing at the University of Chicago.

CPSIA information can be obtained
at www.ICGtesting.com
Printed in the USA
FSHW022304300620
71703FS

9 781501 131738